A Publication of the Gensler Research Institute
New York, NY | Washington, D.C.
www.gensler.com/research
gensler_research@gensler.com

Published by ORO Editions
Publishers of Architecture, Art, and Design
Gordon Goff: Publisher
www.oroeditions.com
info@oroeditions.com

Copyright © 2020 Gensler.

10 9 8 7 6 5 4 3 2 1 First Edition

ISBN: 978-1-943532-28-5

All rights reserved. No part of this book may be reproduced, stored in a retrieval system, or transmitted in any form or by any means, including electronic, mechanical, photocopying of microfilming, recording, or otherwise (except that copying permitted by Sections 107 and 108 of the U.S. Copyright Law and except by reviewers for the public press) without written permission from the publisher.

You must not circulate this book in any other binding or cover and you must impose this same condition on any acquirer.

Library of Congress data available upon request.

Color Separations and Printing: ORO Group LLC

Printed in China.

International Distribution: www.oroeditions.com/distribution

ORO Editions makes a continuous effort to minimize the overall carbon footprint of its publications. As part of this goal, ORO Editions, in association with Global ReLeaf, arranges to plant trees to replace those used in the manufacturing of the paper produced for its books. Global ReLeaf is an international campaign run by American Forests, one of the world's oldest nonprofit conservation organizations. Global ReLeaf is American Forests' education and action program that helps individuals, organizations, agencies, and corporations improve the local and global environment by planting and caring for trees.

*Cover illustration:* Urban Futures (2019), *digital illustration of combined urban landscapes, collaboration by Shuli Sade and designers from the Gensler Research Institute. In a unique collaboration to create the cover of this Catalogue, Shuli Sade_Sade Studio incorporates imagery adapted from cities around the world with an infographic representing the Catalogue's contents.*

*Inside cover illustration:* Night vision, (2014), *120 x160 Pigment print on archival paper by Shuli Sadé_Sadé Studio unveils an urban grid of a city made of retraced and reconfigured memory. The geometry of missing particles unveils a grid of architectural rhythms that belong to large modern cities.*

# Gensler
# Research
Catalogue Volume 3
A PUBLICATION OF THE GENSLER RESEARCH INSTITUTE

## SHAPING THE FUTURE OF CITIES

**Every research project at Gensler has a common goal: to uncover insights that help us shape the future of our cities and build a great experience for the people who live in them every day.** This work is particularly poignant in today's changing world. With a global population shift toward cities, issues such as urbanization, climate change, mobility, connected city technology, housing, and homelessness represent growing challenges. Many of our clients recognize the change and they see an uncertain future because of it.

At Gensler, we believe it's our responsibility to take on tough challenges and make a positive difference in our cities and communities. We're also uniquely positioned to do just that. We have a breadth of expertise as a global collaborative of 6,000 architects and designers in over 50 cities around the world that is second to none. We also do the research.

Since we published the last volume of this Catalogue, our research program has grown exponentially in both breadth and scale, including becoming a formal Research Institute in 2018. Our research spans more countries and disciplines than ever before. We're integrating traditional research methods with cutting-edge technologies that establish new connections between people and place, giving us unprecedented access to behavioral and real-time data. But Gensler's culture of curiosity is, and always has been, the true momentum behind what we do. We ask first what people need, and then how design can positively manifest change.

It is by leveraging our research, our people, the scale of our expertise, and the power of our innovation platform that we will make a positive difference in the world and help our clients navigate an uncertain future. The 54 projects documented in this catalogue each explore an aspect of our cities and environments. Building on the first two volumes of the Gensler Research Catalogue, each entry is organized around a simple framework that outlines the methods, context, results, and next steps of each project. As these projects demonstrate, we are unwavering in our commitment to use design and research to take on the toughest challenges facing cities; to connect people and build community; and to design an inclusive, purposeful, and impactful future for all.

Diane Hoskins, FAIA, IIDA
Co-CEO

Andy Cohen, FAIA, IIDA
Co-CEO

# TABLE OF CONTENTS

## SHAPING THE FUTURE OF CITIES

**THE GENSLER CITY DESIGN INDEX**
10  The Gensler City Design Index

**HOMELESSNESS**
12  Design Solutions for Homelessness

## TACKLING CLIMATE CHANGE

**DESIGNING FOR RESILIENCE**
56  Impact by Design
60  A Path Toward Net Zero Energy Buildings
66  Designing Dynamic Facades to Conserve Energy

**URBAN ECOLOGY**
70  Urban Strategies for Coastal Resilience
74  Preserving Urban Ecosystems
78  Underground Retail and Rooftop Farming

## ENHANCING URBAN MOBILITY

**CARS AND PARKING**
94  Forecasting Design Shifts Under Future Vehicle Technologies
100  Projecting Future Parking Demands of Autonomous Vehicles
106  Investigating Parking in the Age of Automation

## SHIFTING THE WORKPLACE NARRATIVE

**THE GLOBAL WORKPLACE SURVEYS**
122  U.S. Workplace Survey 2019
128  Germany Workplace Survey 2019
132  Latin America Workplace Survey 2017
136  History of the Global Workplace Surveys

**WELLNESS IN THE WORKPLACE**
138  Emotional Security in the Workplace
140  Prioritizing Psychological Well-Being

## CREATING A RICH URBAN EXPERIENCE

**THE EXPERIENCE INDEX**
180  Retail Experience Index 2018
184  Museums Experience Index 2019
188  Hospitality Experience Index 2018

**TRAVEL AND LEISURE**
194  Exploring Multigenerational Travel
198  The Impact of AirBnb on Hospitality

## BUILDING INTELLIGENT CITIES

**SENSED ENVIRONMENTS**
234  Designing Intelligent Retail Places
238  Spatializing Our Data
240  IoT Technology in the Workplace

**MACHINE LEARNING**
244  The Value Opportunities of Machine Learning Design Strategies

### HOUSING
- 18 A New Model for Intergenerational Living
- 22 Designing Intergenerational Communities
- 26 Hong Kong's Next Generation of Senior Living
- 28 Converting Office Buildings for Residential Use

### DIVERSITY AND INCLUSION
- 32 Achieving Inclusivity in the Design Process
- 38 Designing Gender Inclusive Restrooms

### EQUITABLE DEVELOPMENT
- 42 Local Development in Sub-Saharan Africa
- 46 Investigating Downtown Neighborhood Resurgence
- 52 A Framework for Holistic Urban Planning

### RESILIENCE IN THE WORKPLACE
- 82 The Effects of Living Walls
- 88 Implementing the Circular Economy

### AIR AND RAIL
- 110 Understanding Airports through Social Data
- 116 Japan's Railway Retail Hubs

### EMPLOYEE ENGAGEMENT
- 146 Balancing Density and Employee Engagement
- 152 Work Styles and Spatial Preference
- 154 The Value of Customer Experience Centers

### SPACES FOR SCIENCE
- 156 Designing Effective Research Buildings
- 158 Adaptable Life Science Lab Design

### EVOLVING THE DESIGN PROCESS
- 164 Narrative-Driven Design
- 166 Rapid Workplace Redesign
- 170 Building Repositioning Strategies
- 174 Future-Proofing Design Strategies

### ENHANCED EDUCATION
- 202 A Toolkit for Active Learning Environments
- 208 A Comparative Analysis of Enhanced Classrooms

### COMMUNITY INSTITUTIONS
- 212 A New Model for the Public Library
- 216 The Future of USPS Real Estate

### OPTIMIZING HEALTH CARE
- 220 A Model for Integrated Ambulatory Care Clinics
- 224 Enhancing the Waiting Room Experience
- 228 Optimizing Exam Room Design

### CONNECTED REAL ESTATE
- 248 Real Estate and the Intelligence Economy

## APPENDIX
- 255 History of the Gensler Research Institute
- 256 About Gensler
- 258 Bibliography
- 268 Index
- 272 Acknowledgments

This third volume of our Research Catalogue is a compilation and celebration of the research initiatives we have undertaken over the past three years. Building on over a half century of designing the places and spaces that shape the future of our cities, our latest research tackles major issues facing our communities, and captures the shifts taking place in how we live, work, and play. The 54 research projects featured in the catalogue are unified by a common purpose: to help create places that elevate the human experience and make a positive contribution to our clients, communities, and cities.

## SHAPING THE FUTURE OF CITIES

Cities are only 3% of the world's landmass but generate over 80% of GDP. As they continue to grow, how do we make sure the design of cities helps people thrive?

**THE GENSLER CITY DESIGN INDEX**

**HOMELESSNESS**

**HOUSING**

10 **The Gensler City Design Index**

**Research Team**
Christine Barber
Andre Brumfield
Justin Chase
Andy Cohen
Carlos Cubillos
Michelle DeCurtis
Mark Erdly
Diane Hoskins
Lin Jia
Brian Ledder
Lawrence Ler
Zheyu Liu
Ian Mulcahey
Tim Pittman
Oliver Schaper
Sofia Song

12 **Design Solutions for Homelessness**

**Research Team**
Russell Baker
Nancy Foster
Aaron Gensler
Christopher Gray
Audrey Handelman
Rob Jernigan
Brandon Larcom
Allison McElroy
Mina Noorbakhsh
David O'Brien
Roger Sherman
Eric Stultz

18 **A New Model for Intergenerational Living**

**Research Team**
Tama Duffy Day
Laura Latham
Lee Lindahl
Erik Lucken
Olivier Sommerhalder
Amy Weinstein

22 **Designing Intergenerational Communities**

**Research Team**
Tama Duffy Day
Scott Hampton
Wesley Hiatt
Laura Latham
Lee Lindahl
Olivier Sommerhalder
Summer Yu
Daquan Zhou

## DIVERSITY AND INCLUSION

**26 Hong Kong's Next Generation of Senior Living**

**Research Team**
David Frank
Callum MacBean
Cheryl Martirez
Christy Wong

**28 Converting Office Buildings for Residential Use**

**Research Team**
Jeff Barber
Derek Gilley
Duncan Lyons
Sarah Palmer
Bill Talley
Greg Zielinski

**32 Achieving Inclusivity in the Design Process**

**Research Team**
Gail Napell
Karen Pedrazzi
Amy Pothier
Oliver Schaper
Vivian Schapsis

**38 Designing Gender Inclusive Restrooms**

**Research Team**
Nick Bryan
Chad Finken
Melissa McCarriagher
Kathryn Moore
Katy O'Neill
Haley Campbell
Mara Russo
Pia Sachleben
Stephen Swicegood
Jennifer Thornton

## EQUITABLE DEVELOPMENT

**42 Local Development in Sub-Saharan Africa**

**Research Team**
Lisa Amster
Thabo Lenneiye
Simi Marinho
Erica Oppenheimer
Levi Schoenfeld
Carolyn Sponza

**46 Investigating Downtown Neighborhood Resurgence**

**Research Team**
Mitchell Bobman
Andre Brumfield
Alice Davis
Wes LeBlanc
Nic Pryor
Steve Wilson

**52 A Framework for Holistic Urban Planning**

**Research Team**
Sumita Arora
Jessica Galeazzi
Brenden Jackson
Carolina Montilla
Naomi Sakamoto
Sarah Szekeresh

# The Gensler City Design Index

How does the design and form of our cities impact the human experience?

**WHAT WE'RE DOING**

**We are exploring the impact of city design on the human experience by integrating original research and feedback from the residents of cities around the world with data gathered about the design and physical form of cities, as well as cities' performance on a variety of socioeconomic factors.**

Our goal is to understand how our cities are working directly from the perspective of the people who live, work, and play in them every day—and to create new insights that bring the voice of the people to shift conversations about what really makes cities thrive and grow.

The study is structured to understand the city through the lens of people's daily behaviors in cities, and the places they spend their time in—where they live, work, learn, connect, stay healthy, and move throughout the city. This "people" data—50,000 survey responses gathered across 50 cities—will then be integrated with data gathered on the aspects of city place and performance to create a full picture of the urban experience.

**THE CONTEXT**

Cities today account for only 3% of the world's landmass, but generate over 80% of global GDP and use 70% of the world's energy. And as the world's population continues to flock to cities—well over half of the global population already lives in urban areas, with a projected 70% living in cities by 2030—it's clear these trends are poised to continue. Cities around the world are major drivers of innovation and opportunity for both individuals and businesses; but they also come with unique challenges.

The challenges faced include providing affordable housing, reducing homelessness, and improving the quality of life around the globe—all while addressing the pressing issues of climate change. Our research will help us capture deeper data and insight to understand how our cities really work, and uncover unique opportunities for design to optimize the human experience and help build a better world.

**WHAT'S NEXT**

The Gensler City Design Index is the most ambitious, integrated research project the Gensler Research Institute has ever undertaken. By integrating original survey data with place and performance data captured from a variety of datasets, we hope to uncover insights connecting the physical and spatial characteristics of place directly with how people experience space, and its impact on their overall health, happiness, and success. These insights will in turn inform the future of Gensler's work across myriad project types and scales as we partner with our clients and communities to build the cities of the future.

**PEOPLE**

Data capturing the human experience directly from the behaviors, perceptions, and day-to-day experiences of the people who live in each city.

**PLACE**

Measuring the aspects of physical place in all dimensions—from land use and zoning, to the age and height of buildings, to the form and quantity of open spaces.

**PERFORMANCE**

Variables measuring a city's performance from a social, economic, and public health standpoint—quantifying aspects of business performance and human well-being.

# Design Solutions for Homelessness

How do we quickly create cost-effective Permanent Supportive Housing (PSH) for the homeless?

### WHAT WE DID

**We developed a plan to design, develop, and oversee a prefabricated, modular approach to house Los Angeles' homeless population.** Our team met and discussed our ideas with stakeholders including permanent supportive housing (PSH) developers, the city, the county, for-profit developers, real estate brokers, PSH operators, nonprofit groups focused on homelessness, other architects, and prefabrication manufacturers.

We started by focusing on four sites in Lincoln Heights that the city identified for PSH. Our design solution involved prefabricated modular units to make the construction of the four buildings faster and more cost-effective. The idea of prefab construction for multifamily housing was not new, but it catalyzed our thinking for how to house Los Angeles' 10,000 chronically homeless people.

We knew a one-project-at-a-time approach was inadequate, so we looked to the retail industry for inspiration: in retail architecture no retailer ever wants just one store, they want hundreds. To solve homelessness, we need hundreds of PSH projects. So we conceptualized a PSH approach that would resemble a retail rollout. Essentially, our system procures all materials in high volumes to realize the cost benefits of economies of scale.

### THE CONTEXT

The lack of permanent supportive housing in the market leaves chronically homeless people without shelter and on the streets—and the problem is particularly dire in Los Angeles. In November 2016, 76% of L.A. voters passed the $1.2 billion bond measure, Proposition HHH, to fund the construction of 10,000 units of PSH. However, recent efforts to leverage funds for constructing projects have dragged with delays and have not gained the scaled momentum necessary to combat the epidemic of homelessness and all the resultant effects.

### THE RESULTS

We proposed a holistic approach to engage an umbrella organization that works on a program level to coordinate, track, and manage the entire real estate process to support the mass construction of hundreds of permanent supportive housing buildings throughout L.A. PSH has funding available, but without a sustainable approach, that funding is going untapped. Our framework responsibly accounts for all resources.

Our focus pivoted from a single, project management oversight (PMO) operation to the PMO team managing the execution of a prefab solution through the manufacturing industry. Projects will realize economies of scale and time savings at an exponential pace. This will reduce the cost, the construction timeline, and the risk to developers.

# THERE ARE 53,000 PEOPLE EXPERIENCING HOMELESSNESS IN LOS ANGELES COUNTY

**DESIGN IMPLICATIONS**

Our initiative is based on the following core principles:

## WORK DIRECTLY WITH LOCAL STAKEHOLDERS TO IDENTIFY SITES NEAR EXISTING HOMELESS COMMUNITIES, MASS TRANSIT, AND HOMELESS SERVICES

Through the PSH Ordinance, the entitlement process can either be by-passed or become a more expedient approval for these sites. The PSH Ordinance was passed in May 2018, but was almost immediately challenged in court. As such, its status remains in limbo. If this ordinance is not upheld, we would propose to do a mass entitlement of the selected sites. This will produce a pipeline of land ready to have PSH built on it.

## STREAMLINE THE CONSTRUCTION PROCESS

For individual projects, developers are responsible for sitework and building the ground floor to contain supportive services for the formerly homeless and desired amenities for the community, such as a grocery store or laundromat. They will then install the modular units in any configuration and quantity that works for the site. Building can then be finished with a facade that fits in the visual fabric of the surrounding community.

## CENTRALIZE PROGRAM MANAGEMENT OVERSIGHT

A new holistic view of the overall process is needed to properly coordinate, track, communicate, and deliver finished developments to meet the demand. A PMO is needed to establish the goals, success factors, metrics, and management routines around the program as a whole and into each of the key phases of the delivery cycle. The phases of the delivery cycle are property acquisition, entitlement, funding and developer selection, design, fabrication, construction, and operations.

## DESIGN PREFABRICATED MODULAR UNITS IN COLLABORATION WITH A RESIDENTIAL FABRICATION MANUFACTURER

The use of modular construction provides the ability to manufacture high-quality and lower-cost residential dwellings with quicker speed to market. By going with this delivery method, costs can be reduced by 20% to 30%, and schedules can be reduced by about six months vs. a traditional "stick built" delivery. Additionally, in a controlled assembly-line type of manufacturing environment, the quality and efficiency improve dramatically. Other benefits include a significantly reduced impact to the neighborhood surrounding the construction site as there is a shorter site construction duration, and a streamlined permitting and inspection process.

A rendering of the Skid Row Housing Trust Ambrosia project.

# Proposed Prefab PMO Org Chart

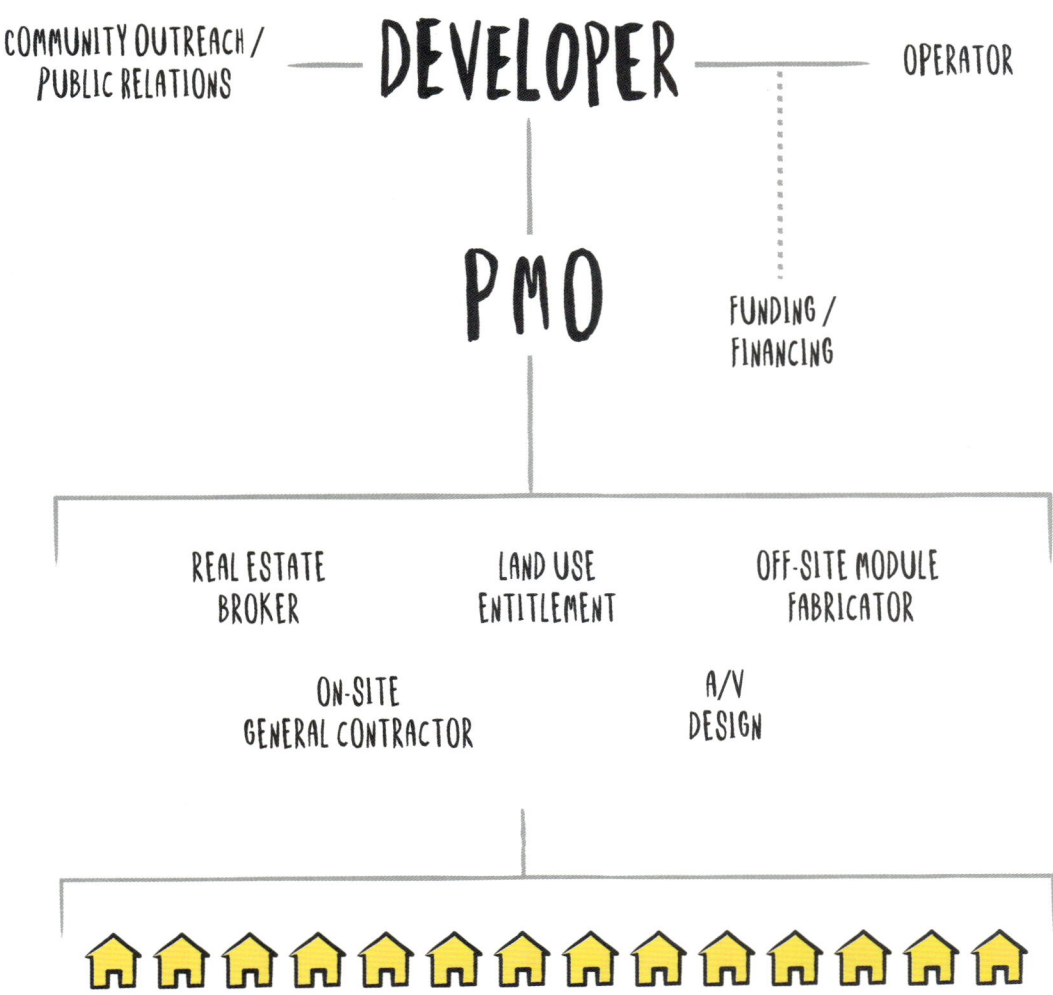

**WHAT'S NEXT**

Our work is ongoing. We are meeting with several prefab manufacturers to understand the path toward opening a factory in Los Angeles. This will help develop an inventory of affordable PSH units for purchase/use by a multitude of developers. Concurrently, we are working with Skid Row Housing Trust, a leading PSH developer, to design and construct four projects that will provide proof of concept for our rollout solution. Each of these projects will house approximately 70 to 100 formerly homeless residents. Looking forward, we will be attuned to how our strategies are adopted, the industry changes, and what new innovative approaches communities employ to combat homelessness.

Homelessness is not an LA phenomenon; we look next to other areas for application and inspiration. With this unified strategy and a single point of oversight, we can implement an innovative solution to address chronic homelessness in major U.S. cities. The success of prefab manufactured projects will be game-changing for the residential industry—an industry that has been stagnant—for decades as the supply and subsequent cost of units skyrocket.

16  Shaping the Future of Cities

**El Puente Bridge Home**
Los Angeles, California

Connected by a 7,000-square-foot deck, the El Puente Bridge Home is a welcoming and inclusive space that houses 45 people. Temporary housing provides a short-term solution—but a crucial step in the path toward permanent housing for the city's homeless population.

# A New Model for Intergenerational Living

Are today's communities prepared for our rapidly growing, healthy, and savvy aging population?

**10,000** baby boomers turn 65 every day

The number of renters ages 55+ rose **28%** between 2009 and 2015

Americans ages 55+ will be **25%** of the U.S. workforce by 2024

**WHAT WE DID**

**Our team conducted secondary research on aging, and reviewed Gensler's relevant project work, to develop a knowledge foundation for our study of "intergenerational communities," or a location that promotes the well-being, contributions, and mutual support of all age groups.** Next, we interviewed experts across myriad industries that are, or will soon be, subject to the upcoming surge of boomers—from real estate developers to health practitioners. We explored trends and policies in senior living, community development, health and wellness, longevity, and living and working environments. Our questions related to best practices, industry trends, and how each industry is addressing multigenerational wants and needs.

We then took the current framework of intergenerational communities a step further, and developed our BoomTown Community model: a community for all ages that fosters interaction across generations as they live, work, and play. Our design strives for a diverse environment that promotes healthy living, provides choices in working and playing, and offers vital services that address the changing needs of the community. The culmination of our research was a salon dinner held at Gensler's D.C. office, attended by many thought leaders in the region. Our goal was to document current best practices and thinking around the formation and design of these communities. Ultimately, our discussion crystallized our shared vision for a BoomTown future.

> The sheer size and new demands of the baby boomer generation should compel industry leaders to work together to create new inclusive, holistic community models.

**THE CONTEXT**

The U.S. is shifting toward a demographically older population: in the last century, the number of Americans ages 65 or older increased tenfold. What's more, the older population segment is now living longer than previous generations entering this age bracket—and in more comfort and with better health.

Getting older no longer means a slow trek toward infirmity. In fact, many of those approaching retirement want the same city-based amenities that younger generations prefer. While many seniors choose traditional senior-living, assisted-living, or aging-in-place models, many boomers have a different vision of the ideal community that will serve them today and as they age.

But the concept of aging remains stuck in age-old stereotypes like infirmity and passivity, which can relegate older people to the periphery—both dynamically and geographically. It's important instead that they feel in control through a personalized atmosphere that feels central to a community's mission.

To create such an environment, we need to shift to a more optimistic perception that emphasizes longevity and encourages intergenerational collaboration. That perception will naturally flow into communications among the generations, and serve as a powerful driver of an inclusive community.

> We need to shift our communication style and cultural symbols away from infirmity and passivity and toward integration and proactivity.

**THE RESULTS**

**The desire for an authentic, productive, and interconnected lifestyle transcends older and younger generations.** Most soon-to-be retirees want to stay active past when they retire, and they take pleasure in the same amenities as millennials do. But current lifestyle typologies segregate generations. Multipurpose communities attract millennials, while most senior-living models cater to only older generations.

**Intergenerational social structures are key to our vision.** According to Generations United, intergenerational communities have many benefits. Older adults who interact regularly with younger people are less socially isolated and more likely to promote their physical and mental health. For younger individuals, interactions with older adults can enhance communication skills and provide a sense of purpose and community service. These benefits can help preserve cultural traditions and strengthen partnerships among community organizations and individuals.

**BoomTown, our prototype community, is our vision of a progressive future where both people and property types are integrated.** The ideal community is located close to commercial, medical, and recreational facilities, and includes areas with the design flexibility to enable multiple uses for changing needs. Universal design principles, such as design features and products that make a home safer and more comfortable for all residents, should drive community development. The promotion of independence and personal satisfaction, even as daily activities become more physically challenging, is paramount.

**DESIGN IMPLICATIONS**

We know the mechanics of what will make BoomTown tick. Through our research, we established an overhauled paradigm of community development that includes three focus areas: physical architecture, social architecture, and economics & policy. Over an evening of discussion at our BoomTown dinner event, we came to understand the nuts and bolts of realizing a new community. Each industry player offered a unique perspective. We found six underlying subareas of focus (see diagram on opposite page) that will be integral in the next step of creating BoomTown—and a better future for all ages.

# BOOMTOWN FRAMEWORK

**PHYSICAL ARCHITECTURE**

### DESIGN-CONSCIOUS

The implementation of design principles that seamlessly integrate adaptability and ease of use into all aspects of the built environment.

### EVOLVING TECHNOLOGY

App-based access to everything from health care to everyday services to drastically change the delivery of supportive care.

### PURPOSE-CENTERED

Coworking spaces, maker spaces, incubator offices supporting entrepreneurship, flexible spaces for community gatherings, and other interests.

### WELLNESS-FOCUSED

Incorporation of community gardens, walking trails, fitness centers, and targeted wellness services from acupuncturists and masseuses to counseling.

### SMART DEVELOPMENT

Leverage the repurposing of existing building stock to ensure the preservation of existing community aesthetics and promote sustainability.

### MIXED-USE CONVENIENCE

Provide quick and easy access to retail, transportation, health care, and nightlife.

**SOCIAL ARCHITECTURE**  **ECONOMICS & POLICY**

### WHAT'S NEXT

Regardless of where or what we build, our plans are meant to find common ground on what makes us happy. Importantly, we need to create space for shared affinities that connect across generations—ranging from interest in the outdoors to artistic endeavors and educational opportunities.

In our next research phase, we will apply the BoomTown framework to neighborhoods that are ripe to benefit from an intergenerational community model. We will bring together designers, planners, and stakeholders to envision a path for development that leverages neighborhood strengths to enhance the bonds between all community members.

# Designing Intergenerational Communities

What elements are essential to make our existing communities livable for all ages?

MacArthur Park, Los Angeles

**WHAT WE DID**

**After bringing together industry experts to discuss, envision, and create a framework for BoomTown, we tapped Gensler design teams from Los Angeles and Washington, D.C., to create visualizations for two communities: MacArthur Park (see images below and at right) and Ivy City in Washington, D.C. (see images on pages that follow).**

Our conceptual designs are tools for changing the built environment to expand opportunities for existing community members and encourage intergenerational living and connections.

**THE CONTEXT**

BoomTown is a new community model for all ages. Our goal is to implement transformative solutions for all people within existing urban communities. The built environment must be planned and developed to support interactions across generations, cultures, and socioeconomic groups. Stakeholders—including developers, investors, policy leaders, and local community members—are turning to multigenerational community solutions that drive collaborative innovations that can improve residents' health and longevity.

**1**
*Encourage safe and calm traffic patterns using audible signals and clear pavement transitions for pedestrians. (below)*

**2**
*Integrate and coordinate surrounding residential, business, and health care networks for people of all ages throughout their lifetime. (below)*

22   Shaping the Future of Cities | Designing Intergenerational Communities

Support existing local vendors through designated structures and lighting to create a haven for intergenerational engagement. (above)

Establish a sense of place through design elements that celebrate the history and culture of the existing neighborhood. (above)

Provide ample space for the community-conscious programming of events and festivals to minimize isolation and foster social connections. (above)

Leverage existing transportation infrastructure to access services and area amenities. (above)

**THE RESULTS**

We created speculative design solutions for BoomTown in partnership with the Milken Institute's Center for the Future of Aging. In Los Angeles, our proposal would completely reform how MacArthur Park serves its community. Space would be reallocated to accommodate a playground, outdoor classroom, fitness center, and other community-focused amenities. A central hub would then leverage the area's most valuable assets—reasons why people come to MacArthur Park in the first place.

To foster age-inclusive development in Ivy City, Washington, D.C., we reimagined spaces and programs to better meet residential, health care, and educational needs. For both communities, we proposed the creative reuse of space to support the community and facilitate sustainability.

**DESIGN IMPLICATIONS**

## We have to make better use of space.

In Ivy City, significant parcels are dedicated to usage that provides little benefit to community members. Change does not mean outsourcing necessary but unseemly functions, but reappropriating local sites. For instance, vertically storing city-owned vehicles creates additional city blocks for many residential typologies.

*Consolidate industrial and municipal facilities to create hubs for (a) creative work environments, (b) health care, (c) centralized public space, (d) mixed-use residential, and (e) education. (left)*

*Soften and buffer major adjacent highways and rail yard with green space. (left)*

*Revitalize existing residential areas with green pocket parks. (left)*

**Ivy City, Washington, D.C.**

24  Shaping the Future of Cities | Designing Intergenerational Communities

## Community engagement is integral to our vision of change.

In MacArthur Park, we wove street vending into the neighborhood tapestry to explicitly create space for vendors to do business. Our conceptual future for MacArthur Park reimagines the built environment as facilitating what is already in the community—people and the cultures they bring with them.

## No matter which way you look at it, designing for all ages is the right choice.

Health care is moving toward decentralization, digital access, and individual wellness. Technology is providing unprecedented changes to how we access services in our daily lives. Although isolated environments for elders are the norm, we propose smart, integrated living environments as an alternative.

**4**
*Build a rooftop community garden to create spaces for shared affinities across generations. (below)*

**5**
*Strengthen local transportation networks for greater access to hospitals, universities, and local recreation. (below)*

**6**
*Provide a centralized, easily accessible health and wellness center to promote healthy living. (below)*

**7**
*Expand and revitalize the historic Crummell School to foster civic and social engagement. (below)*

**8**
*Create commercial space for coworking, maker spaces, and continued learning. (below)*

**9**
*Devote ample public space for community programming with outdoor exercise equipment for all ages. (below)*

**10**
*Provide affordable residential options that embrace inclusivity and diversity. (below)*

**11**
*Integrate residential housing with retail shops, services, and entertainment venues. (below)*

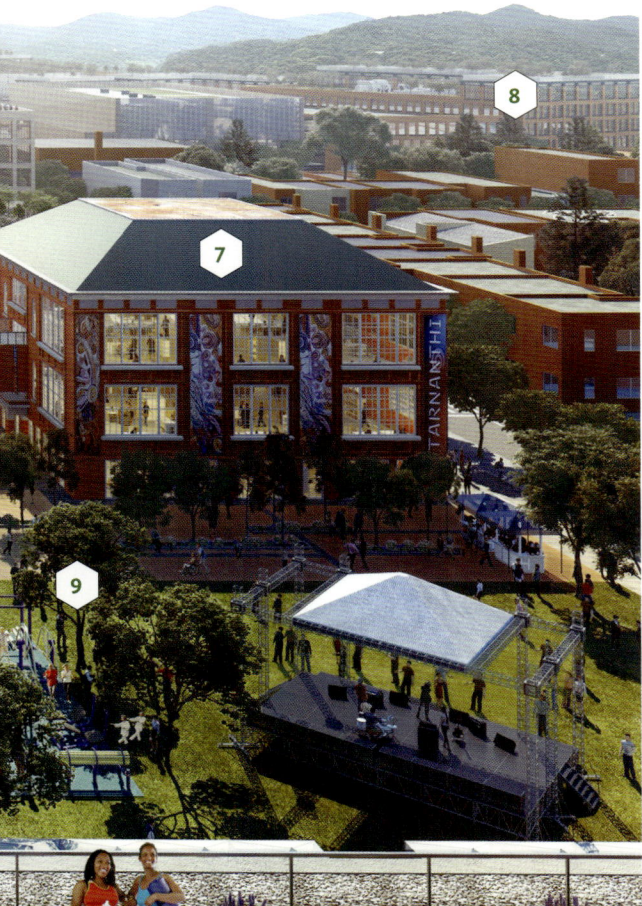

**WHAT'S NEXT**

We continue to share our results with the contacts we made during the research process and engage in follow-up dialogues. With these findings, we also plan to create a guide to share with prospective clients, which will clearly identify the technical and functional issues that need to be resolved to deliver a successful design.

# Hong Kong's Next Generation of Senior Living

How do we address the effect of Hong Kong's density on the region's senior adults?

**WHAT WE DID**

**We explored the adverse effects of Hong Kong's ultra-density on the city's senior adults.** We conducted site visits, analyzing how different housing profiles meet the needs of this group of people. We then interviewed key stakeholders including senior adults, caregivers, subject matter experts, and community organization representatives. After profiling Hong Kong senior-living communities, we created a design toolkit that enhances mobility and accessibility, while addressing local socioeconomic issues.

**THE CONTEXT**

Hong Kong's seven million people live atop a mere 1,100 square kilometers—there are at least six people per meter of land. The island is small but bustling, and it holds the world title for highest life expectancy. But that means by 2050, Hong Kong is forecasted to rank fifth in the world for cities with the largest percentage of senior adults. While the current life expectancy is 87.6 for women and 81.4 for men, in 2034 it will be 90.3 and 84.0 respectively. To meet the demands of changing demographics in the region, the Hong Kong government teamed up with the Hong Kong Housing Society to implement various housing solutions. Specifically, the Ageing in Place Initiative addresses the myriad challenges that senior adults face.

**THE RESULTS**

Our interview process revealed that the headlines are true: senior adults have dynamic needs, and development density is having an adverse effect on those needs. Demographic shifts, real estate premiums, and space constraints are hindering Hong Kong's approach to senior living. Senior people living alone are at a higher risk for many health issues.

We proposed an "action and reaction" strategy to identify and improve the public housing units in most need of improvement. Our proposed model is cyclic—not only testing and learning from changes to design, but engaging with stakeholders to advocate for the most advantageous design principles.

## 7,000,000
people live within Hong Kong's 1,100 square kilometers

## By 2040,
One in three residents will be 65 or older

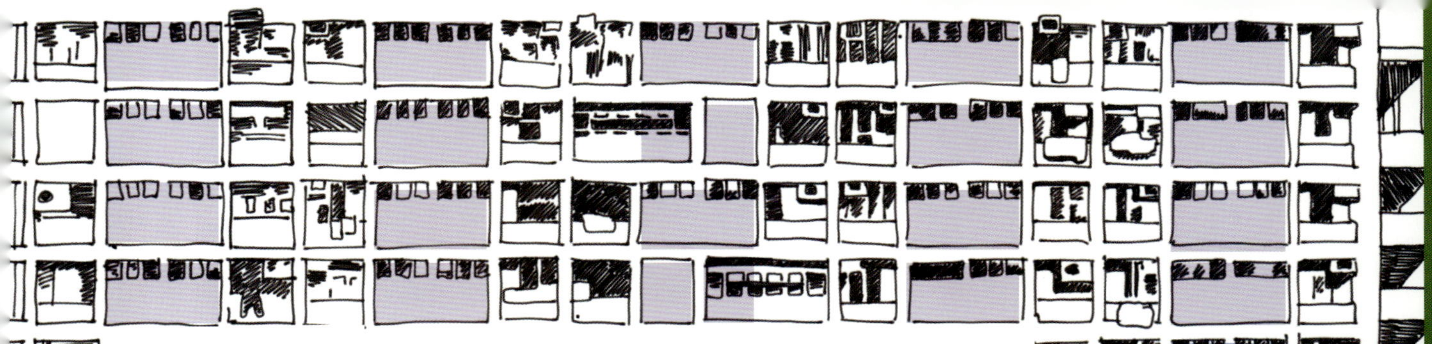

# 81.4% of Hong Kong seniors prefer living at home rather than moving into a residential care home.

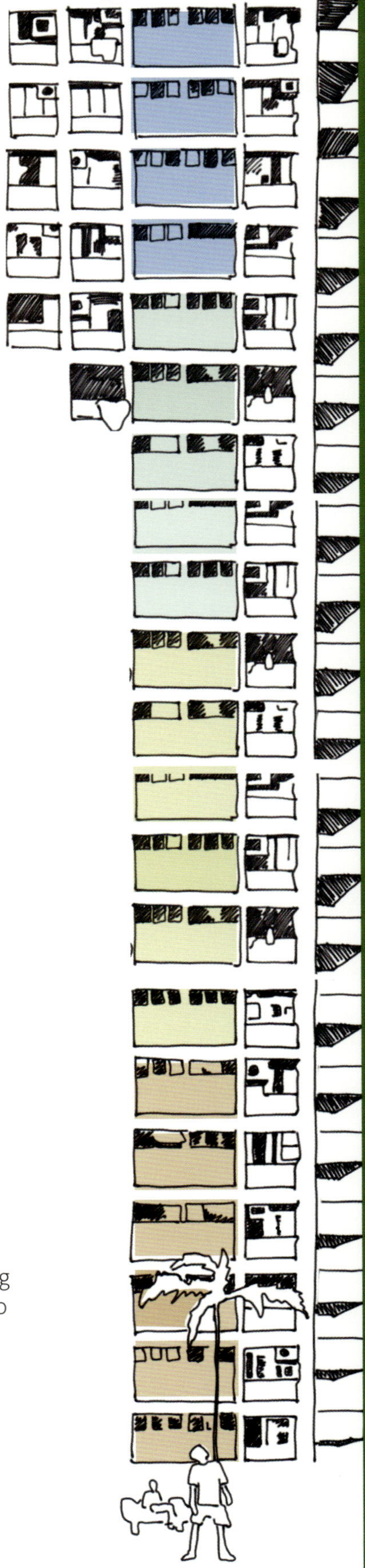

**DESIGN IMPLICATIONS**

**Single units in public housing provided by the Hong Kong Housing Authority are the most problematic housing profile.** These units are designed with issues related to barriers, spatial connectivity, utilities, and functionality. Our action-and-reaction method is calibrated to target these needs through the lens of senior adults, proposing and then testing changes to these units.

**Even those with financial stability often do not know how to access services.** To better integrate housing and services, we need to plan for collaboration and support between disciplines. As a solution, we challenge multiple service providers to work together, streamlining institutional and public resources that pose logistical problems to Hong Kong's older people.

**Barrier-Free Accessibility**

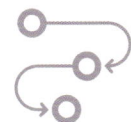
**Spatial Connectivity**

**Utility Compactness**

**Functional Flexibility**

**WHAT'S NEXT**

Our team will discuss our findings with stakeholders in the region. There is scant research related to the effects of ultra-density on senior living—our research is a first step toward creating and standardizing a program of design and policy solutions to help the region's most vulnerable citizens.

# Converting Office Buildings for Residential Use

Can converting underperforming office buildings to residential space increase urban vitality?

Current © Google 2019
Proposed — Washington, D.C. Golden Triangle, Rhode Island Ave. & M St.

### WHAT WE DID

**We built a framework for converting underperforming office buildings to residential use in Washington, D.C.'s Central Business District (CBD).** Within this 175-block area, we categorized each office property according to five archetypes: wedge, cube, light or L-shaped, blinder, and heavy or slight slab. After sorting each office building into a categorical bucket, we mapped out the degree to which each archetype is fit for residential conversion. Further, we evaluated each building in the context of its surrounding neighborhood. This included mapping a network of residential nodes where development could generate a new interconnected community to replace the current office-only landscape.

### THE CONTEXT

**It is imperative to reprogram downtown areas for greater property-type diversity.** The benefits are vast: heterogeneity has the potential to relieve stress on infrastructure and resources, and increases the city's tax base with new residents. Specifically, through office to residential conversions, neighborhoods can attract the commercial amenities that create more active street life—and ultimately support our shared goal of a live-work-play district.

Segregated office and residential environments can have dire consequences. In Mumbai, India, where office and residential environments are separated miles apart, car ownership has risen over 3,700% over the past 60 years. Over that same time period, Mexico City has endured greenhouse gas emission increases of 70% because residences surround the city's periphery rather than the city's center. Design patterns can help or hinder our social lives too. One study noted the ill effects of greater car traffic in cities: residents living on streets with less pedestrian traffic had fewer intimate social relationships.

For better or for worse, property conversions are contingent upon social and economic ebbs and flows. The development boom of the early 2000s was compounded by the Great Recession, creating a problem of excess office supply. Vacancy levels almost doubled from 2006 (5.8%) to 2009 (11.5%).

# Facade modifications create the aesthetic necessary to attract new residents and create vibrant neighborhoods.

While Class A vacancies have rebounded, lower-quality buildings are still stagnant. Our current preferences for office space—which differ from our pre-recession preferences—are partly to blame for the swath of vacancies; the millennial workforce demands working in amenity-rich buildings and alongside amenity-rich environments. While Class A office buildings can satisfy these demands, anything else is deemed inadequate.

In older submarkets, like D.C.'s Central Business District, neighborhoods lack residential stock and have limited retail options. Class B and C office stock has sat unoccupied for an extended period, and despite a demand for conversion, deep or dark floor plates are less than ideal for residential space. Further, landlords may be hesitant to fund the overhaul because office rents average nearly $1 per square foot more per month than apartment rents. While this may be true at a city-level analysis, downtown rents are higher, and additional height or density may be available for residential redevelopment. Walkable, mixed-use neighborhoods average lower vacancy rates, commanding rent premiums for both office and residential space.

### THE RESULTS

**A winning strategy is twofold: focus on the right archetypes, and focus on the right places.** Wedge and cube configurations offer the best ingredients for a convertible archetype, and these archetypes should top the docket for redevelopment in D.C.'s Golden Triangle and downtown neighborhoods.

Building skin is a big consideration in office to residential conversions. Facade modifications are highly contingent on the type of window system, and may be costly. However, we can pinpoint which modifications are most suitable to each facade typology. We expect the return on investment to offset the cost of creating an attractive residential aesthetic.

Interior work prescribes several core strategies such as reconfiguring vertical and horizontal circulation and repurposing core mechanical space, but facade modifications create the aesthetic necessary to attract new residents and create vibrant neighborhoods. Therefore, we created a paradigm of modifications that correspond with different facade typologies. We found the variable elements to be projections and recessions. Modifications are contingent on whether a property includes curtain walls, punched windows, or ribbon windows. Modifications may include balconies, operable windows, or smaller-scale adjustments that include existing ribbon windows.

Finally, we identified clusters of high-potential conversion buildings, or areas with the capacity to convert over 1,000 residential units. We forecast areas within this threshold to help attract commercial amenities. Each converted node will create a network of communities, which in sum will yield a more interconnected cityscape.

**DESIGN IMPLICATIONS**

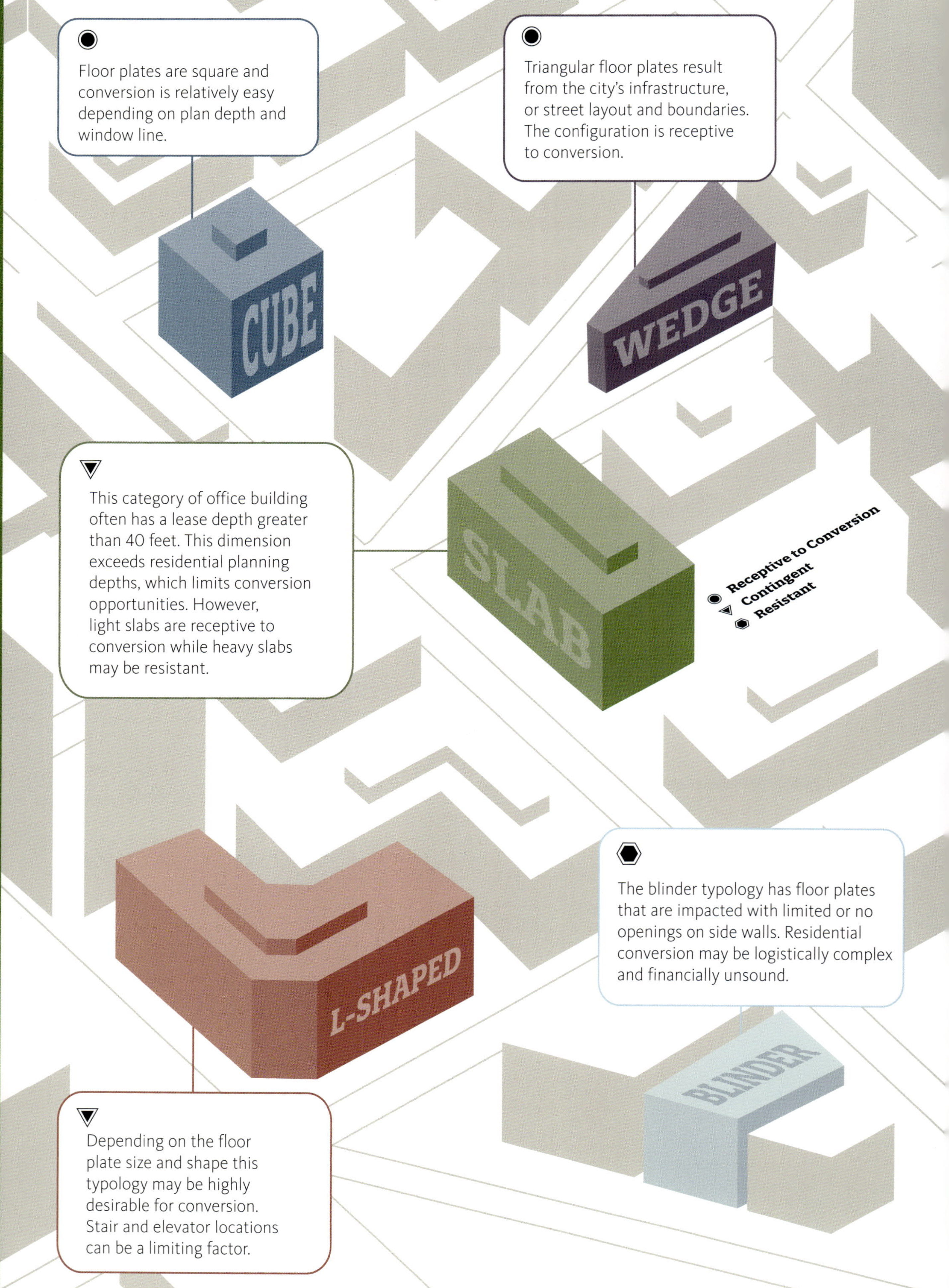

 Floor plates are square and conversion is relatively easy depending on plan depth and window line.

 Triangular floor plates result from the city's infrastructure, or street layout and boundaries. The configuration is receptive to conversion.

 This category of office building often has a lease depth greater than 40 feet. This dimension exceeds residential planning depths, which limits conversion opportunities. However, light slabs are receptive to conversion while heavy slabs may be resistant.

● Receptive to Conversion
▼ Contingent
⬢ Resistant

 The blinder typology has floor plates that are impacted with limited or no openings on side walls. Residential conversion may be logistically complex and financially unsound.

 Depending on the floor plate size and shape this typology may be highly desirable for conversion. Stair and elevator locations can be a limiting factor.

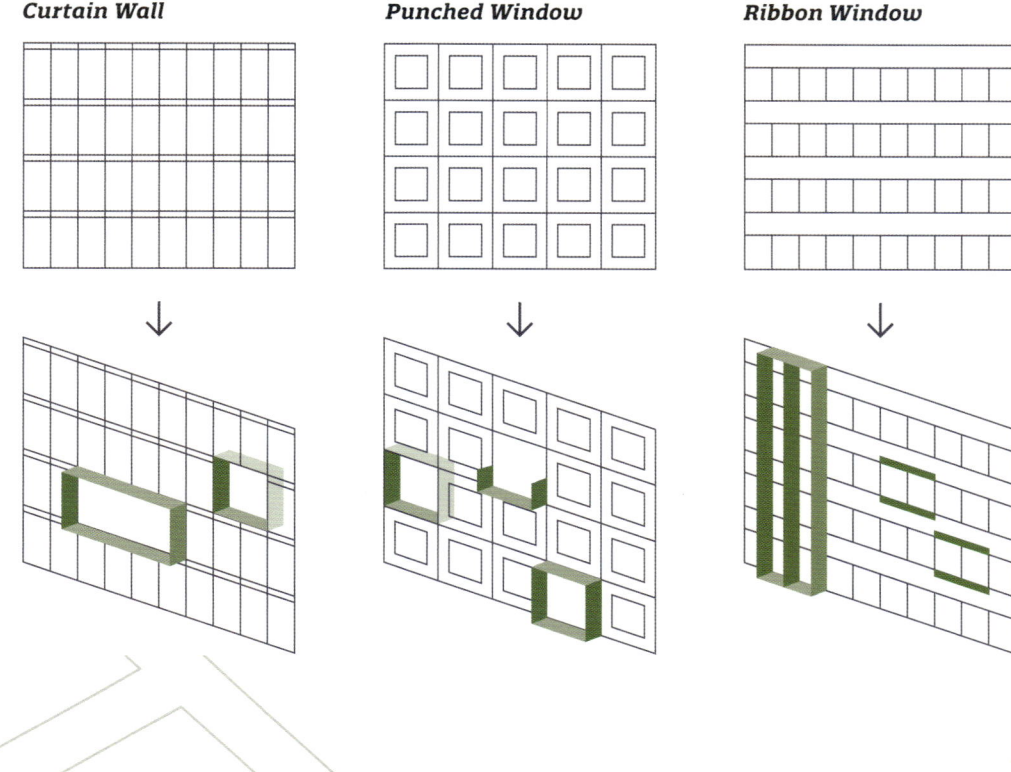

Creating mixed-use neighborhoods also delivers multifamily rent premiums, all while cutting back on underutilized office stock.

**WHAT'S NEXT**

We need to fine-tune the economics of conversion. Going forward, we should map and focus revenue streams and scale cost by complexity and size. To ensure that our community change is all positive, we need to predict broader economic impacts such as increased rent growth that hurts businesses and residents. Substantial rent growth may be a good thing for landlords, but affordable rents are a cornerstone of a healthy urban dynamic.

Owners need up-front capital, and help from D.C. is available. The Golden Triangle and the downtown neighborhood are among Washington, D.C.'s Business Improvement Districts (BID). The BID program encourages economic development through capital improvement projects, funded by a tax paid by local property owners. D.C. is using the BID program to catalyze residential conversions in the CBD area with abatements that could total up to $40 million over 10 years. Creating mixed-use neighborhoods also delivers multifamily rent premiums, all while cutting back on underutilized office stock.

# Achieving Inclusivity in the Design Process

How can designers ensure great experiences for all users?

**WHAT WE DID**

**We began our research by collecting secondary research on how today's designers approach accessibility.**
We hosted a roundtable called Designing Common Ground to discuss the state of the built environment and how we can improve the experience of individuals with disabilities.

We gave the roundtable participants (designers, architects, and people with disabilities) the floor to discuss what design professionals need to know, and how they are missing the mark in rendering design that is inclusive for all.

**Roundtable Participants**

New York City

Gensler

Washington, D.C.

Toronto

"We need to draw on those with expertise in the aesthetics of disability—increasing access and enriching experience."

"We're changing the paradigm of how we look at accessible design."

"The only way to overcome resistance is through education."

Nearly **1/5** in Americans have a disability.

### THE CONTEXT

**Designers have an underlying duty to remove barriers and create an equal experience for all people.** Problems disproportionately arise in certain areas of the built environment, so in the U.S., the Americans with Disabilities Act (ADA) created the ADA Standards for Accessible Design Checklist, which states four priority areas for accessibility in buildings: the approach and entrance, goods and services, toilet rooms, and other relative items such as water fountains and public telephones. Similarly, Canadians have noted several design features that are more likely to pose problems: corridor widths, buildings that lack elevators, and doorways.

Canadian accessibility regulations vary from Province to Province, but there is a growing desire for universal standards. Three in ten Canadians say that accessibility issues limit the places they can visit. Even as the Canadian government moves closer to implementing nationwide laws, policy is not the end-all for equality. Most legislation states that public accommodations must remove architectural barriers if doing so is "readily achievable" or when spaces undergo renovation. That means that if it is financially unsound to make a change, businesses are not culpable. In short, compliance with the law is often not enough—designers must strategize around the experiences of all people.

Nearly one in five Americans have a disability. Increased awareness of the disparities in how people with disabilities experience the built environment has only accomplished so much in righting shortfalls—there are hundreds of civil rights lawsuits each year that target buildings that do not properly accommodate people who are differently abled. When the ADA was signed into law in 1990, its goal was to create equality in the enjoyment of public facilities, enforcing public accommodations to suitably provide for the needs of people with disabilities.

# 3 in /10

Canadians say that accessibility issues limit the places they can visit

### THE RESULTS

**The findings from our roundtable discussions illustrate the need for innovative, experience-based design solutions.** Designers play an integral role in creating equal opportunities for a great experience, but too often do not design for inclusion. According to our roundtable participants, the design community does not adequately empathize with people with disabilities, lacking the foresight to create equitable access to building services and positive building experiences.

Abiding by building codes may technically accommodate people who are differently abled, but mere compliance too often falls short of providing an equal opportunity for a great experience. Progress is not achieved solely through legislation; the design community must have a more proactive hand in encouraging equality. Beyond the scope of building codes and legislation, we found that we need a more systematic way of isolating the design elements that are most likely to be problematic. Design teams must remove—not create—barriers for participating in the built environment.

**DESIGN IMPLICATIONS**

## Designing for accessibility begins when designers are first educated on skills and principles.

Post-secondary design institutions do not teach inclusive design, and this has a cascading effect for the design community's future of making inclusive spaces. Subject matter experts should participate in educating design professionals and design students. Universities are eager to leverage a new framework and apply new teaching methods for accessible design. As a result, the design community will be better able to design for all.

## First-hand perspectives from people who are differently abled are indispensable to designing for accessibility.

Our roundtable event included advocates from the U.S. and Canada who offered diverse perspectives on the issue of accessibility. Rather than starting from the antithesis of ability-versus-disability, we intend to illustrate a method to connect with the experiential design dimension from the perspective of people having diverse abilities, supporting a pathway to accessible design.

## The words we use to discuss accessibility are at issue too.

We must eradicate the belief that inclusive design cannot be achieved while making a beautiful aesthetic. Further, we must remove the thinking that designing for accessibility is not necessary. Effectively, we need a new vocabulary of design, or a rhetorical strategy to help grow positive conceptions around accessibility and to support those who are most vulnerable to inadequate foresight.

**WHAT'S NEXT**

Our research is a message, one that calls for continual checks on designing for inclusion. A theme of our research is questioning how to motivate a community to change. Therefore, our next step is launching a roadshow to demystify and inspire design teams to design for inclusivity. Through this effort, we aspire to build a network of experts we can use as consultants around the world to deliver inclusive projects. With our research as a catalyst, design professionals should be inspired to design by a more robust set of goals for inclusivity.

Shaping the Future of Cities

**The Ford Foundation Center for Social Justice**
New York, New York

The renovation of the Foundation's Manhattan headquarters embraces the dignity of all people. The atrium features a brick pathway that increases wheelchair access by 50% and opens circulation. A touch-and-smell garden takes center stage, including features for the visually impaired and braille signage totems.

# Designing Gender Inclusive Restrooms

How can we design public restrooms to be safe, comfortable, and inclusive?

**WHAT WE DID**

**Restroom access for transgender people has recently entered national conversations and debate.** To contribute to this discourse, we explored the long history of research and historical precedents related to gender-segregated restrooms. We followed this research with a survey of Gensler staff, designed to provide aggregated information on our experiences with restroom design. Our firmwide survey included 966 respondents from 35 offices in seven different countries. We quickly realized that restroom access goes far beyond the transgender community, affecting nearly everyone: parents, caregivers, private people, people with disabilities, and people living with special medical needs, among others.

Our next step was outreach. We held roundtable events in Los Angeles, Chicago, Atlanta, and New York. We wanted to understand a diversity of perspectives on experiences with restroom design, so we invited participants beyond just design and real estate professionals. Roundtables included members of the LGBTQ community to represent their experiences and concerns directly, alongside other community members, educators, industry leaders, and clients.

**THE CONTEXT**

Our modern conception of public restrooms dates back to antiquity—in Ancient Rome, the city installed multi-seat restrooms without partitions. Archeological digs in ancient civilizations demonstrate class distinctions in the restrooms used by upper and lower social strata. Looking to the present, it is impossible to dissociate social influences on restroom design from more practical concerns; our current conception and design of a restroom reflects a long history of building codes, policy, and law.

Throughout the 20th century, restroom access became politicized in the United States through equal rights movements: the repeal of Jim Crow laws, the passage of the Americans with Disabilities Act, and most recently, transgender rights. Today, very few gender-segregated spaces remain in our American landscape—restrooms are one of them. Regulatory codes set by the U.S. Department of Labor and the U.S. Department of Health and Human Services mandate not only separate facilities by gender, but also male to female restroom ratios. Alongside the political and institutional mandates, there are many intangible variables that mediate restroom design. Social and behavioral norms are highly influential forces on any concrete code, law, or design practice.

Many transgender people either face harassment and violence when seeking to use public restrooms, or are excluded entirely from their restroom of choice by policies or staff. Lack of safe restroom access has been linked to medical problems such as kidney infections, urinary tract infections, and other stress-related conditions.

As we face the challenge of restroom access and equity domestically, we should also recognize the broader challenges of restroom access and sanitation that continue to be pervasive globally. According to a World Health Organization study, over 30% of the global population does not have an adequate restroom as of 2015. Further, 2.4 billion people still do not have basic sanitation needs such as toilets.

**>30%** of the global population does not have an adequate restroom.

**2.4 billion** people still do not have basic sanitation needs such as toilets.

### Ancient Rome
Multi-stall restrooms without partitions are introduced.

### 1739
First gender-segregated public restroom exhibited at a ball in Paris. People thought it was eccentric and fun.

### Victorian Era
Male-only public restrooms dominate public access.

### 1870–1960s
In the U.S., Jim Crow laws required restrooms to be segregated by race.

### 1887
Massachusetts passed a law requiring workplaces that employed women to have separate restrooms for them.

### 1964
Title VII of Civil Rights Act passed. Many courts have interpreted Title VII to prohibit discrimination based on gender identity or transgender status.

### 1990
Americans with Disabilities Act passed, transforming restrooms.

### 2009
Kyle Giard-Chase spoke to the Vermont Human Rights, launching a new campaign on the importance of gender-neutral restrooms in public schools.

### 2012–2013
150 university campuses installed gender-neutral restrooms, along with a number of high schools.

### 2013
Portland approves law that requires gender-neutral signage on single-occupancy restrooms.

### 2014
Executive Order 13672 extends protection against discrimination in hiring on the basis of gender identity and sexual orientation.

### 2015
First gender-neutral restroom in the White House is introduced. Justice Department agrees with high school student Gavin Grimm, who is transgender and argued for right to use restrooms that match his gender identity.

### 2016
President Obama issues *Dear Colleague* letter directing public schools to allow students to use facilities consistent with their gender identity.

North Carolina passes HB2, which requires that people use the restroom of the sex indicated on their birth certificate.

### 2017
President Trump issues *Dear Colleague* letter rescinding rules on restrooms for transgender students, deferring to state governments.

SCOTUS defers pending Gavin Grimm v. Gloucester County School Board to lower courts.

Newly elected North Carolina governor, Ray Cooper, working with lawmakers, repeals HB2 after public outcry.

### 2018
International Building and Plumbing Codes will include "gender-neutral" restrooms as proposed by the AIA (403.1.2; IBC 2902.1.2).

Hygienic sanitation facilities are crucial for public health. Since 1990, the number of people gaining access to improved sanitation has risen from 54% to 68% but some 2.3 billion people still do not have toilets or improved latrines.

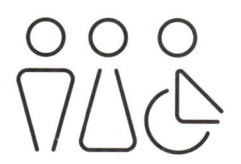

**62%**
of respondents would use a gender-inclusive restroom if it is closer than a gender-specific restroom.

**THE RESULTS**

Our survey and subsequent roundtable discussions found many prevalent, universal themes. In particular, proximity and privacy emerge as key concerns when designing any restroom for inclusivity.

Despite expressed trepidation for use of a gender-inclusive restroom, most survey respondents noted they would choose an inclusive option if it's the most expedient.

Privacy was probably the most noted consideration across our data and discussions. Universally, people want to feel safe and comfortable—particularly in the restroom. In this regard, single-occupancy stalls are ideal, but not always feasible. More than half of survey respondents stated openness to using a gender-inclusive restroom that is not single occupancy. However, lighting, ventilation, and maintenance pose constraints to universal, single-stall solutions. Floor-to-ceiling stalls require additional lighting, ventilation, and potentially structural support. Considerations for additional security with single-stall solutions also cannot be overlooked.

When single-occupancy stalls aren't possible, privacy can be achieved in more nuanced ways. Respondents noted that ambient noise and floor-to-ceiling doors, with amenities such as full-length mirrors, towels, and hygiene products, are quick and effective means of creating a sense of comfort and privacy. Outside a restroom unit, signage should be gender-inclusive, and policies that allow usage based on gender identity should be clearly communicated and multilingual when appropriate. For added security, each stall should have a visual lock that displays occupancy.

**DESIGN IMPLICATIONS**

**Design for privacy, proximity, and cleanliness.** Many people of all backgrounds plan their days around using the restroom, often having to research restroom availability. But what they're looking for is universal—privacy, proximity, and cleanliness matter to everyone choosing a restroom. Features like floor-to-ceiling stalls that maximize privacy are ideal, but maintenance is also a consideration—will the cleaning equipment be able to reach the corners?

**Don't assume; accommodate.**
Designing for inclusivity from the beginning (instead of waiting for issues to arise) not only reinforces cultural tolerance and organizational values, but also saves money by avoiding the need to redesign or add new facilities in the future. Inclusive policies also attract the best talent and promote diverse points of view.

**Language is powerful.**
"Gender inclusive," or "all gender" is preferred. "Gender neutral," is considered problematic by some in the transgender community—the term erases gender identity. Signage and pictograms should also be considered carefully, and within the cultural context. What works for a North American workplace may not for an international airport or highly trafficked museum.

**Provide options for all users.**
There is no one-size-fits-all solution. Single-user, hybrid, and multi-stall options should all be considered. If providing amenities, such as hygiene products, they should be provided equally in all environments.

40  Shaping the Future of Cities | Designing Gender Inclusive Restrooms

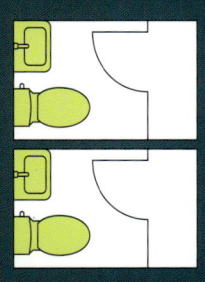

## Single User

Only single-occupancy stalls are provided, maximizing privacy and flexibility and coupled with policy allowing usage based on gender identity. Appropriate for small work environments or low-traffic areas.

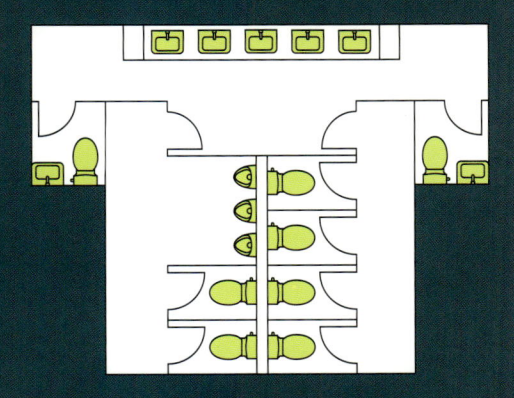

## Hybrid

Single user options are provided alongside gender-segregated facilities and shared sinks. Appropriate for work environments, public institutions, and high-traffic areas.

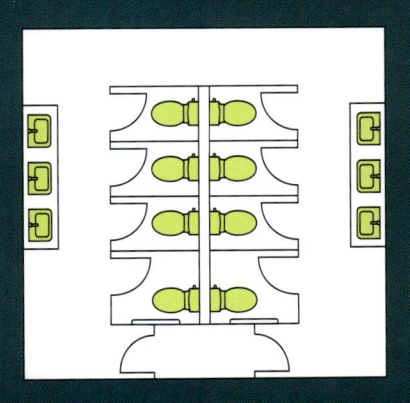

## Multi-Stall

Floor-to-ceiling stalls with visible locks are available to people of all genders. Appropriate for highly trafficked, well-secured public spaces and with additional single user, or gender-segregated spaces. Signage should clearly communicate usage policy and locations of nearby restrooms with alternative layouts.

**WHAT'S NEXT**

Restroom access continues to be ingrained in controversy; near-term solutions are marred by both practical considerations and social issues. As designers and architects, we have an opportunity to pave the way for open communication—informing clients of the requirements by law, but also proposing creative options for inclusive design solutions. Although many states have pending restrictive measures to limit individuals to using facilities that correspond to the sex indicated on their birth certificates, such legislation is increasingly unpopular.

But ultimately, laws alone aren't going to change design. Forward-thinking corporations and institutions must be at the forefront of change. A movement toward inclusive restroom design will require change management, and designers need to help facilitate productive discussions with clients and building users.

Broadly, restrooms should not be viewed as an inconvenience, or a place to cut costs, but rather as an opportunity to forge a cohesive building aesthetic, and a place to signify inclusion. There is an enormous landscape of laws and policies, but also solutions whose only bounds are creativity. Because of this, we are not limited to one prescriptive solution. With careful consideration, we can continue to evolve in the right direction to provide better experiences for all.

### Ideal Amenities

- Stalls
- Full-length mirrors
- Towels

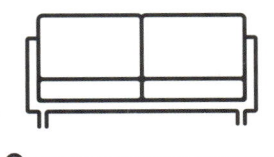

### Amenities to Avoid

- Attendants
- Urinals
- Seating

# Local Development in Sub-Sahraran Africa

What role should design play in Sub-Saharan Africa's growing markets and economies?

**WHAT WE DID**

**We aggregated research on two major Sub-Saharan economic hubs—Nairobi, Kenya and Lagos, Nigeria—investigating the unique social and economic elements in how design can help the region.** Our research is differentiated from past work on this topic by a focus on the human experience. We held a design strategy workshop, or a paneled discussion, to ensure our vision reflected the most pressing regional concerns. Our inaugural workshop included 28 attendees representing various stakeholders of positive change in the region: IDB, Deloitte, Accenture, IADB, IFC, Commerce, Tiphub, and DBIA. Finally, we synthesized our findings and socialized our work among clients and the design community.

**THE CONTEXT**

Sub-Saharan Africa is vast and diverse—no singular research project can account for the successes and challenges of the entire region. For a manageable approach, we focused our attention on two economies with enormous upside potential. According to the Ibrahim Index of African Governance (IIAG), a tool that measures and monitors governance performance in African countries, Nigeria—the largest economy in Sub-Sarahan Africa valued with a GDP of over $1 trillion USD—ranks highly in rule of law, participation, and human rights. Kenya outperforms other African nations on human development and health. Currently both are outranked by South Africa in terms of where global companies are located, but these emerging economies are far outpacing South Africa's annual growth and are poised to increase in global significance.

**THE RESULTS**

One point of agreement for all panelists/participants: the region does not have the infrastructure it needs. One solution is quality public-private partnerships that engage national, state, and local tiers of government. Deloitte has noted the benefit of public-private partnerships in orchestrating business opportunities in Sub-Saharan Africa. Further, such partnerships may reap enormous tax incentives for companies to expand in Nigeria in underutilized industries.

**We need a broader range of statistics to gauge performance and pursue positive growth.** Economic indicators, such as GDP, do not tell us the full story of a region's well-being. Both Kenya and Nigeria rank in the bottom quartile of the Human Development Index, an aggregation of life expectancy, education, and per capita income. Incremental improvements under each targeted problem area is the right approach to the long term.

> Integrating design with local development can significantly improve the human experience in Sub-Saharan Africa.

# NAIROBI KENYA

**Development abounds, but social, economic, and infrastructural problems remain.**

## Infrastructure & Environment

**1.5+ hours**
work commute into Nairobi

**Hydro & fossil**
primary energy sources

**30x worse**
air quality than London

**15%** private vehicles
**41%** walk
**43%** informal buses (matatus)
**< 1%** bus rapid transit (BRT)
**30%** daily income spent on transit (lowest income group)

## Economic Development | Services & Access

**Majority**
have Internet access

**$1,081 USD GDP**
per capita

**15k housing units**
developed annually

**200 Settlements**
60% of population live on 6% of land

**Cheaper real estate**
for startups

**696 km²**
land in 85 wards

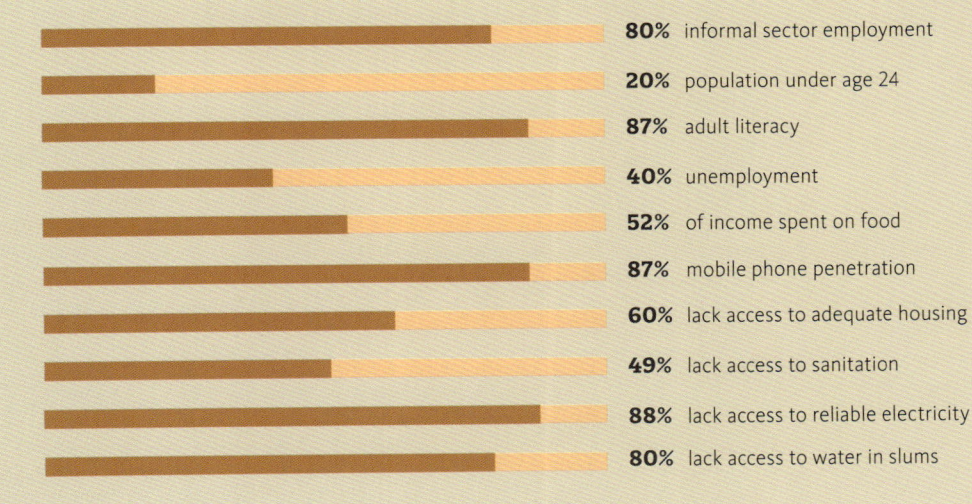

**80%** informal sector employment
**20%** population under age 24
**87%** adult literacy
**40%** unemployment
**52%** of income spent on food
**87%** mobile phone penetration
**60%** lack access to adequate housing
**49%** lack access to sanitation
**88%** lack access to reliable electricity
**80%** lack access to water in slums

# LAGOS NIGERIA

Lagos is Nigeria's economic engine. Future prosperity should be pursued through considering all socioeconomic levels.

## Infrastructure & Environment

**Up to 4 hours**
commute into CBD

**Diesel generators**
primary energy sources

**Higher emissions**
than Beijing, China, at 1.44 trigrams per year

- **11%** private vehicles
- **40%** walk
- **45%** informal buses (danfos)
- **> 1%** bus rapid transit (BRT)
- **54%** of daily income on bus fare (lowest income group)

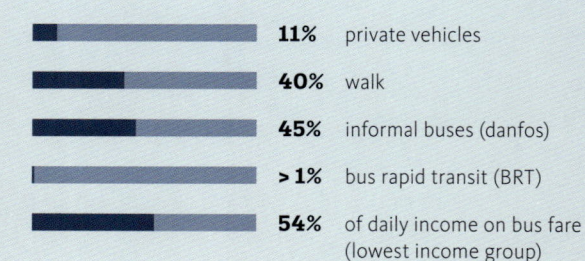

## Economic Development | Services & Access

**Introduction**
of high-speed Internet

**$80.1 Billion USD**
2010 GDP, 36% of Nigerian GDP

**100k housing units**
estimated

**250k jobs**
estimated

**Largest city globally**
without a mayor

**100 slum communities**
153,182 average people per slum

**Cheaper real estate**
for startups

**9 km²**
land in 10 urban districts

**2 of 3 college-age students**
cannot find a spot at a Nigerian University

**25/54**
Participation & Human Rights Score among peers according to Mo Ibrahim Index for Nigeria

- **0.8%** GDP derived from Internet enterprise
- **+60%** population under age 24
- **70%** of Nigeria's industrial capacity is in Lagos
- **63%** lack rights to occupancy
- **70%** lack access to adequate housing
- **69%** lack access to sanitation
- **88%** lack access to reliable electricity
- **84%** lack access to water

## The Market Approach

- BUILT
- SOCIAL
- ECONOMIC
- DEVELOPMENT
- POLICY
- DESIGN

**DESIGN IMPLICATIONS**

**Development abounds in the region, but many projects lack a focus on the human experience.** There is an opportunity to bring design experience into the conversation on the region's path forward. This means bringing together the right people. Many global companies are already working in the region, all of whom should be involved in a meaningful dialogue about the people, place, and profit dynamic in each emerging market.

**Access to basic needs is an issue for most people of this booming population.** Nearly three-quarters of those in Nairobi and Lagos lack access to sanitation and adequate housing. For the impoverished, the cost of living is nearly insurmountable. In Nairobi, bus fares can account for over 50% of an individual's income. But there are upsides to consider too. The district of Yaba in Lagos is quickly becoming a hub for technology. And unlike most of Nigeria, Lagos is not entirely dependent on oil.

**Framing the correct problem statement will save a lot of time and resources.** This is especially salient in a market that is challenged with limited resources. In times of booming growth, markets must ensure intelligent design, integrating sustainability and the human experience. Only recently have the markets we explored initiated a turn toward ameliorating grand problems on a massive scale.

**To enact grassroots change, we must recognize local "change agents."** Panels of community, public, and private sector leaders must be responsible for advocating and moving the agenda forward, regardless of the political environment. To realize a future-thinking vision, we must create small, impactful, multidisciplinary interventions throughout the region's local government areas.

**WHAT'S NEXT**

The World Bank reports that both Nigeria and Kenya are moving in the right direction for more ease in doing business. On variables such as obtaining credit, enforcing contracts, starting a business, and dealing with construction permits, the organization reports that both countries are moving in a positive direction.

# Investigating Downtown Neighborhood Resurgence

How can we systematically track and analyze the indicators that lead to neighborhood development?

**WHAT WE DID**

**We analyzed the factors driving the resurgence of downtown and adjacent neighborhoods in the Midwest.**
We focused on seven Midwestern cities—Minneapolis, Milwaukee, Chicago, Cincinnati, St. Louis, Detroit, and Cleveland—including 56 neighborhoods under our assessment. We tapped multiple data sources such as median age, household growth, economic diversity, transportation accessibility, rental rates, and apartment occupancy to investigate the range of preconditions that yield neighborhood development.

Based on our initial analysis, we then used two case studies—Corktown, Detroit, and Walker's Point, Milwaukee—to test the scalability and applicability of our findings. With these case studies, we were able to identify key themes around the process of neighborhood change. For further insight into market nuances, we interviewed two key area stakeholders: Farpoint, a development trust in Chicago, and the Department of City Development in Milwaukee.

**THE CONTEXT**

Downtown core neighborhoods in cities around the U.S. are experiencing growth, aligned with the ongoing trend of the world's population shifting toward urban areas. The growth in downtown core neighborhoods, in particular in Midwestern and Rust Belt cities that have often experienced cycles of disinvestment, is now putting downtown-adjacent neighborhoods in flux too.

As major employers are expanding their footprints in urban centers, the focus on these neighborhoods is only poised to increase—though these areas often encounter higher vacancy rates and less positive socioeconomic indicators. When positioned historically, the trajectory of adjacent neighborhoods shows prime suitability for redevelopment. Considering the impact of a significant makeover on the community at large, stakeholders—including development authorities, private developers, real estate professionals—must work in tandem to create a sustainable development path forward.

# The right mix of assets and preconditions can catalyze development.

- Transportation
- Public Schools
- Real Estate Vacancy
- Adjacencies
- Population Density
- "Trendiness"
- Education
- Diversity

## 56 neighborhoods across 7 cities classified by status

*By understanding where a neighborhood lies within its development cycle, planners and policymakers can encourage development.*

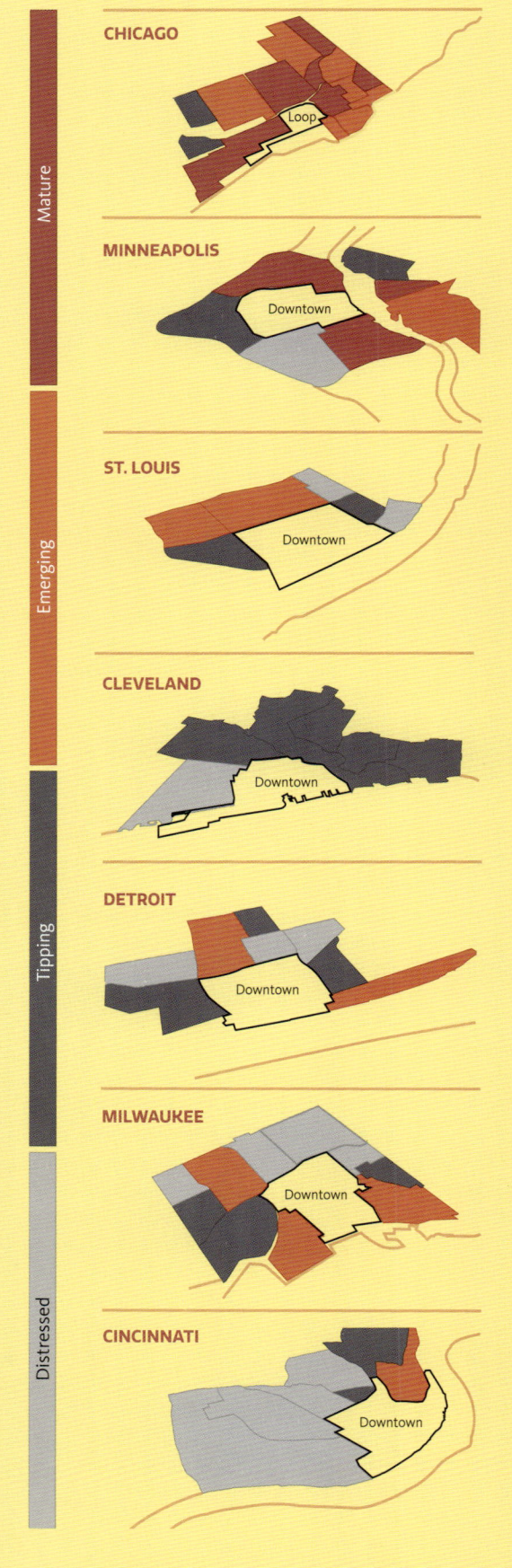

CHICAGO

MINNEAPOLIS

ST. LOUIS

CLEVELAND

DETROIT

MILWAUKEE

CINCINNATI

Mature | Emerging | Tipping | Distressed

### THE RESULTS

**We created a framework that classifies urban neighborhoods into four potential development states: distressed, tipping, emerging, and mature.** The largest contingent, tipping, is represented in each of the seven downtowns we studied. We found that neighborhoods categorized as tipping are often areas with the most development potential—or vice versa, are areas at risk of becoming distressed. Common themes among the tipping neighborhoods with high development potential include adjacent emerging or peaking neighborhoods, transportation access, public school quality, high commercial occupancy, trendiness, and social and economic diversity. Therefore, we systematized available socioeconomic, real estate, and financial data to help drive data-driven development decisions.

Our interview process provided insights into areas of opportunity. Many city governments or development authorities lack the quantitative tools to forecast trends and scenarios, and have no framework to compare metro regions. As a solution, they need predictive models in their decision-making process. Our research can help to achieve this goal through integrating data types specifically around Esri Tapestry Segmentation and proprietary data from the city.

Our interviews with developers and community stakeholders revealed a similar dynamic: development decisions often rely on too much anecdotal evidence, operate under time constraints, and are hampered by the contextual complexity of different neighborhoods. There is an opportunity to create quantitative precedents and case studies of neighborhoods, with application to other secondary cities. This could also create baseline information to support neighborhood-specific growth and conversion strategies. We can do this through empowering equity and ownership within communities, identifying quantitative indicators, and determining tipping point neighborhoods.

**DESIGN IMPLICATIONS**

**Corporate investment can be a positive driver for growth.** Corporate moves and population growth from a young demographic are driving Corktown's neighborhood transition in Detroit, for example. The area holds a large concentration of management, education, and public administration jobs, demanding high levels of educational attainment and young professionals. Large corporations such as Ford and Quicken Loans have opened offices and have invested heavily in the area. In Walker's Point, Milwaukee, companies from adjacent neighborhoods are moving in, opting for more space and less expensive rental rates and seeking to create a similar dynamic.

**A positive economic outlook increases apartment demand.** Net migration and economic upsides have driven rising apartment rents and new, quality apartment developments. In Corktown, large swaths of vacant publicly owned land mean an opportunity for further revitalization. Despite new multifamily inventory added in response to growing demand in Walker's Point, vacancy continues to fall.

**Target underutilized land to optimize impact.** The Harbor District in Walker's Point represents a unique opportunity for the City of Milwaukee to repurpose underutilized industrial land and drive economic growth on the near south side of the city. As a result of the port and manufacturing legacy of the district, an overwhelming majority of the Legacy Industrial District is reserved for industrial uses but represents a future opportunity for a mixed-use development. Here, approximately 13% of the land is vacant, and much more is underutilized.

**WHAT'S NEXT?**

Developers, city entities, urban policy groups, think tanks—all have a vested interest in improving the planning and development process. Our next steps include collaborating with all stakeholders to develop further case studies and a finely tuned framework for implementation. Our framework must holistically fuse residential and commercial needs to create the opportunity for informed development decisions and policy proposals.

Shaping the Future of Cities

**Crystal City Repositioning**
Arlington, Virginia

Gensler's repositioning strategy envisioned the transformation of an underutilized city block into a thriving, pedestrian-oriented destination. The strategy maximizes the street retail envelope creating a continuous retail experience, defines street edges with new architecture, and increases urban density. Gensler envisioned a new metro transit plaza, movie theater, infill retail, and the repositioning of four existing office buildings.

# A Framework for Holistic Urban Planning

How can we encourage a responsible approach to urban planning?

## WHAT WE DID

**We believe that urban planning projects should not place financial concerns above all others; social and environmental concerns can be taken up without sacrificing financial returns.** To test that thesis, we set out to create a tool that both encourages more holistic development and quantifies a project's socio-economic and ecological impact. As a starting point, we reviewed the United Nations Sustainable Development Goals (SDGs), which serve as an outline for a more just and sustainable development model.

We then identified those SDGs that coincide with architecture and planning. Next, we conducted an extensive review of the metrics of existing rating and certification systems to guide how we measure progress toward an SDG target. **Ultimately, we created a set of key performance indicators that became the basis of the Socio-Economic Ecological Performance Index (SEPI)**—a tool for measuring a project's performance across the quadruple bottom line of people, planet, policy, and profit.

◇ No poverty

◇ Zero hunger

◇ Good health & well-being

◇ Quality education

◇ Gender equality

◇ Clean water & sanitation

◇ Affordable & clean energy

◇ Decent work & economic growth

◇ Industry, innovation & infrastructure

◇ Reduced inequalities

◇ Sustainable cities & communities

◇ Responsible consumption & production

◇ Climate action

◇ Life below water

◇ Life on land

◇ Peace, justice & strong institutions

◇ Partnerships

## THE CONTEXT

In a future where megacities are widespread, sustainable and human-focused development should be the centerpiece of a responsible growth strategy. By 2030, there are expected to be over 40 megacities; i.e., metropolitan areas with more than 10 million inhabitants. According to the World Migration Report, the number of people living in cities will almost double by 2050, reaching 6.4 billion people. Yet many new city dwellers will find themselves in environments that are starkly unequal, as evidenced by the global epidemic of socio-economic and spatial inequality. Given these developments, we began to explore methodologies for measuring a project's socio-economic and ecological performance, and incentivizing projects to better engage with their local communities.

**THE RESULTS**

SEPI is designed as an anticipatory toolkit that can help any locale grow responsibly, sustainably, and justly. To gauge the impact of every new project, SEPI employs a survey tool based on 25 key performance indicators for pre-occupancy and 25 key performance indicators for post-occupancy. Successful projects score well across the entire multifaceted framework. Its performance indicators address everything from how a project will play into public transportation to the diversity of personnel creating a project. **By synchronizing best practices at the local level with aspirational targets, SEPI helps drive toward meaningful long-term impacts.**

For example, SEPI asks whether the project has a life-cycle plan to reuse, recycle, or upcycle all building equipment materials. In considering this question at a project's inception, designers will be better able to forecast costs and community involvement and tap the necessary partner organizations.

## Our model operates by a quadruple bottom line of people, planet, policy, and profit.

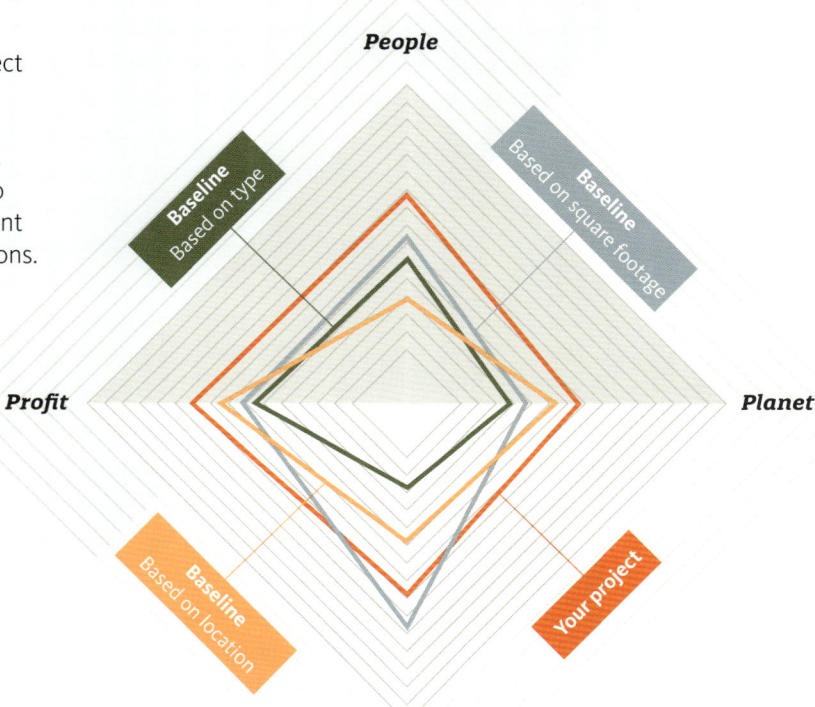

*People*

*Profit*

**Baseline** Based on type

**Baseline** Based on square footage

*Planet*

**Baseline** Based on location

**Your project**

*Policy*

**DESIGN IMPLICATIONS**

**Responsible design is not achieved by financial incentives alone.** It is achieved through efforts that incentivize a more comprehensive and human-centered approach. That means we need new tools—such as SEPI—for engendering more responsible outcomes and new guidance for how we measure those outcomes. Yet such tools cannot stand alone if we are to spur truly holistic development.

**Ultimately, we envision SEPI as part of a collaborative, multipronged approach.** Such an approach will involve multiple stakeholders working together and merging data streams, intellectual property, and any tools necessary for a unified system. Thus, SEPI will play a key role in helping architects, owners, developers, and others synchronize their efforts according to the quadruple bottom line of social, economic, ecological, and performance considerations.

**WHAT'S NEXT**

Looking to the future, we see our tool as a launch point of advocacy in pushing policy and financial incentives toward more responsible design practices, and therefore, more holistic community growth. To realize that vision, we will use SEPI to rapidly collect robust and meaningful data across a broad project portfolio. Our objective is to build a database of project information that will allow us to provide benchmarks and actionable recommendations. We believe that such data mining and benchmarking will definitively show that when projects achieve goals tied to socio-economic and ecological issues, they also open up new avenues for financial gains.

# TACKLING CLIMATE CHANGE

Building materials and operations are currently one of the largest contributors to greenhouse gas emissions worldwide; smart design strategies can minimize their impact.

## DESIGNING FOR RESILIENCE

56 **Impact by Design**

**Research Team**
David Briefel
Anthony Brower
Nick Bryan
Chang-Yeon Cho
Kevin Craft
Stella Donovan
Paula Eleazar
Christopher Gray
Lance Hosey
Ken Sanders
Leonard Sciarra
Kyle Sellers
Rives Taylor
Richard Tyson

**Research Partner**
Jerde Analytics

60 **Gensler's Path to Net Zero**

**Research Team**
Anthony Brower
Brian Ledder
Gail Napell
Gregory Plavcan
Leonard Sciarra
Mallory Taub
Rives Taylor

66 **Designing Dynamic Facades to Conserve Energy**

**Research Team**
Jeff Barber
Mark Bassett
Zhifei Cheng
Adam Simmons
Daniel Walsh

## URBAN ECOLOGY

**70 Urban Strategies for Coastal Resilience**

**Research Team**
Ana Benatuil
Corina Benatuil
Corina Ocanto
Carlos Valera

**Research Partners**
Florida International University Professor and Associate Dean Marilys R. Nepomechie, FAIA, DPACSA, NCARB

**Students**
Yailyn Barrera
Jose Diaz-Rivera
Vanessa Estevez
Verlan Eugene
Mylene Feng
Nicole Franzese
Marcela Gavilanez
Cristina Gomez
Stevenson Jean
Kaitie Fuson
Celine Mazhar
Marie Mondiere
Esther Triana
Valeria Zavatti

**74 Preserving Urban Ecosystems**

**Research Team**
Ned Dodington
Brandon Hendricks
Scott Magnuson
Rives Taylor

**78 Underground Retail and Rooftop Farming**

**Research Team**
David Glover
Robert Hughes
Maja Jasniewicz
Ian Kim
Emmanuel Ramirez Muro
Adham Refaat
Leonara Bustamante Sauma

**Research Partners**
OJB Landscape Architecture
Saiful Bouquet Structural Engineers
Syska Hennessy Group

## RESILIENCE IN THE WORKPLACE

**82 The Effects of Living Walls**

**Research Team**
Daichi Amano
Hisayuki Araki
Tatsuya Oi
Taro Uchiyama
Nachiko Yamamoto

**88 Implementing the Circular Economy**

**Research Team**
Jane Christen
Jane Greenthal
Marcus Hopper
Gail Napell
Kirsten Ritchie
Michael Saunders
Allie Trachsel

# Impact by Design

How can we expand our resilience efforts beyond just energy and efficiency to include broader areas of impact?

We must broaden the discussion of resilience beyond just energy efficiency.

**WHAT WE DID**

**We assessed the resilience and sustainability of Gensler's portfolio to understand the impact our work is having on the environment and the world, and how we are tracking as a firm against the industry's broader goals for improvement.** We then identified elements of a comprehensive strategy to expand the discussion of resilience beyond just energy efficiency to encourage broader adoption of resilient methods.

**THE CONTEXT**

By mid-century, our urban areas will account for over three-quarters of the world's population. This urbanization will come with a huge amount of new building; it is estimated that 2.5 trillion square feet of new space will be built in the next 40 years. Nearly half of greenhouse gas emissions come from the built environment. Finding ways to better integrate our buildings and cities with the natural world is the clearest path to addressing today's most urgent challenges.

**THE RESULTS**

Truly resilient places today—whether interior retail or workplace environments, new or renovated buildings, neighborhoods, or city districts—represent the culmination of design strategies that work in concert to maximize both performance and the human experience. We identified six topics that we believe have the greatest potential for positive impact in the coming years:

## FORM

At every step of the design and decision-making process—from the location of a building, to its orientation on site and its shape, size, and ability to respond to its environment—the decisions designers make are crucial to creating high performance buildings with minimal environmental impact.

## ENERGY

Minimizing energy usage, and therefore operational carbon impacts, is a key first step to acheiving net zero. In a traditional net zero approach, the amount of energy a building needs is then created on-site via renewable energy sources. The conversation also includes how to procure renewable energy from utilities in markets where buyers can specify their energy source.

## MATERIALS

More energy is expended during the production of materials than at any other point during a project's lifestyle. Ultimately, if we specify materials that minimize carbon production, select locally sourced materials, use resilient materials, and consider material life cycle, then we significantly lessen the environmental impact of our buildings.

## WATER

Cities should consider strategies specifically designed to combat sudden or gradual influxes of sea water, such as cut/fill canals, constructed coastal dunes, and dedicated wetlands. Finally, the designers, owners, and operators of the built environment must determine the strategies that best suit their location, such as raising ground floors to flood-proof existing structures.

## ADAPTATION

Significant design interventions can present a whole new character or experience for users without starting over. These "hacked" buildings can preserve materials to reduce environmental impact while adjusting the building's form to accommodate new use cases or operational realities.

## INTELLIGENCE

Our spaces, buildings, and cities will learn to leverage real-time data concerning occupant behavior and air quality and temperature to dynamically optimize space performance and experience. This responsiveness will significantly reduce the amount of energy required to operate the built environment.

**DESIGN IMPLICATIONS**

**The business case for sustainable design has never been clearer, even though the specifics of how to achieve higher levels of sustainability are evolving.** State and city governments are driving many of these changes. Taking cues from progressive design firms and nonprofit organizations, states and municipalities are implementing increasingly stringent building codes. These shifts will be the basis on which performance is judged in the future.

**Whenever possible, we should design our buildings for a future in which their use is potentially unknown.** Human behavior, technology, and the ways in which we use and inhabit physical space will continue to evolve. Whether designing buildings in a way they can be easily deconstructed and reconstructed with reusable or reused materials, or creating flexible and reconfigurable spaces that easily adapt to new needs, this approach to an unknown future should increasingly be part of the resilience narrative.

# Gensler's 2018 portfolio is estimated to save 14.6 billion kWH/year, offsetting approximately 10.3 million metric tons of CO2 emissions.

**BUILDING PERFORMANCE
ENERGY USE INTENSITY (EUI)**

Our 2018 building projects represent a 48% improvement over our calculated CBECS 2003 equivalent.

*EUI is a measure of energy use. Typically, and as used in this publication, EUI represents an estimated number based on a building's design and energy model. It is measured in kBtu per square foot per year.*

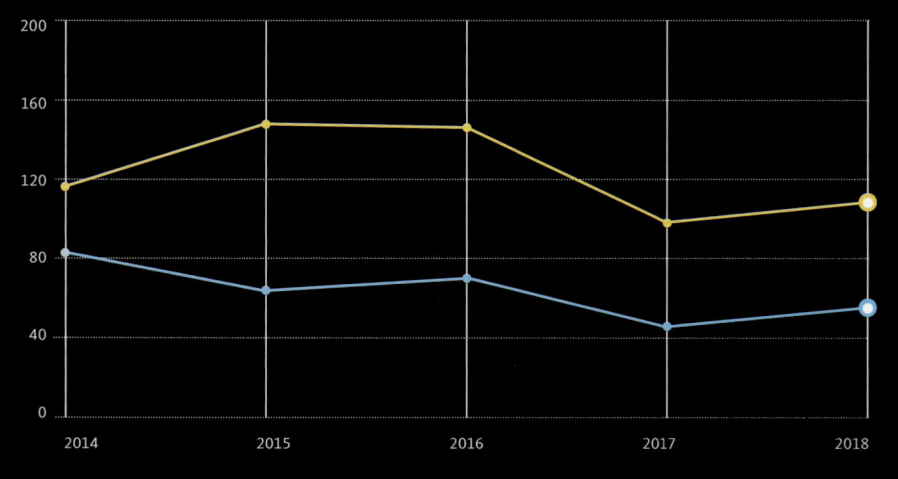

CBECS 2003 Average
112.8 kBtu/sf

Gensler 2018 Portfolio Average
58.4 kBtu/sf

58  Tackling Climate Change | Impact by Design

**Overall, we must prioritize life cycle thinking for every design we create and every material, furniture, and fixture that we specify.** It is important to understand not only the energy and carbon expended in the creation of an object or place, but the expenditure at the end of that life cycle. This means planning for reuse of materials and buildings whenever possible—whether via refurbishment, recycling, or adaptive reuse—and having a careful approach to waste management when materials do need to be discarded.

**WHAT'S NEXT**

In today's economy and climate, things seem to be moving and changing faster than ever. As a firm and an industry, we need to move just as quickly. Ambitious targets set by the World Green Building Council's Net Zero Building Challenge, the UN Global Compact, and the Architecture 2030 Challenge are fast approaching—but may not be enough. Gensler has set our own targets for improving the performance of our work: the Gensler Cities Climate Challenge launching in 2020. As the world continues to cluster into urban areas, we will continue to rethink the built environment with an eye toward resilience and preservation.

## INTERIOR PERFORMANCE
## LIGHTING POWER DENSITY (LPD)

Our 2018 interiors projects represent a 43% improvement over our calculated ASHRAE 90.1 2007 equivalent.

*LPD is a calculation of the installed lighting power of an interior environment, and is measured in watts per square foot. An LPD score is generated through adding all of the lighting in a floor plan and dividing the total wattage generated by these lights by the floor plan's total square footage.*

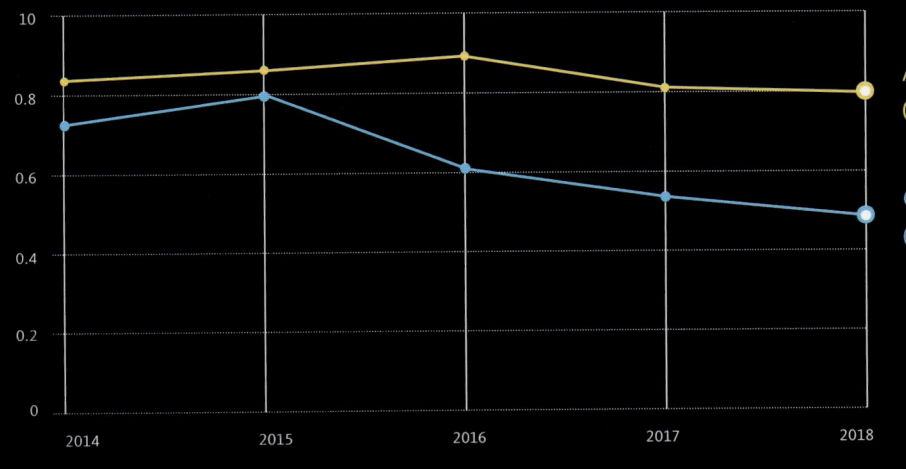

ASHRAE 90.1 2007 Average
0.84 watts/sf

Gensler 2018 Portfolio Average
0.55 watts/sf

# A Path Toward Net Zero Energy Buildings

How can Gensler achieve a carbon-neutral portfolio by 2030?

**Commitment: AIA 2030 Challenge**

**80% reduction in predicted EUI by 2030**

**WHAT WE DID**

**Prior to announcing the Gensler Cities Climate Challenge, our research provided insights to help Gensler make significant year-over-year progress toward our AIA Challenge commitment, which is to reduce the predicted energy performance of our projects by 80% by 2030 compared to a 2003 baseline.** While the Gensler Cities Climate Challenge goes beyond this commitment by declaring all of our work will be completely carbon neutral in 2030, this project focused on setting targets for reducing predicted energy performance.

As part of our project, we drafted a proposed roadmap for our energy reduction goals, and created a tool to empower managers to provide customized energy use intensity (EUI) and lighting power density (LPD) targets at the start of a project. The 2030 roadmap identifies the annual percentage improvement in predicted energy performance needed to meet the AIA 2030 Challenge. It then establishes a front-loaded strategy to accelerate sustainability efforts in the next five years to encourage quick progress. The tool goes beyond existing publicly available energy target tools by integrating into Gensler project workflows and including performance data from Gensler's portfolio.

We began by analyzing Gensler's performance and baseline data to develop energy targets for new projects based on their typology, size, climate zone, and projected completion date. We also met with project managers to understand the needed resources for net zero performance, and analyzed portfolio-wide strategies for achieving the identified improvement targets. From this research, we developed a proof of concept for the project startup tool that empowers project managers to make well-informed, sustainability related design decisions up front.

✓ **Analyzed Gensler's performance and baseline data**
*to develop energy targets for new projects*

✓ **Met with Gensler's project managers**
*to understand the resources needed to achieve net zero energy performance, and analyzed portfolio-wide strategies for the identified improvement targets*

**Proof of concept for a project startup tool to empower project managers to make well-informed sustainability related design decisions up front.**

## We need a tool to empower our designers with energy performance targets at the start of every project across myriad project types, locations, and budgets.

Gensler is an ongoing participant in the Architecture 2030 Challenge and an initial signatory of the Paris Pledge for Action signed at COP21. Both represent our commitment in pushing our design solutions toward a goal of drastic energy reductions in our designs by the year 2030. In the majority of regions in which we work, this level of energy performance will be beyond what is required by code. To meet these performance targets, we needed a plan and associated toolset to empower our designers and clients with actionable strategies to improve project performance across myriad project types, locations, and budgets.

Designing for "net zero energy" doesn't mean they use no energy—but it does mean they use significantly less. Net zero energy is made possible by combining minimized energy use with on-site and purchased renewable energy. Following the AIA 2030 Challenge guidelines, off-site renewable energy can account for no more than 20% of the reduction from the 2003 CBECS baseline.

Our first step was to analyze a database of the predicted EUI of every project Gensler designed in 2017. To achieve an 80% reduction in EUI from the baseline, our portfolio average EUI will need to be 22 kBtu/sf/year; our current portfolio-wide average EUI is 70. To reach a portfolio EUI of 22, we need to achieve a 19% improvement beyond industry standard in the next five years. We argue that we should be aiming for a 38% reduction in our portfolio average in the next five years to lead the market. We have a huge amount of data from past projects to help us understand our performance to date. And this data can be leveraged to inform a strategic roadmap for the next 11 years to drive sustainability performance further toward our ambitious goal.

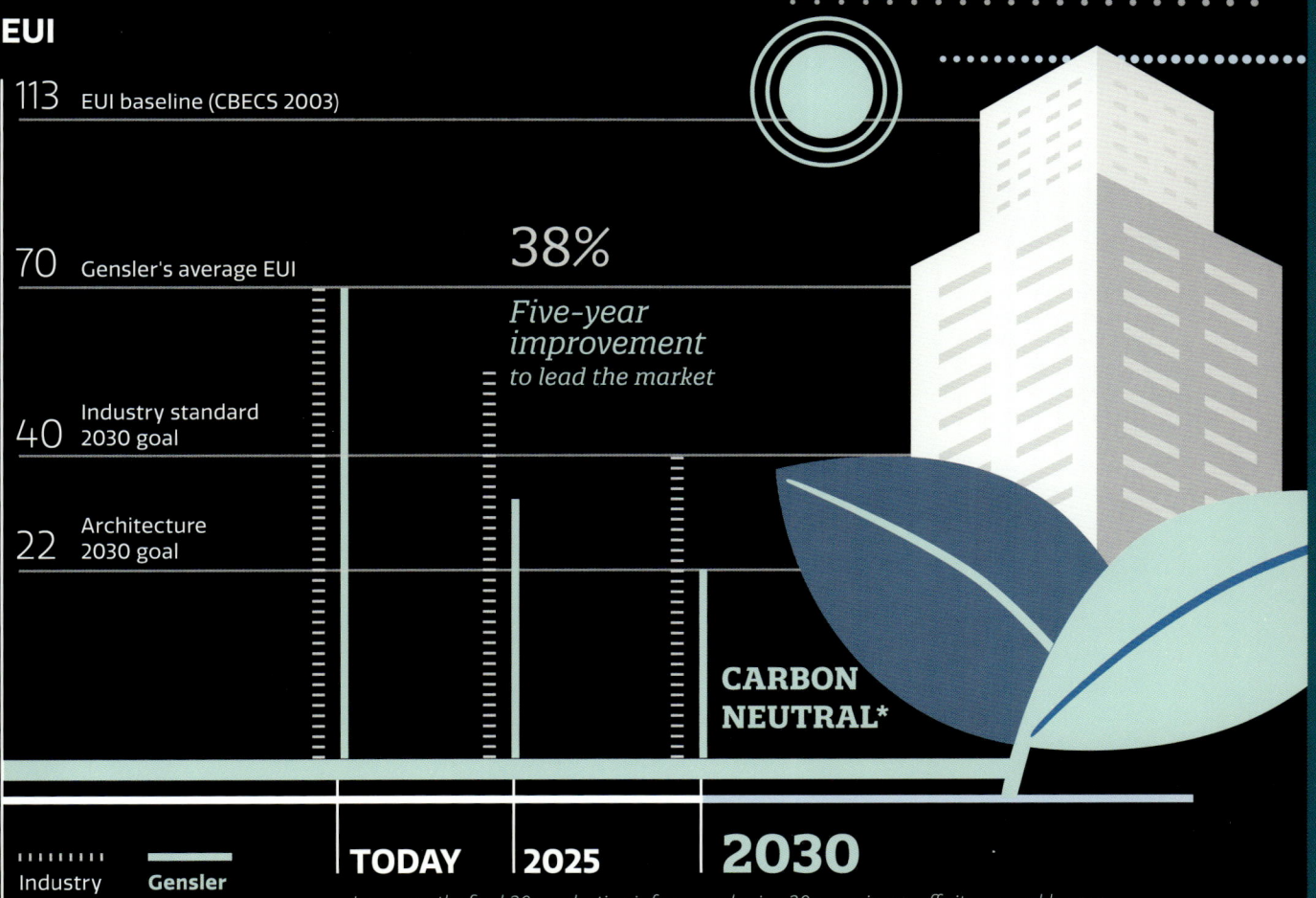

**EUI**

113 — EUI baseline (CBECS 2003)

70 — Gensler's average EUI

**38%**
*Five-year improvement*
*to lead the market*

40 — Industry standard 2030 goal

22 — Architecture 2030 goal

**CARBON NEUTRAL***

Industry | Gensler | **TODAY** | 2025 | **2030**

*\* assumes the final 20% reduction is from purchasing 20% maximum off-site renewable energy*

**THE RESULTS**

# To meet our goals, we need education and tools to help designers better understand, and communicate, net zero commitments and strategies.

Importantly, these discussions must happen in tandem with strategies that optimize design and the human experience—our conversations with project managers, design experience leaders, and design realization leaders emphasized that Gensler must sell experience alongside high performance. Clients often have an entrenched belief that net zero costs more and looks worse, so we need cost- and experience-based methods to improve client pitches. These tools include cheat sheets for teams so they can confidently discuss net zero goals internally and externally, and also simple strategies to achieve net zero energy and low energy by project type.

These tools also need to integrate with existing Gensler processes to be successful. When Gensler project managers begin a new project, they are required to enter the project size, type, zip code, and end date in an intranet form to set up the project on our network. Our tool leverages this information, along with data from various Gensler and national databases, to provide a customized energy target specific to each project. After submitting this required form, project managers will receive an automated email with a customized energy target.

By providing this target relative to AIA baseline data, estimated code requirements, Gensler's past performance, and net zero goals, the tool puts the information in easy context for discussion

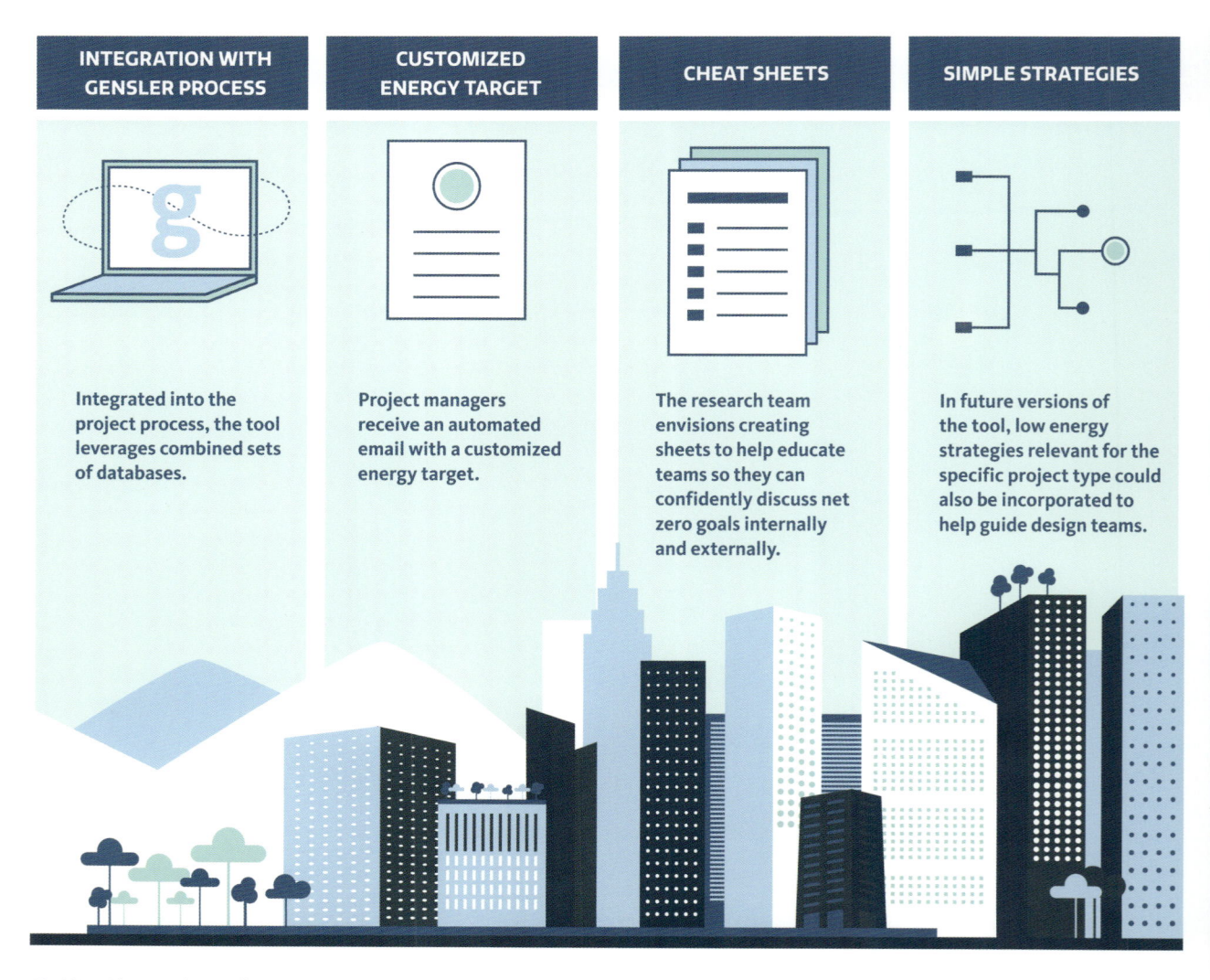

| **INTEGRATION WITH GENSLER PROCESS** | **CUSTOMIZED ENERGY TARGET** | **CHEAT SHEETS** | **SIMPLE STRATEGIES** |
|---|---|---|---|
| Integrated into the project process, the tool leverages combined sets of databases. | Project managers receive an automated email with a customized energy target. | The research team envisions creating sheets to help educate teams so they can confidently discuss net zero goals internally and externally. | In future versions of the tool, low energy strategies relevant for the specific project type could also be incorporated to help guide design teams. |

Tackling Climate Change | A Path Toward Net Zero Energy Buildings

**DESIGN IMPLICATIONS**

### Project-specific insights can inspire meaningful sustainable performance in every project, no matter the scale.

As our projects successfully meet or exceed energy targets, our designers will be able to access information about similar projects in their region. Teams can connect with others in the firm who have delivered high-performance designs across all sectors and practice areas. These collaborative opportunities will help accelerate projects.

### Opportunities vary by project type—so should our reduction targets.

Using Gensler's firmwide data, we measured the effect of various scenarios to understand what tools or conversations are needed for high-impact results. Our wide-ranging portfolio of strategies identifies energy targets specific to different project types to make achieving our goals more actionable.

### Our data helps increase awareness of our highest-performing projects and strategies.

This customizable tool will allow us to provide insight into the most impactful, and economical, high-performance solutions based on our portfolio of data and our most successful projects. Increasing awareness of Gensler's high-performance projects will continue to advance conversations with clients and the marketplace around sustainability.

### Benchmarking our practice area performance metrics provides our clients with context.

Custom benchmarking enables clients to consider their projects in the context of other similar, real-world design solutions. Drawing these comparisons makes the data more accessible, and helps clients understand their projects within broader trends around building performance.

---

**WHAT'S NEXT**

We plan to launch the tool, monitor its effectiveness, and make improvements as needed based on feedback we receive over the coming year. We have just scratched the surface of the substantial changes needed to produce net zero designs. We will define concrete steps in greater detail and identify resources, people, strategies, and buy-ins that will help us manifest these changes.

64  Tackling Climate Change

**Peoples Energy Welcome Pavilion at Navy Pier**
Chicago, Illinois

The Peoples Energy Welcome Pavilion is the first stop for the 9 million people that visit Navy Pier each year. The pavilion maximizes the guest experience while minimizing environmental impacts. It features a green roof that rises from a ground-level garden, and sustainable features—like low-flow plumbing and LED lights—that contribute to a 21% reduction in energy usage compared to a traditional building.

# Designing Dynamic Facades to Conserve Energy

How can we quickly create and select building facade options through comparative analysis?

**WHAT WE DID**

**To save energy and time in the exploration of high-performance building facades, Gensler developed a propriety algorithm and streamlined process built on the Dynamo visual programming tool with Revit software.** Within these platforms, we built a parametric, pattern-generating system that analyzes and compares dynamically responsive facade options in relation to solar insolation and daylight penetration, improving the designer's ability to rapidly create and test multiple scenarios.

We simplified prior workflows by replacing several platforms and programs with a single Revit-based tool set, consisting of prebuilt, parametric shading components and Dynamo scripts that users can easily integrate into their work process.

Our tool prioritizes speed and simplicity. We identified the need for improved building skin design through case studies and secondary research that involved kinetic and responsive facades. Building on previous work in this field, our research provides a new workflow through the rapid generation of geometric models, running simulations of them, and performing comparative analysis of the results.

**THE CONTEXT**

A building facade is the combination of three components: an underlying form that hosts a pattern of panels; a modular pattern of shaped panels applied to the form's surface; and for dynamic facades, movement applied to the panels. Current approaches to the design of facades incorporate static elements such as sunshades for solar deflection or operable windows to utilize natural ventilation—the performance of which is influenced by local climatic conditions. Since weather continuously changes, it is difficult to sustain adequate dynamism. An optimal solution at any given time or place is achieved through environmentally responsive facades that react in real time to stimuli.

In 2015, residential and commercial buildings amassed 40% of overall energy consumption in the United States. By allowing heat to enter or exhaust, building facades are the frontline of healthy energy performance. Fixed facades are a limited answer to environmental ebbs and flows, but new, flexible technologies shift with day-to-day and season-to-season fluctuation. Solar shade and other external building technologies either dampen sunlight in the summer or maximize radiation during the winter. Older, tested-and-true technologies may work too: operable windows are easy-to-use sources of natural ventilation.

Residential and commercial buildings are a significant draw on energy consumption in the United States.

By allowing heat to enter or exhaust, building facades are the frontline of healthy and efficient energy use.

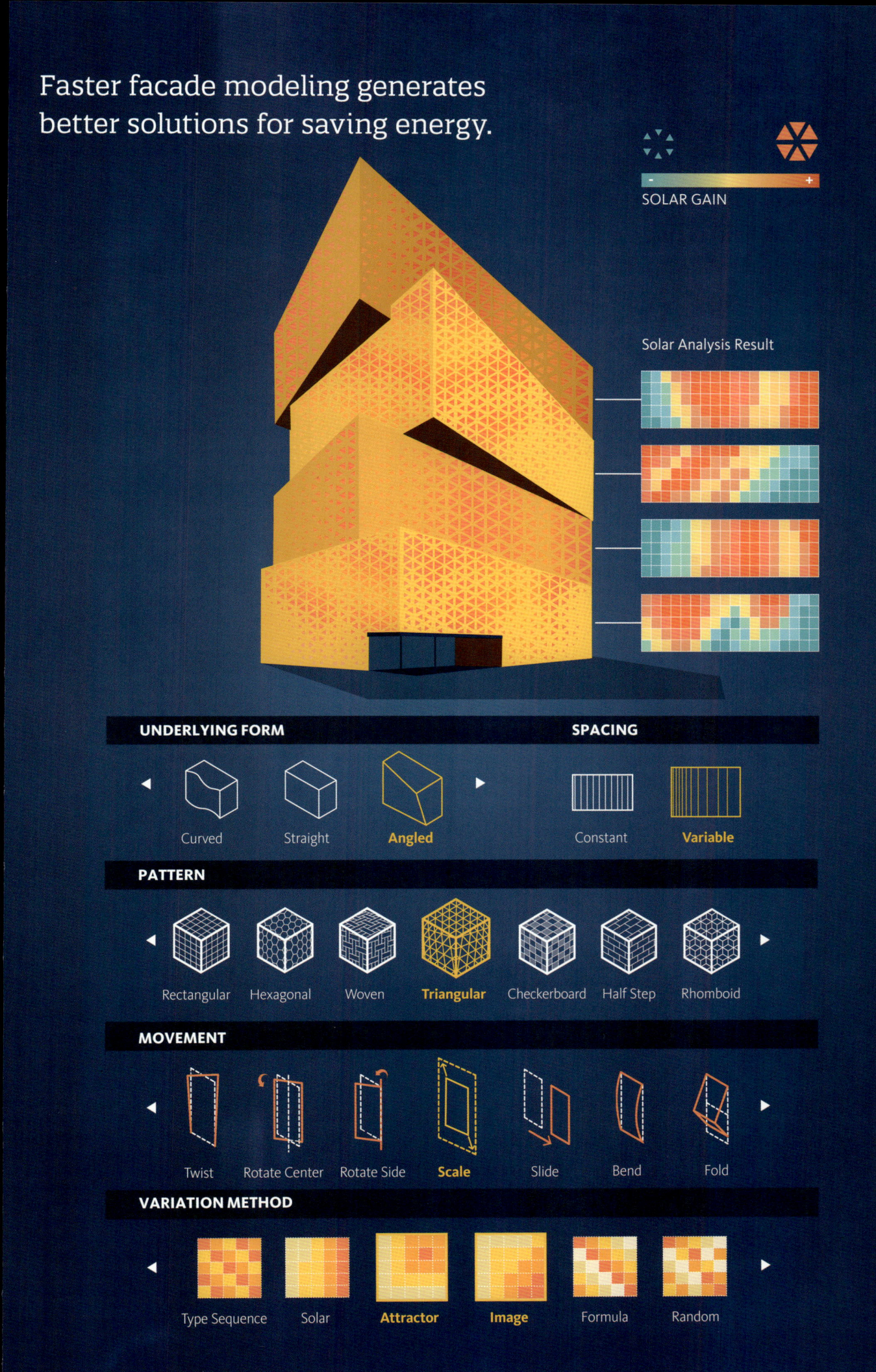

# Faster facade modeling generates better solutions for saving energy.

SOLAR GAIN

Solar Analysis Result

## UNDERLYING FORM

Curved · Straight · **Angled**

## SPACING

Constant · **Variable**

## PATTERN

Rectangular · Hexagonal · Woven · **Triangular** · Checkerboard · Half Step · Rhomboid

## MOVEMENT

Twist · Rotate Center · Rotate Side · **Scale** · Slide · Bend · Fold

## VARIATION METHOD

Type Sequence · Solar · **Attractor** · **Image** · Formula · Random

**THE RESULTS**

# The Super Panel is a prebuilt template for panel construction, or the starting point for dynamic facade creation.

By our design, the user achieves an extraordinary range of geometric shapes through modifying predesigned geometric panel parameters. This predesigned template, called a Super Panel, has an interior and exterior component, infilled with changeable baseline parameters in common configurations. After the user designates panel shape and characteristics, the panel supports six separate kinetic response options: rotation, twisting, sliding, bending, folding, and scaling. The Super Panel alteration process is user friendly: there is no scripting, nor any manual geometric shape design. A user-controllable grid can be applied to the surface—and once a final grid design is complete, a script automatically places panels on the grid. The panel parameters can be adjusted to tune the shape, orientation, and movement of the panel if it is to respond to environmental factors.

Users can also conduct further environmental analysis. Facade analysis can be performed through analyzing environmental stimuli on a building cell, or a zone defined by a column bay and a floor-to-floor height where solar insolation accumulates on the adjacent facade over time. The cell consists of a weather-tight skin forming the exterior of the building. The skin is then shielded from the environment by a secondary system of shading panels outboard of that skin.

Dynamically responsive facades include panels that respond to an arcing sun. A base case of an unprotected building skin is performed, followed by a static shading system, or a panel motion that is determined by sun location or the external stimulus. In addition to a baseline, the analysis should include an optimized static case and a no-build alternative.

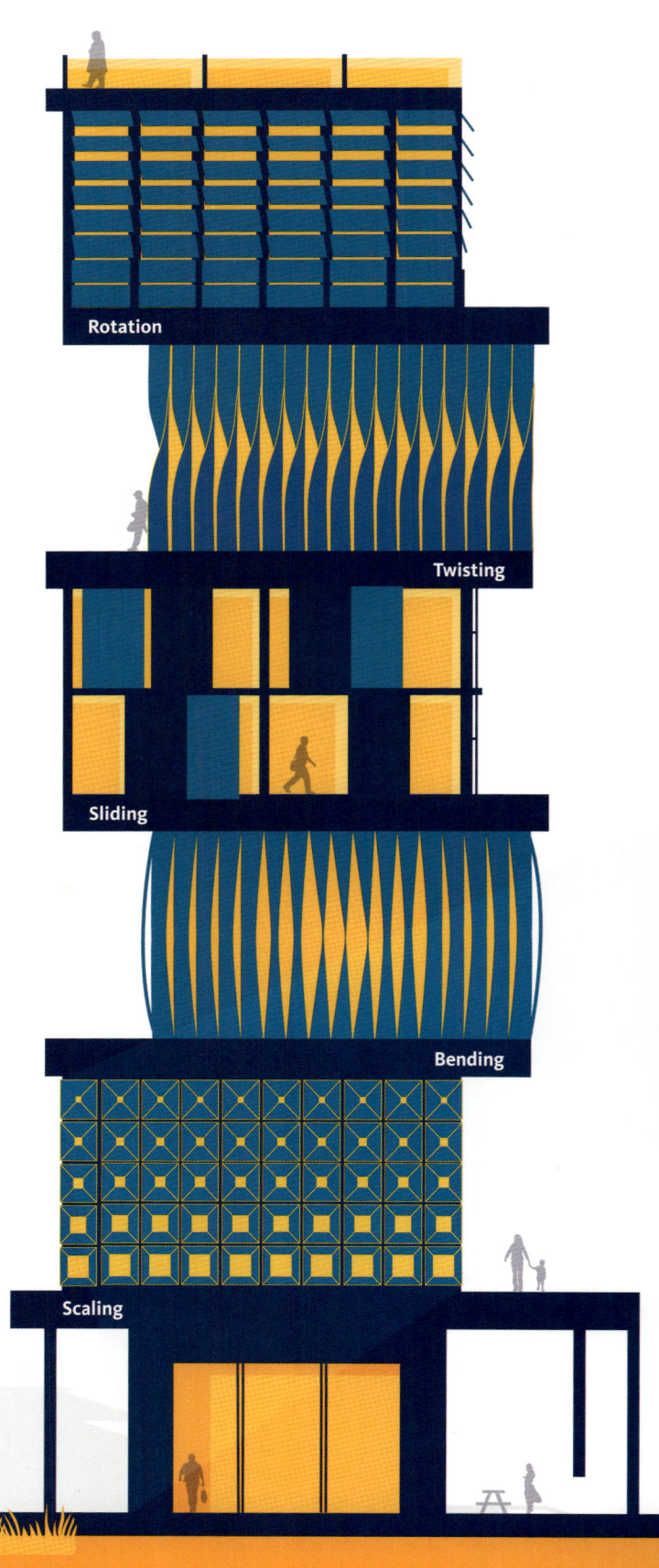

Tackling Climate Change | Designing Dynamic Facades to Conserve Energy

**DESIGN IMPLICATIONS**

## Save time.

Our case studies showed an 80% reduction in design and consulting coordination time. Our tool creates more options and better decision-making in early design phases. Where designers had previously created models from scratch and updated construction administration documents manually, designers use pre-generated parametric models to create multiple facade types and have their work automatically updated in construction administration files. Further, our process eliminates arbitrary or unempirical decisions, by forecasting thermal and ventilation impacts.

## Save energy.

Our digital models are supported by an aggregated system of panels. We model panel movement, and through our observed responses to parametric behavior, we document how a stimulus leads to different parameters over time. When we put our models into action, environmentally responsive facades react to stimuli in one of two ways. Depending on our inputs to the building interior environment, facade components either physically move or undergo material change.

**WHAT'S NEXT?**

Our next step is to distribute our tool to colleagues, and effectively communicate its full suite of abilities. Once we reach a wide audience, we will encourage feedback, because it is in how the user engages our tool that we envision future software changes.

By reducing end-use consumption caused by cooling, heating, and ventilation, there are increased thermal comfort, improved air quality, and direct cost savings. As added value, our tool combines aesthetic value and functionality to create iconic appearances, sustainability, and brand value.

Increased thermal comfort

Improved air quality

Direct cost savings

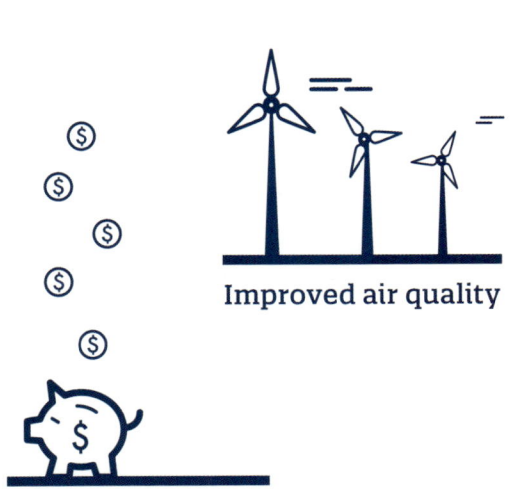

# Urban Strategies for Coastal Resilience

How can we address sea level rise and major storm threats in vulnerable cities?

**WHAT WE DID**

**We partnered with the Florida International University School of Architecture in teaching a thesis class focused on researching coastal climate challenges in major cities across the country and developed a framework for local partnerships to scale the development of responsive design strategies.** With students in FIU master's program, we identified current risks and projected vulnerabilities due to sea level rise and climate events in Washington, D.C., New York City, Houston, Boston, San Francisco, Tampa, London, and Miami. This investigation was done in collaboration with multiple Gensler offices, leveraging our local presence in these cities. The students then focused on Miami and developed strategies on how to address these challenges at the regional, city, and neighborhood levels through the lens of the development codes.

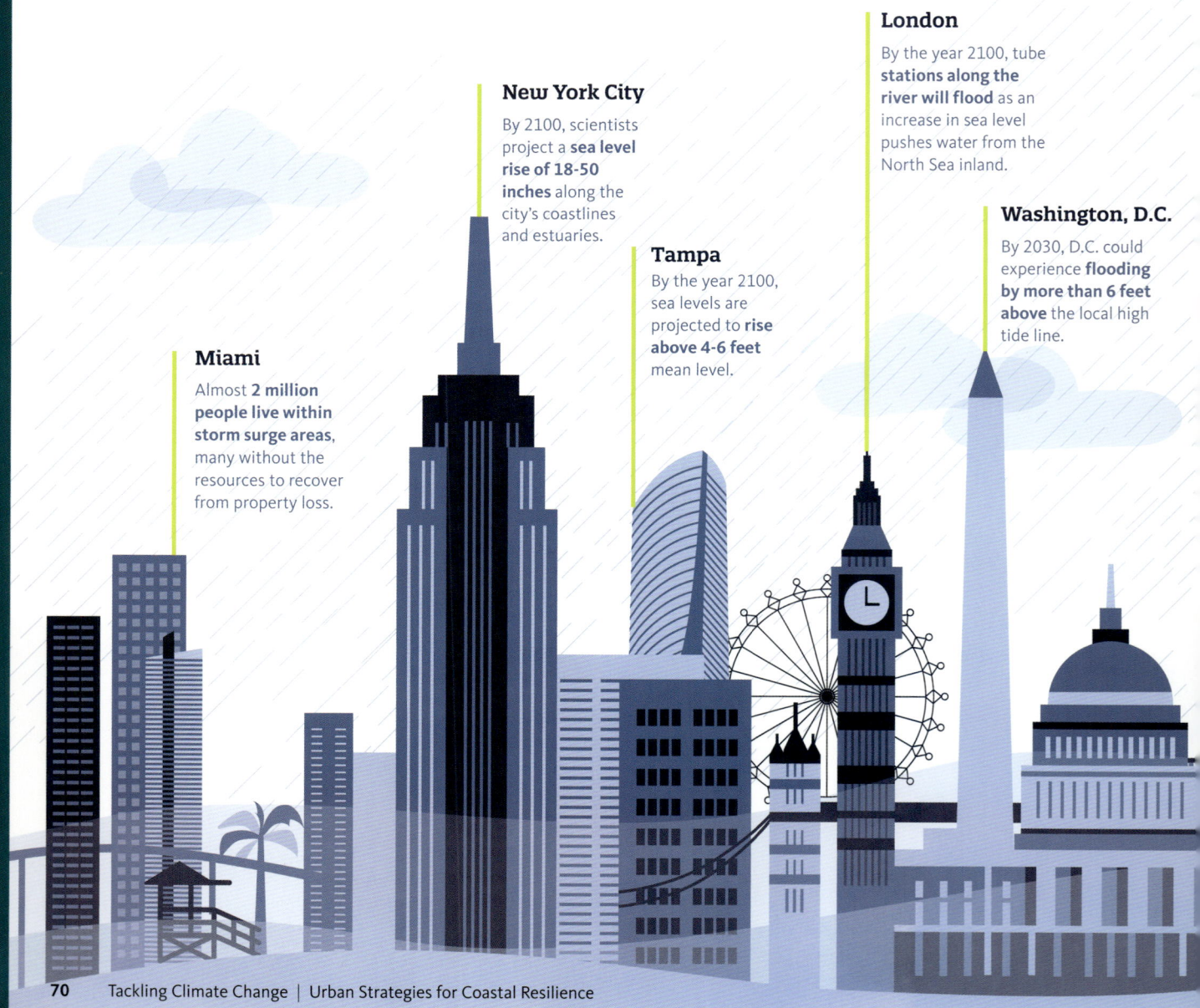

**Miami**
Almost **2 million people live within storm surge areas**, many without the resources to recover from property loss.

**New York City**
By 2100, scientists project a **sea level rise of 18-50 inches** along the city's coastlines and estuaries.

**Tampa**
By the year 2100, sea levels are projected to **rise above 4-6 feet** mean level.

**London**
By the year 2100, tube **stations along the river will flood** as an increase in sea level pushes water from the North Sea inland.

**Washington, D.C.**
By 2030, D.C. could experience **flooding by more than 6 feet above** the local high tide line.

# In the greater Miami area alone, almost 2 million people live within storm surge areas, many without the resources to recover from property loss.

**THE CONTEXT**

Coastal cities continue to face the impacts of flood risks, including sea level rise, storm surges, inundation, erosion, and salt water intrusion. Failure to respond to these risks will impact every aspect of cities, including buildings and public spaces, historic structures, new developments, infrastructure, and levels of social vulnerability.

The economic impact is also undeniable: New York City, for instance, has incurred over $7 billion in flood-related losses.

San Francisco has projected that over $55 billion of public and private property is at risk if the city does not respond adequately to flood-related dangers. Cities that take a proactive response to designing for rising sea levels will better ensure the security of their residents and businesses.

As architects we have a responsibility and a unique opportunity to have a strong voice in our communities to influence how our cities are shaped and can have positive impact.

**San Francisco**
Half of San Francisco International Airport runways are **likely to be underwater by 2100**.

**Houston**
Hurricane Allison and Hurricane Harvey each **displaced over 30,000 people and destroyed thousands of homes**.

**Boston**
3,303 properties **will face chronic flooding** by 2030, with a combined value of $2 billion.

**THE RESULTS**

## Build knowledge with local primary and secondary partners to gain a specific understanding of the issues caused by sea rise.

Architecture is not the only aspect of a city affected by sea level rise, and it cannot be the only solution to its challenges. Creating a multidisciplinary team can help determine relevant outcomes and deliverables, and also develop holistic points of view. Consider engaging engineers, land-use attorneys, city planning departments, universities and other educational institutions, local resilience task forces, and other city-specific experts.

## Teams should get familiar with the research and resources that are already in place for their cities.

They should make connections with people already invested in addressing climate change challenges in their locations. This will help them understand what is already being done to address existing concerns and where potential gaps in impact exist. For instance, greater Miami has joined the 100 Resilient Cities initiative, bringing together three chief resilience officers for the county and the city. Local AIA and ULI chapters focus on resilience, sea level rise, adaptation, and recovery after disasters. Working with these organizations can expedite intervention efforts.

## Identify where team and partner stakeholders can have real-world impact on the issues.

Outcomes should be focused around boosting resilience against sea level rise. This requires identifying areas of impact based on research and conversations with partners, and then developing relevant deliverables. Our team identified that what drives the shape of our city is the zoning code, so we focused on exploring how the development codes could potentially shift and adapt to increasing challenges in the City of Miami. The solutions and deliverables will vary between cities. It is important to remember that the overall goal is to lead the way in real-world impact for architecture and related industries.

72 | Tackling Climate Change | Urban Strategies for Coastal Resilience

**DESIGN IMPLICATIONS**

We need to think globally, but the action will happen at the local level. Different cities will encounter different challenges, so it is crucial to understand the threats of coastal climate change that are specific to a city. With the FIU students, we looked at the City of Miami at an urban scale, at the neighborhood scale, and at the building scale:

## Urban Scale

- Restack zoning densities to respond to higher/lower ground.
- Repurpose industrial areas in the city with urban agriculture to offset increased risks of agricultural land.
- Reduce social vulnerability through new models of affordable housing.

## Neighborhood Scale

- Utilize energy nodes to create energy independent city blocks.
- Redesign the edge between water and land.
- Preserve Historic Districts in the midst of sea level rise.

## Building Scale

- Can water redefine the ground level?
- Rethink the commercial realm at the ground level in urban districts.
- Use local biomimicry to respond to sea level rise.

Images by FIU Master Student: Marcela Gavilanez

**WHAT'S NEXT**

Phase II of this project will focus on consolidating the design implications through an exhibition at the local AIA chapter venue to engage with the community and serve as a platform to engage our multidisciplinary team of partners and local stakeholders. The team will continue working to understand the Miami Zoning Code and its limitations in adapting to challenges related to sea level rise. Through various workshop sessions, we plan to elevate the strategies into actions and make real impact in the way our city is shaped. The team will also work to create a scalable model and process that can be replicated across Gensler offices.

# Preserving Urban Ecosystems

How can we take a resilient and holistic approach to urban ecology?

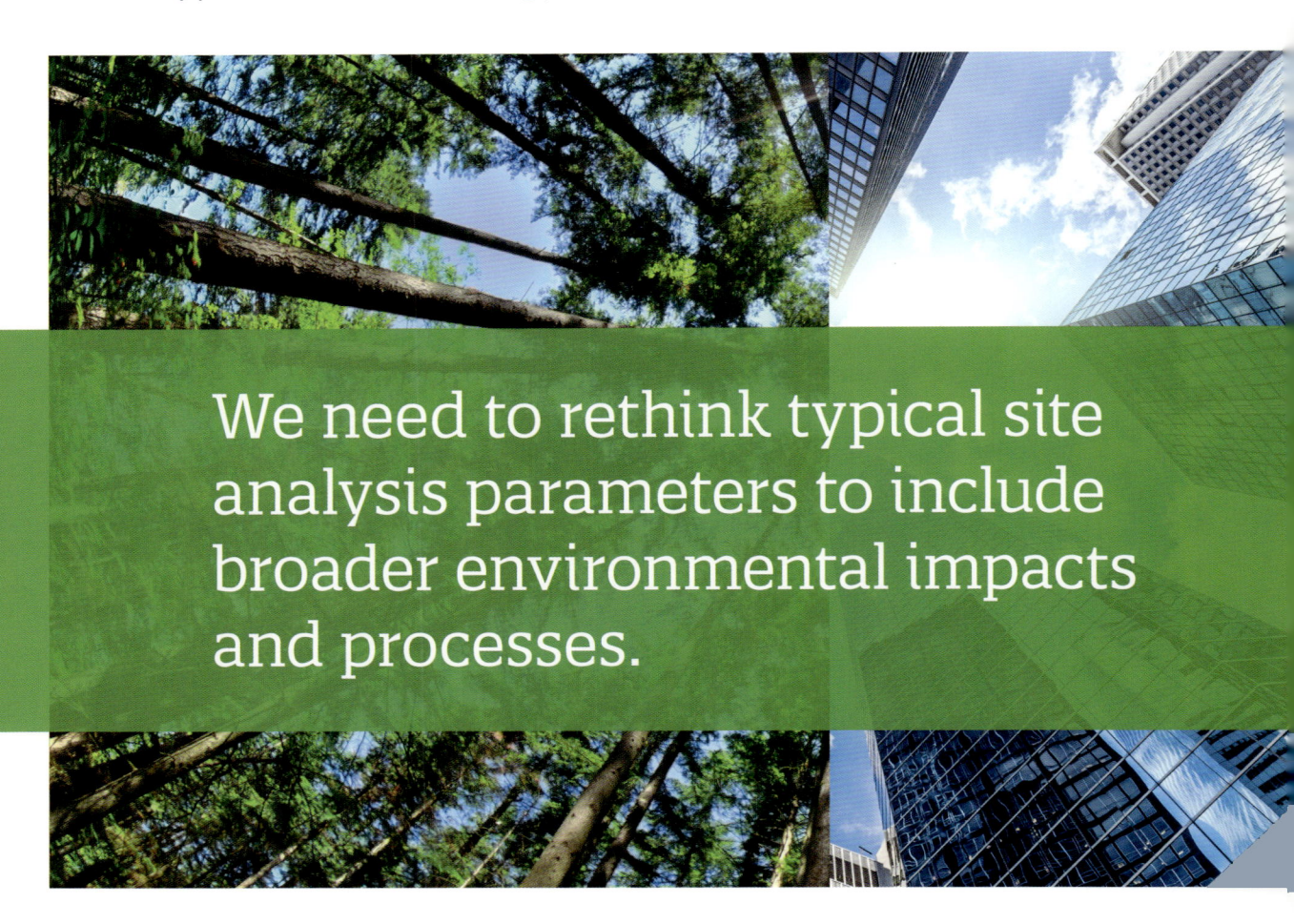

> We need to rethink typical site analysis parameters to include broader environmental impacts and processes.

**WHAT WE DID**

**We conceptualized a mapping tool to forge a holistic approach to ecological processes in urban centers.** While there is a clear benefit to analyzing a specific natural resource or species, we found a dearth of information on processes that are holistic. To address this gap, we developed a methodology that studies a broad range of ecological processes rather than overly focused indicators.

To test our conceptual tool, we conducted a site analysis of a two-block plot formerly developed. Our analysis went well beyond the scope of environmental regulations, and well beyond the site boundaries, considering the site's context within a 20-block radius to understand how it fits within community-level environmental processes. After aggregating information and experimenting with illustrating methods, we developed an approach to the challenges we face, and a path forward.

In a sense, we need corrective lenses for our approach to urban ecology. We embraced resiliency for assessing urbanism—we need resilient designs to foster a sustainable environment. Through understanding the environment in which we operate, we can implement progressive design practices.

**THE CONTEXT**

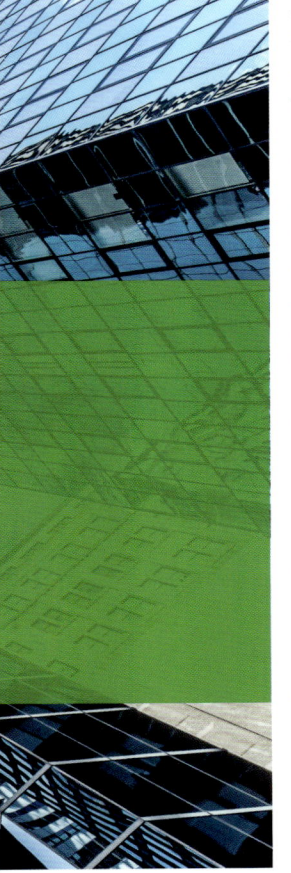

A hallmark of urban areas is interdependency—among residents, the built environment, and ecology. Unfortunately, throughout the 7,000-year history of urbanity, ecology has often been treated as an afterthought. Models of economic stability are built from an "empty world" concept, or the idea that our urban areas are impeded only by costs and growth rates. GDP and healthy growth are important, but our paradigm fails to consider a key component: our natural world. Often it is not until biodiversity shrinks, or our environment shifts, that we acknowledge our need for a new outlook.

More often than not, today's design solutions continue to create truly non-resilient environments. Environmental considerations are widely viewed as downward pressures on ROI. Further, environmental regulations lack standardization across regions. However, the public's growing exposure to and concern for environmental impacts and climate change are pushing cities, and properties, to embrace sustainability and resilience. And this goes beyond altruism: ecosystem services is an emerging field to draw the connections between resilience and profitability.

**More and more, we are recognizing that respecting our natural systems isn't just a moral imperative, it is an economic one too.** Consider Houston as a prime example. An urban ecosystem analysis by American Forests showed that lost tree coverage over 25 years cost the community about $50 million from consequences such as stormwater runoff, heightened noxious airborne chemicals, and increased costs in air-conditioning. With scientific and technological advancements, our knowledge of how our urban ecosystems function—and how we are influencing them—has never been greater. With this knowledge, a failure to act is negligent. For instance, there is rapid population growth in major hubs such as Salt Lake City, Denver, and Albuquerque, with each one dependent on major waterways like the Rio Grande and Colorado River. Growth without forethought—and compounded by drought—is leading to overburdened ecosystems, with symptoms including flash floods and wildfires increasing in frequency. Creative solutions are mandatory to sustain both local ecologies and healthy urban growth.

**URBAN HEAT ISLAND EFFECT**

*"Heat islands do not just cause a bit of additional, minor discomfort. Their higher temperatures, lack of shade, and role in increasing air pollution have serious effects on human mortality and disease."*

–Lisa Mummery Gartland, *Heat Islands: Understanding and Mitigating Heat in Urban Areas*

## THE RESULTS

Cities are heterogeneous by nature: we found significant value in conducting our own site assessments and broadening the range of variables considered. To assess the impact of future projects, we conceptualized an integrated mapping tool. Our goal is to instill decision-making with multiple ecological considerations. The approach is twofold and spans macro- and micro-level scrutiny: our proposed tool includes macro-scale ecological overlays on GIS maps, in addition to site-specific survey inputs.

We found that the best way to map ecological processes is through integrating available technologies. **We have the technology to create change; it is simply a matter of implementation. Drones, GPS systems, infrared cameras, and satellite imagery are at our disposal.**

While major cities understand the risks of deferring ecological issues, we found that there is no central tool for policymakers and designers to make informed decisions.

Every city has a biological legacy that our framework aims to sustain and make more resilient. We found the need to incorporate data from a host of ecological issues: stormwater retention, reduced heat island effect, air purification, carbon sequestration, and increased wildlife habitats. Even though our tool encompasses a limited radius, a site analysis should recognize wider urban trending. For example, it is at the property level that design will combat urban heat island effect, or heat-producing infrastructure that causes a suburban-urban temperature variance that can differ by nearly 10 degrees Celsius.

**Drones**      **GPS**      **Infrared**      **Satellite**

## DESIGN IMPLICATIONS

### Expand efforts to quantify the benefits of local ecologies.
We share in the benefits of green space, and ecology-friendly urban planning solutions and design practices. The opportunities are bountiful, but not fully understood and therefore not fully integrated into decision-making processes. Designers, developers, and cities need to work many ecological considerations into plans along with other factors. We believe that by integrating wide-ranging overlays into a singular mapping tool, we can create a robust resource to embrace resilient designs.

### Emphasize a dynamic, process-based system at the community level.
Ecological issues are diverse by nature, and our challenges will inevitably change. For instance, in a city that is as large as New York, there are many different moving parts. New York has created long-term planning documents, PlaNYC and the NYC Infrastructure Plan that are being used as a long-term strategy for a greener NYC. Many designers are faced with community-level concerns alongside these macro-level goals. Design solutions will be a balancing act of macro- and micro-level requirements.

# Our goal is to instill decision-making with multiple ecological considerations.

### Provisioning services
Material products gathered from ecosystems *(genetic resources, food and fiber, and fresh water)*

### Regulating services
Benefits derived from the regulation by ecosystem processes *(regulation of climate, water, and some human diseases)*

### Cultural services
Nonmaterial benefits people obtain from ecosystems *(spiritual enrichment, cognitive development, reflection, recreation, knowledge systems, social relations, and aesthetic values)*

### Supporting or habitat services
Those that are necessary for the production of all other ecosystem services *(biomass production, nutrient cycling, watercycling, provisioning of habitat for species, and maintenance of genetic pools and evolutionary processes)*

**WHAT'S NEXT**

First and foremost, we need to foster resilience—in our ecological systems and through our design practices. Our approach is seemingly altruistic. However, there are serious financial impacts to consider. Designers need to open a dialogue with clients as to how an environmental framework is both sustainable and financially preferable.

At this point, we have more questions than answers. The first step forward is building tangible, quantifiable tools. Yet finding ecological information can be quite difficult, since urban ecology literature operates on the outskirts of policy. It is time that we welcome such policies to the forefront of our thinking.

# Underground Retail and Rooftop Farming

What are the benefits and challenges of "urban farmification?"

*Citrus orchard* | *Vertical farming towers* | *Restaurant terrace*

**Test site**

*Glendale, CA
17.5 acres*

**WHAT WE DID**

**We explored the opportunities and realities of submerging big box retail centers to support rooftop farming.** Big box retail centers are demonstrably ripe for this process: they have large roofs, generally do not have windows, and are ubiquitous across the United States. The first big boxes, Walmart, Kmart, and Target, opened in 1962 on a promise of mass production and efficiency. For this property type, we need to rethink a sustainable and inclusive integration into the surrounding community.

After choosing our site, a big box near Glendale, California, we created a practical, but inviting design for submergence. To promote openness, we leveraged daylighting when allocating vehicular entryways, truck-loading areas, and store entrances. Aboveground, our design aims to be community-centric—an open invitation to social space through rooftop farming.

Our design features a decisive shift away from inexpensive materials that characterize big box stores. Robust structural materials for the underground space were needed, such as a protection slab and waterproofing membrane, as well as a reinforced skeleton that can bear additional weight. We conducted a preliminary building performance analysis through Syska Hennessy Group, Inc., which included a climate, energy efficiency, and daylighting analysis. The large roof area of this project offered a perfect fit for powering the building with solar energy—and could potentially achieve net zero energy, our efficiency goal.

**THE CONTEXT**

Urban sprawl is necessitating creative community planning, alternative design solutions, and a reinvigorated agriculture industry. In our subject city, Los Angeles, urban sprawl has excised farming from a city that was once home to one of the nation's largest concentration of dairy farms. The Inland Empire is now crowned the big box capital of the United States. Across the U.S., we are losing more than an acre of

Present

Future

Welcome pavilion   Farming plots   Opening to below

# Integrating farming with big box stores can mitigate the negative consequences of urban sprawl.

farmland every minute. Urbanization and rural restructuring mean that large cities will have trouble sustaining an adequate level of produce. Urban centers are reworking consumption patterns by creating alternative food networks like farmers' markets and food cooperatives. These shifting consumer behaviors, paired with ag-tech innovations, are laying the groundwork for a progressive agriculture industry.

Markets exist in a social context—so big box districts can boost efficiency of their space through meaningful social connections. To understand how our design decisions affect the surrounding community, we utilized the term "social capital," or the norms and networks that facilitate collective action toward shared goals. Abundant evidence draws on the relationship between social capital and positive social goods like charities, nonprofits, public parks, and other media that facilitate interpersonal interactions out in the community. Social capital has also been correlated with community-level financial performance. Counties with a higher Social Capital Index tend to have a higher-value cash ratio, lower deficits as a percentage of total municipal budgets, more accurate expenditure forecasts, and greater spending on services per capital.

Image by: Calzada Visualization

**THE RESULTS**

Our proposed design solution would result in energy savings of 10% compared to a typical big box. A subgrade structure makes it easier to bring the interior temperature to within the optimal comfort parameters because there is less fluctuation in ground temperature. Further, the earth-sheltered solution achieves a low environmental impact, even while using high-energy consumption materials like concrete, steel reinforcement, and masonry. Depending on rooftop space allocation, previous research has established that if about 50,000 square feet were devoted to solar panels, the building could achieve close to net zero energy. We estimated our total construction cost at $65 million with a 25-year time to profitability.

Our plans call for a Cartesian planting system with the flexibility for different crops. For a ballpark idea of revenue generation, a typical 1-acre plot of avocados or peaches can reach about $100,000 annually. This flexible space for community engagement not only is income generating, but is expected to increase profits for the business underfoot, and serve as a social capital creation system for the surrounding community.

**DESIGN IMPLICATIONS**

### Early adopters will have to take the long view on investment.

To achieve faster profitability, our plans must leverage all sources of income and cost saving. Notably, the cross effects of urbanization and rural restructuring are yielding new legislative solutions. The Urban Agriculture Incentive Zones Act aims to increase the use of privately owned, vacant land for urban agriculture and improve land security for urban agriculture projects. Additionally, our clients are integral to our cost-saving paradigm. All experiences and perspectives are needed to realize our design plans.

### Our design achieves a compelling aesthetic.
Underground architecture does not have to be stylistically inert. There are multiple ways of instilling creative surface-to-subsurface relationships through features like penetrational wall openings and nondisruptive features, or subgrade components that integrate with the surrounding environment.

November

October

September

## WHAT'S NEXT

Big box retail is far from the only property type that includes rooftop farming—some of our projects add another element to the conversation on sustainable and community-building design solutions. In London, Growing Underground recently opened its first underground farm through converting air-raid shelters from World War II into a 7,000-square-foot tunnel filled with sprouting herbs. The Washington, D.C.–based company Up Top Acres has brought rooftop farming to both residential and office projects. Up Top Acres opened The Farm at 55 M Street in April 2016, and includes a 15,000-square-foot farm. In addition to cost savings for the property, this project supports a 35-member CSA program and a weekly market stand.

In Los Angeles, the opportunities for urban farmification are endless. To reinvigorate communities with wide implementation of our design solutions, we need to investigate contiguous lots across districts—and identify areas where parcels can be joined. There are 8,600 empty lots in Los Angeles, and more than 63 million square feet available for potential "Big Box Underground" space in Los Angeles County.

> Urban farming is not only a sustainable solution, but one that creates new communities.

### Annual planting
*Farming in cycles*

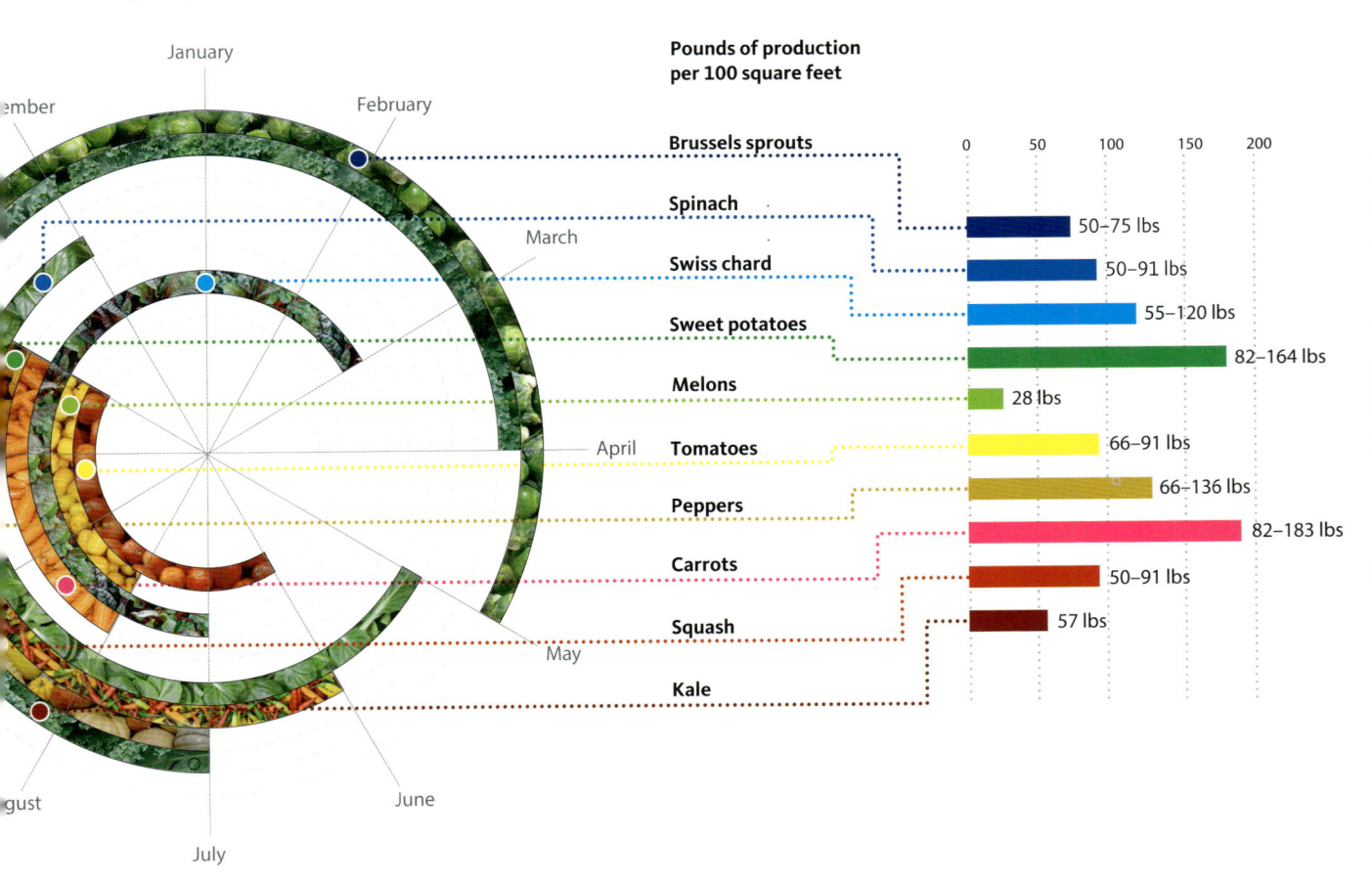

**Pounds of production per 100 square feet**

|  |  |
|---|---|
| Brussels sprouts | 50–75 lbs |
| Spinach | 50–91 lbs |
| Swiss chard | 55–120 lbs |
| Sweet potatoes | 82–164 lbs |
| Melons | 28 lbs |
| Tomatoes | 66–91 lbs |
| Peppers | 66–136 lbs |
| Carrots | 82–183 lbs |
| Squash | 50–91 lbs |
| Kale | 57 lbs |

Image by: OJB Landscape Architecture

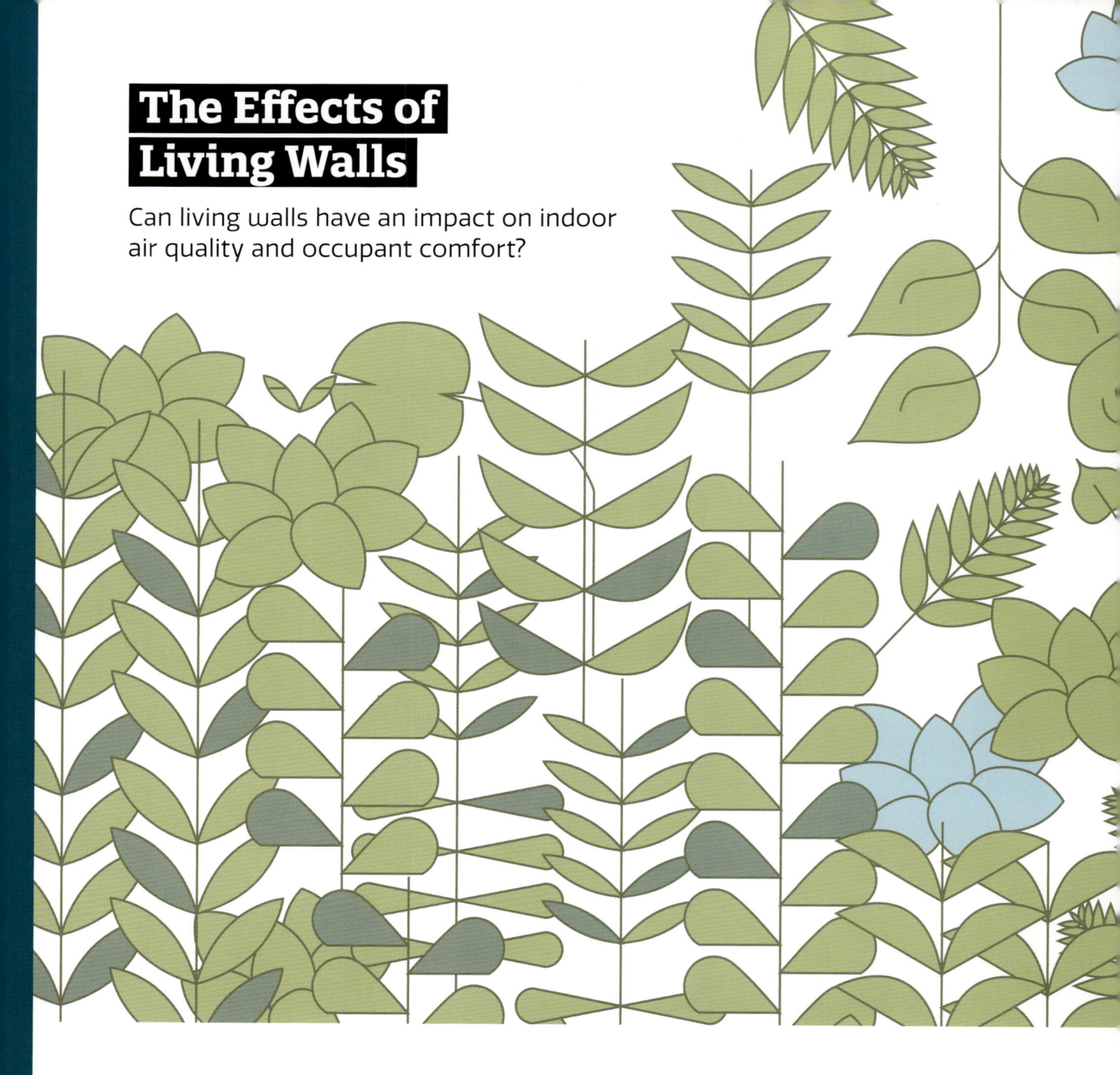

# The Effects of Living Walls

Can living walls have an impact on indoor air quality and occupant comfort?

**WHAT WE DID**

**We conducted an experiment to test the effect of a living wall on indoor air quality and thermal comfort of occupants in a real-life working environment.** We used two conference rooms in Gensler's Shanghai office—one served as the control room. For the other room, we created a "green" room by installing a living wall, specifically using plant species known to target indoor air pollutants and improve indoor air quality (IAQ) levels. The plans, furniture fit-out, and ventilation of the two rooms were identical, and differences in lighting plans were only slight.

The living wall was installed in February 2015. Over the course of six months—March to August 2015—we monitored levels of $CO_2$, particulate matter (PM2.5), total volatile organic compounds (TVOC), relative humidity, and temperature in the two rooms. We used this data to conduct a detailed comparative analysis at the conclusion of the study, uncovering measurable impacts of living walls on the workplace environment, as well as areas in which additional research is needed. We also surveyed 60 members of Gensler Shanghai, who used the two rooms to gather input on their experience and preferences related to the green room.

Living walls can dramatically improve indoor air quality—but their effects may go far beyond just filtering air.

**THE CONTEXT**

Addressing the mounting issues of pollution and air quality is of paramount concern to human health, particularly in cities like Shanghai that suffer from consistently substandard air quality. And the problem isn't only outside the buildings, it's also within. Indoor air quality (IAQ) is of particular concern today: workers spend the majority of their waking hours in the office, and some even note finding refuge at the office when air quality outside or within other places is particularly bad.

Today, IAQ is most often managed via mechanical ventilation systems to address levels of $CO_2$, PM2.5, and TVOC in the air. This approach has a significant downside, however: managing air quality via mechanical systems increases the energy required to manage buildings, with a negative impact on overall sustainability and resilience (as well as operating costs). In the long run, these systems ultimately contribute to the problems of pollution they are meant to solve because of higher fuel use.

If we instead could manage indoor air quality by introducing living or "green" walls into indoor environments, the impact on the health and experience of the occupants—as well as overall building operation—could be significant. Indoor potted plants have been shown to reduce levels of $CO_2$, PM2.5, and TVOC in prior studies. We seek to not only confirm this effect, but quantify the impact of indoor plantings to inform future use.

## THE RESULTS

**The living wall showed significant, positive improvements to IAQ over the course of our study.** The greatest observed effects were on overall levels of CO2 and PM2.5, which showed overall average reductions of 24% and 21%, respectively, compared to our control. Importantly, the effect of the living wall is positive not only in the long term, but also over short periods of time. The living wall also proved more resilient. When a disruption occurred, resulting in a spike in measured levels of CO2 and PM2.5, the control room was slower to return to baseline levels than the room with a living wall. This ability to mitigate change is particularly important on days when outdoor air quality is poor, as this has a direct impact on the quality of air indoors.

**The green room also had higher overall temperature and humidity.** The presence of the living wall, and the added lighting needed to maintain it, kept the green room comparatively warmer than the control room. This is likely due to the added heat generated by the plant lights, as well as heat released from plants in the form of water vapor. We observed a similar trend for the relative humidity of the two rooms as well—the green room's humidity was comparatively higher. The gap in humidity appeared to be falling over the course of our study, however, and the green room humidity levels overall became less volatile with time, so the humidity impact may be temporary.

*Percent reduction of CO2, PM2.5, and TVOC levels from March to June, 2015*

**Users see health benefits from the living wall, but challenges to thermal comfort.** Two-thirds of users surveyed (65%) preferred the green room to other conference rooms, noting that they enjoyed the presence of plants and found the greenery relaxing. Users also felt the air quality in the green room was superior, and four in five (79%) believed the room was an overall benefit to their health. However, users noted the higher temperature and humidity of the room as negative impacts of the living wall. The smell of the room was also noted by many users, potentially an impact of the soil mix used.

**79%** Feel like there are health benefits from using the green room

**76%** Sense a reminder of nature from view of plants, inspiring a mindful break

**70%** Feel happy working in the green room

**70%** Feel that the green room is more humid than other conference rooms

**65%** Prefer the green room with the living wall

84    Tackling Climate Change | The Effects of Living Walls

## DESIGN IMPLICATIONS

**Living walls provide a significant opportunity to improve indoor air quality.** Not only did we observe an overall positive effect on IAQ, but the room also showed a greater ability to bounce back from events negatively impacting air quality. As a result, the green room recorded significantly less time that IAQ would be considered dangerous to human health than the control room.

**The greatest health and bottom-line impact may come from distributed greenery.** When contained within individual spaces, as in our study, the effects of the living wall were significant, but also easy to negate if the rooms were not kept properly sealed (for example, doors left open). The enclosure of the rooms was necessary for our study, but for a broader and more sustained impact on indoor environments, distributed installation of plants may prove beneficial.

**Building systems and sensors must be well coordinated with living wall installations.** The secondary effects of the living wall—higher temperatures and humidity, and the added smell—must be mitigated by building HVAC systems. If handled well, the overall impact of the added heat and humidity could prove to be neutral or even positive over the course of a full year, depending on climate.

**User perception and behavior may be a challenge for broad adoption.** Direct user input showed a preference for the green room aesthetically, but also the need to manage its thermal comfort as previously noted. We conducted additional analysis of users' actual behavior via the office's conference room reservation system, and saw no significant increase in utilization of the green room over the control room.

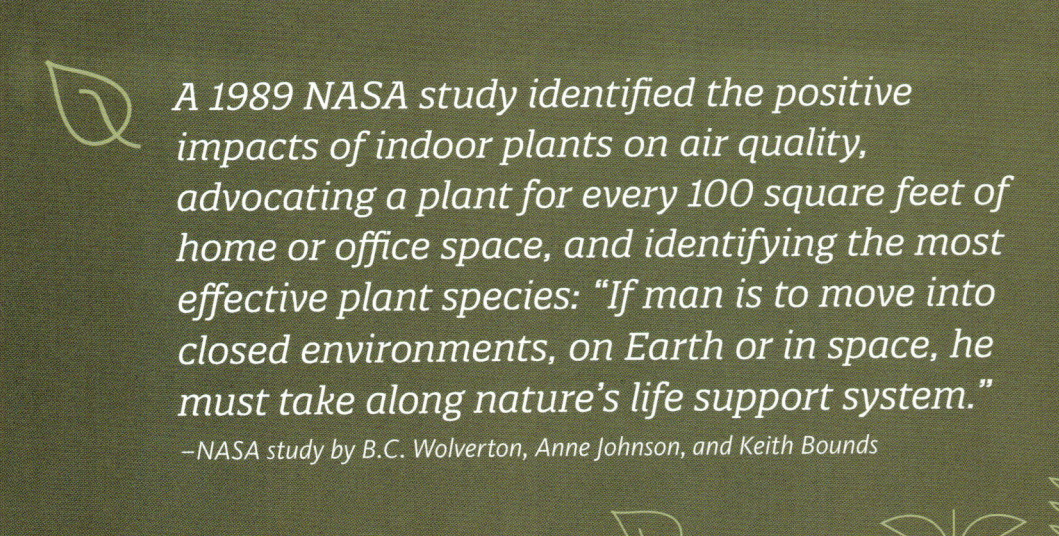

---

*A 1989 NASA study identified the positive impacts of indoor plants on air quality, advocating a plant for every 100 square feet of home or office space, and identifying the most effective plant species: "If man is to move into closed environments, on Earth or in space, he must take along nature's life support system."*
–NASA study by B.C. Wolverton, Anne Johnson, and Keith Bounds

---

### WHAT'S NEXT

Our study showed the significant benefits of green or living walls installed within office environments, but also raised a number of questions warranting further analysis. The inconclusive effects on TVOC levels are of particular interest and concern. Understanding how to mitigate the effects on thermal comfort and smell via different plantings and soil mixes will also be key to broader adoption.

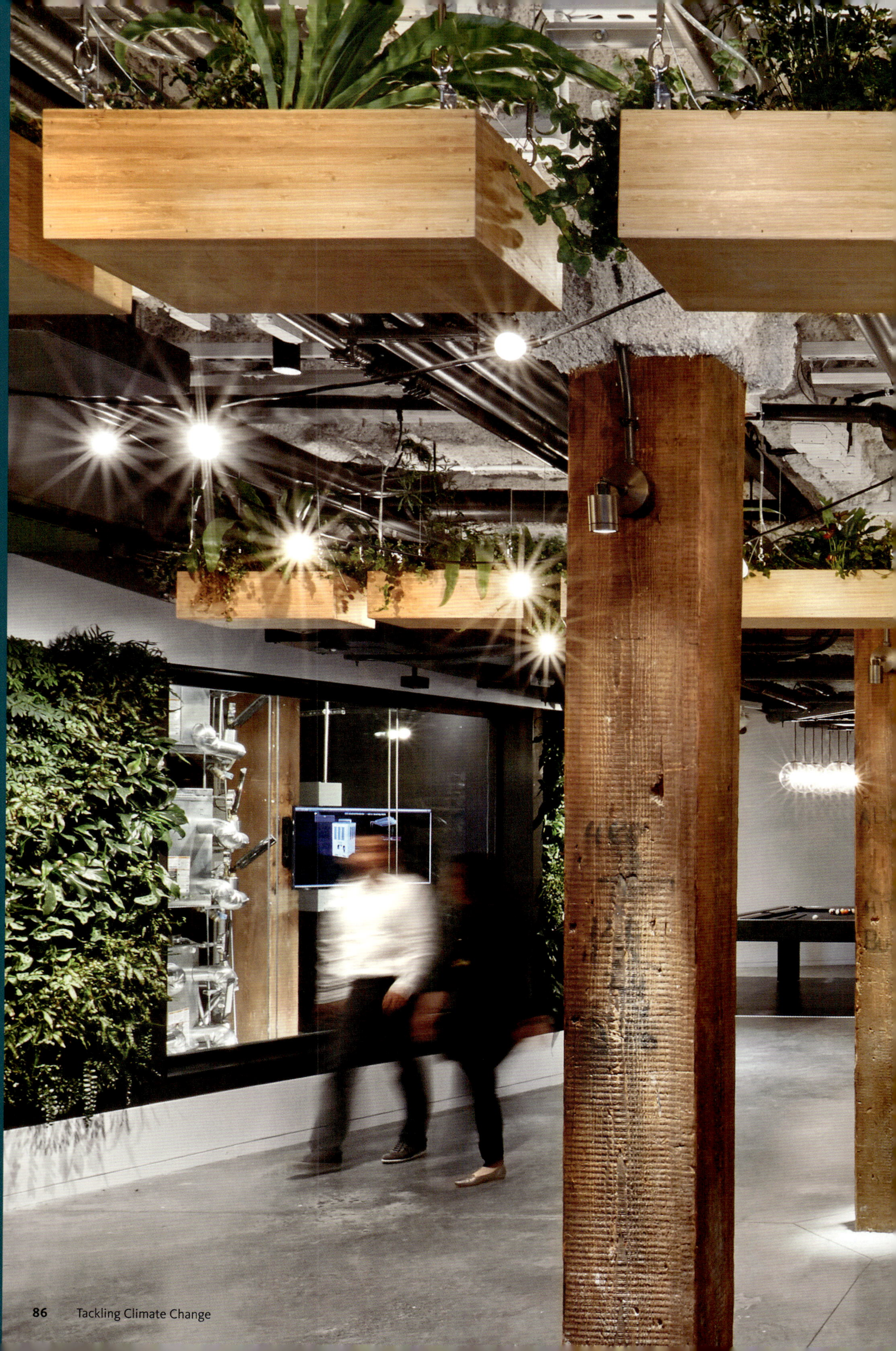

**United Technologies Digital Accelerator**
Brooklyn, New York

The new United Technologies Digital Accelerator, located in a renovated warehouse, is designed to embrace the space's original architecture while incorporating natural elements and a green wall.

# Implementing the Circular Economy

How can materials recovery and reuse steer our industry's resiliency efforts?

**WHAT WE DID**

**We studied five Gensler offices that have recently undergone a move and renovation, or are currently in the process of designing a new space, to assess process and see how reused materials played a role.** The goals of this research are to bring awareness to the circular economy and identify how the industry can bolster and encourage reuse processes within design work. We hope that by understanding current industry dynamics and salvage trends, we can develop a framework and platform for the efficient exchange of reusable materials.

Our research was conducted at Gensler locations in San Francisco, Denver, London, San Diego, and New York. We supplemented our observations with literature analysis, qualitative data from interviews, and case studies to gain an overview of existing circular reuse models in the United States and the United Kingdom for furniture and interior materials. After analyzing the current client interest in the circular economy, we tracked the waste stream of recycled materials and began to assess typical constraints on materials reuse.

**THE CONTEXT**

A circular economy focuses on the renewal, resilience, and repurposing of materials and parts. It represents a deliberate disruption to the "take, make, dispose" method of linear industrial production. Although a relatively recent framework, Accenture Strategy states that 94% of companies surveyed for a recent report practice circular strategies. However, 44% of those companies identified recycling as their area of concentration, and only 18% reuse or refurbish end-of-life materials.

While recycling is an important component of waste elimination, corporations must take more comprehensive steps. Only a fraction of the businesses focused on product life extension. And nearly half of those programs only recycle base materials, ultimately wasting more than 60% of reclaimed resources. This problem is especially prevalent in the furniture/interior materials sector. According to the Disposal-Facility-Based Characterization of Solid Waste in California, construction and demolition materials are estimated to account for between 21.7% to 25.5% of the municipal waste stream. Additionally, the three million tons of discarded furniture from U.S. businesses each year incurs disposal costs of over $100 million.

> **Office moves create a substantial amount of waste that could be reduced or avoided.**

**GENSLER NEW YORK**
120,000 sf, completed 2016

# 91%
of waste was recycled or donated

## THE RESULTS

Implementing the circular economy in the architecture, engineering, and construction industries contributes to economically sustainable growth and savings across multiple sectors. Clients can see an average savings of 30% to 50% by purchasing recycled office furniture. Simple reuse of office desks can reduce carbon footprint by 36%.

Office moves create a substantial amount of waste that could be reduced or avoided. By aggregating the total waste and estimated carbon footprint metrics estimates at each location we surveyed, we can assume that each office move (based on square footage) generates approximately 269.53 tons of waste and 1,462 metric tons of carbon. This waste could be diminished if we rethink methodologies, processes, and project goals.

Waste streams are largely undefined. The current reuse landscape is highly localized. It requires time to understand and coordinate where materials finish their life spans. There is no simple answer to what this process looks like, or how it is decided. An accessible framework needs to be set in place that clearly articulates the best practices around how to properly reuse a material, or discard a material to be reused.

### Carbon Impact

# 36%

Simple reuse of an office desk can cut its carbon footprint by up to 36% from 292 to 187 kg CO2e.

Center for remanufacturing and reuse, 2012

### Economic Impact

# 30-50%

Our clients can see an average savings of 30-50% by purchasing recycled office furniture.

Herman Miller, 2017

### Waste Stream Impact

# $100 mil

Three million tons of furniture is discarded from U.S. businesses each year, incurring disposal costs of $100 million.

EPA, 2015

**DESIGN IMPLICATIONS**

**Reuse strategies can be implemented at every phase of the design process.** Designers can develop strategies for the reuse of existing furniture within the design of clients' new space; identify and secure contracts for waste/reuse materials; and determine the success of the design by tracking relative metrics. Activities such as creating a spec sheet of existing furniture in a space for designers to reuse; exploring existing manufacturing/take-back programs that would benefit from unused resources; and providing carbon savings calculations can encourage and support circular strategies.

**Partnerships are essential for the circular economy to evolve and gain traction within the architecture, engineering, and construction industries.** To transform the design process into an increasingly reuse-friendly, circular network, the industry will need to develop policies, re-create processes, and encourage reuse on internal and external projects.

**Development of reuse networks will thrive on a local level through design, planning, removal, and transportation structures.** Through our internal and external interview process, we identified numerous potential partners that either already work in the reuse and exchange realm, or have expressed interest in becoming a key player.

Best practices involving reuse can be incorporated into the design process. Similar to the ambiguity surrounding waste streams, there is no formalized approach to reuse during the design process. However, we can pose questions and guidelines in each phase of the design process to help direct stakeholders toward reused resources and products. As we look to develop a more streamlined approach to material reuse, preparing our designers, consultants, and contractors with a standard set of questions will help ensure the awareness and implementation of circular strategies.

**GENSLER DENVER**
19,963 sf, completed 2015

**68%**
of waste was recycled or donated

**GENSLER LONDON**
37,670 sf, completed 2017

**90%**
of movable furniture, fixtures, and equipment was reused

## WHAT'S NEXT

Looking ahead, there are clear corporate incentives for bolstering and participating in the short- and long-term circular economy. The model of the circular economy encourages untapped revenue streams while enhancing the inherent worth of the material or furnishing. We outline the following four implementation models, while acknowledging that each approach has a variety of barriers and stakeholders:

**Circular supply**—provide renewable input materials that replace single life cycle inputs.

**Product as a service**—an external company retains ownership of the product and internalizes the benefits of circular resource possession and care; similar to a lease agreement.

**Product life extension**—repair, tune, and upgrade various product components to extend the life of a material or furnishing.

**Resource recovery**—retrieve and recover useful resources and/or energy from end-of-life products that would otherwise be destined for landfill.

Ultimately, more industry and consumer research is needed to gauge interest in circular thinking. Such future research could analyze the current state of reuse in local markets and further scrutinize concerns and motivation.

**GENSLER SAN DIEGO**
18,322 sf, completed in 2017

**60% FF&E** reused in the project

*"We will consume three planets' worth of resources by 2050."*
—The Circulars 2018 Yearbook: An Initiative of the Forum of Young Global Leaders

**GENSLER SAN FRANCISCO**
54,284 sf, completed 2017

**60%** of FF&E reused in the project

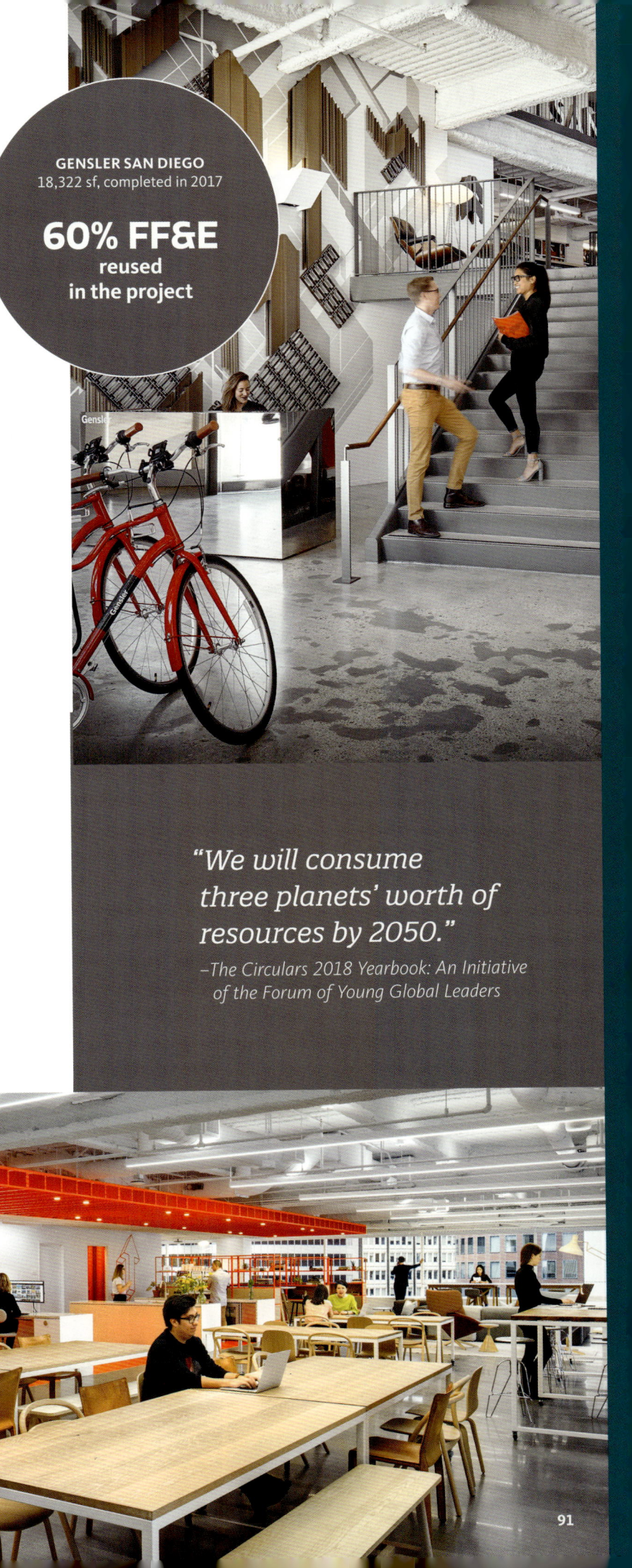

## ENHANCING URBAN MOBILITY

Innovations in transportation and mobility are creating opportunities to rethink the design of our cities and improve the urban experience.

| CARS AND PARKING | AIR AND RAIL |
|---|---|

94 **Forecasting Design Shifts Under Future Vehicle Technologies**

**Research Team**
Jeff Barber
Laura Carey
Claire Kang

100 **Projecting Future Parking Demands of Autonomous Vehicles**

**Research Team**
JF Finn III
Kevin Kusina
Karina Silvester
Andrew Starr
Diana Vasquez

**Research Partner**
Ira Winder

106 **Investigating Parking in the Age of Automation**

**Research Team**
Andrea Peterson
Daniel Ranostaj

110 **Understanding Airports through Social Data**

**Research Team**
Andy Huang
Kate O'Connor
Keith Thompson
Justin Wortman

**Research Partner**
Charles Le Grosse (Lexalytics)

116 **Japan's Railway Retail Hubs**

**Research Team**
Anna Demuth
Kelly Guo
Melissa Mizell
Daisuke Okazaki
Marco Troncarelli
Nagato Uematsu

# Forecasting Design Shifts Under Future Vehicle Technologies

What are short- and long-term responses to shared, electric, and autonomous vehicles on the built environment?

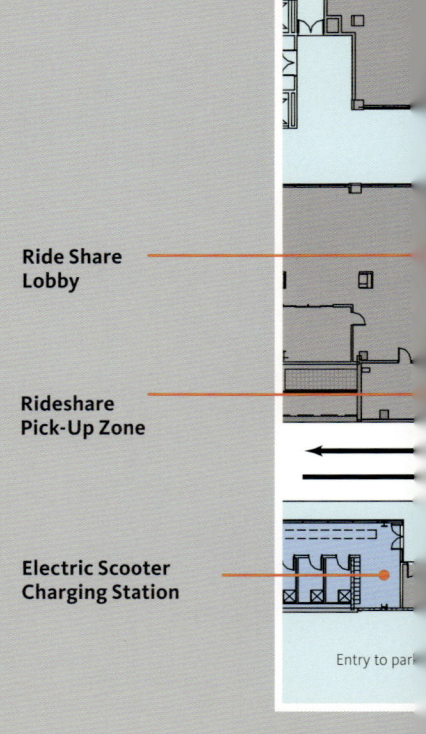

**Ride Share Lobby**

**Rideshare Pick-Up Zone**

**Electric Scooter Charging Station**

Entry to par[k]

### WHAT WE DID

**We created a spatial projection model that helps predict parking, queueing, and electric requirements for the next 25 years.** With simple inputs, the user achieves square-foot estimates as related to parking, queueing, and electric demands in the short, medium, and long term. Essentially, our model reflects building-specific projections according to future trending.

Curbside demand is expected to increase, so we developed a toolkit for adaptive reuse strategies and programming alternatives for parking garage space that will soon become available. This toolkit for convertability is built around a range of solutions that anticipate changes for various timeframes. We created a simple set of convertibility metrics to gauge the feasibility of multiple scenarios to reclaim residual parking space in the future.

### THE CONTEXT

Despite the optimistic tenor of conversations on the development of driverless vehicles, manned autonomous vehicles have so far failed to perform safely and consistently on the road; doubt remains about the actual timeline of full-scale adoption.

For now, shared and electric car adoption is expected to yield the most significant change in the short term. There have been drastic jumps in shared-car service usage, and while the market share of the plug-in electric car segment only passed 2% in 2018, forecasters project significant gains throughout the 2020s.

The rise of transportation network companies (TNCs), such as Uber and Lyft, are already having a significant impact on the built environment causing cities like San Francisco, New York, and Washington, D.C. to develop ways of managing increased curbside demands such as geofencing, dynamic pricing, and regulating the number of shared vehicles on the roads. Further, policy changes to reduce emissions and automotive companies' strategic decisions to increase production of electric vehicles will fundamentally change the course of transportation.

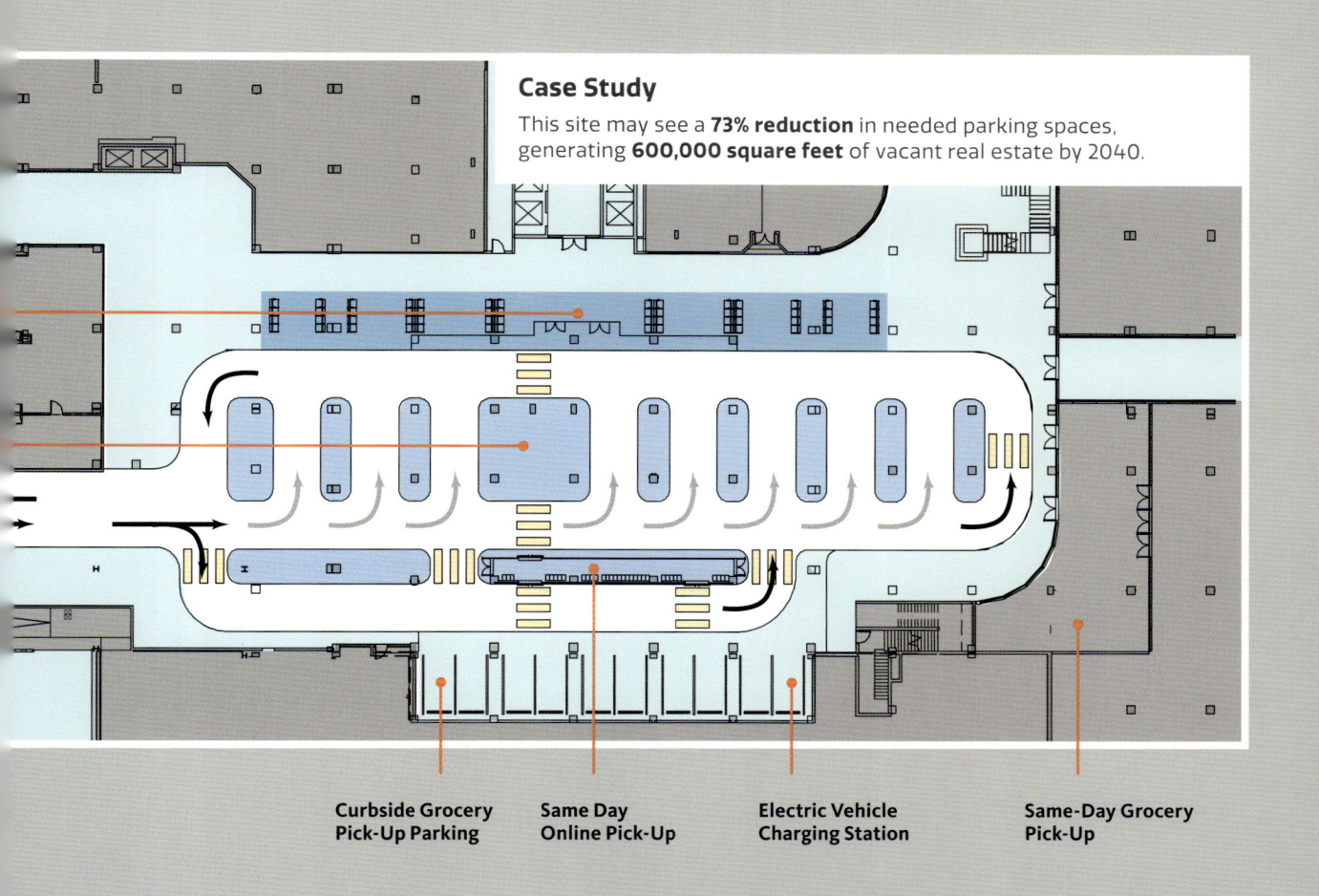

**Case Study**

This site may see a **73% reduction** in needed parking spaces, generating **600,000 square feet** of vacant real estate by 2040.

**Curbside Grocery Pick-Up Parking**

**Same Day Online Pick-Up**

**Electric Vehicle Charging Station**

**Same-Day Grocery Pick-Up**

# Each step along the path to autonomous vehicles demands a new way of envisioning space

## THE RESULTS

We developed a model that quantifies the spatial implications of different car-usage projections to demonstrate how needs might fluctuate over time. The requirements of our model are simple: the user inputs a building's total number of parking spaces or required parking ratio. The model can then be run according to many adoption-rate scenarios, and users receive an estimate of how much space should be allocated to parking under different futures and how much of the present-day parking space will become available.

We explored a range of programmatic alternatives to visualize a future with diminishing amounts of real estate devoted to parking. Density, existing transportation networks, and demographics will play a role in alternative options. Acknowledging that adoption rates for shared, electric, and autonomous vehicles will vary significantly by location we categorized sites into urban, ex-urban, suburban, and rural. We focused first on the areas with greatest potential: urban and ex-urban locales, and residential and commercial office buildings that have parking within the building's footprint and limited curbside frontage.

We applied our tool as a case study for National Landing, a transit-oriented development (TOD) situated next to Reagan National Airport, approximately four miles from downtown Washington, D.C. With the anticipated changes to parking real estate, this site would see a 73% reduction in needed parking spaces, generating 600,000 square feet of vacant real estate by 2040.

DESIGN IMPLICATIONS

## Building owners should begin a phased, parking-conversion plan.

Rethinking pickup and drop-off areas may be the first priority based on the current and projected increase in ride-sharing. Managing for peak times and varying usage will be crucial; for office buildings, AM and PM peaks can vary significantly based on the time differences in drop-offs and pickups. Space implications will also bleed into ther adjacent building areas with potential to become pickup and drop-off areas. For example, "rideshare lobbies" are a potential alternative to first-level parking garages.

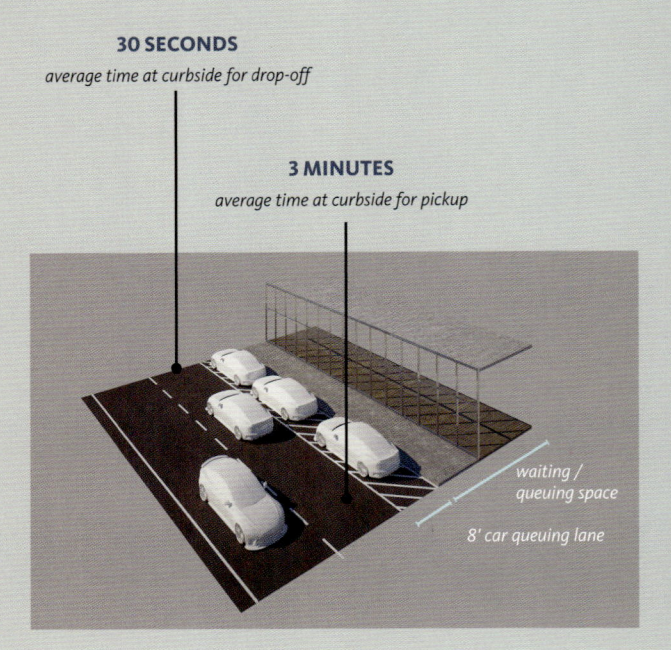

**30 SECONDS**
average time at curbside for drop-off

**3 MINUTES**
average time at curbside for pickup

waiting / queuing space

8' car queuing lane

## More and more space will become available as parking demand progressively decreases.

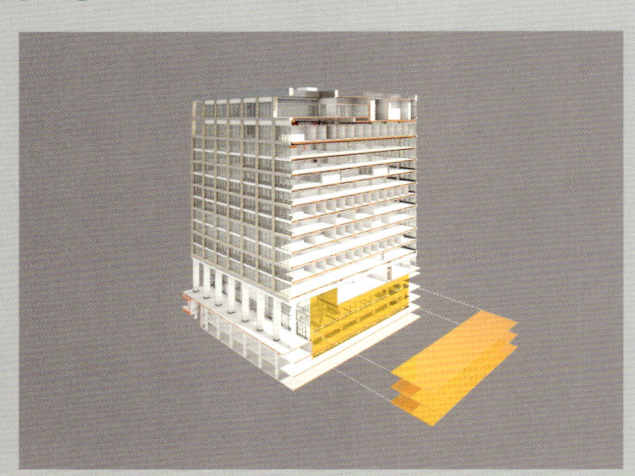

There are myriad options for the reuse of reclaimed parking space. For instance, a landlord may choose to move MEP equipment to below-grade parking, or increase the overall usable space in a building by adding below-ground atriums or amenities.

## We need to outfit buildings to better accommodate electric cars.

The quantity of electric vehicles is increasing; that means we need not only charging stations, but an increase in energy services for electric vehicles. On average, electricity costs $0.11 per kWh, and for an electric car, that means a price-point twice as low as gasoline. If monetized, charging stations are profitbale and sustainable programmatic options. Alternatively, financial incentives from government agencies may also be able to offset costs.

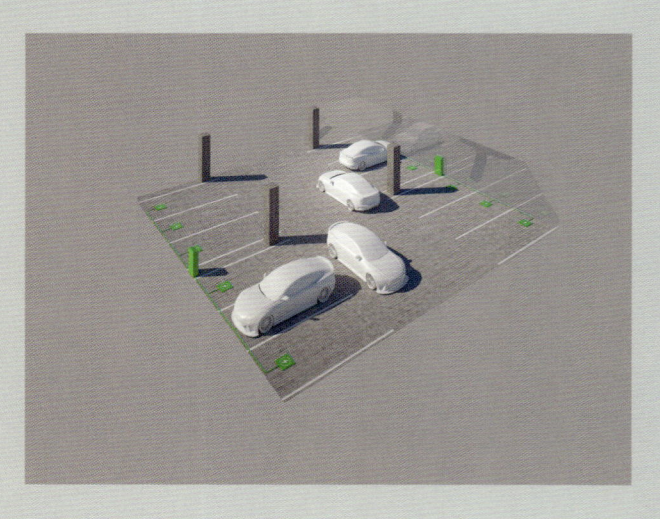

Enhancing Urban Mobility | Forecasting Design Shifts Under Future Vehicle Technologies

# Toolkit for Convertibility
*Design explorations for the conversion of parking garages to other uses.*

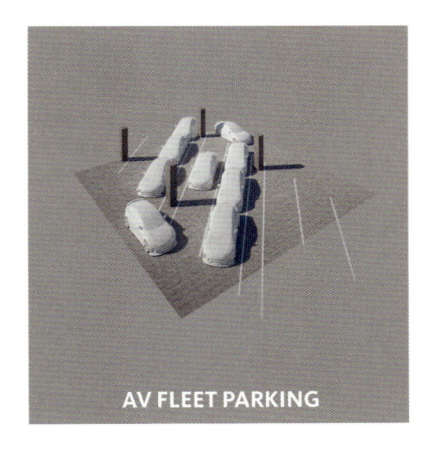

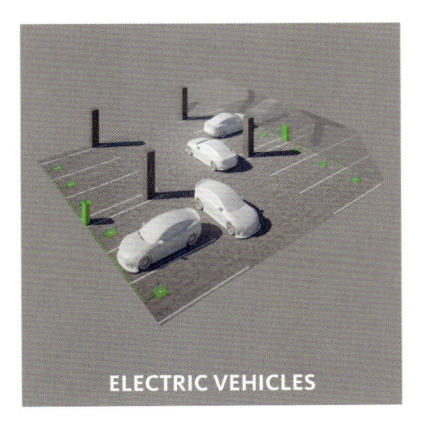

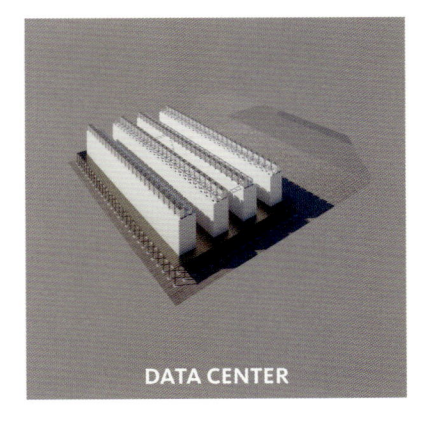

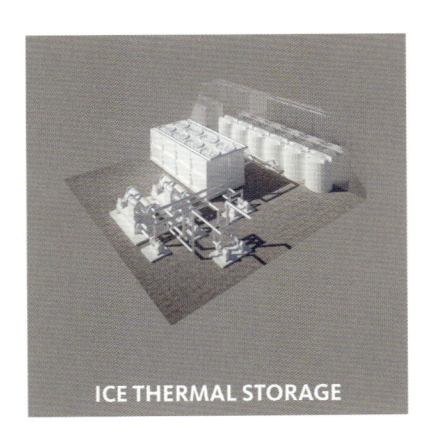

| | | |
|---|---|---|
| **AV FLEET PARKING** | **FITNESS CENTER** | **APP-BASED SELF-STORAGE** |
| **ELECTRIC VEHICLES** | **SQUASH COURT** | **DATA CENTER** |
| **ICE THERMAL STORAGE** | **HYDROPONIC FARMING** | **RAINWATER STORAGE** |

**WHAT'S NEXT**

Our next phase of research is to continue to work with clients to antipate the impact of future mobility—whether it be autonomous, shared, or electric vehicles, e-scooters or drones—and its impact on the built environment.

Enhancing Urban Mobility

**Skyport Mobility Hub**

The Skyport Mobility Hub imagines tomorrow's mobility through a community destination and connection concept. The Mobility Hub is equipped to handle passengers arriving on e-bikes, e-scooters, public transit, traditional ride-sharing vehicles, and—eventually—autonomous vehicles. This design solution is a pivotal piece of the urban fabric, binding the neighborhood together with a central place to shop, dine, and engage while reducing congestion across the city.

# Projecting Future Parking Demands of Autonomous Vehicles

How will new vehicle technologies impact real estate?

**WHAT WE DID**

**We researched the impact of increased autonomous vehicle (AV) adoption on real estate with a particular focus on parking.** We first gathered information from developers and consultant groups to calibrate our orientation toward the future impact of this technology. Parking is a shared urban amenity with many stakeholders; we met with myriad groups to gather diverse perspectives on this topic.

We synthesized secondary research, stakeholder communications, and client workshops, identifying drivers of AV adoption rates and how they may influence future investments in real estate. We added a quantitative foundation to our research using data from Gensler's project work, establishing baseline real estate metrics. We applied this conception to an interactive tool to model various AV adoption scenarios. Our model uses manual inputs for parking structure typologies, AV adoption timeline, rideshare percentage used, and other operable variables to illustrate various scenarios over time.

**THE CONTEXT**

Changes to transportation are coming at a fast clip. Uber and Lyft came less than a decade ago, and the ride-sharing services are now the norm. Electric-car sales in the United States are oft-cited to be 2% of total market share; however, that number is misleading as reported electric-car sales peaked 10% in some US cities. There is one charging station for every gas station in the US right now, but that ratio is shifting as consumers become more likely to favor environmentally-friendly options.

Electronic vehicles are projected to last for one million miles, ten times the average car using an internal-combustion engine— that means financial upsides significantly favor the former. Ride-sharing and AV adoption are integral to a trend toward transportation as a service (TaaS) and away from private ownership. TaaS and AV adoption coincide with the innovation and adoption of electric vehicle (EV) technology. Consider the mash-up of ride-sharing services with electric and autonomous vehicle technology: ride-sharing services may buoy electric vehicles in the short term and autonomous vehicles in the long term.

These trends mean not only a shift in behaviors, but a rethinking of infrastructure and how it relates to newly prioritized forms of transportation. Our conception of how we use space expands with new modes of transportation, their implications for traffic patterns, and the subsequent need to address parking utilization on and off the street. The transition to a TaaS, AV, and EV future requires new collaboration between public, private, and academic stakeholders—partnerships that our research looks to facilitate.

*5,000,000 miles*

*4,500,000 miles*

*4,000,000 miles*

*3,500,000 miles*

*3,000,000 miles*

*2,500,000 miles*

*2,000,000 miles*

*1,500,000 miles*

*1,000,000 miles*

*500,000 miles*

*Annual miles driven*

| 2020 | 2025 | 2030 | 2035 | 2040 |

**2040**
Shared mobility accounts for ~80% of miles driven

*Shared autonomous vehicles*

*As the mobility landscape shifts, we must address the value assigned to parking infrastructure over time.*

*Private autonomous vehicles*

*Shared vehicles*

**2025**
Shared driver–driven vehicles account for > 10% of miles driven

**2022**
Use of personally owned driver–driven vehicles begins to decline

**Introduction of shared (2020) and personally owned (2022) autonomous vehicles**

*Private vehicles*

Source: Deloitte's "Gearing for change: Preparing for transformation in the automotive ecosystem."

# The Future of Parking

*This simulation tool evaluates key assumptions about behavior and technology, and can ultimately influence parking demand and vehicle traffic into the future.*

## 2030

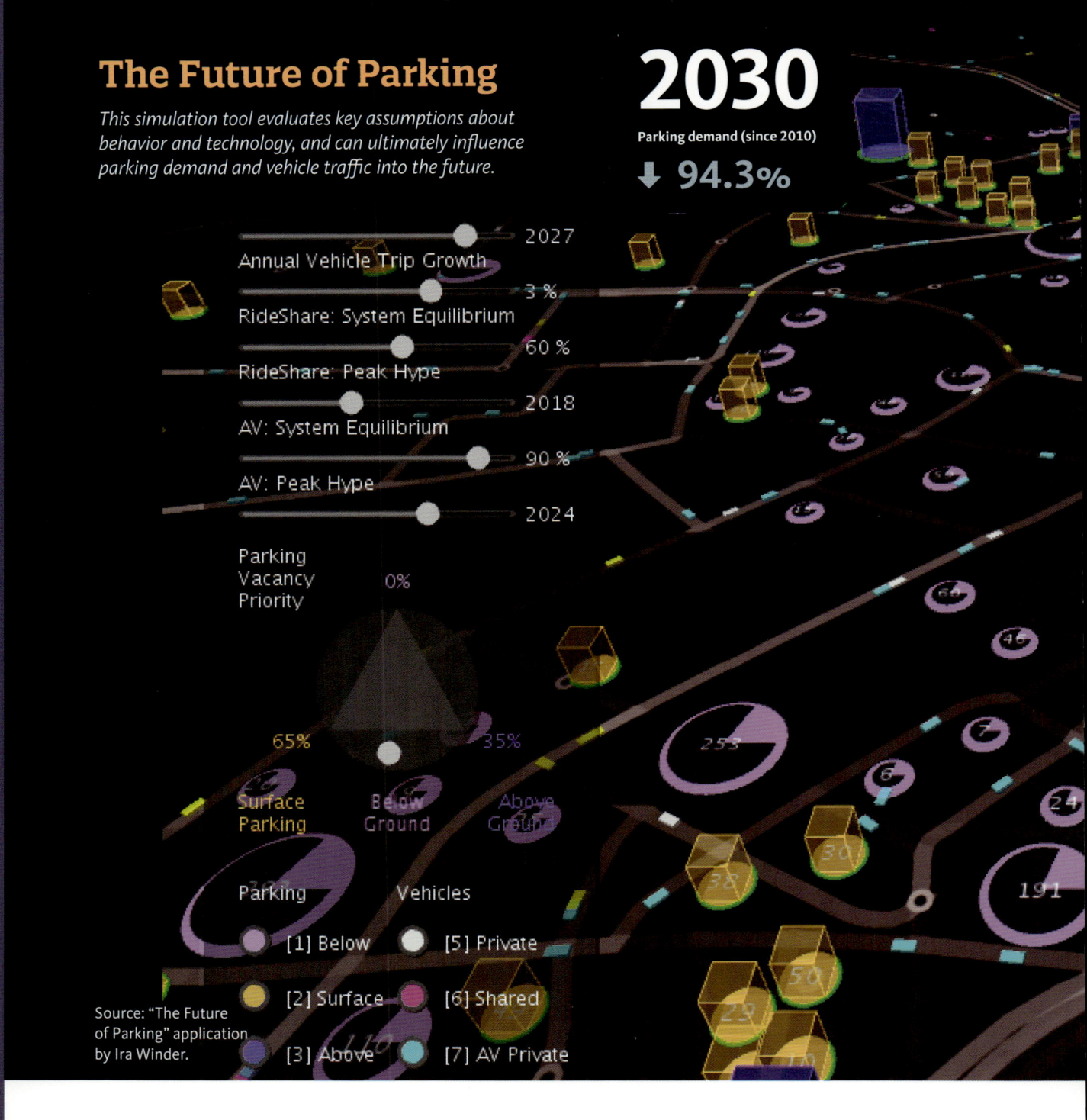

Parking demand (since 2010)

↓ **94.3%**

- Annual Vehicle Trip Growth: 2027 / 3%
- RideShare: System Equilibrium: 60%
- RideShare: Peak Hype: 2018
- AV: System Equilibrium: 90%
- AV: Peak Hype: 2024
- Parking Vacancy Priority: 0%

Surface Parking 65% / Below Ground 35% / Above Ground

**Parking**
- [1] Below
- [2] Surface
- [3] Above

**Vehicles**
- [5] Private
- [6] Shared
- [7] AV Private

Source: "The Future of Parking" application by Ira Winder.

## THE RESULTS

We created an application called *The Future of Parking* to simulate parking utilization for passenger vehicles in hypothetical scenarios. To do this, we defined parking typologies and their role in the adoption of autonomous vehicles in downtown Boston. In our beta release, the application framework supports a data import from GIS road networks and parking that can be populated with simulated agents. We designated four main parking structure typologies: surface, below grade, above grade, and standalone. We visualized each parking property by capacity, which across time may change according to manual inputs. By clicking on each parking area, a display shows the parking capacity at each location and the proportion that each area represents. The simulation includes fully reconfigurable, multimodal vehicles that travel to and from parking structures along shortest-route trajectories. It also allows the user to prioritize which types of structures are more relevant for use over time. Our case study has 3D visualization, with clarity at multiple scales, or zoom levels.

[Analysis] System Projections

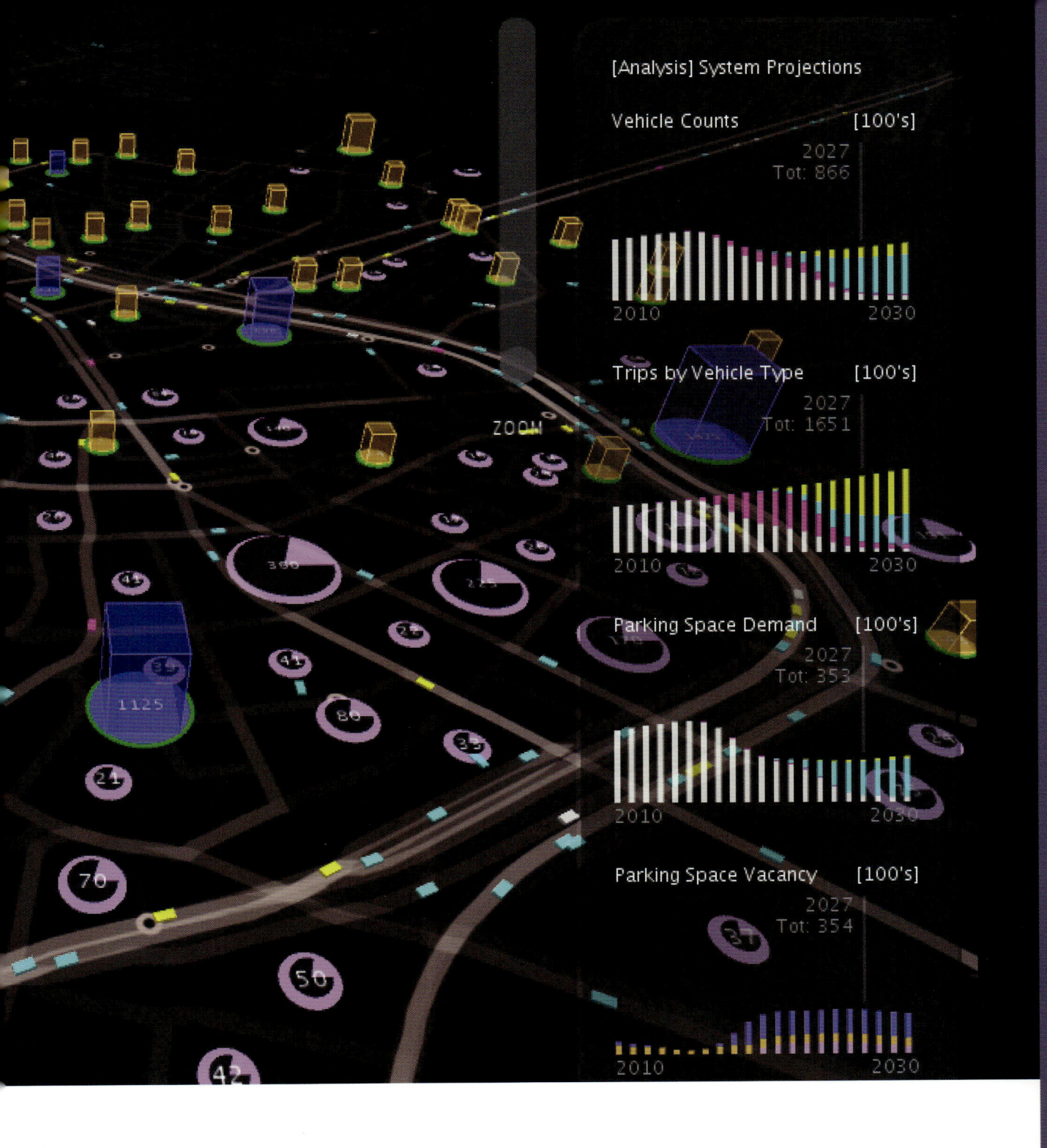

Vehicle Counts          [100's]
                        2027
                        Tot: 866
2010                    2030

Trips by Vehicle Type   [100's]
                        2027
                        Tot: 1651
2010                    2030

Parking Space Demand    [100's]
                        2027
                        Tot: 353
2010                    2030

Parking Space Vacancy   [100's]
                        2027
                        Tot: 354
2010                    2030

Through our tool, we provide a better understanding of the value of real estate. The most useful metrics, or our most impactful outputs, may be the sheer quantity of liberated square feet in the next ten years—a number with a direct financial impact—and how rideshare could have the same or greater impact today. As we apply our framework and tool to new case studies and partner with stakeholders to solve new real-estate questions, we will hone our capacity to support evolving client needs. That means our approach will be fine-tuned with time. Future releases will incorporate more economic inputs that will offer granular simulation of parking and utilization under various AV and shared vehicle adoption scenarios.

The key to our model is adjustable variables: years of analysis, annual vehicle trip growth, rideshare and AV equilibriums, and peak adoption years. The model works in real time to demonstrate how a city behaves according to unique situations. The model includes projections for vehicle counts, vehicle types, parking space demand, and parking space vacancy.

103

# Developer Checklist

We created a versatile checklist to adapt a long-term vision at the inception of each new project. The checklist considerations are meant to drive the conceptualization of novel design solutions, not one-size-fits-all answers.

## Future Proofing

What design considerations should we make for future flexibility?

- Conversion or alternative use of infrastructure
- Modular infrastructure
- Changes to parking garage density
- Frontage and amenity locations

## Public Policy

What is the public policy landscape of innovation and investment?

- AV and rideshare regulations
- Local support for alternative transportation systems and public transportation
- Incentives for investment in new technologies

**User Experience**

## Risk & Benefit

Which risk and value structures will change over time?

- Revenue plan length
- On-site parking, alternative parking, and infrastructural changes
- Construction costs
- Alternative land uses

## Environmental Impact

What are the target areas for improved environmental impact?

- Private and public transportation balance
- Ground water recharge and stormwater runoff
- Potential spaces for diverse flora and fauna
- Reduced urban heat island effect

**DESIGN IMPLICATIONS**

**New technologies will facilitate large-scale change in the real estate industry,** pushing stakeholders to reimagine how to manage public policy, land use, development, infrastructure, space utilization, and human experience. These topics found what we call a "developer checklist," or an outline for project visioning sessions. The checklist includes targeted considerations that may flex to accommodate any project requirement.

**Parking space liberation is the future. As a general rule, we need to stop investing in parking.** About 10% of office building developer revenue comes from parking; however, that stream is bound to become a trickle as even ten driverless ride-sharing cars could reduce the need for parking by 500 stalls. If parking is needed, flexible parking solutions should be considered.

**We must program real estate with a greater emphasis on a multimodal understanding of future transportation,** considering privately owned user-driven vehicles are trending down. We expect a city landscape to accommodate more drop-off areas and charging stations, which means that commercial buildings will repurpose ground-level space, reimagining the entry experience and parking space for these needs through higher-density parking and conversion-capable design.

**WHAT'S NEXT**

We are planning for a dashboard that fully reflects the dynamism of the urban environment. While area utilization—defined as vacancy—will be the primary output of our model, we plan to design for targeted specifications that drill down further into each pressure on parking demand. Over time, vehicle passenger demand growth may be flat or robust and the ratio of traditional vehicles, autonomous vehicles, and ride-sharing service vehicles may fluctuate. We need to account for each of these scenarios moving forward. More advanced economic inputs to our interactive model mean we will move toward a more accurate picture of tomorrow's structural changes.

SURFACE    ABOVE-GRADE    BELOW-GRADE

# Investigating Parking in the Age of Automation

How can we optimize parking in the built environments of today and tomorrow?

**WHAT WE DID**

**We collaborated with engineers, parking designers, and urban planners to review secondary research and achieve a holistic understanding of what tools we have to tackle our present and future parking needs.** After gathering and analyzing this information, we documented present trends in technology and design that are molding how and where we park, and emerging technologies that are poised to have significant effects on parking in the future. The goal of our research was to discover ways in which innovative designs, and new technologies, will drive change, and speculate on how we can best design buildings and cities today to accommodate potential changes in the future.

**THE CONTEXT**

Since the advent of Ford's Model T, cars have played a central, and often dominant, role in urban design and planning. And while cities will not shrug off parking concerns any time soon, new urban design solutions are emerging that trend away from traditional parking arrangements. Why? Our needs are changing and we are met with competing demands: increase parking capacity and lower congestion, while not sacrificing prime real estate.

Our current model for parking isn't working—the need to appease parking has grown out of control. Parking provisions can command up to 50% of programmed space in buildings today. Increased demand for parking is therefore putting how we park under increased scrutiny. Finding new solutions to parking can help address this demand without increasing space allocated to parking—and ideally, even help free up current parking space(s) for other uses.

One-third of the typical American city is asphalt, but this may change as new technologies continue their drive toward dynamic mobility and streamlined methods getting from Point A to Point B. As we look to the future, our design logic needs to follow the principle of maximizing mobility rather than simply creating, or allocating, more space to parking.

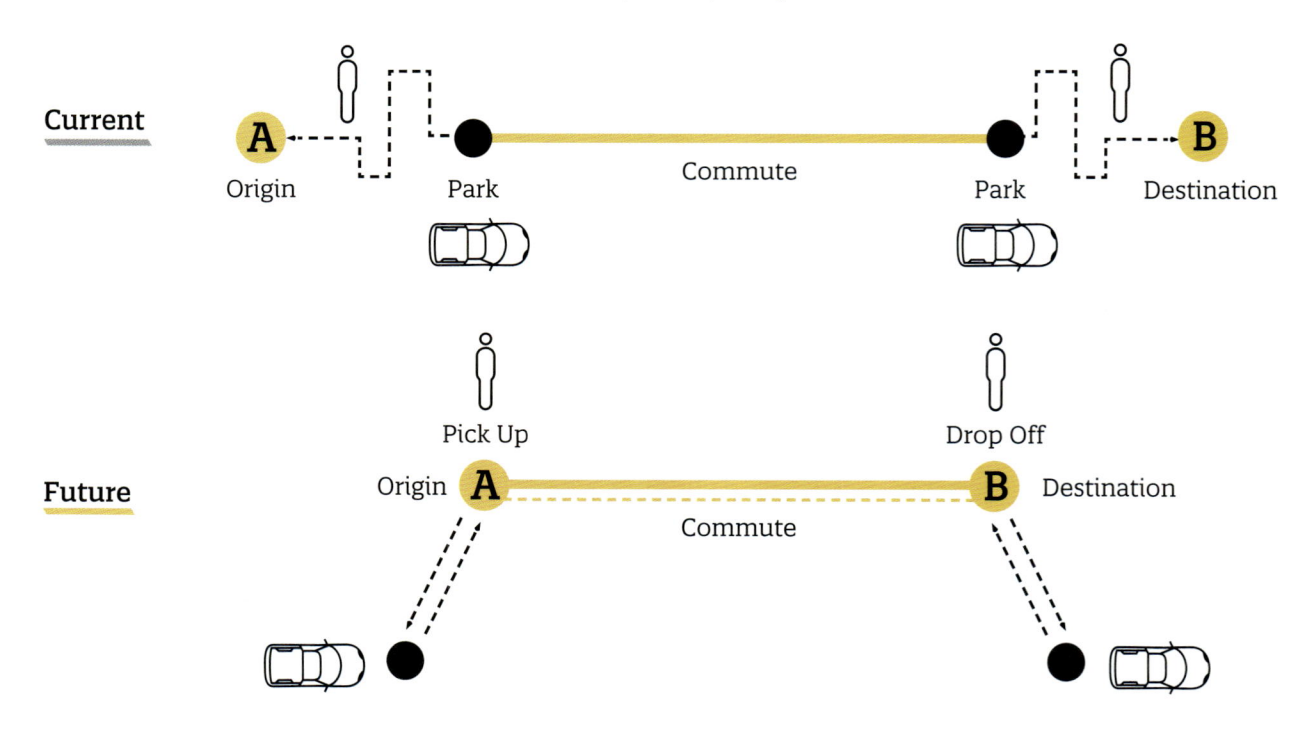

**Current**

Origin — A — Park — Commute — Park — B — Destination

**Future**

Origin — Pick Up — A — Commute — B — Drop Off — Destination

Enhancing Urban Mobility | Investigating Parking in the Age of Automation

*Driverless cars are capable of sensing the environment and navigating without human input.*

820 ft

490 ft

200 ft

260 ft

164 ft

330 ft

**THE RESULTS**

We began our research focused on parking, but evolved toward the adaptation of our design processes and solutions for evolving mobility patterns rather than simply rendering less parking. Undoubtedly, it is important to modify existing inventory to maximize usage, but we found that newer technologies that address how we travel rather than just the end point, or the parking space, are our areas with greatest potential.

In the near-term, solutions from city policies and startups are already pointing the way toward more efficient parking. Something as simple as managing parking costs can make a big impact—studies have shown that free parking induces demand and exacerbates the parking problem by oversupplying needed spaces. In San Francisco, under the project title of SFPark, the city installed sensors and variable meters to detect parking space occupancy rates, and adjusts prices in real time.

Reducing time spent looking for parking can also have a big impact on overall traffic congestion and reduce latent capacity. ParkiFi, a Denver-based mobile application, allows users to find available parking spaces in Denver's Downtown area. The company has been implanting sensors, and coordinating a cloud-based system, to discern when and where parking spots are vacated or occupied. The app elaborates on existing apps that help drivers find parking garages based upon price and location.

Technology innovation will push us well beyond these solutions however. Autonomous vehicles (AVs) and automated garages are the end game. By fully automating parking, the typical garage floor plan would be able to accommodate over 50% more cars. Because of the costs and pragmatic considerations, the most optimistic forecasts do not call for full implementation of automated parking any time soon. AVs are also slated for an exponential increase in use. Looking ahead, AVs could relieve up to 90% of parking demand—meaning the solutions we design today need to not only be more efficient in their capacity, but also plan for a future in which current parking needs are dramatically reduced.

**11.8 million**
Self-Driving Cars
2030

↑

**50x**

↑

**230,000**
Self-Driving Cars
2020

## Optimization of Parking Structure Design

To future-proof development, parking structures with flat floors and higher floor-to-floor distances are recommended. These layouts allow for more flexibility and adaptability to a wider range of future potential uses.

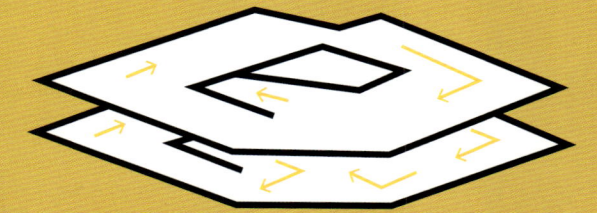

**Sloping Floors:** Parking structures with sloped floors are incredibly hard to retrofit.

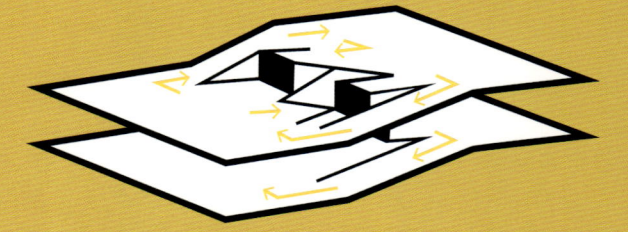

**Staggered Floors:** Staggered floors offer limited opportunities to repurpose.

### DESIGN IMPLICATIONS

**Parking design and infrastructure should be designed to accommodate emerging technologies.** There is a growing need for new infrastructure and property designs to better accommodate innovations in parking and transport, while planning for a future with much less parking need. Creative floor plate design should not be inhibitive to robotic parking, full automation, or shrinking parking space requirements.

**We must identify and anticipate future infrastructural needs in our design process and show how these are possible in our projects.** New technologies such as increased use of AV will decrease parking footprints, but the implications remain largely unknown. What would we do with all that space? Although the typical parking garage may be on a path toward obsolescence, we do not expect that this space will be supplanted with only city amenities, or green space. For instance, if we move in the direction of "smart cities," we will have a greater need for support infrastructure and services. In short, instead of restricting parking garages to their definition, consider them to be "empty shells" with numerable purposes—and design them accordingly.

**We may know tomorrow's technologies, but we need to figure out the nuts and bolts.** Future research needs to create effective trajectories to transport consecutive passengers. If an AV reaches a destination with a first passenger just to commute all the way back to its initial starting point to retrieve a second passenger, there is a "doubling effect" on infrastructure. The scope of this research spans algorithms to better understand behavioral patterns when it comes to commuting.

**Finally, any modifications to parking habits and physical space will reshape how we interact with the built environment.** Cities will have to create designated pickup/drop-off spaces, reconfigured building entrances, loading zones, and other new features to accommodate new technologies and designs. Now consider a cityscape once these modifications are made. Although small in scale, reclaiming street parking spaces for green space, pedestrian traffic, or pickup/drop-off spaces would abridge a city's aesthetic.

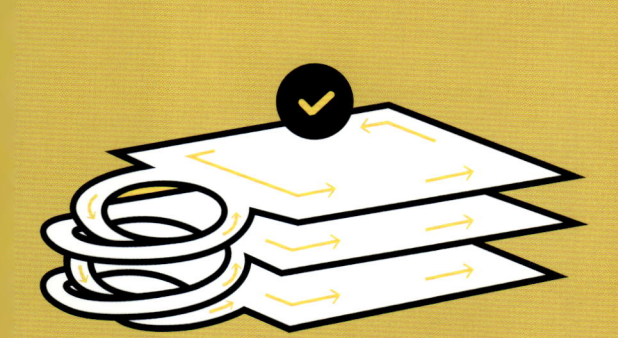

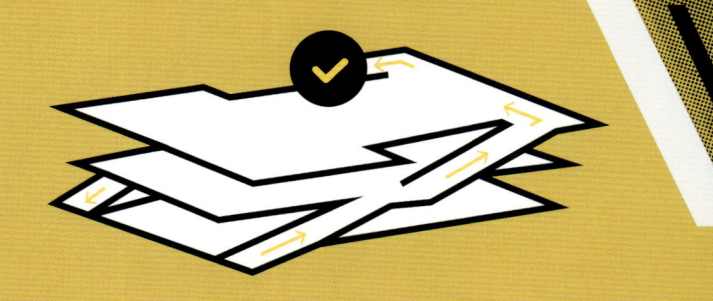

**Flat Floors (helical):** Helical ramps can be designed to be removed in the future to support other uses.

**Flat Floors (one-way ramps):** Structures with flat floors and one-way ramps minimize sloped floor space to maximize future reuse.

*"Creative floor plate design should not be inhibitive to robotic parking, full automation, or shrinking parking space requirements."*

–Arup, "Intelligent Connectivity for Seamless Urban Mobility," 2015

**WHAT'S NEXT**

Parking is part of a broader discussion on mobility and transportation. And put into an even broader context—a long and unpredictable series of consequences following any technological or behavioral change. For example, on a pro forma basis, incorporating new technologies could lower the footprint of parking spaces while requiring greater resources and money. How can we adapt to new parking typologies that command higher investments and rents?

Conversely, how will we adapt to stubborn populations and policymakers? If policymakers alleviate parking requirements from new buildings, as they have been doing in many cities across the U.S., how will designers and urban planners accommodate? We need to be practical with change. Even though we can design new typologies that automate garages, we must project our investments against a future with decreased parking demand.

# Understanding Airports through Social Data

What do people value in American airports?

**WHAT WE DID**

**We mined data from online review websites to investigate opportunities to improve the airport experience.** We organized that information in Excel, and partnered with Lexalytics to perform a sentiment analysis, algorithmic categorization, data visualization, and statistical analysis. Our data mining effort included documents from websites such as Yelp, Twitter, Facebook, and TripAdvisor. Our research culminated in the groundwork for an automated process to analyze user sentiment toward airports using social media data.

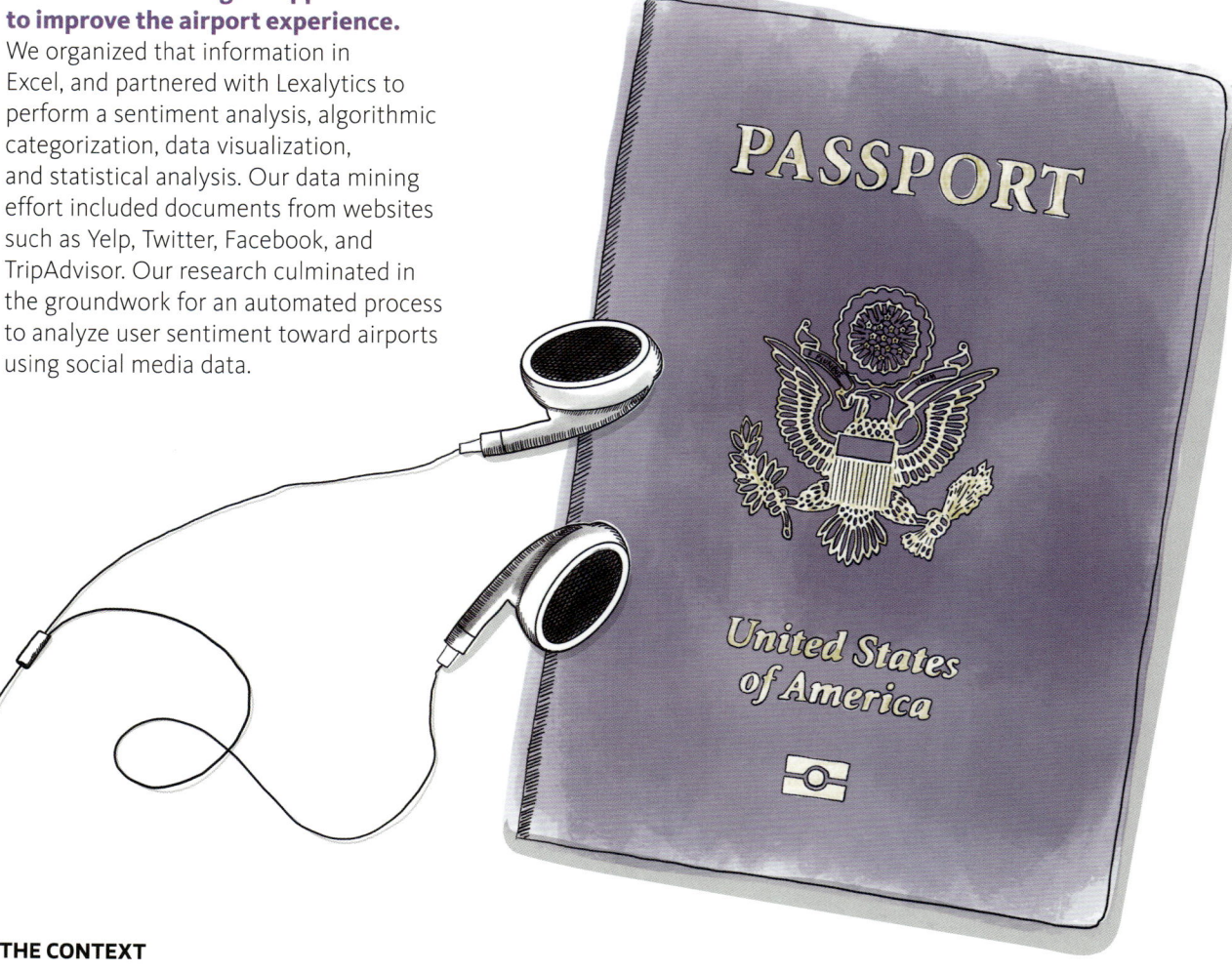

**THE CONTEXT**

It's not easy to capture and analyze the truth of how people feel about the airport experience. Airport vendors, airlines, and other stakeholders do not readily offer their data, so capturing and analyzing user sentiments is difficult. But we are not in a data vacuum, and in fact, there is no shortage of individuals posting their hot takes of an airport experience online. People visit websites for different reasons, and the ebb and flow of website popularity is a certainty. Yet when we put all that information in one place, we create the starting point for analysis.

Airports are limited in their feedback channels. Airlines use disaggregated information such as customer satisfaction surveys, compliments and complaints, social media feedback, airport comment cards, and mystery shopping (people given a script for a visit). Our research suggests using real-time feedback and real-time intelligence that can demonstrate trending data over time. We will need to focus on formulating the right algorithms, which take into account the nudges or biases embedded in people's comments.

# We created an architecture paradigm to drill down into how people talk about specific airport design features.

**THE RESULTS**

A sample of discussions about baggage fees served as our first pilot. In 2008, American Airlines introduced the first baggage fees—which helped offset the rising cost of fuel and declining profits from the recession. In 2017, the industry collected $57 billion in additional fees, including $4.6 billion in baggage fees. The average number of carry-on bags (3.4) has doubled over the past five years. We hypothesized that baggage fees have an impact on how customers experience the built environment of airports.

Our results showed that travelers who commented negatively about carry-on baggage were 95% less likely to review food, while customers who talk about checking bags are more likely to discuss shopping or food. The implication is clear that those free of their baggage did not go directly to the gate—and that the frustrations of unchecked baggage are likely to influence how someone experiences the airport environment.

We analyzed and visualized the data using an interactive dashboard. At first, we mined the data looking for a topic's sentiment. Topics ranged from food to lounge areas, parking, noise, lighting, and staff interactions. We then analyzed the polarity of sentiments by coding them with a value that ranges from very positive to very negative, through targeting words that have an emotional connotation.

We created an architecture paradigm to drill down into how people talk about specific airport design features, and we compared architecture sentiment to other experience categories to find correlations. For instance, at SFO Airport, negative architecture sentiments correlate with other categories such as attitude, wayfinding, food and drink, baggage, and bathrooms. At the same airport, a positive view of architecture is related to better perceptions of other airport features, services, and staff interactions.

We found that people on social media use very different language to refer to spaces than designers. We must stay in tune with how people refer to design. Not only must we understand what a "chill vibe of this place" means, but we must stay at the forefront of evolving phraseology. Importantly, we need to be aware of the words that customers actually use to describe their environment.

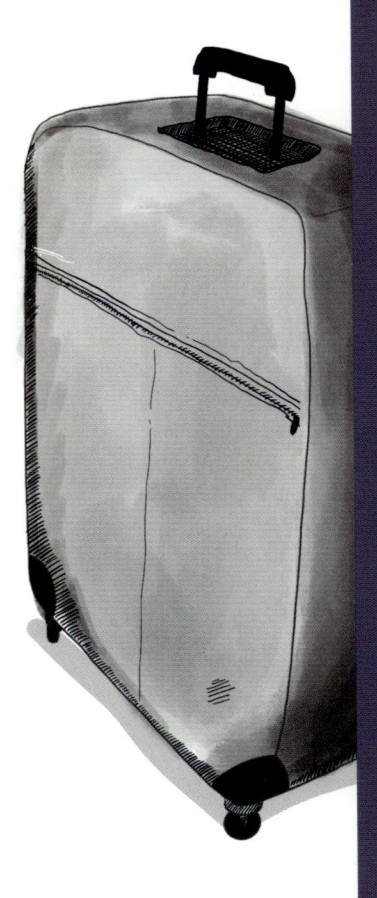

DESIGN IMPLICATIONS

## People—and the tools we use to analyze them—are imperfect.

Lexalytics found that people conflate negative feelings about a city with its airport. In fact, conflation is a serious issue as customers have a propensity to fuse their thoughts about the airlines and the roads leading to the airport with the quality of the airport.

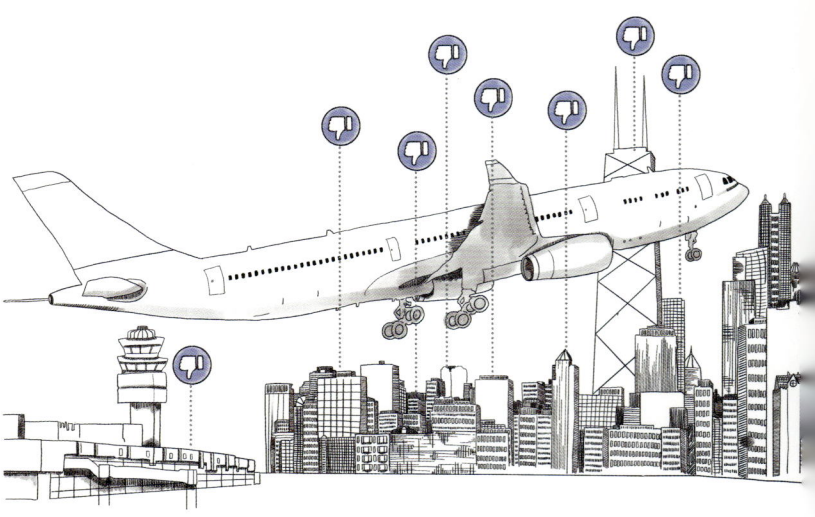

## One bad aspect of an experience can bring down attitudes about the whole experience.

For instance, if bathrooms are unclean, people are far more likely to report a poor overall airport experience. We found that people aren't necessarily having an overall bad experience, even though their sentiment may swing negative. The reality is they have frustrations targeted at one specific aspect of their experience.

## Over time, people are mentioning overhead bin space and crowded hold rooms at a higher frequency.

The 15,000 documents we analyzed spanned 13 years of user sentiments toward airports. Not only is a user sentiment from last month incongruous with a user sentiment 13 years ago, we also must tune our analytical systems by the motivations of why users issue feedback on certain websites at any given time.

# Data processing: sentiment analysis output

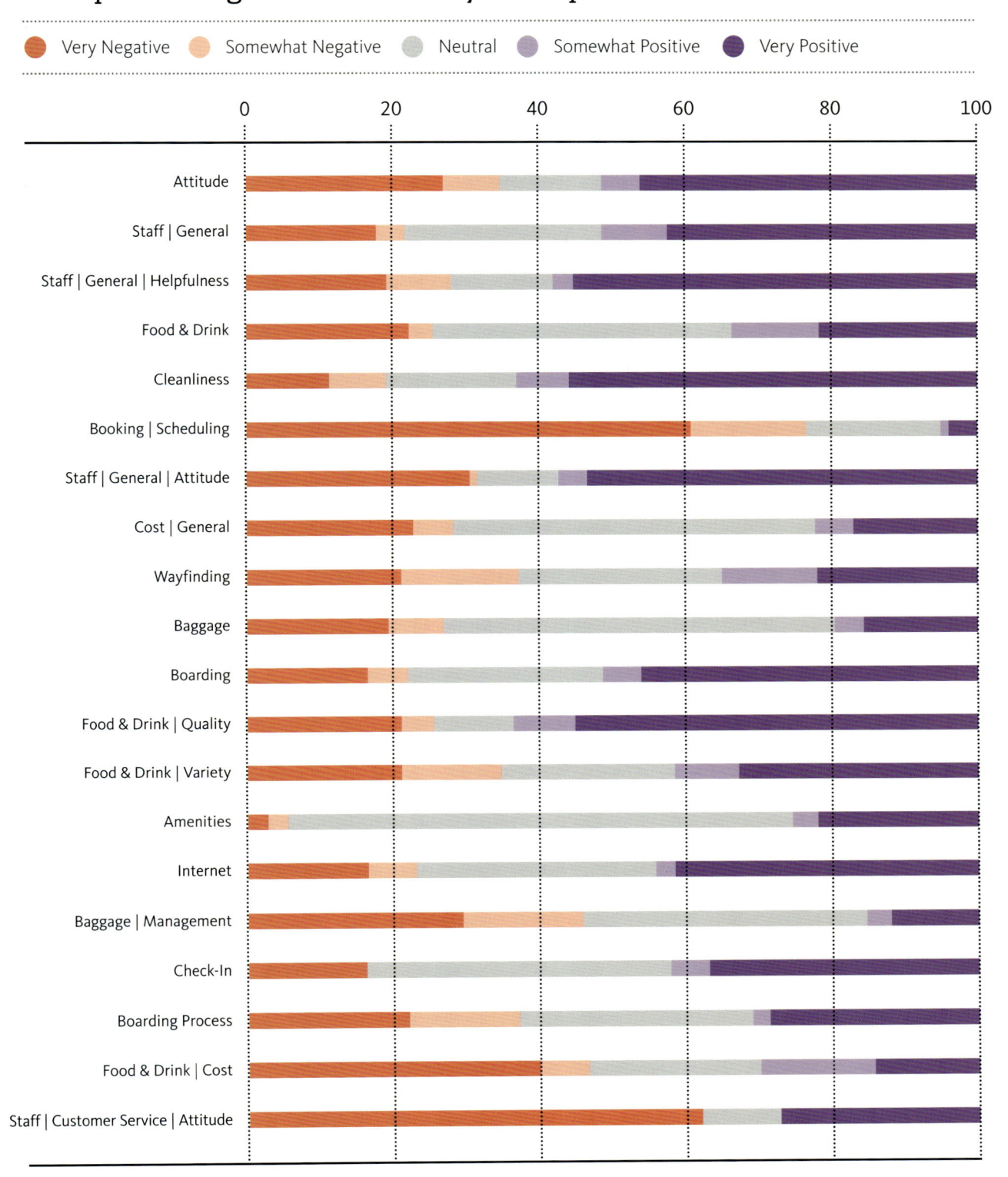

● Very Negative  ● Somewhat Negative  ● Neutral  ● Somewhat Positive  ● Very Positive

|  | |
|---|---|
| Attitude | |
| Staff \| General | |
| Staff \| General \| Helpfulness | |
| Food & Drink | |
| Cleanliness | |
| Booking \| Scheduling | |
| Staff \| General \| Attitude | |
| Cost \| General | |
| Wayfinding | |
| Baggage | |
| Boarding | |
| Food & Drink \| Quality | |
| Food & Drink \| Variety | |
| Amenities | |
| Internet | |
| Baggage \| Management | |
| Check-In | |
| Boarding Process | |
| Food & Drink \| Cost | |
| Staff \| Customer Service \| Attitude | |

**WHAT'S NEXT**

Our research has faced the unique challenge of creating a dataset, despite some clients' reluctance in sharing data relevant to our design decisions. Although we were successful in tapping into and mining useful information, there are limitations in the platforms we use to scrape and analyze data. Grabbing and cleaning data is difficult. In coding sentiments, nuances are often lost. Certain websites are harder to transform into data than others. Yelp star ratings, for example, are embedded images, so developing a software package to transform that information into data is cumbersome.

Enhancing Urban Mobility

**Auckland Airport**
Auckland,
New Zealand

Gensler led the international airport departure area upgrade for Auckland Airport. Notably, the upgraded area comprises three distinct spaces that impact the visitor journey: a reconfigured landside farewell area, a new and expanded security screening and processing area, and a new departure passenger lounge and retail hub.

# Japan's Railway Retail Hubs

How can Japanese train station retail spaces improve their experience for local and foreign visitors?

## WHAT WE DID

**We conducted an in-depth assessment of the Japanese railway retail system, its local and foreign users, and current development efforts in the area.** We then completed field studies of two Tokyo railway stations to understand how their retail hubs could better serve their users. We selected Gotanda (a small-scale station) and Shimbashi (a medium-scale station) for our blind studies. Over the course of 45 minutes, volunteer participants explored the stations and reported their impressions and experiences. To supplement these findings, we collected and analyzed data about the shopping experience from internal workshops conducted with native Japanese citizens and foreigners living in Japan. We also developed a survey based on Gensler's Experience Index algorithm and posted it on websites targeting both Japanese citizens and foreign visitors to gather public responses.

## THE CONTEXT

Using railway services is an integral part of the daily life of most Tokyo residents. In Tokyo, shopping is heavily done in department stores and small shops in and around subway stations. These stores tend to sit directly atop or below large subway stations, particularly in central business districts—and the presence of these stores is a major reason why Tokyo's private rail lines are so successful. Large passenger traffic flows at stations provide more opportunities for retail businesses to have direct distribution access to a mass of general consumers in transit.

However, many consumers feel that these retail spaces have become over-congested and unintuitive. We felt that by studying Gotanda, a small-scale station, and Shimbashi, a medium-scale station, we could identify ways to boost the positive aspects of the shopping experience (such as convenience, increased ease of payment, and outstanding sales techniques), while alleviating some consumer pain points (such as uninspiring product selection, language barriers for foreign shoppers, lack of greenery, and a fading sense of community).

The results of an internal SWOT analysis shed light on the current shopping experience at retail hubs.

### STRENGTHS
- The stores offer limited edition items that are only available in Tokyo
- The hubs provide a convenient shopping experience

### WEAKNESSES
- Products lack a strong brand identity
- Retail hubs with limited access to the public spaces that enhance shopping experience

### THREATS
- Most digital services are only provided in Japanese
- Many payment systems are cash-based or use a locally based credit system

### OPPORTUNITIES
- Many retail stores can improve the user journey
- Considering wayfinding, product selection, and authenticity can improve Tokyo's retail experience

新橋

1. JR Lines
2. Ginza Subway Line
3. Asakusa Subway Line
4. Yurikamome Subway Line
5. Shimbashi Ekimae Building
6. Plaza
7. Shiodome City Center

SHIMBASHI

GOTANDA

五反田

1. JR Lines
2. Femy Shopping Plaza
3. Atra Shopping Plaza
4. Red Light District
5. Meguro River
6. Begami Line
7. Undertrack Retail/F&B

**Shimbashi Station** is close to Ginza, Tokyo's upscale shopping hub, and is a major transfer station (daily approx. 280,000 passengers) between several rail and subway lines. There are connections to both major airports. It is primarily known as a business and entertainment district, so it is not optimally organized for shoppers. However, there are still many small cafés, restaurants, and bars around the station and underground passage connected to the station that locals use on a daily basis. We selected this station for its potential: we felt that with a few design improvements, it could attract a lot of foreign visitors.

**Gotanda Station** serves around 140,000 passengers daily and is located in a primarily business area with residential in close proximity. On weeknights, the area is active with business people and commuters, but there is less activity on the weekends. Budget-friendly hotels and major airports are easily accessible to this station. Because of recent local community development, we were curious to uncover how Gotanda could be a good role model for other similar-sized stations.

## Japan's rail stations are major retail hubs, but many are congested and unintuitive.

**Divisional Profit**

Retail's contribution to the profits of Japan's top-three rail companies in 2017.

| | TRANSPORTATION | REAL ESTATE | RETAIL | HOTEL | OTHER |
|---|---|---|---|---|---|
| JR EAST | | | | | |
| KINTETSU | | | | | |
| TOKYU | | | | | |

0 — 100

117

# 五反田

**80%**
OF PARTICIPANTS USE THE STATION FOR TRANSFER

*"Feels crowded"*

*"Lacks a compelling point of interest"*

*"Signage is in Japanese only"*

*"Does not feel authentic or unique"*

**THE RESULTS**

**Gotanda Station** is failing to create a sense of community, connect with consumers, and provide a stimulating experience. Gotanda is missing an opportunity to use area-specific landmarks, such as an adjacent river, to convey the local culture. The random assortment of shops alienates shoppers and travelers. Additionally, the shopping experience at Gotanda fails to stimulate the senses. It is important for consumers to smell, touch, hear, and taste the products whenever possible to spark unanticipated purchases.`

# 新橋

**70%**
OF PARTICIPANTS THOUGHT SHIMBASHI STATION IS UNIQUE

*"Unorganized"*

*"Minimal activity for children"*

*"Nothing visually appealing to post on social media"*

**Shimbashi Station** creates a sense of togetherness, authenticity, novelty, and community. This made more of an impression on study participants than efforts to beautify or renovate the station. Respondents identified that sitting elbow to elbow among the local workers in intimate shops and restaurants/bars, and being welcomed into conversations, contributed to a positive, authentic experience. Additionally, the warren of tiny bars and restaurants found off of an underground passageway between train lines made participants feel like they were stepping back in time to a Tokyo that is slowly slipping away. However, both the authenticity and effectiveness of the space feels compromised by a newly renovated retail passageway. Although bright and clean, it lacks visual appeal and retail that attracts business people and foreign visitors.

**60% OF PARTICIPANTS THOUGHT IT WAS MISSING AUTHENTICITY**

😉 *"Convenient and easy to use"*

*"Vibrant night scene"*

*"Could offer a great place to meet for drinks/food and run errands"*

*"Opportunity to eat at Japanese restaurant and pub"*

😉 *"Local prices"*

*"There are a variety of activities"*

*"Friendly atmosphere"*

**60% OF PARTICIPANTS THOUGHT IT WAS MISSING A STRONG SENSE OF COMMUNITY**

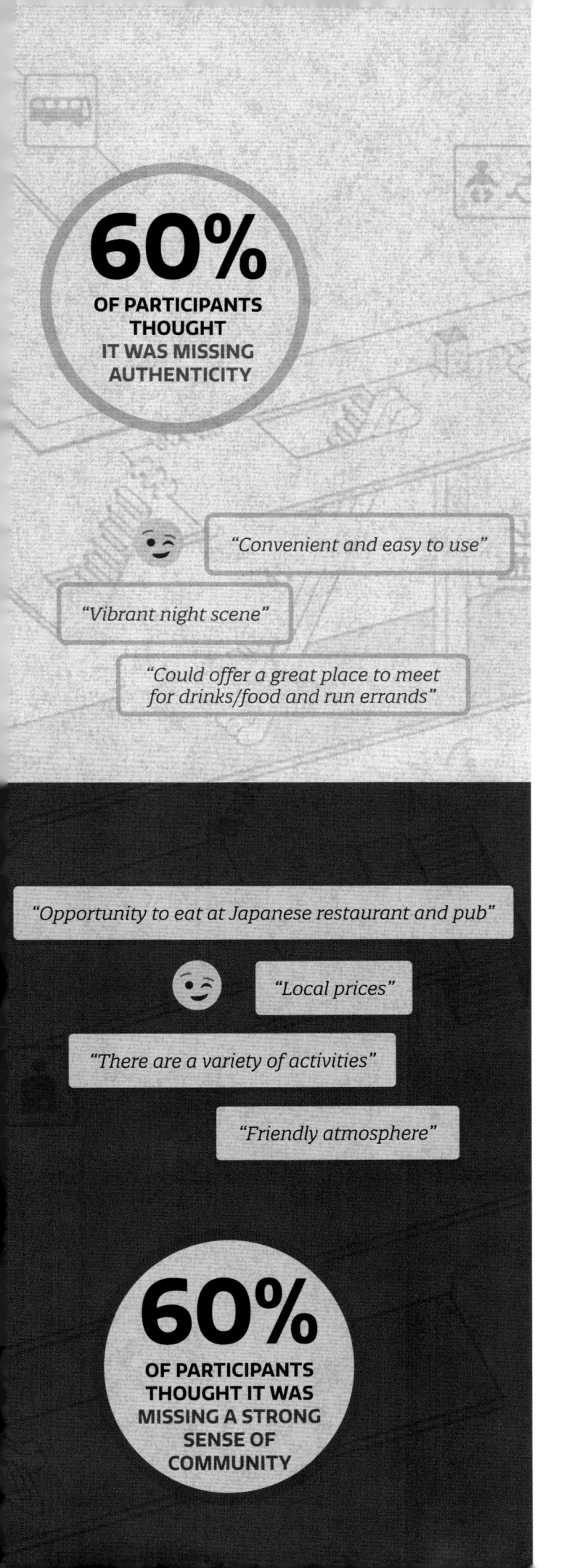

## DESIGN IMPLICATIONS

Our exploration of these stations informed the development of strategies that can be broadly applied to Japan's other retail/transportation hubs:

### Renovate…with tweezers.
Acknowledge the elements of authenticity that can't be replicated in a space, and juxtapose them against simple and modern design moves that improve the physical space around them.

### Create a sense of community and release its hidden gems.
Spark interest in the neighborhood by highlighting exciting places while shopping in the station. If a station is in proximity to other public spaces or landmarks, take advantage of opportunities to create pop-up and relaxation spaces.

### Create shareable experiences.
Social media shares and recommendations will help drive traffic to and improve visibility of retail outlets. Strive to make railway stations exploratory, photographable destinations, rather than just areas of convenience.

### Ensure that the shop assortment is intentional and attracts the right customers.
Stores tailored to clear customer types enhance the shopping experience. Look for opportunities to link appropriate retail to established station activities. For instance, if a station like Shimbashi is most known for food and beverage, add retail that offers sake by the bottle, local products, and small gifts.

### Improve wayfinding whenever possible.
The number of tourists that visited Japan in 2018 rose to 31.9 million, far exceeding the government's projections. Providing multilingual information on signage and packaging will help demystify the complexity of station passageways and the navigation of retail spaces.

### WHAT'S NEXT

We hope to continue applying these lessons to additional mixed-use transit stations around Tokyo and Japan. We also plan to continue to socialize our findings with the industry and our clients and city stakeholders, including setting up a roundtable with several different groups: developers, community users, and government representatives.

# SHIFTING THE WORKPLACE NARRATIVE

The continued evolution of work is driving a profound shift in the design and dynamics of today's work environments.

## THE GLOBAL WORKPLACE SURVEYS

**122 U.S. Workplace Survey 2019**

**Research Team**
Amrapali Agarwal
Michelle DeCurtis
Stella Donovan
Janet Pogue McLaurin
Kyle Sellers
Nicholas Watkins

**128 Germany Workplace Survey 2019**

**Research Team**
Amrapali Agarwal
Izabella Barlog
Leeann De Barros
Michelle DeCurtis
Aina Ito
Janet Pogue McLaurin
Chandkiran Nath
Peter Schaefer
Kyle Sellers
Philip Tidd

**132 Latin America Workplace Survey 2017**

**Research Team**
Amrapali Agarwal
Jessica García
Francesca Poma-Murialdo
José Luis Sánchez-Concha

**132 History of the Global Workplace Surveys**

Research teams noted in individual reports.

## WELLNESS IN THE WORKPLACE

**138 Emotional Security in the Workplace**

**Research Team**
Meaghan Beever
Joel Fariss
Garima Gupta
Jacob Simons
Andrew Yang

**140 Prioritizing Psychological Well-Being**

**Research Team**
Ankita Dwivedi
Namrata Krishna
Emer Lynam
Zsuzsi Nagy
Claudia Poma-Murialdo
Philip Tidd

## EMPLOYEE ENGAGEMENT

**146** **Balancing Density and Employee Engagement**

**Research Team**
Chris Jerde
Adriana Phillips
Yana Ronin
Gervais Tompkin

**152** **Work Styles and Spatial Preference**

**Research Team**
Sara Anderson
Cindy Coleman
David Crabtree
Janet Pogue McLaurin
Tom Mulhern

**154** **The Value of Customer Experience Centers**

**Research Team**
Kloey Battista
Daniel Bender
Robert Cohen
Michael Schneider

## SPACES FOR SCIENCE

**156** **Designing Effective Research Buildings**

**Research Team**
Beth Gibb
Maria Herrero
David Johnson
Michael Martin
Pixy Peng
Brett Riegler
Deborah Shepley
Julia Spackman
Kelly vanOteghem

**158** **Adaptable Life Science Lab Design**

**Research Team**
Alfred Byun
Kenneth Fisher
Adam Harper
Erik Lustgarten
Cerise Marcela

## EVOLVING THE DESIGN PROCESS

**164** **Narrative-Driven Design**

**Research Team**
Shamus Halkowich
Allison Wong
Richard Zapata

**166** **Rapid Workplace Redesign**

**Research Team**
Jackson Fox
Sven Govaars
John Haba
Dean Strombom
Jeannie Wu

**170** **Building Repositioning Strategies**

**Research Team**
James Frankis
Erin Saven
Thomas Vecchione
Scott Wilson

**174** **Future-Proofing Design Strategies**

**Research Team**
Laura Coyne
Chesley McCarty
Levi Schoenfeld
Deanna Siller

# U.S. Workplace Survey 2019

How is the open office impacting U.S. worker experience?

**MOSTLY OPEN**
With on-demand private space; offices only when required by role

**TOTALLY OPEN**
No walls—everyone in the organization sits together

7%

MOST OPEN

### WHAT WE DID

**The workplace is getting better, but significant room for improvement still exists. In this report, we frame progress and future goals within a dual narrative—a focus on both effectiveness and experience in the workplace.** Our U.S. Workplace Survey 2019 expands our purview to codify and measure the entire employee experience. By analyzing effectiveness and experience together—as quantified by our proprietary Workplace Performance Index℠ (WPI) and Experience Index℠ (EXI) scores—we are able to explain a larger portion of employee engagement and performance.

### THE CONTEXT

The U.S. workplace has improved in recent years, with 2019 registering our highest effectiveness scores of any Workplace Survey over the past 15 years. While this may be partially attributable to an extended economic expansion, it is also connected to improvements in the physical and experiential nature of the workplace itself. A greater portion of people today report working in a balanced workplace. People today also report greater levels of choice and autonomy at work—45% of U.S. workers now report having choice in where they work within their office.

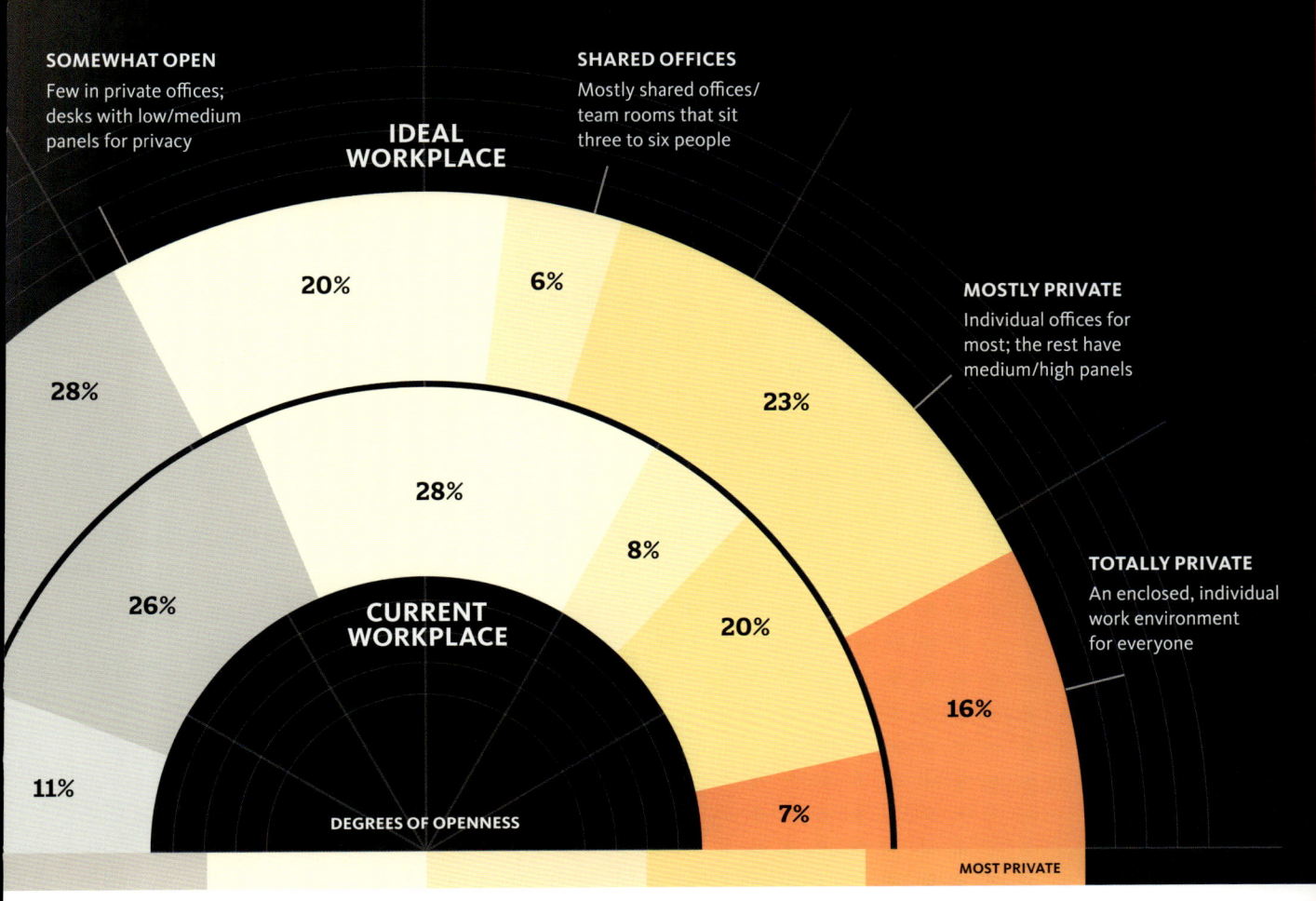

# Very few people say their ideal workplace is "totally open"

**SOMEWHAT OPEN**
Few in private offices; desks with low/medium panels for privacy

**SHARED OFFICES**
Mostly shared offices/team rooms that sit three to six people

**MOSTLY PRIVATE**
Individual offices for most; the rest have medium/high panels

**TOTALLY PRIVATE**
An enclosed, individual work environment for everyone

IDEAL WORKPLACE: 28% | 20% | 6% | 23% | 16%
CURRENT WORKPLACE: 11% | 26% | 28% | 8% | 20% | 7%

DEGREES OF OPENNESS — MOST PRIVATE

## THE RESULTS

**People are asking for more private space at work.** Only a fraction of people would prefer working in a totally open or a totally private environment; over two-thirds (77%) consider environments that fall between these extremes to be ideal. To capture this nuance, we measured "degrees of openness" with six variables, from "totally open" workplaces with no walls, to "totally private" workplaces in which all employees have individual offices. Environments that are mostly open environments but provide ample on-demand private space have both the highest effectiveness and the highest experience scores.

**Not all amenities are worth the investment.** The workplace is becoming more choice-based and amenity-rich. But every workplace can't, and shouldn't, have every amenity.

To target the right investments, we must understand the impact of individual amenities and alternative workspaces on people's performance. The amenities that deliver the greatest impact connect directly to people's most salient needs and preferences: spaces directly connected to innovation, making, and collaboration; and quiet places to perform focused or individual work.

**Of the employees at large companies, 14% use coworking spaces.** For the majority of these users, coworking appears to be part of their company's broader plan to facilitate autonomy and mobility instead of acting as their primary workspace—and our data suggests this is the right strategy. Coworking adds value as an alternative work setting, but only to a point. Spend over a day a week in coworking spaces, and they lose their luster.

## The amenities that deliver most on effectiveness and experience

WPI and EXI score comparisons for each amenity: differences in scores between people who have the amenity in their workplace and those who do not.

**EFFECTIVENESS (WPI)** | **EXPERIENCE (EXI)** | **GREATEST VALUE**

| Effectiveness (WPI) | Experience (EXI) | Amenity |
|---|---|---|
| +11 (those who have this amenity vs. those who do not) | +16 | INNOVATION HUB* |
| +11 | +14 | MAKER SPACE* |
| +10 | +14 | QUIET/TECH-FREE ZONE |
| +9 | +13 | OUTDOOR WORKSPACES |
| +9 | +13 | FOCUS ROOMS |
| +8 | +12 | WORK CAFÉ |
| +7 | +10 | PHONE ROOM |
| +7 | +9 | LIBRARY |
| +4 | +6 | CAFETERIA |
| +1 | +2 | BREAK ROOM/LOUNGES |

*Innovation hub and maker spaces are most prominent in technology, media, management advisory, and finance firms.

**LEAST VALUE**

### DESIGN IMPLICATIONS

**Open environments should be private too.** Greater degrees of openness are associated with high performance; but noise, privacy, and the ability to focus remain key determinants of workplace effectiveness. A choice-based strategy that provides a variety of spaces and different types of enclosure can reconcile these needs.

**Amenities are not about escaping work—they're about optimizing it.** People are working from everywhere—and greater mobility is associated with greater performance and engagement. The best amenity strategies prioritize anywhere-working, creating hybrid settings that deliver both an amenity and a workspace: work cafés, quiet/focus zones, and innovation hubs, among others.

## Invest in the amenities that deliver the highest impact— those that directly support work process have the most value.

124  Shifting the Workplace Narrative | U.S. Workplace Survey 2019

**Time spent in coworking spaces**

Number of days spent in coworking spaces during an average week, by percent of respondents.

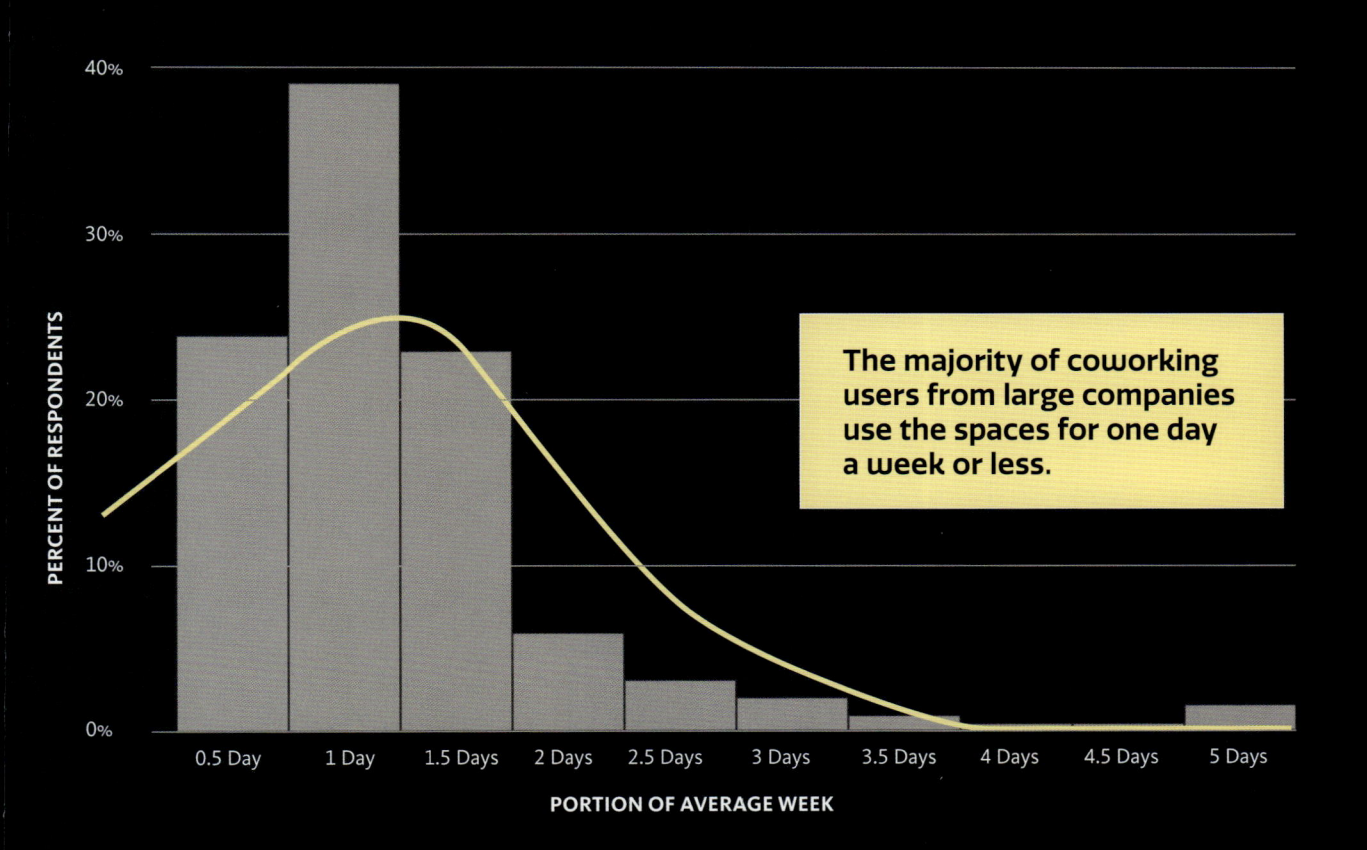

*The majority of coworking users from large companies use the spaces for one day a week or less.*

**Coworking is a supplement, not a replacement, for a great workplace experience.** Coworking does not yet contend as a primary work setting—but as a high-value amenity it delivers. Our data shows distinct benefits from giving people access to coworking spaces; but the effect diminishes for those spending significant amounts of time coworking, and most still spend more time in the primary offices.

**WHAT'S NEXT**

The pace of change is increasing in the U.S. workplace. Our work will continue to evaluate how worker satisfaction, effectiveness, and overall happiness change according to varying degrees of openness, new amenities packages, and the ebbing influence of alternative workplaces.

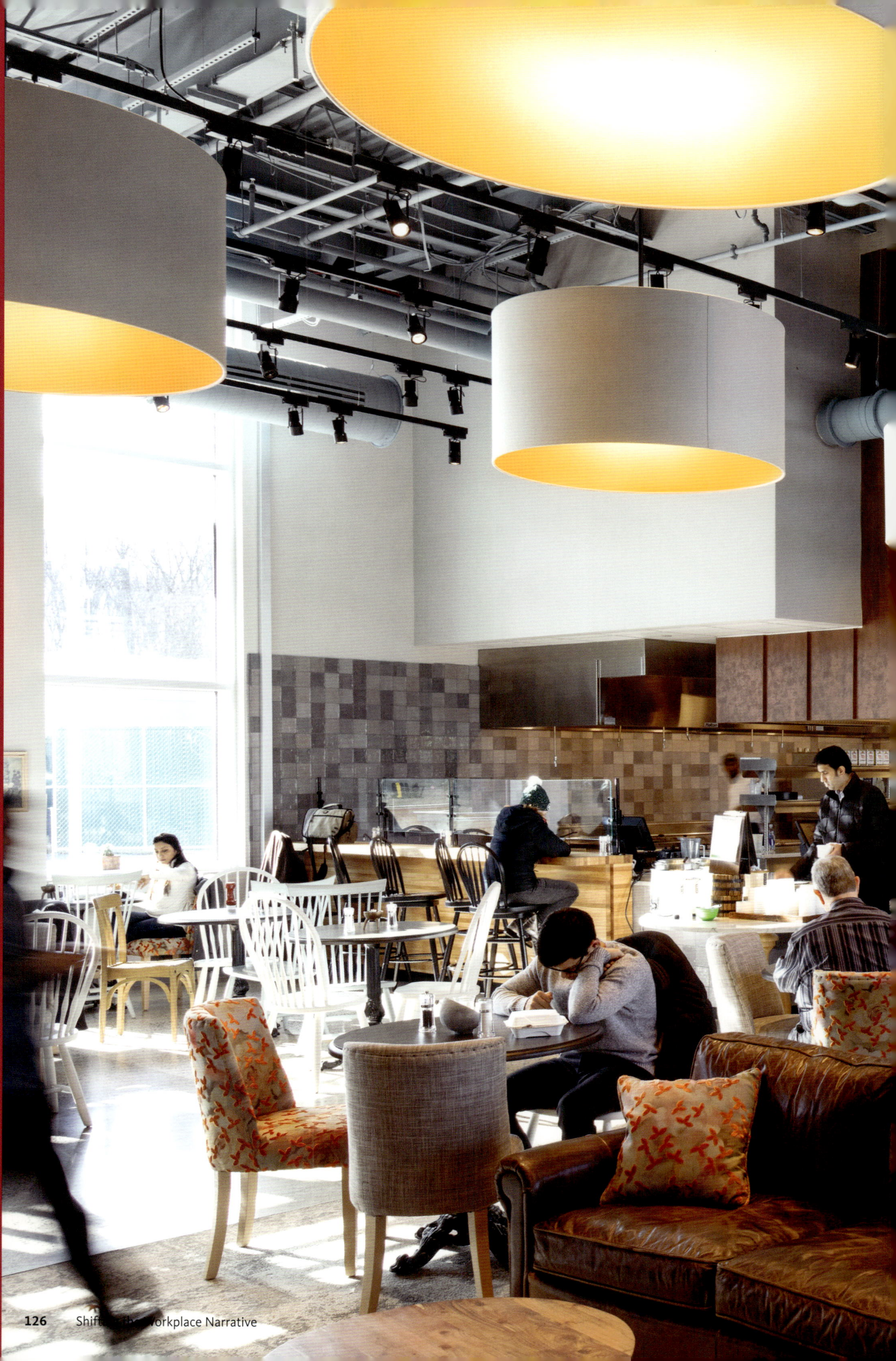

**Confidential Client**
Whippany, New Jersey

For this campus repurposing we created a robust amenity program, a green transportation hub, and an array of outdoor amenities and spaces across 65 acres. The transformation is driven by multiple business goals: reuse and revitalize obsolete real estate, strengthen the real estate portfolio in a cost-effective way, expand a technology branch, attract top talent, and create a community-facing workplace.

# Germany Workplace Survey 2019

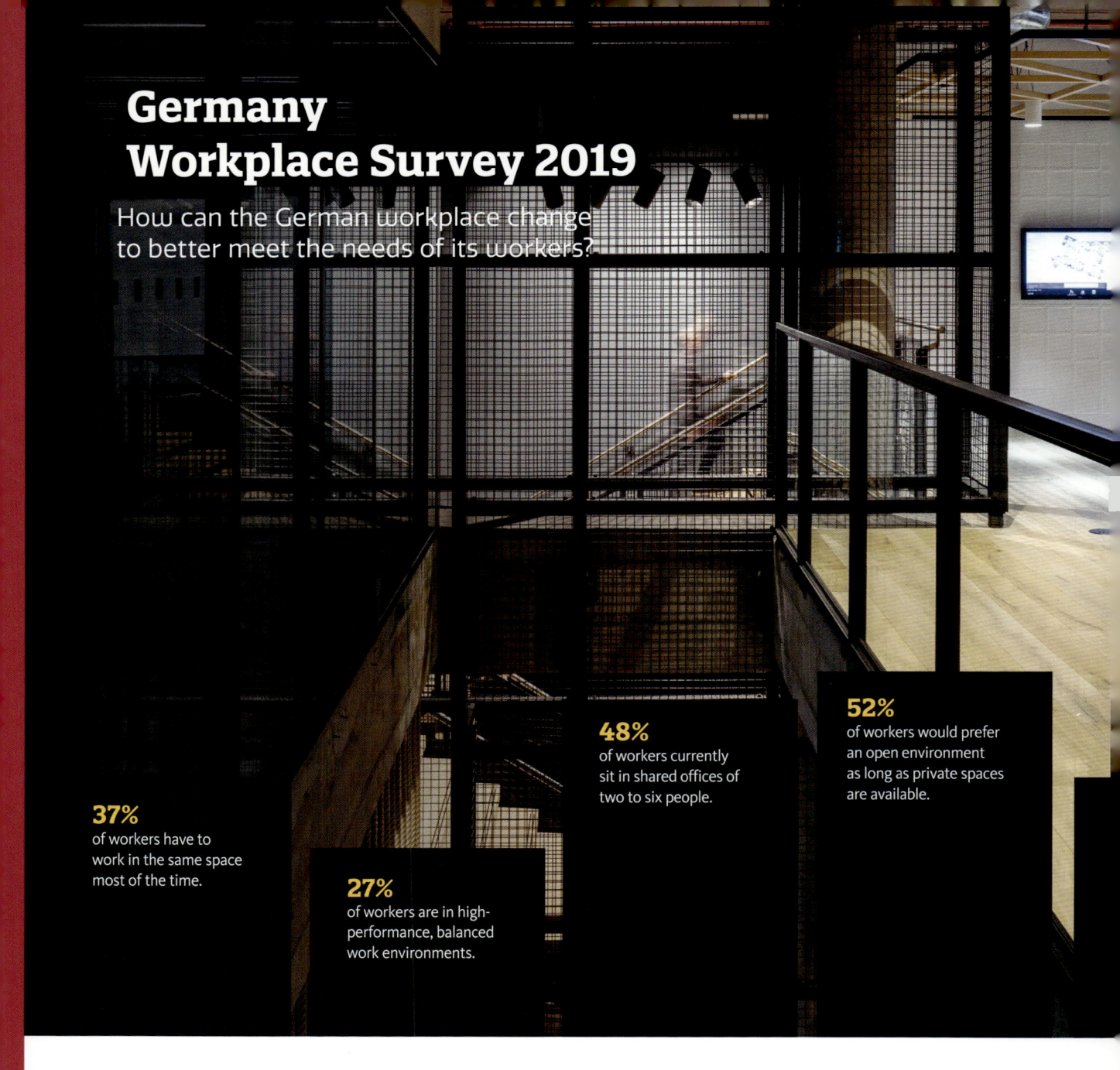

How can the German workplace change to better meet the needs of its workers?

**37%**
of workers have to work in the same space most of the time.

**27%**
of workers are in high-performance, balanced work environments.

**48%**
of workers currently sit in shared offices of two to six people.

**52%**
of workers would prefer an open environment as long as private spaces are available.

**WHAT WE DID**

**We surveyed 2,250 German workers that represent a diverse cross section of the German workforce.** We found that Germany needs a new approach to the workplace. Germany invented the open office, but they aren't using it. With the concept of Bürolandschaft, Germany once led the world in moving toward a dynamic, open space office environment. Today, however, the German office is dominated by shared and group offices, a typology that underperforms from the standpoint of effectiveness.

**THE CONTEXT**

Germany is a global powerhouse that combines economic diversification with a skilled labor market. While the country is revered for novel approaches to many things that make the German economy tick, workplace innovation lags. Workplace design and dynamics have not progressed to reflect the average German worker's expectations. Traditional hierarchical organizational structures may have yielded the meticulousness and rigor we have come to expect from German organizations; however, the German workplace must incorporate a more flexible paradigm to move forward.

# Germany has double the number of employees in shared office settings compared to the U.S. or UK.

**Individual Space Types**

Percent of respondents in each type of individual workspace.

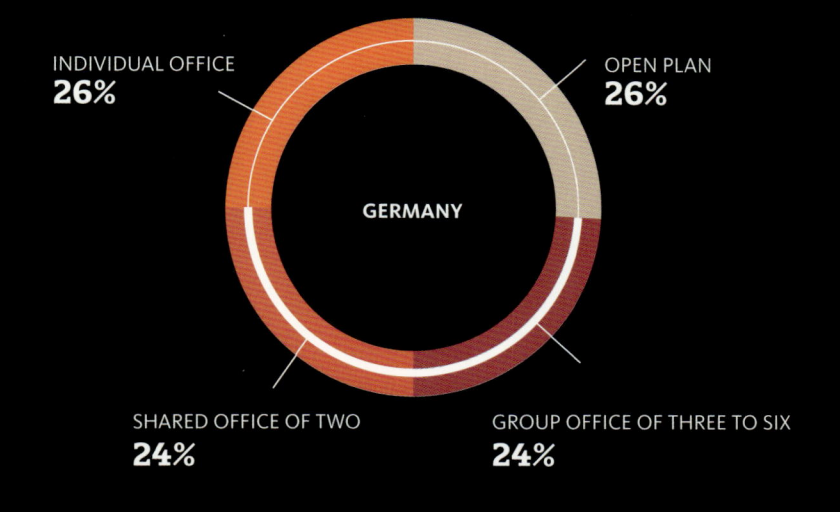

**GERMANY**

INDIVIDUAL OFFICE
**26%**

OPEN PLAN
**26%**

SHARED OFFICE OF TWO
**24%**

GROUP OFFICE OF THREE TO SIX
**24%**

**THE RESULTS**

**German workers are asking for more open, collaborative spaces.** Given the opportunity, only a fraction of German workers would choose a work environment that uses private offices exclusively. Over half of our survey respondents would prefer a more open work environment, but today three-quarters of those same respondents work in an enclosed office type. This approach to the workplace is the crux of what we call "balance." A balanced workplace is one that prioritizes both focus work and collaborative work.

**German workers need a workplace that prioritizes well-being.** German workers ranked health and wellness as the most important attribute of a great workplace. Looking beyond functional factors to issues of behavior and experience, German workers today are falling short on well-being, despite identifying it as a priority. At the end of a typical day at the office, German workers are likely to feel accomplished, but feel depleted and lacking a sense of individual accomplishment.

# 52%

**of German workers choose mostly open environments as the best workplace type.**

## Employee Well-Being

Rating of how energized, purposeful, and productive respondents feel at the end of a typical day on a five-point scale.

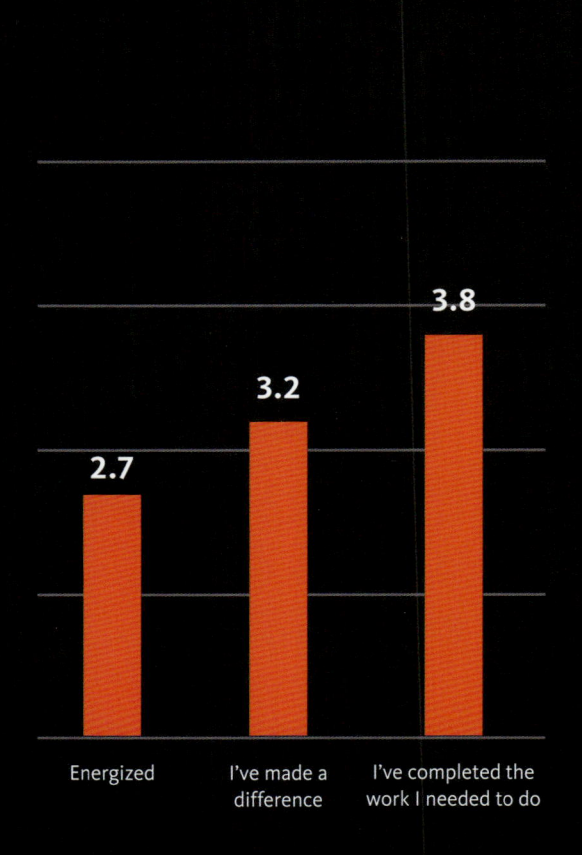

- Energized: 2.7
- I've made a difference: 3.2
- I've completed the work I needed to do: 3.8

## Well-Being and Balance

Percentage of respondents in a balanced workplace, defined as workplaces that effectively prioritize both individual and collaborative work.

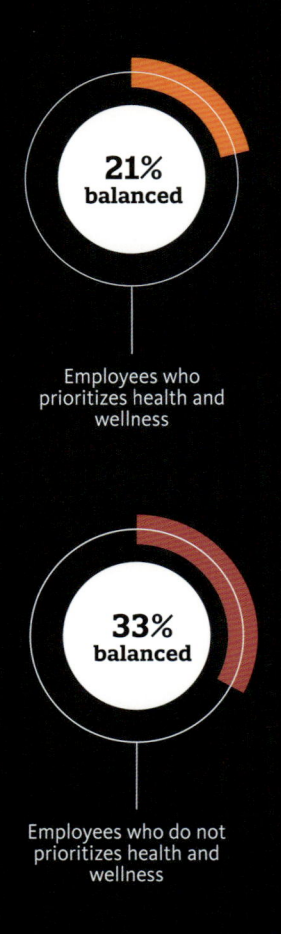

**21% balanced** — Employees who prioritizes health and wellness

**33% balanced** — Employees who do not prioritizes health and wellness

### DESIGN IMPLICATIONS

**Group offices aren't working for German workers; it's time for a new approach.** We know the attributes of the physical environment that maximize workplace effectiveness and experience—and we also know that the global community is transitioning to more open, more collaborative office environments. By listening to the German worker, the design community can help realize an imminent change away from shared and group office types to a workplace that fosters both focus work and collaboration.

**Give German workers the balanced, collaborative environments they're asking for.** We must create a more dynamic, multimodal workplace landscape to reflect the needs of the German workforce. That means treating the workplace as an ecosystem of spaces, and investing at the scale of the team or group as well as the individual. The drivers of balanced workplaces offer a roadmap here—greater space variety, and spaces that feel welcoming and offer the latest technology.

## 1.3x

**Workers in balanced workplaces rate their ability to experiment with new ways of working 1.3 times higher.**

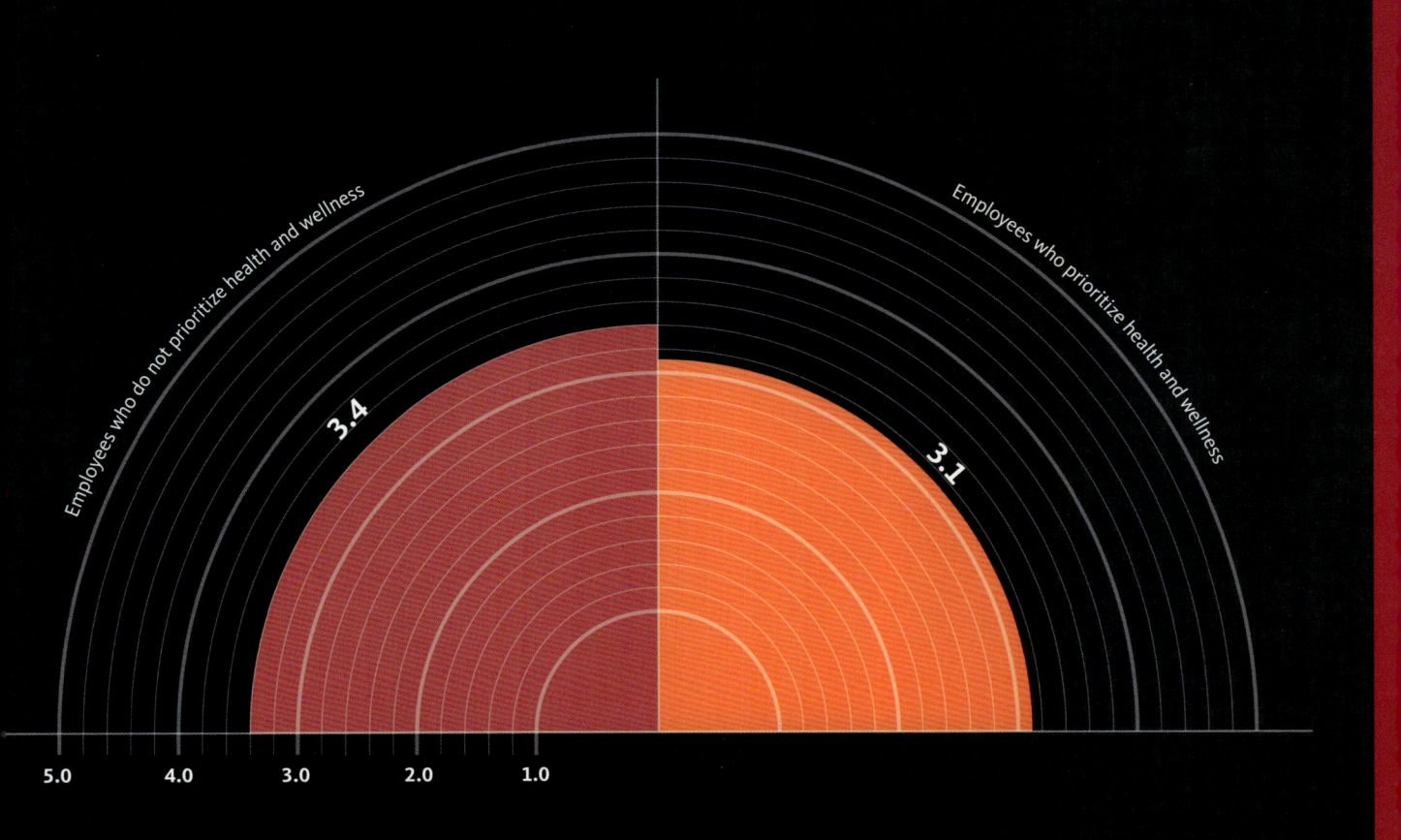

**Workplace Variety**

Respondent rating of whether their workplace has a good variety of spaces on a 5-point agreement scale.

Employees who do not prioritize health and wellness: 3.4
Employees who prioritize health and wellness: 3.1

5.0  4.0  3.0  2.0  1.0

### Workers expect the office to deliver on health and well-being; make it a priority.

The German workforce is serious about health and wellness—the workplace needs to keep up. A well-being focused culture, and the institutional power to back it, means that the basics of health and wellness are met—but Germans expect more. A comprehensive amenity and workspace strategy focused on physical and psychological well-being is a must.

### WHAT'S NEXT

Most German workers want a better workplace experience, and our findings show how workplace dynamics can change for the better. Shared offices are the norm, and importantly, they are not meeting the needs of German workers. We will track whether more effective workspace types emerge, and whether German employers come to prioritize what workers want from their workplace.

# Latin America Workplace Survey 2017

How well is the Latin American workplace supporting the region's knowledge workers, and what are the opportunities to improve?

**CITIES SURVEYED**

**México City,** México

**San José,** Costa Rica

**Medellín and Bogotá,** Colombia

**Lima,** Perú

**Santiago,** Chile

**Rio de Janeiro and São Paulo,** Brazil

**Buenos Aires,** Argentina

**WHAT WE DID**

**We surveyed an anonymous, panel-based sample of over 4,000 office workers across nine major cities in Latin America.** As with Gensler's other Workplace Surveys, we gathered responses using our proprietary Workplace Performance Index® (WPI℠) survey tool. Our goal is to further develop our understanding of how and where people are working, and how well their spaces support that work. We use this information to understand the differences (and similarities) between Latin American workers and others around the world; and to identify targeted strategies to improve workplace design and maximize employee and business performance in the region.

# Latin American workers and organizations must search for a culturally relevant approach to the workplace.

**How workers spend their time**

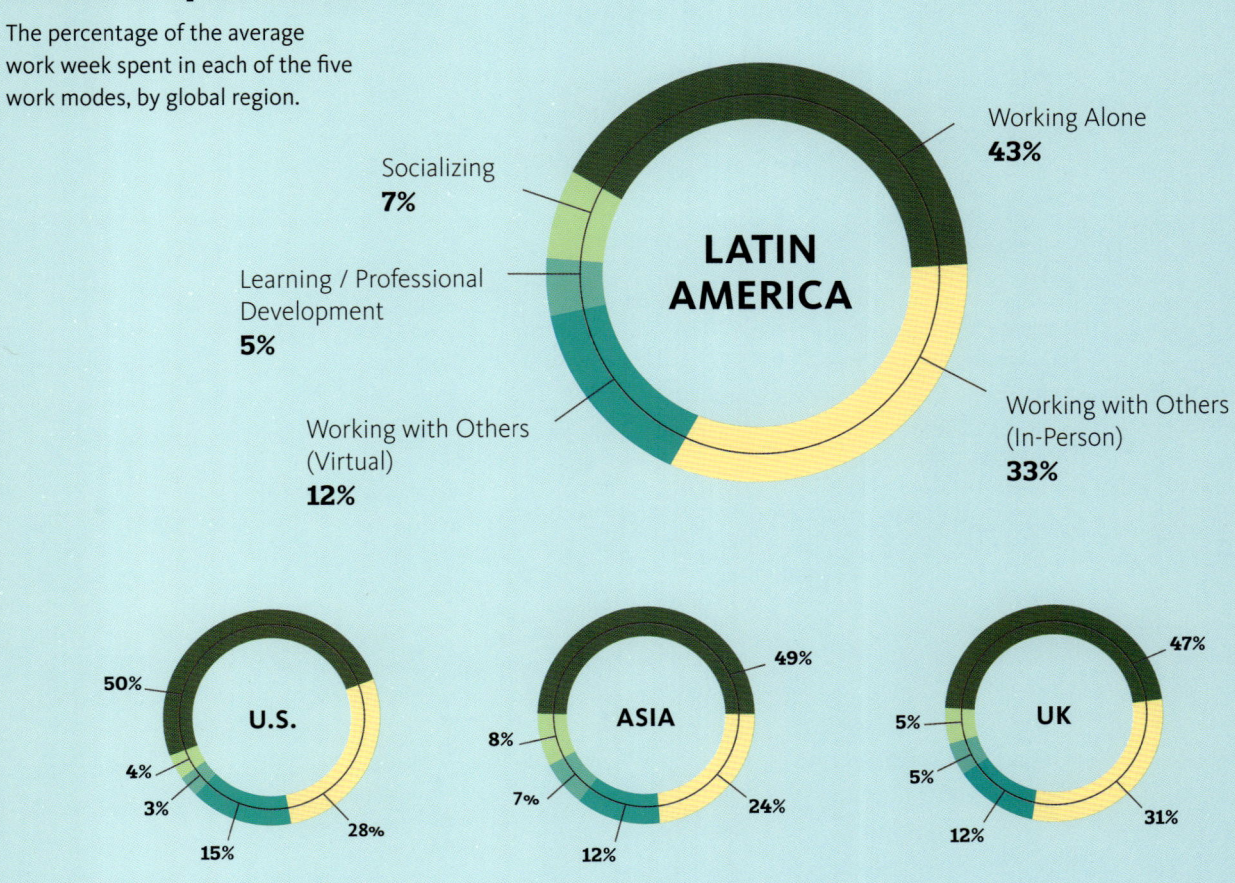

The percentage of the average work week spent in each of the five work modes, by global region.

### LATIN AMERICA

- Working Alone **43%**
- Working with Others (In-Person) **33%**
- Working with Others (Virtual) **12%**
- Learning / Professional Development **5%**
- Socializing **7%**

### U.S.
- 50%
- 28%
- 15%
- 3%
- 4%

### ASIA
- 49%
- 24%
- 12%
- 7%
- 8%

### UK
- 47%
- 31%
- 12%
- 5%
- 5%

## THE CONTEXT

Latin America is a mix of Spanish- and Portuguese-speaking countries with a rich cultural legacy. The food, music, and people who populate these dynamic countries and global cities—two of the ten largest cities in the world are located in the region—bring deep influences that impact how, and where, work is done throughout the region.

Yet for many years, Latin American workplace strategies have been largely informed by information and research-based trends from other countries. As many global companies migrated to the region to expand their businesses or strategically transform their delivery models, their global standards often set a precedent for local workplace models. The local culture still tends to resist more modern open office designs, even those offering a choice of complementary workspaces that are often well-received and desired by workers around the world. To find success, Latin American companies must find new workplace models that can help them achieve business success.

# DRIVERS OF INNOVATION

**WORKPLACE** + **MEANING** + **RELATIONSHIPS** + **WORKPLACE TECHNOLOGY**

Workplace design prioritizes collaboration | Making a difference, personally and organizationally | Management cares about job satisfaction and career development | The quality of technology at individual and group workspaces

## THE RESULTS

**Latin Americans work with others more than they work alone.** Typically known for their social nature, Latin American workers are very effective when working together—and it shows in how they spend their time. Compared to the other global regions surveyed in 2016 (U.S., UK, and Asia), Latin American workers report spending the least time working alone (43% of an average workweek), and the most time working with others (45%, combining both in-person and virtual collaboration).

**For Latin American workers, an additional driver also proved crucial: the quality of collaborative technology.** Having technology that supports collaborative work, both for meeting spaces (technology to support group work) and individual workspace (integrated technology and connectivity), has a distinct effect on the level of innovation employees ascribe to their companies. The behaviors and characteristics of the most innovative employees illustrate the point—the most innovative have better collaboration spaces and greater access to technology.

**Collaborative technology is a key innovation driver.** A common theme among all 11,000+ workers surveyed across the globe in Gensler's 2016 Workplace Surveys is the power of workplace design, the importance of seeing meaning in one's work, and the value that at-work relationships bring. These factors were key drivers of performance and innovation across all our surveys.

**Local companies have an opportunity to improve.** Global companies are currently scoring higher on workplace effectiveness and innovation scores as compared to their local peers. Global companies are also scoring higher on measures of job satisfaction and choice than their local/regional peers, and employees are more likely to report their workplace is effectively balancing collaboration and focus work.

LOCAL COMPANIES **64** | REGIONAL COMPANIES **69** | GLOBAL COMPANIES **73**

50 — 60 — 70 — 80

**DESIGN IMPLICATIONS**

Increased, and more effective, collaboration continues to be exhibited by the most innovative companies around the world—and Latin American workers are some of the best at it. High-performance workplaces support this preference to work in teams, while also employing targeted strategies to ensure that individual, focused work has a place in the office too.

**Provide places to work alone, together.** While employees in the region love to work together, our data also shows they love to work from home. While only a minority of their time is spent working from home, it has some of the highest effectiveness ratings. This speaks to the challenge of doing focused work in a vibrant office where everyone is collaborating.

**Leverage global workplace trends to stay competitive.** Global companies are currently setting the pace on space planning and technology. Given the importance of meaning and relationships to the employee experience, local companies should have a leg up on their global competitors if they are able to provide a physical environment that not only provides the right mix of spaces, but also reflects local culture and values.

**Technology investments set innovators apart from the rest.** Overall, technology and tools in Latin America are undersupported. But the region is also poised to get the most benefit out of greater technology investment and use. Companies should acknowledge the inherently social behavior of their workers and support it through workplace design and policy.

**WHAT'S NEXT**

Understanding the work behaviors and environments at the national and regional level is a first step to identifying opportunities to improve the Latin American workplace. To drive more targeted conversations, these insights should be considered in light of the specific needs and work processes of individual organizations and work groups. By working directly with our clients in this manner, we can find the best solutions to the challenges and opportunities they face.

**History of the Global Workplace Surveys**

The Gensler Workplace Surveys are the industry's foundational research connecting workplace design, employee experience, and business performance. They offer actionable insights for how to optimize your workforce using workplace design and strategy, and leverage anonymous survey data from around the globe to document the current state of the workplace and identify the biggest opportunities to improve as we look to the future.

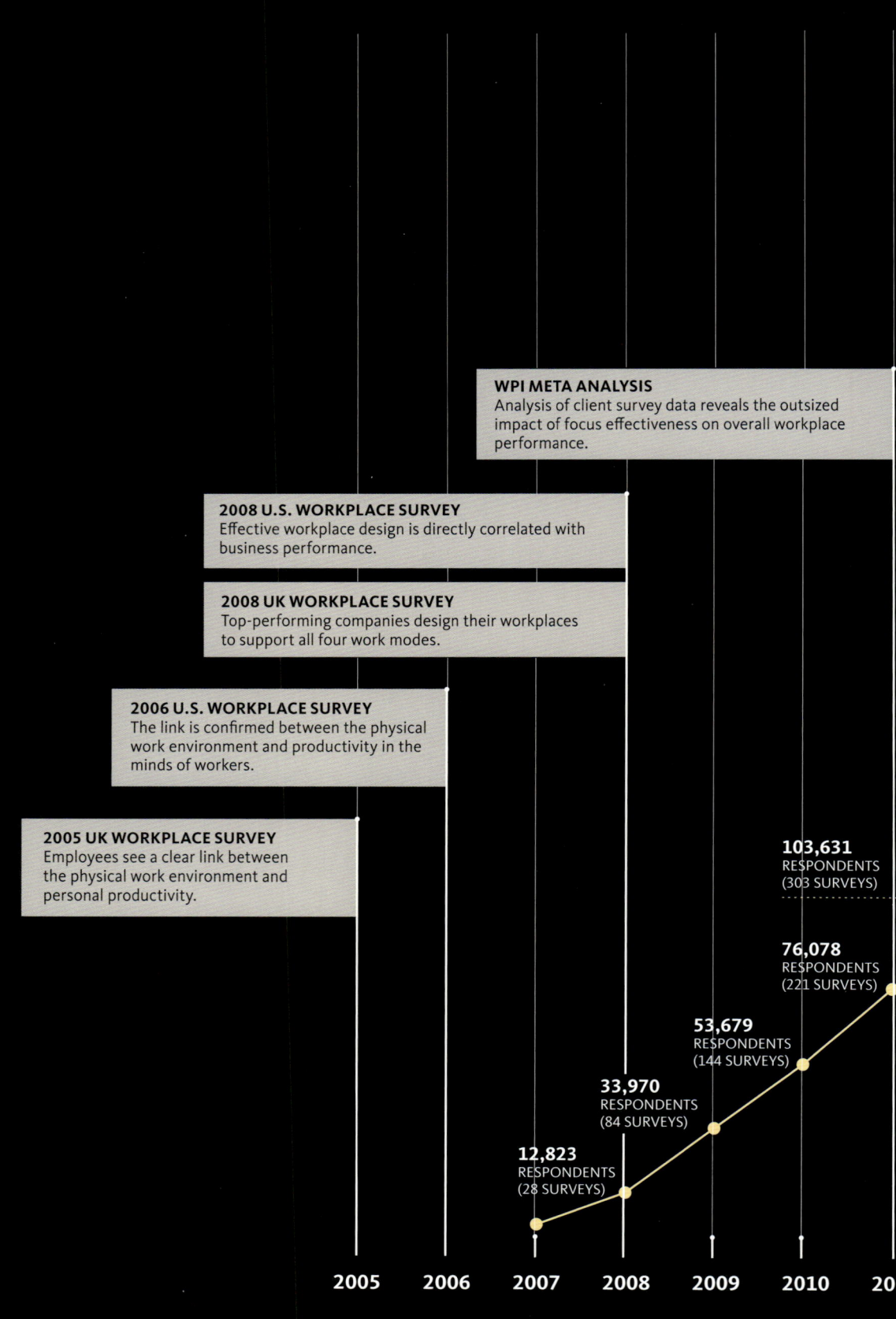

**WPI META ANALYSIS**
Analysis of client survey data reveals the outsized impact of focus effectiveness on overall workplace performance.

**2008 U.S. WORKPLACE SURVEY**
Effective workplace design is directly correlated with business performance.

**2008 UK WORKPLACE SURVEY**
Top-performing companies design their workplaces to support all four work modes.

**2006 U.S. WORKPLACE SURVEY**
The link is confirmed between the physical work environment and productivity in the minds of workers.

**2005 UK WORKPLACE SURVEY**
Employees see a clear link between the physical work environment and personal productivity.

**103,631** RESPONDENTS (303 SURVEYS)

**76,078** RESPONDENTS (221 SURVEYS)

**53,679** RESPONDENTS (144 SURVEYS)

**33,970** RESPONDENTS (84 SURVEYS)

**12,823** RESPONDENTS (28 SURVEYS)

2005    2006    2007    2008    2009    2010    20

136  Shifting the Workplace Narrative  | History of Global Workplace Surveys

**370,631**
RESPONDENTS
(1,121 SURVEYS)

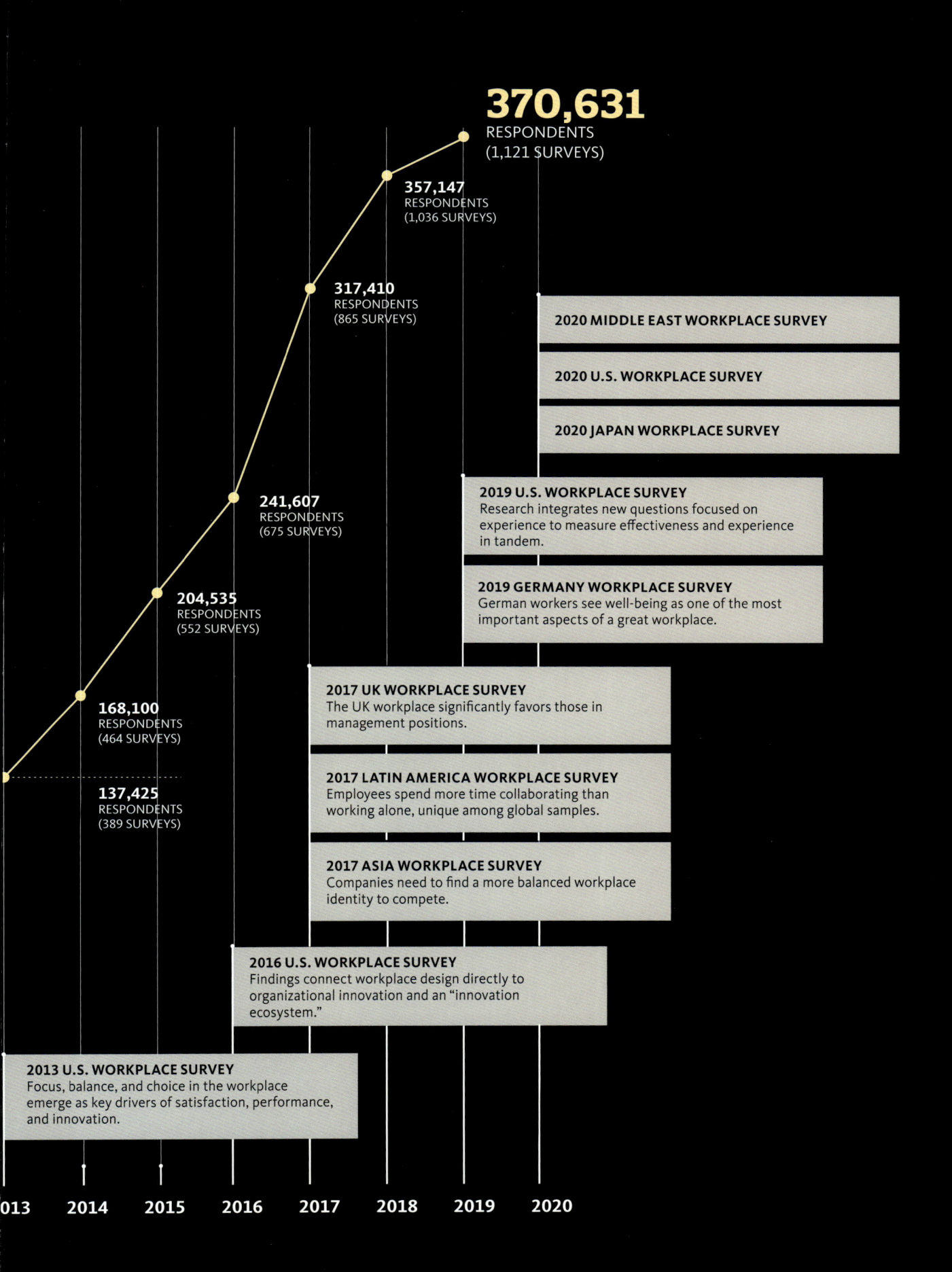

**357,147**
RESPONDENTS
(1,036 SURVEYS)

**317,410**
RESPONDENTS
(865 SURVEYS)

**241,607**
RESPONDENTS
(675 SURVEYS)

**204,535**
RESPONDENTS
(552 SURVEYS)

**168,100**
RESPONDENTS
(464 SURVEYS)

**137,425**
RESPONDENTS
(389 SURVEYS)

**2020 MIDDLE EAST WORKPLACE SURVEY**

**2020 U.S. WORKPLACE SURVEY**

**2020 JAPAN WORKPLACE SURVEY**

**2019 U.S. WORKPLACE SURVEY**
Research integrates new questions focused on experience to measure effectiveness and experience in tandem.

**2019 GERMANY WORKPLACE SURVEY**
German workers see well-being as one of the most important aspects of a great workplace.

**2017 UK WORKPLACE SURVEY**
The UK workplace significantly favors those in management positions.

**2017 LATIN AMERICA WORKPLACE SURVEY**
Employees spend more time collaborating than working alone, unique among global samples.

**2017 ASIA WORKPLACE SURVEY**
Companies need to find a more balanced workplace identity to compete.

**2016 U.S. WORKPLACE SURVEY**
Findings connect workplace design directly to organizational innovation and an "innovation ecosystem."

**2013 U.S. WORKPLACE SURVEY**
Focus, balance, and choice in the workplace emerge as key drivers of satisfaction, performance, and innovation.

2013  2014  2015  2016  2017  2018  2019  2020

# Emotional Security in the Workplace

What relational conditions are needed to foster exploration, creativity, and innovation in organizations?

**WHAT WE DID**

**We identified the relational conditions necessary for organizations and professional networks to thrive.**
We began by analyzing existing literature on relational dynamics in organizations. We then interviewed a diverse group of theorists and practitioners in the worlds of business, sociology, psychology, academia, and corporate leadership. Finally, we conducted an interactive group interview with academic researchers and professors at the University of Washington to understand the emerging expectations of students regarding the relationship they seek with new employers.

**SAFE HAVEN**
Accessibility and responsiveness when in distress

**SECURE BASE**
Confidence and safety in exploration

DISTRESS

EMOTIONAL SECURITY

**THE CONTEXT**

The global conversation about the future of work is largely focused on how new technology and nontraditional business approaches will change how organizations operate. Navigating decentralization and mobility, talent wars, and the gig economy are important considerations as we enter an increasingly automated and agile age. However, it's difficult to find nuanced conversations about the emerging role of organizations to nurture and support a fundamental element of the human experience: relationships.

As social creatures, we are defined by our relationships—our relationship to ourselves, to others, and to the world around us. We often spend more of our waking hours with our colleagues than we do with our families, friends, and romantic partners. As a culture, we tend to avoid emotional conversations in the workplace. Organizations are primarily thought of as platforms for efficiency and productivity. However, in this age of innovation and creativity, it is imperative that workplaces support not only good thinking but good feeling. It is critical to understand the relational conditions that will equip us to do engaging, meaningful, and valuable work.

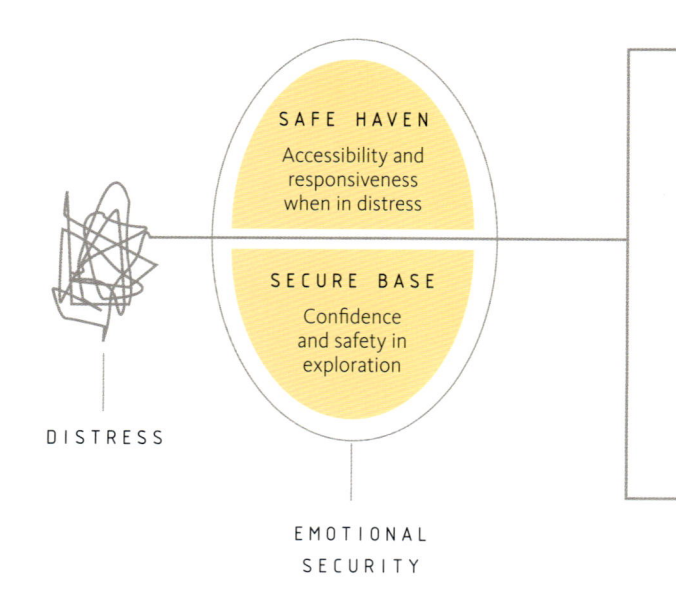

**THE RESULTS**

Adopting relational homeostasis—or the processes that support stability within interpersonal relationships—matters in the workplace, and plays a pivotal role in the efficacy of an organization. As humans, we have internal working models that define our relationship expectations. Our emotions detect and diagnose the ways in which our reality is (or is not) aligned with our needs and expectations. Security and shame are the two predominant and opposing valences that determine how we feel in the workplace, and need to be nurtured carefully in order for organizations to thrive.

**People need to feel deep emotional security to embrace the innate risks of exploration, creativity, and innovation.**
Emotional security is the source of healthy personal agency and team cohesion. Security in the workplace is nurtured when leaders are both a Safe Haven and a Secure Base, being accessible and responsive to distress and instilling confidence that exploration is safe. This allows for what psychologists call "rupture and repair": the process by which a team member can express distress—which momentarily creates relational imbalance—but subsequently receives a reparative response.

PEOPLE MUST FEEL DEEP EMOTIONAL SECURITY
TO STRIVE PAST "TASKS" AND ACTIVELY THINK AND DO WITHIN
THE EXPANSES OF THEIR CREATIVE POTENTIAL

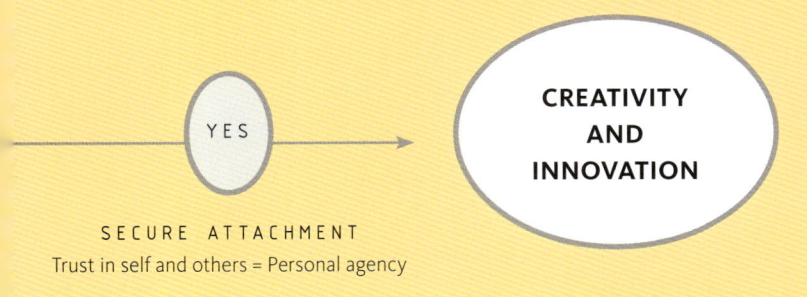

**YES** → **CREATIVITY AND INNOVATION**

SECURE ATTACHMENT
Trust in self and others = Personal agency

**Security is the foundation of diversity.** Emotionally secure individuals don't feel obligated to subscribe to homogeneous norms. They feel empowered to integrate their own preferences for working effectively into wider team or organizational processes. This comfort negates the fear of social exclusion and supports creativity and risk-taking. It also enriches the social ecology of the team.

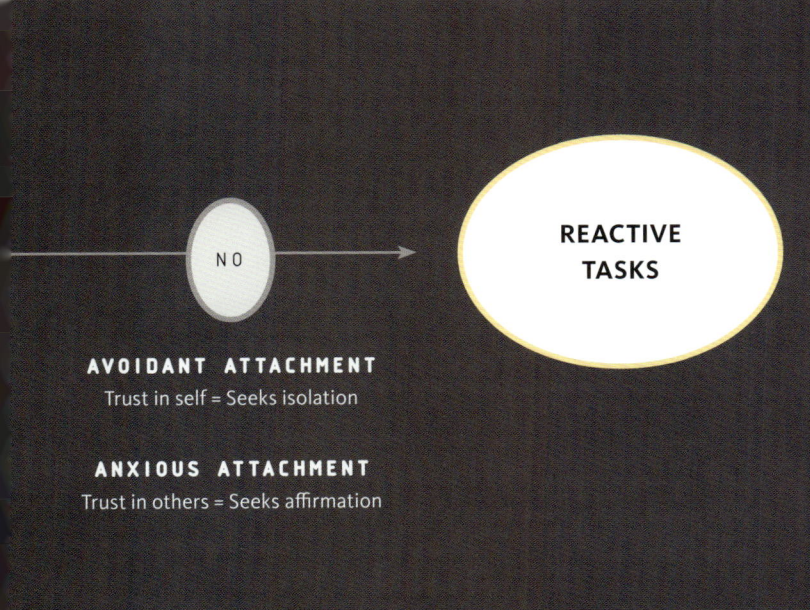

**NO** → **REACTIVE TASKS**

AVOIDANT ATTACHMENT
Trust in self = Seeks isolation

ANXIOUS ATTACHMENT
Trust in others = Seeks affirmation

**Feelings of shame drastically inhibit an individual's ability to complete creative and effective work.** Shame is perpetuated by the absence of safety and security, reinforcing an individual's perception that they have failed to meet an organization's "conditions of belonging." This leads to feelings of exclusion and isolation with immense emotional energy spent on "earning" the responsiveness of others, engaging in unhealthy pursuits of affirmation, and disregarding their own needs. These behaviors degrade security and undermine an individual's creativity, originality, and willingness to take risks.

### DESIGN IMPLICATIONS

**Designers, consultants, thought leaders, and strategic advisors must understand how to promote emotional security if they want to foster innovation.** Emotional security must pervade every aspect of an organization, from building and interior design to HR policies and leadership practices. Individuals working to enhance the creativity of their organizations and employees must understand how to orchestrate places, cultures, and experiences that promote emotional security.

**Organizations that invest in relational and emotional security will be more resilient in the face of a radically transforming world.** In the future, smart machines will process and complete tasks at a rate that human knowledge workers will be unable to match. The value that humans create will shift toward storytelling, meaning-making, empathy, and imagination. This exploratory and creative work will require relational and emotional security to exist at every level of an organization.

### WHAT'S NEXT

We are developing a cultural diagnostic tool to help clients identify the facets of their culture that need to evolve in their pursuit of innovation. The insights gained from this research can go on to inform and complement other research efforts concerning organizational culture.

# Prioritizing Psychological Well-being

What tools can encourage designers to consider users' psychological needs?

**WHAT WE DID**

**We developed a toolkit to help designers, strategists, and clients understand and prioritize psychological well-being throughout the design process.** This toolkit—comprised of collaborative activities, worksheets, and multisensory prompts—builds on three years of joint research with the Royal College of Art (RCA). We partnered with RCA's Helen Hamlyn Centre for Design to understand how employees can have better and more productive experiences in their workplaces.

This project occurred in three phases. In Phase 1, we conducted an extensive literature review and interviewed employees at four newly modified offices in/around London. In Phase 2, we guided an organization through a Participatory Design Project and evaluated how employees' participation in the design of their workplace influenced their well-being. The findings from the first two phases enabled us to develop a "workplace well-being conceptual model" that demonstrates the need to balance an individual's functional and psychological needs. In Phase 3 of the project, we identified six emotional states that are key components of psychological well-being: belonging, serenity, recognition, influence, stimulation, and awe. Because well-being is so subjective and there is no one "formula," we set out to build a toolkit that would help designers and clients quickly understand and reflect upon those emotional states in relation to live projects.

**THE CONTEXT**

Most employees spend one-third of their waking hours in their workplace. Evidence suggests that workplace surroundings have a substantial impact on employee fulfillment, wellness, and productivity, and can also influence team collaboration and unity. However, most workers are not experiencing feelings of connection and positivity in their work environments. In a recent study, 6 out of 10 workers in major global economies reported increased levels of workplace stress. As long-term stress is known to negatively impact physical and mental health, this added strain can affect both individual and organizational functioning.

In the United States alone, mental illness is the single greatest cause of worker disability. Additionally, absences from work due to mental illness typically require a greater amount of time away from the office than physical illness. This "well-being deficit" is one of the most urgent problems facing organizations and employees today. In the UK alone, 30.7 million working days are lost every year due to work-related depression, stress, anxiety, and muscular-skeletal disorders. Such absences carry an annual cost of $16 to $81 (small employer) and $17 to $286 (large employer) per employee per year. The Centre for Mental Health in UK reports that mental health problems at work cost 35 billion in the UK, in recent years.

While these numbers seem bleak, employee well-being doesn't have to drain company resources. According to a 2014 report, every dollar dedicated to creating a mentally healthy workplace generates $2.30 in organizational benefits. And the case for healthy employees is compelling. Employees who have strong overall well-being are twice as more likely to be engaged in their jobs (compared to employees with moderate well-being) and 39% less likely to be diagnosed with a new disease in the next year. Designers have a unique opportunity to provide a foundation for well-being in the environments they create for their clients.

**Understand the Emotion**
The workshop process includes visual, tactile, and audio materials to evoke and understand the emotional states.

> We need a framework to integrate emotional well-being in the design process.

What makes you feel safe/peaceful?

When/why would you need serenity?

Is this about being alone or being with other people?

**SERENITY**

Where and when have you felt awe?

Can you describe this word/feeling?

What does it trigger in you?

**AWE**

**RECOGNITION**

Can you recall when you felt a sense of recognition?

Was it about you as an individual?

How could recognition be represented?

How would you like to be acknowledged?

Think of an example of when you have been able to affect change. How did it make you feel?

If you could change/control your environment, would you? How often? Why/When?

How would you like to be able to change/control your environment?

**INFLUENCE**

**BELONGING**

What makes you feel connected to something/someone? Why?

Where do you feel a sense of belonging?

How do you make yourself "at home" somewhere?

**STIMULATION**

What gets you excited at work? What do you feel enthusiastic about?

What would encourage you to become active?

*"People felt better about work when invited to participate in the design of their work environment, and unfairly excluded from decision-making processes when not given a voice."*

—Jeremy Myerson, Chair of Design, Helen Hamlyn Centre for Design, RCA

**Six emotional state cards**

These cards define each emotional state of well-being and provide reflective prompts to engage workshop participants.

**THE RESULTS**

**We completed six 90-minute workshops in San Francisco and London with designers and non-designers.** The workshops combined a variety of different activities and prompts. Each session began by introducing the project and identifying the design problem. We then defined psychological well-being and discussed its design-related contexts. For reference, we provided six cards (shown at left) that outlined the key emotional states of psychological well-being in the workplace.

After participants identified the emotional states that were most important to address in their projects, they completed a series of worksheets and engaged with multisensory prompts to create a moodboard. Both the worksheets and the visual, audio, and tactile prompts challenged participants to think more deeply about how to manifest the emotional states in the workplace design. Participants then broke into small groups to present their moodboard, discuss their experiences, and generate and evaluate ideas.

It was necessary to have a tangible outcome to the workshop, so we created the emotional brief. The emotional brief developed organically from the completed worksheets and contains potential solutions to the design problem identified at the start of the workshop. It should stand alongside, or be integrated into, the design brief, and can be referenced and/or revised throughout the design process as needs evolve.

**DESIGN IMPLICATIONS**

**A sense of control is the most important contributor to perceived well-being.** This manifests itself in the workplace environment, but also in the creation of the workplace design. Employee participation in the design process increases their feelings of belonging and attachment to the workspace, which in turn can boost productivity. Interestingly, it was not the degree of participation, but rather the simple fact of being invited to participate in co-design that had a positive impact.

**It is important to give workers freedom to reconfigure and personalize their space.** Incorporating design elements such as rearrangeable artwork, accessories, and furniture positively correlates to employee autonomy and competence.

**Well-being is a huge priority for many clients.** When designers become experts on psychological well-being, it increases the value and longevity of their designs and perspectives. Introducing interactive, collaborative elements such as the toolkit at the beginning of the design process is beneficial to both the client and the designer.

**The toolkit can be used by designers alone, or in conjunction with clients.** Designers can utilize the tool by themselves to catalyze the brainstorming process and spark new ideas. The emotional brief is a great reference throughout the project, to make sure that the evolving design is addressing and supporting the key emotional states. Designers can also use the toolkit with clients to facilitate conversations about psychological well-being and help them identify which aspects of psychological well-being most align with their future vision.

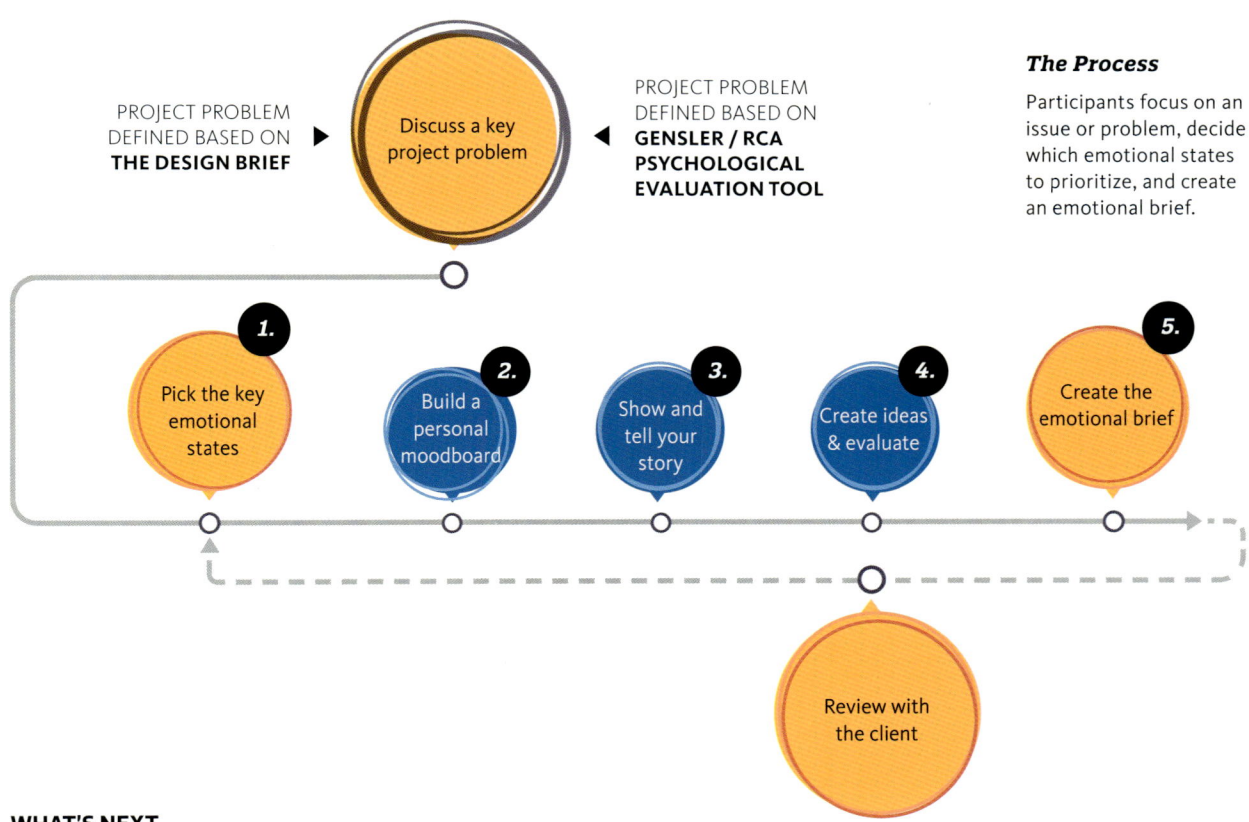

*The Process*

Participants focus on an issue or problem, decide which emotional states to prioritize, and create an emotional brief.

PROJECT PROBLEM DEFINED BASED ON **THE DESIGN BRIEF** ▶ Discuss a key project problem ◀ PROJECT PROBLEM DEFINED BASED ON **GENSLER / RCA PSYCHOLOGICAL EVALUATION TOOL**

1. Pick the key emotional states
2. Build a personal moodboard
3. Show and tell your story
4. Create ideas & evaluate
5. Create the emotional brief

Review with the client

**WHAT'S NEXT**

Having iteratively tested the toolkit with volunteers using imaginary design briefs, we are now ready to test it on live projects and identify potential areas of improvement. Validating toolkit activities and determining the optimal multisensory prompts are essential to growing a collection of ideas and best practices. We are working to introduce additional sensory experiences and tactile prompts to enrich the workshop experience. Additionally, we plan to design branding and packaging for the toolkit to ensure a polished presentation of the product.

Shifting the Workplace Narrative

**Shaw Create Centre**
Cartersville, Georgia

With appreciation for Shaw Create Centre's setting in a rural locale, Gensler designed it as a place to transcend brands—collaborating and innovating across multiple creative groups. This center of excellence set out to attract top talent, demonstrate domestic and global leadership, highlight design and performance leadership, and support well-being in the workplace.

# Balancing Density and Employee Engagement

How do different workplace configurations influence real estate value and employee engagement?

**WHAT WE DID**

**We developed conceptual workplace design scenarios and used them to establish and test different value propositions.** In the context of a broad transition toward more open environments, we built a framework that references not only typical value considerations—real estate, capital, and operational costs—but also the impact of workspace layout on employee engagement. We measured different design scenarios according to value, a dynamic of both people-driven and cost-driven inputs, so as to uncover a better understanding of what design may achieve.

The three design scenarios included an open, closed, and flexible workspace type. While we maintained the same floor plate square footage, the amount of enclosed, open space, and mobile pods differed in each workspace type. Because of the different design features, we hypothesized that cost and engagement would vary by degree of openness.

**VALUE AND COSTS WILL BE ASSESSED USING DESIGN CONCEPTS (20,000 sf FLOOR PLATE)**

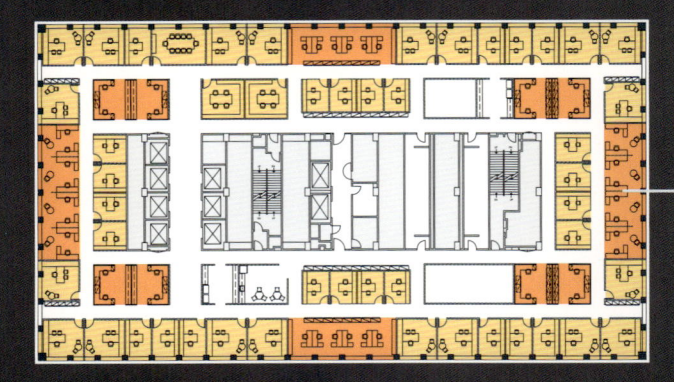

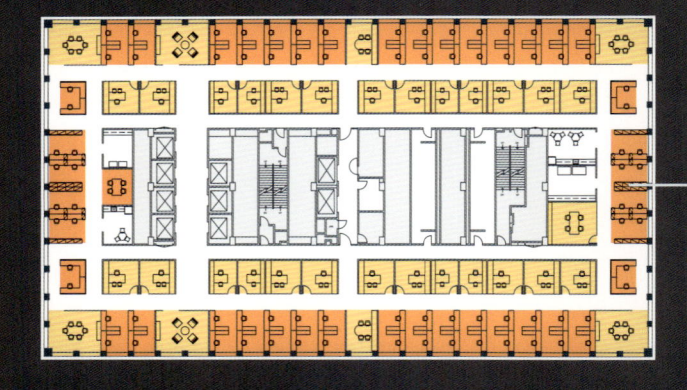

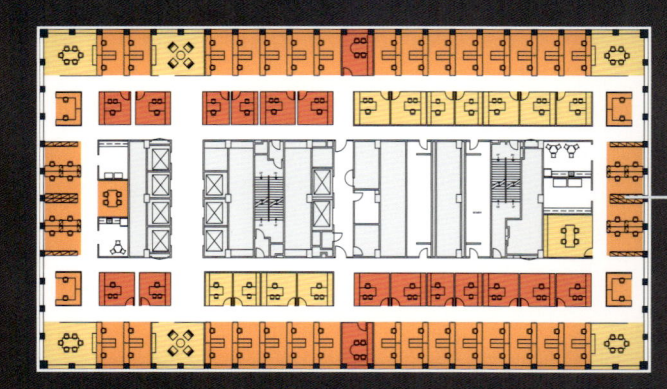

# A truer conception of value challenges the typical open versus closed dialogue.

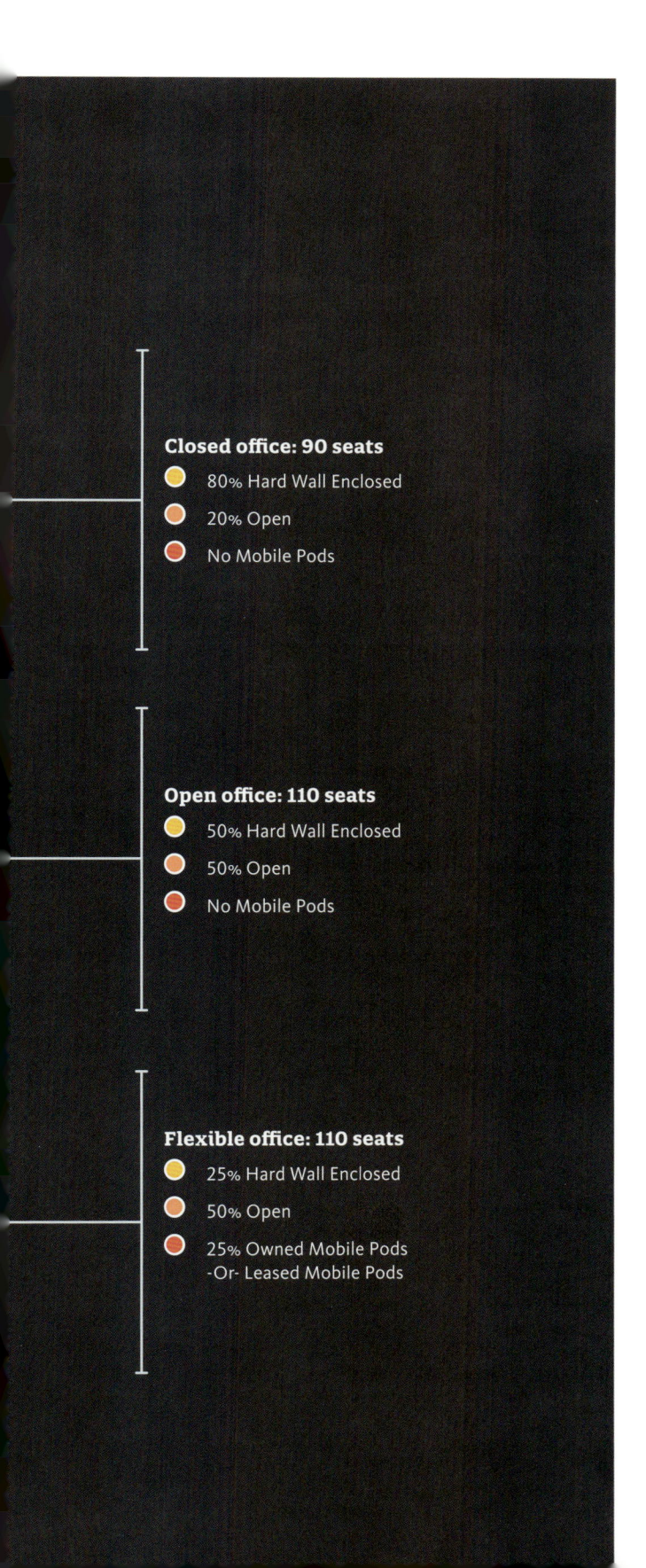

**Closed office: 90 seats**
- 80% Hard Wall Enclosed
- 20% Open
- No Mobile Pods

**Open office: 110 seats**
- 50% Hard Wall Enclosed
- 50% Open
- No Mobile Pods

**Flexible office: 110 seats**
- 25% Hard Wall Enclosed
- 50% Open
- 25% Owned Mobile Pods -Or- Leased Mobile Pods

**THE CONTEXT**

We must challenge commonly held assumptions about the workplace. For one, we need to expand our definition of value beyond construction costs and operating expenses to include employee engagement, or the extent to which employees feel passionate about their work and their organization. Employee engagement is strongly correlated with productivity. According to a 2012 Gallup Survey of 1.4 million employees, companies in the top quartile of employee engagement have 65% less turnover, 22% more profitability, 21% more productivity, and 37% less absenteeism—all indicators of a healthy culture at work.

Employee-per-square-foot ratios may vary by industry, region, and motive, but there is an overall trend toward more open space configurations. As a rule of thumb, open plan concepts decrease construction costs because of comparatively fewer walls, doors, and frames, and simpler plumbing, HVAC, and electrical systems. Typically, as construction costs decrease, soft costs, which include consulting, strategy, and legal fees, decrease too. The relationship between worker productivity and open plan environments is complicated. Open plans are likely to foster collaborative work and increase sociability, but focus work and privacy are threatened. All things considered, there is an elusive balance to pursue that considers employee engagement and cost. And achieving that balance must be assessed through the prism of workplace configurations.

**THE RESULTS**

We broke down three expense types: real estate, operational, and capital. Real estate costs decrease in denser environments because the employee-per-square-foot ratio is higher. Greater density floor plans also have lower construction costs initially but higher capital expenses over time. Since there are fewer personal offices in flexible work environments, communal areas require higher articulation, and furniture will come at a higher cost and require higher maintenance. Overall capital costs increase through more wear and tear on assets, and higher administrative costs are required to coordinate and change equipment and furnishings. Operational costs increase in denser environments because more people are generating business costs under one roof.

Ideally, we want to decrease costs while increasing employee engagement. Our test case was an international technology company that had renovated its offices from an enclosed, private office environment (235 sf/person) to an open, flexible environment (180 sf/person). In doing so, the layout increased from 426 seats to 556 seats.

## The Impact of Density on Cost

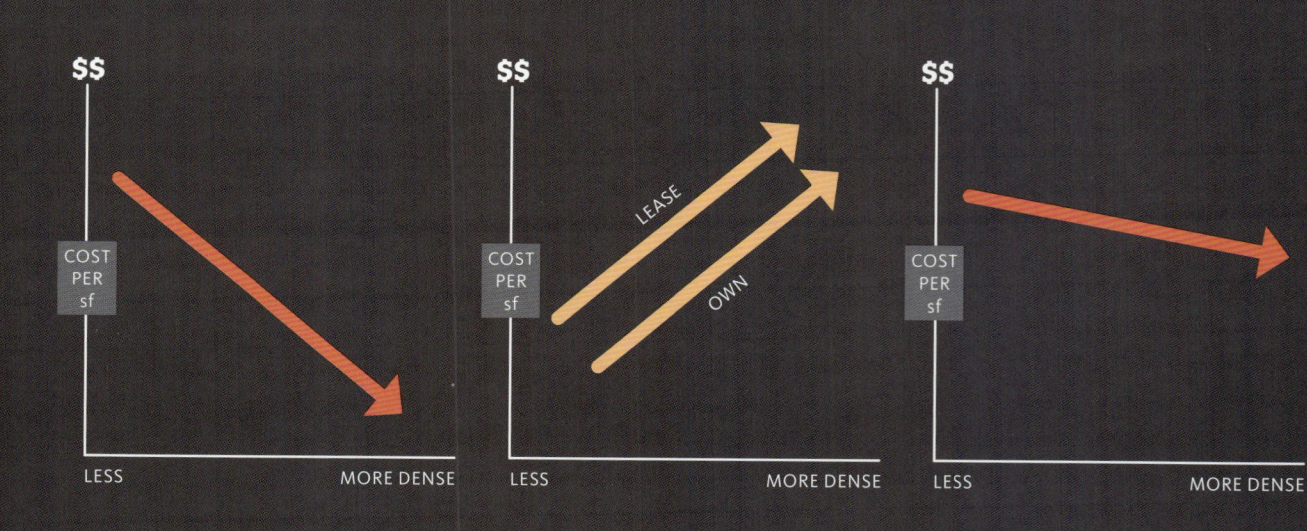

**Real Estate**
Greater density means more people in the same or less sf

**Operational**
Greater density means more people generating business expenses

**Capital**
Greater density means lower construction costs but higher furniture costs

148  Shifting the Workplace Narrative | Balancing Density and Employee Engagement

The company saved 10% on total construction cost in the first year and experienced increased employee engagement. However, over a 10-year period, operating costs were projected to outpace the cost of the former configuration, an enclosed workplace. We projected a 2.2% total cost increase over a 10-year period for the open, flexible space despite up-front cost savings.

In general, our data suggests that both decreased costs and increased employee engagement may be hard to achieve.

That does not mean that businesses should not consider alternatives. A business may choose short- or long-term savings according to unique financial positions. The key is aligning a design scenario with cost modeling, and either maintaining or increasing employee engagement. As our case study demonstrates, this is difficult and end-user contingent. There may not be a universal standard, but there may be a case-by-case golden ratio.

**Savings due to open plan over 10 years, compared to 100,000 sf workspace with 100% private offices at 235 sf/person**

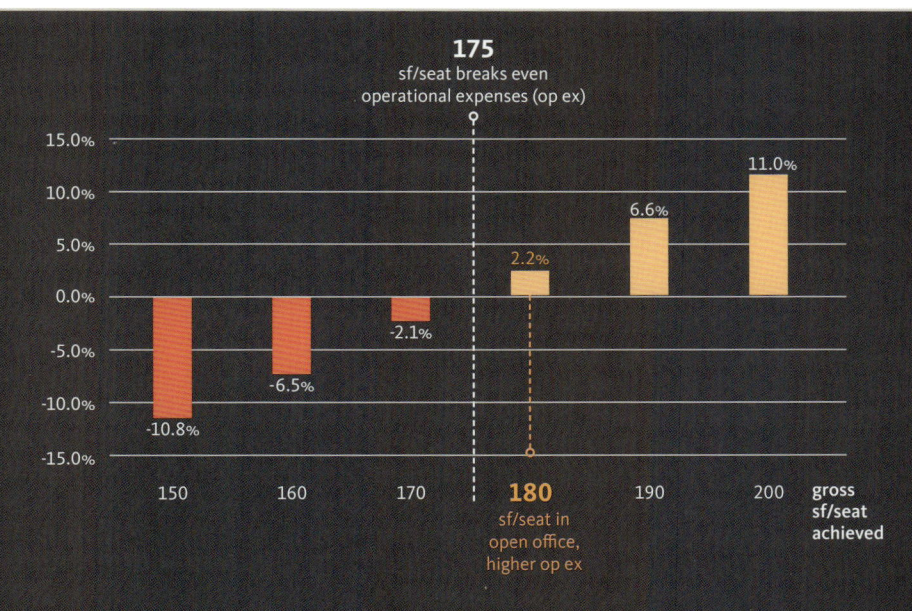

175 sf/seat breaks even operational expenses (op ex)

| gross sf/seat achieved | 150 | 160 | 170 | 180 | 190 | 200 |
|---|---|---|---|---|---|---|
| % | -10.8% | -6.5% | -2.1% | 2.2% | 6.6% | 11.0% |

180 sf/seat in open office, higher op ex

**Savings in operational expenses over 10 years, drops significantly after five years compared to ongoing expenses associated with enclosed (legacy) space**

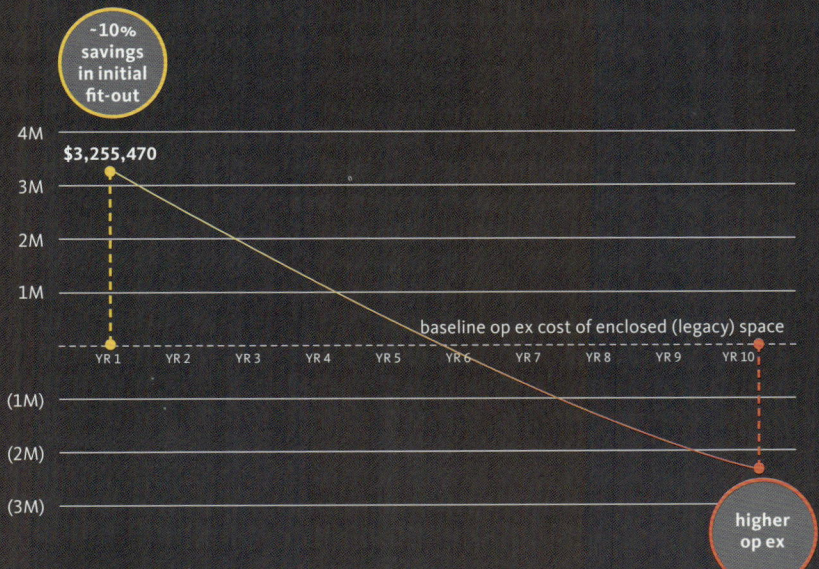

~10% savings in initial fit-out

YR 1: $3,255,470

baseline op ex cost of enclosed (legacy) space

YR 10: higher op ex

**DESIGN IMPLICATIONS**

**Aligning the optimal value range for both engagement and cost is hard as our case study demonstrates.**

Businesses approach the engagement versus cost question through different lenses. Depending on a firm's unique standpoint, however, there can be different successful business strategies. Value ranges are flexible, and cost and engagement shift according to each design scenario.

**OPTIMAL COST**

Up-front costs decrease and operational expenses increase with greater floorplan density. The optimal strategy balances initial build out costs with a projection for expenses incurred by flexible seating arrangements.

## The companies in America with happier or more engaged employees have better financial performance than your average company, quantified by long-term stock growth.

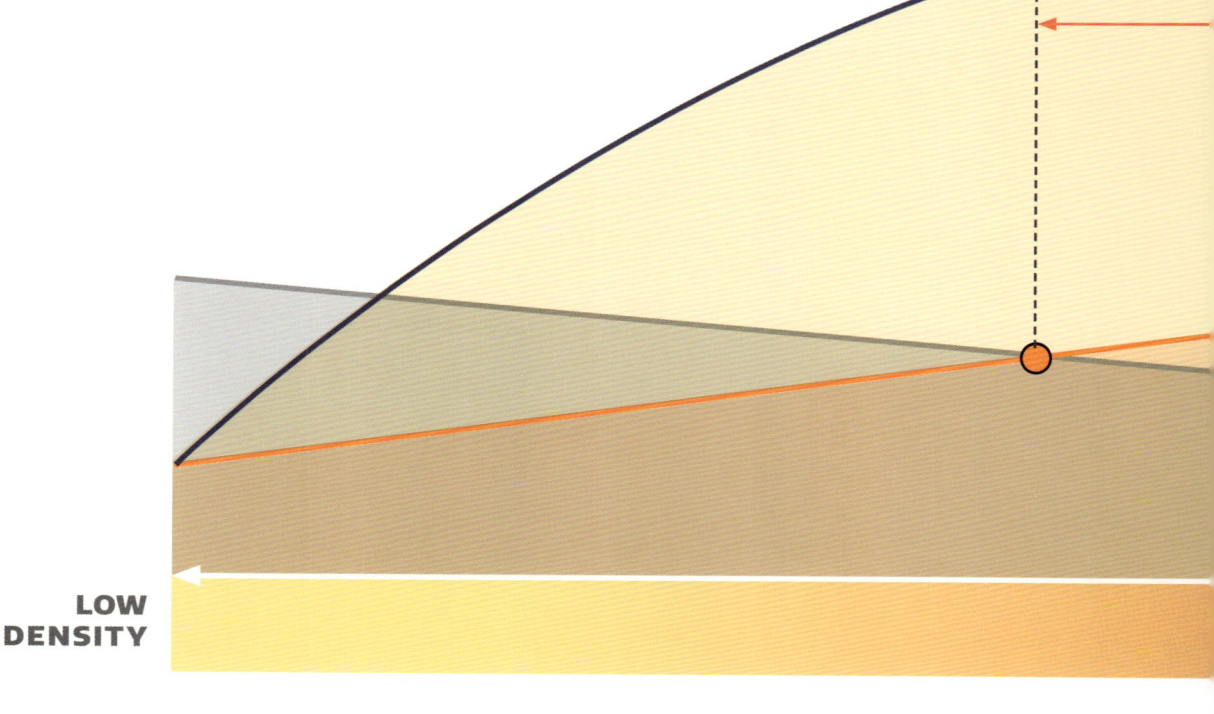

**LOW DENSITY**

**WHAT DOES SUCCESSFUL OUTCOME LOOK LIKE?**

Success looks different depending on the lens

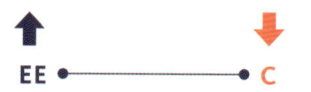

EE ⬆ ● ———— ● C ⬇

**The "Dream"**
Improve engagement while reducing costs

EE ▬ ● ———— ● C ⬇

**Cost-Driven**
Reduce cost without negatively affecting engagement

150  Shifting the Workplace Narrative | Balancing Density and Employee Engagement

## OPTIMAL ENGAGEMENT

Increased density means more opportunity for employee collaboration and interaction; however, there is a point at which density negatively impacts engagement.

## WHAT'S NEXT

While the present study is a work in progress that will help establish a unique and optimal baseline, our research efforts need to be replicated with different clients across different industries and office types. The client used for our case study forecasts lower costs through a new density target of 160 square feet per person. After another design change, the company will reanalyze employee engagement trending and costs. Finding the golden ratio of density, cost, and employee engagement requires multifactor data and long-term operational cost considerations.

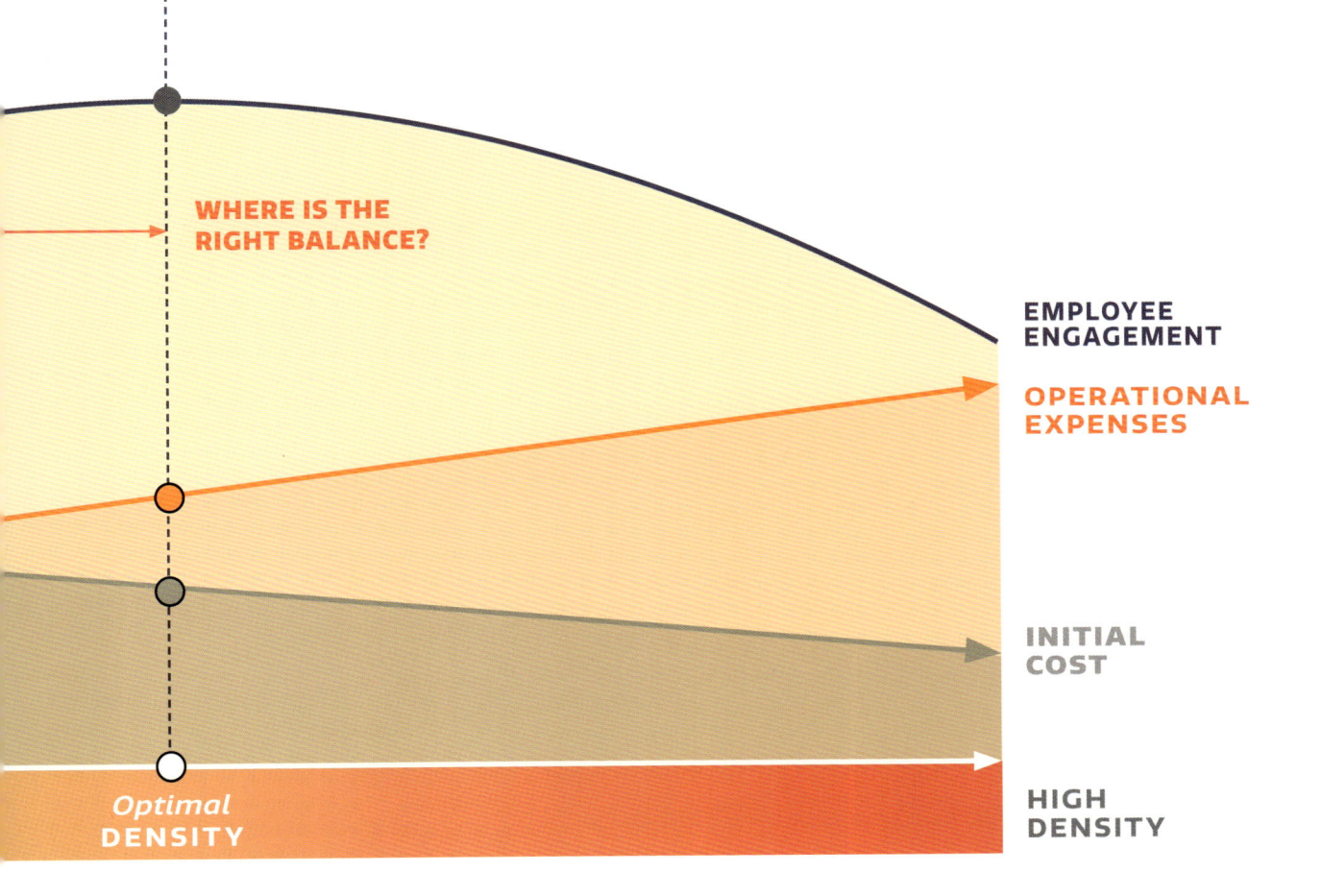

**WHERE IS THE RIGHT BALANCE?**

EMPLOYEE ENGAGEMENT

OPERATIONAL EXPENSES

INITIAL COST

*Optimal* **DENSITY**

**HIGH DENSITY**

**People-Driven**
Modest investments for significant engagement gains

**People & Cost**
Increase engagement without increasing cost

EE  EMPLOYEE ENGAGEMENT

C  COST

# Work Styles and Spatial Preference

Is there a link between a person's learning style and their workplace preference?

## Respondent Overview

**41**
respondents from Chicago, IL

**45**
respondents from Charlotte, NC

**78**
respondents from Washington, D.C.

### WHAT WE DID

**We built upon Gensler's Workplace Performance Index by creating a survey based on Dr. Howard Gardner's Multiple Intelligences concept.** Our goals were to identify alignments, trends, and patterns that exist between work modes and intelligence dominance. To establish these correlations, we surveyed 164 respondents at three Gensler offices.

### THE CONTEXT

The U.S. is currently facing an employee engagement crisis. According to a recent Gallup survey, only 33% of workers are engaged. Research shows that actively disengaged employees cost the U.S. $483 billion to $605 billion a year. Organizations need to examine how they entice and retain their employees. We are among the first to investigate the intersection of intelligence and physical space, and to see if it is possible to design workspaces to complement the unique cognitive profiles of employees.

### THE RESULTS

After answering survey questions about personality, skill sets, and workspace preferences, participants were qualified as falling into one of Gardner's intelligence dominances:

**Intelligence dominance does not appear to influence workplace preference.** Instead, many universal preferences emerged. For independent work activities, respondents prefer intimate spaces without a door, followed by home and informal, calm spaces. Third spaces (i.e., coffee shops) were not a desirable setting for the majority of participants. For collaborative work, most intelligence dominances preferred enclosed and/or intimate spaces. Across all intelligence styles, there was little preference for completing collaborative work in the home.

**Intelligence dominance may play a role in perceived workplace effectiveness and satisfaction.** Interpersonal, kinesthetic, and linguistic learners reported the highest levels of impact when relating the workspace to job satisfaction. The physical work environment is perceived to be a less important part of overall job performance to intrapersonal, math-logical, musical, and spatial-visual learners.

### DESIGN IMPLICATIONS

**Choice and variety are important, regardless of intelligence type.** Multimodal workers require multimodal offices. Employees need creative spaces that foster connectivity, brainstorming, interaction, and decision-making, as well as private spaces and areas geared toward rejuvenation.

**Positive outcomes are associated with allowing employees to maintain their individual identities in the workplace.** Integrating adjustability and personalization into workplace design boosts employee engagement. Designers should consider incorporating "hackable" furniture, movable artwork, and other customizable elements in their designs.

### WHAT'S NEXT

We hope to broaden our data by involving select clients as research partners. More research is needed to fully understand the connection between intelligence dominance and the perception of a current workspace's effectiveness.

| | 1 | 2 | 3 | 4 | 5 |
|---|---|---|---|---|---|
| | *No Impact* | | | | *High Impact* |

**Impact of Physical Work Environment on Job Satisfaction**

### SPATIAL / VISUAL
Facility with the interpretation and creation of visual images.

### LINGUISTIC
Facility with ideas and information via written and spoken language.

### MATH / LOGICAL
Facility with logic, patterns, scientific reasoning and deduction.

### MUSICAL
Facility with awareness, appreciation, and use of sound.

### KINESTHETIC
Facility with movement control, dexterity, agility, and balance.

### INTERPERSONAL
Ability to perceive other people's feelings.

### INTRAPERSONAL
Facility with self-awareness and personal cognizance and objectivity.

# The Value of Customer Experience Centers

What are the benefits of enhanced digital experiences within a customer experience center?

**WHAT WE DID**

**We interviewed customer experience center (CEC) experts to understand why companies pursue CECs and the various approaches to their development.** In addition to these interviews, we conducted qualitative and quantitative research with client experts, expanding our understanding of the CEC design process and the use of success metrics beyond the Gensler community. We hypothesized the components needed to build a successful CEC and tested our hypotheses by interviewing senior leadership and management of six different CEC types. We then sent the subjects a set of follow-up questions to dive deeper into common trends we uncovered during the interview process. Based on our findings, we established distinctive CEC types and common threads between them.

**THE CONTEXT**

With 75% of companies looking to improve customer experience, there is growing interest in digital experience design—an avenue for brand, engagement, and business value. Because CECs represent a company's identity and culture, they offer an opportunity to understand how digital activations add experiential value in other environments—such as the workplace—by improving engagement and experience.

### THE RESULTS

Most subjects had no formal method of measuring ROI, focusing instead on the value created by forming a deep connection with users through a meaningful, personalized experience. User experience was the predominant indicator of success within CECs, measured by a "return on experience" (ROE). While ROE is difficult to measure, many subjects stated users commonly have a visible "a-ha" moment, and it is in this moment that they develop a deep and personal connection with the brand.

CECs can serve as unique and controlled environments to deliver an elevator pitch. To form a deep connection between the audience and the brand, the CEC must tell a compelling story. Investing the time and resources to craft a compelling story early in the CEC development process creates a higher likelihood that users will identify with the brand and its community. Many subjects stated that companies have a hard time concisely telling their story—and the CEC provides an opportunity to focus resources and develop a meaningful and engaging story that synthesizes their mission.

### DESIGN IMPLICATIONS

**CECs are an opportunity for brands to put their best image forward.** CECs offer chances to explore new content delivery systems, design visualization mechanisms, and advanced technology materials that best communicate each company's capabilities and message. Developing showcase materials in a way that makes them readymade for incorporation into a company's CEC can be an efficient way to keep products and content feeling fresh.

**Customized experiences are successful experiences.** Whether they had a guide choreograph a custom presentation from a standard set of content or set up entirely custom content for each user, all of our subjects customized the user experience to some degree. Customization is a critical component for an engaging storytelling experience, helping to create the "hook" that connects the subject with the brand.

**A CEC also provides an opportunity to strengthen the connection between an organization and its employees.** The companies that invested the resources to develop state-of-the-art, authentic CECs saw a positive ripple effect across their corporate cultures. These seemingly isolated spaces consistently elevated employees' expectations around technology, design, and their company's overall "cool factor."

### WHAT'S NEXT

In our second phase of research, we will distribute an experience survey to the 300 attendees of the Association of Briefing Program Managers 2019 spring conference. This will provide us with a robust dataset around how companies developed various components of their CECs and what methods they use to determine their CEC's success. Responses from the survey will also help us target subjects with unique approaches to their CECs for an additional round of interviews. These richer insights will ensure we are better equipped to determine the business drivers behind CECs and efficiently translate them into a story arc and design expression.

# Designing Effective Research Buildings

How does the design of science and laboratory buildings drive innovation, creativity, and collaboration in scientific research?

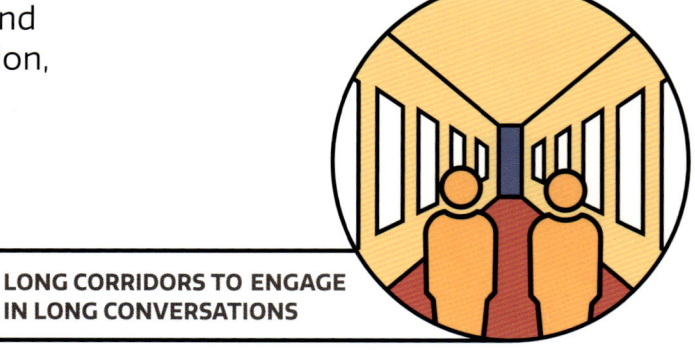

**LONG CORRIDORS TO ENGAGE IN LONG CONVERSATIONS**

### WHAT WE DID

**We studied different approaches to the design of laboratory and scientific buildings to identify how architecture supports collaboration and innovation in the sciences.** We conducted interviews with leading scientific program directors in academic, industry, government, and privately funded research institutes. We surveyed users of both wet and dry labs, identifying both successful and unsuccessful models of research communities. We also analyzed how lab users spend their time within a framework specific to scientific research. Finally, we created architectural diagrams and illustrations to discover the pattern language of successful research institutes.

### THE CONTEXT

There's a well-documented link between in-person collaboration and scientific innovation. Isaac Kohane, a researcher at Harvard Medical School, recently examined the effect that physical proximity had on the quality of research conducted by two or more authors. The highest-quality, most-cited research was consistently produced by teams working within less than 10 meters from each other. Collaborators working a kilometer or more away from each other produced the least cited papers. When interviewed about the study, Kohane remarked, "If you want people to work together effectively, these findings reinforce the need to create architectures that support frequent, physical, spontaneous interactions."

### THE RESULTS

Creating a space that fosters innovation requires creating a common language between the scientists and the architect. We found that many scientists and researchers are frustrated with the functionality of their laboratory's architecture, and feel unheard throughout the design process. Designers must grasp the intricacies of a lab's technical processes and also consider critical organizational structures such as culture, discipline, institution type, and funding source. Additionally, determining the optimum density of people in the building is critical to creating productive collaborations and is a key concern of effective design.

Unsuccessful models prioritized aesthetics over function and adaptability. In some cases, having an "underdesigned" lab proved to be an asset to scientific innovation. Spatial "inefficiencies" can actually facilitate interdepartment collaboration and the cross-pollination of ideas. This is especially true of MIT Building 20, a makeshift space constructed during World War II that was originally intended to be a temporary structure. Users often got lost trying to navigate its confusing, sprawling layout. The building's long corridors enabled long conversations and exchanges between colleagues who might not have met otherwise.

**FUNNEL USERS INTO COMMUNAL AREAS**

**QUIET SPACES FOR INTENSIVE WRITING**

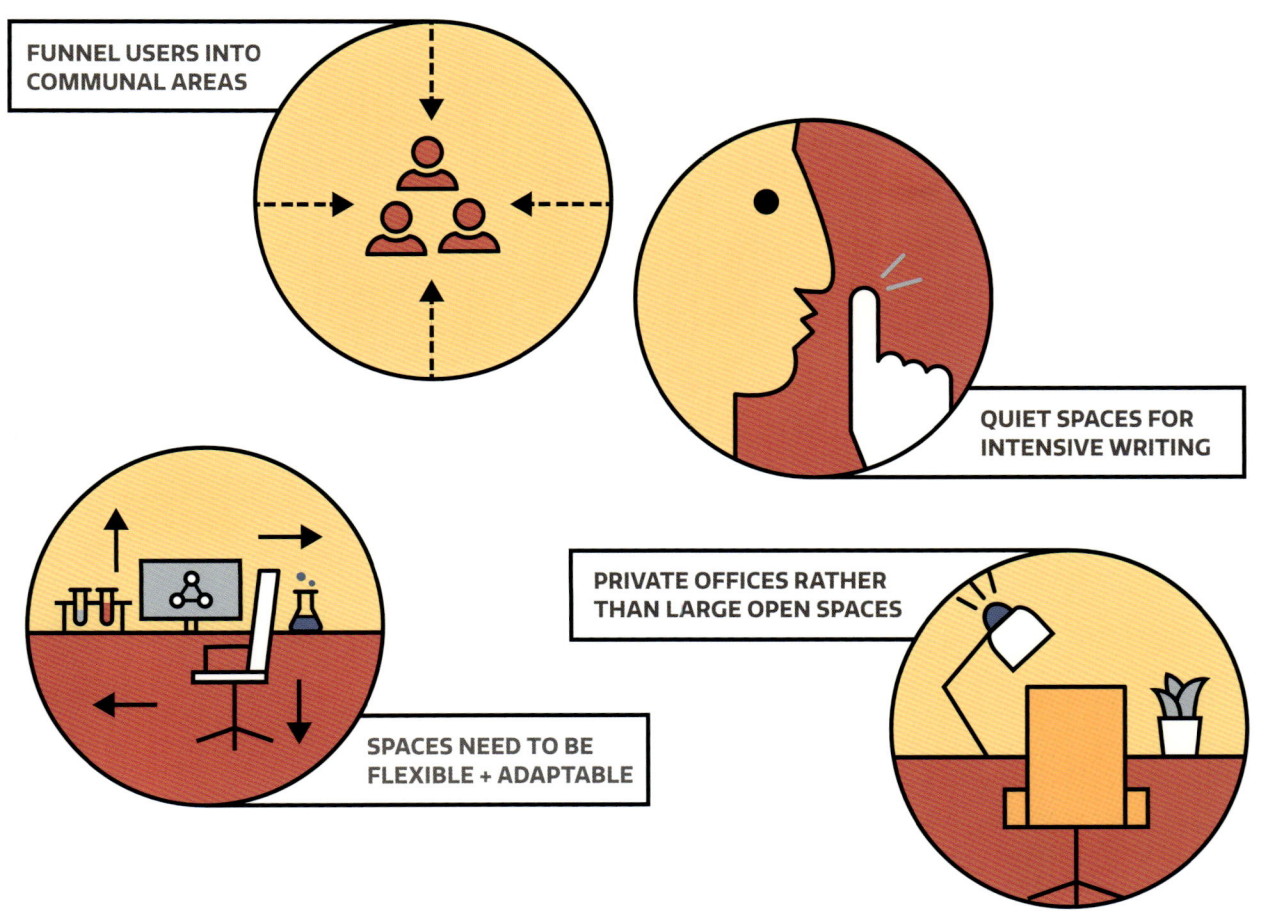

**SPACES NEED TO BE FLEXIBLE + ADAPTABLE**

**PRIVATE OFFICES RATHER THAN LARGE OPEN SPACES**

# Spatial "inefficiencies" can lead to collaboration and cross-pollination

**DESIGN IMPLICATIONS**

**Designs that support collaboration deliberately weave circulation paths within spaces to encourage interaction.** We found that users often preferred and congregated in informal spaces. Designers should identify ways to funnel lab users into communal areas or spaces that are outside of their normal work zones. These increased opportunities for spontaneous interaction will deepen potential collaborative connections.

**Expansive, atrium-like collaboration zones are rarely used.** We found that scientists prefer intimate work spaces, such as their private offices, to large, open areas. There are a variety of reasons why this might be true across laboratories, from the nature of the research being conducted to the perceived lack of privacy.

**Research buildings need more quiet writing spaces.** Across all disciplines and areas of specialization, we found that lab users lacked areas for focused work on their theses and papers. Quiet spaces to complete intensive writing work are a necessary element of successful lab design.

**WHAT'S NEXT**

We aim to use these findings to produce a document to share with prospective clients that clearly identifies the technical and functional issues that need to be resolved in order to deliver a successful design. We will also use the material we have to refine the pattern languages for specific desired outcomes within laboratory spaces.

# Adaptable Life Science Lab Design

What is a value-driven solution to maximizing our needs for flexible life science lab design?

**WHAT WE DID**

**We researched the space typologies typical of life science labs and arrived at a set of archetypes differentiated by functionality, flexibility, and cost-effectiveness.** Our research tested three life science lab design types: traditional/fixed, flexible, and adaptable. In order to scrutinize variances in design, we created a survey. Each participant was a stakeholder with unique design priorities, and these differences contributed to a broad-based understanding of the concerns facing scientific organizations.

Our goal was to establish both financial and experiential value in lab design—a balance between efficient work and healthy margins. We believe there is an intersection where efficient work overlaps with prohibitive costs, a point where more flexibility yields diminishing returns. We created a user-generated list of priorities that encapsulate the drivers of experiential value—and in doing so, we discerned what is necessary and what is not necessary in building ideal life science labs.

**FLEXIBLE AND ADAPTABLE LABS**

○ Mobile casework: tables on levelers or castors are easy to move around, enabling reconfiguration of a lab floor plan without much effort.

Small things matter: integrating pipette holders, glove dispensers, or hazardous waste disposal with furniture systems makes benches more efficient and saves space.

⬡ Utilities are easily accessible using connectors from the ceiling or wall.

158  Shifting the Workplace Narrative | Adaptive Life Science Lab Design

**THE CONTEXT**

Demand is hot for lab space. In major hubs like San Francisco and Boston, vacancy rates are hitting cyclic lows. With greater competition for space, there is greater scrutiny into the dynamics of lab space itself—a need to push for innovative solutions. Other market forces are at work here too: pressure from health care policies and from insurance and consumer groups mean that costs need to be kept in check. There is a premium on efficiency.

Because of the nature of work conducted in life science facilities, the nuances of design have a greater impact than other space types. There are day-to-day consequences in slight variations of structural bay spacing that impact partition, corridor, workstation, and even outlet positioning. To innovate, we need to forge a value-driven conception of design—one that relates experiential markers like productivity and efficiency with both foreground design and elements that users do not interface with, like mechanical, electrical, and plumbing (MEP) systems. An analysis of the interrelationships and distinctions between these variables is necessary to prioritize the constituents of life science facility design.

# Flexibility and cost compete in a zero-sum balance depending on unique user needs.

From genomics to biochemistry, creating a paradigm of empirically driven life science facility design is a tall order. Even though life science labs may differ greatly in nature, our research aims to establish a transcendent baseline. Different lab types can vary substantially by cost. For instance, a cGMP Production Facility Class 100 can range to over $1,000, while a technology development lab generally costs below $300/sf. There is a point where design considerations intersect to generate the most value. Our research aims to guide clients to that point for their organization.

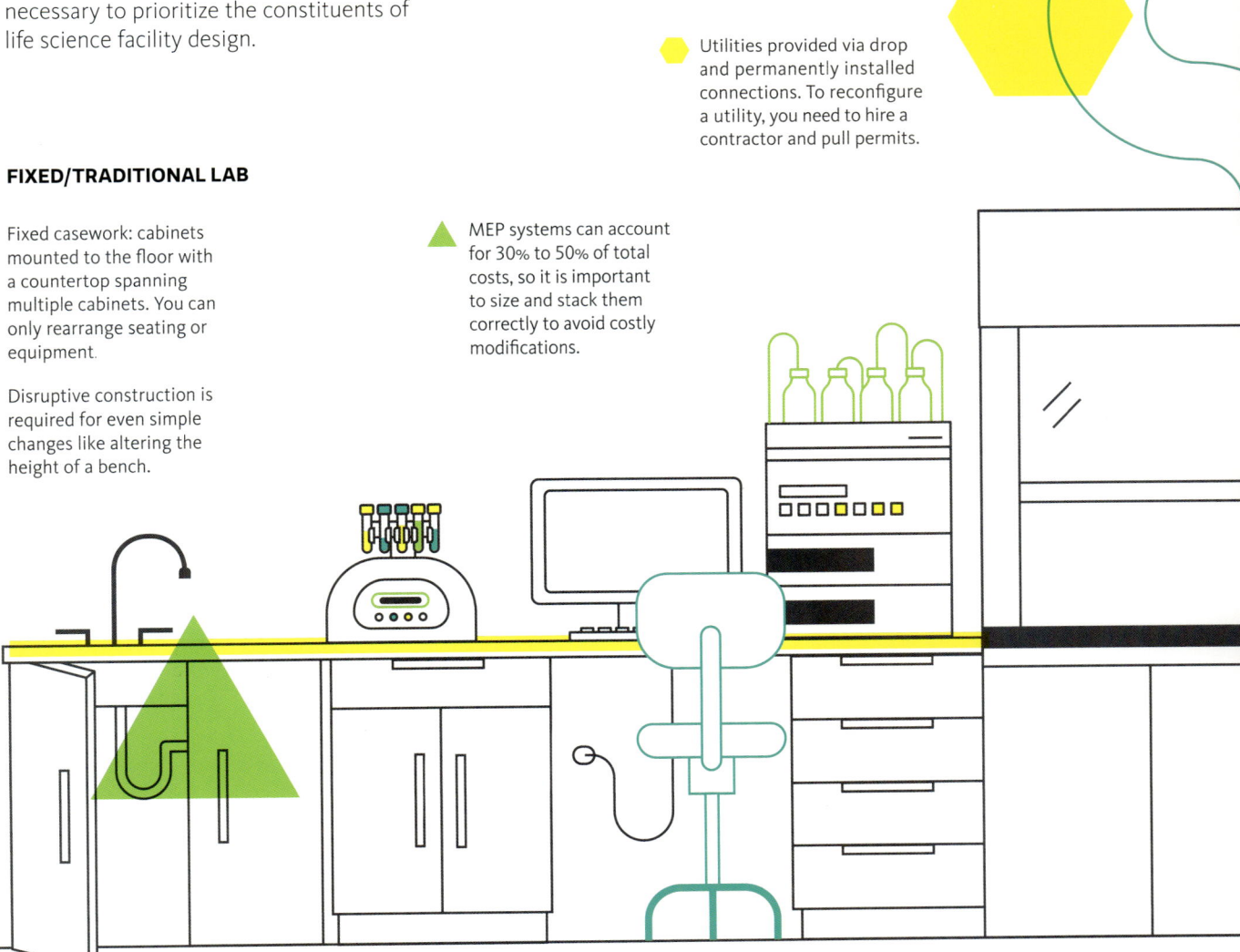

Utilities provided via drop and permanently installed connections. To reconfigure a utility, you need to hire a contractor and pull permits.

**FIXED/TRADITIONAL LAB**

Fixed casework: cabinets mounted to the floor with a countertop spanning multiple cabinets. You can only rearrange seating or equipment.

Disruptive construction is required for even simple changes like altering the height of a bench.

MEP systems can account for 30% to 50% of total costs, so it is important to size and stack them correctly to avoid costly modifications.

**THE RESULTS**

A well-designed lab can reduce the need to invest in costly flexible lab space elements. Lab space is generally balanced: meaning that a lab-to-office ratio usually falls 60:40 or 40:60. The proportion varies depending on the scientific discipline, the level of artificial intelligence, the automation embedded in scientific processes, and the culture of the organization.

Survey respondents and focus group participants indicated that investment in a well-planned open lab allows it to remain relatively unchanged over time, whereas the supporting spaces for functions like cell culture, analytics, and automated processes tended to change more frequently in configuration and infrastructure. The ability to make incremental changes to accommodate new technology and systems is critical.

The traditional lab with fixed casework and lab systems is still a simple, functional model that works for many user needs. When presented with other options, however, users reported higher levels of functionality and efficiency for both adaptable and flexible lab types. Traditional/fixed labs have their shortcomings. Changing labs to offices and vice versa require costly system changes, and disruptive construction is required for even simple changes like altering the height of a bench.

As the name implies, flexible labs are situationally adaptive to a wide variety of work-type needs. They provide mobile benching and easier rearrangement, but at a high premium on initial investment.

## The ability to make incremental changes to accommodate new technology and systems is critical.

Adaptable labs are the next step up from traditional/fixed labs through providing a template for labs that can be rearranged with reduced disruption.

Flexibility and cost are somewhat of a zero-sum balance. Therefore, through our survey, we established a framework for prioritizing design objectives. Work-related priorities topped the hierarchy: survey participants placed a resounding emphasis on functionality and efficiency. The nature of day-to-day work varies between scientific uses; therefore, the ability to easily modify the lab at the user interface, distribution, and building systems levels of intervention allows functional and efficient work.

Finances are a top concern too, however, as cost is grouped into the same conversation on practicality. As a first cost, traditional/fixed labs have relatively low construction costs. However, as demand for change increases over time, rigidity causes new expenditures at a greater cost. Lower-priority goals for survey respondents included design parameters that are more abstract or do not coincide with day-to-day work requirements. Examples included resiliency, sustainability, and aesthetic choices, or the look and feel of lab space.

**LAB PRIORITIES**

Rank of priorities among the top primary goals for a new lab.

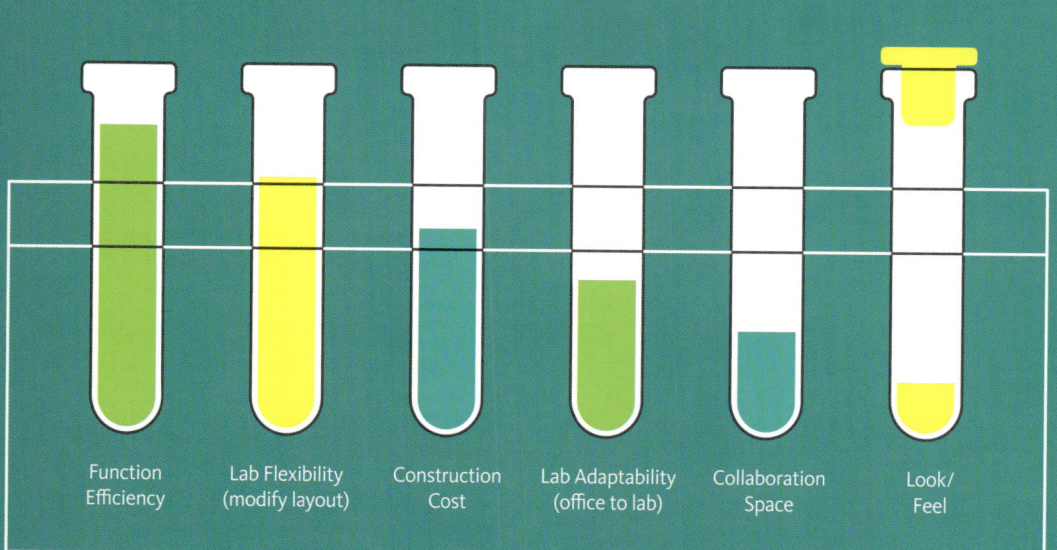

- Function Efficiency
- Lab Flexibility (modify layout)
- Construction Cost
- Lab Adaptability (office to lab)
- Collaboration Space
- Look/Feel

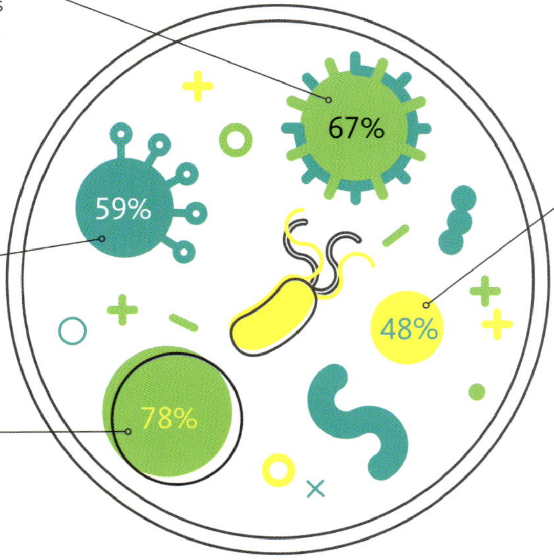

- Three-zone configuration lab (lab/flex zone/office) is the most effective design. **67%**
- Ability to maintain operations during lab renovation is critical. **59%**
- The needs of an individual lab will change frequently. **48%**
- Office/lab adjacency should be maximized. **78%**

### What people told us
Percentage of people who agree to some of the topics that were presented to them.

**67%** It's critical to maximize flexible lab area.

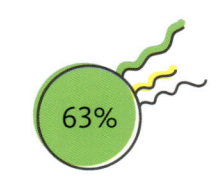

**63%** Large spaces should be flexible; small spaces should be fixed.

**44%** Lab-related building systems have the best ROI.

**67%** Shared lab support spaces increase collaboration.

## A well-planned open lab can remain relatively unchanged over time.

### DESIGN IMPLICATIONS

**A three-zone configuration is an optimal configuration for most scientific uses.** An approach that allows for a flex zone between lab and office space allows proportions to change with less capital investment over time, without an overwhelming investment in lab infrastructure for an entire floor. The needs of an individual lab will change frequently, so a design with effective proportionality can relieve the pressure of needing an overly flexible lab.

**Future-proofing life science labs requires mapping current and future MEP system configurations.** Even though end users are not concerned with building systems after cutting the weighty check to build them, routine efficiency is stymied without considering the inevitability of maintenance to these systems and changes to accommodate future uses.

**At the individual scientist level, the cost of lab furniture/casework (which amounts to 7% to 12% of initial construction cost) should be considered in the context of its life cycle.** It is twice as expensive to install mobile casework as fixed casework, but the former has lower life cycle costs because modifications generally do not require construction. The case for mobile casework is even more compelling in Europe, where vertical adjustability of the work surface for ergonomics is required by law. As is true with MEP systems, the mix of lab-furniture approaches to support a flexible and adaptable design is dependent on the type of scientific use and anticipated need for change over time.

**We should not overplan for flexibility.** We must anticipate change over the short term, and this includes forecasting anything from technological change to installing the right MEP systems. In proper forecasting, adaptable and flexible life science lab design can create greater value than traditional labs over time. We recognize the potential to overbuild up front because it may be hard to conceptualize what is needed in the long term. A risk to flexible or adaptable lab types is sunken costs from depreciation.

### WHAT'S NEXT

As life science labs evolve, we will revisit our taxonomy of space types so that we can better articulate which variables help or hurt our shared design goals. For instance, survey responses de-emphasized the need for larger collaboration spaces; however, as user needs evolve, there may be a reversal in which work zones require a greater allocation of space. In each instance of change, we will continue to quantify and qualify how adaptable and flexible labs ebb and flow to inform our future work.

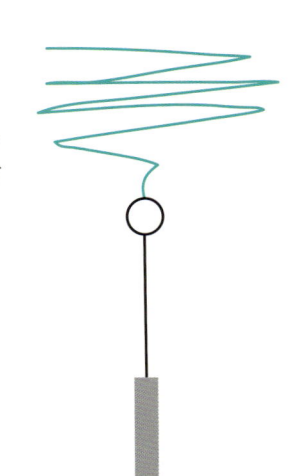

162    Shifting the Workplace Narrative

**Johnson & Johnson Innovation—JLABS**
Toronto, Canada

JLABS @ Toronto was built to attract, support, and inspire emerging pharmaceutical, medical device, consumer and digital health companies. The innovative concept blends a state-of-the-art laboratory environment with a hospitality-centric collaboration and event space, giving startups access to essential infrastructure, educational programs, and a global network of industry experts and venture capitalists.

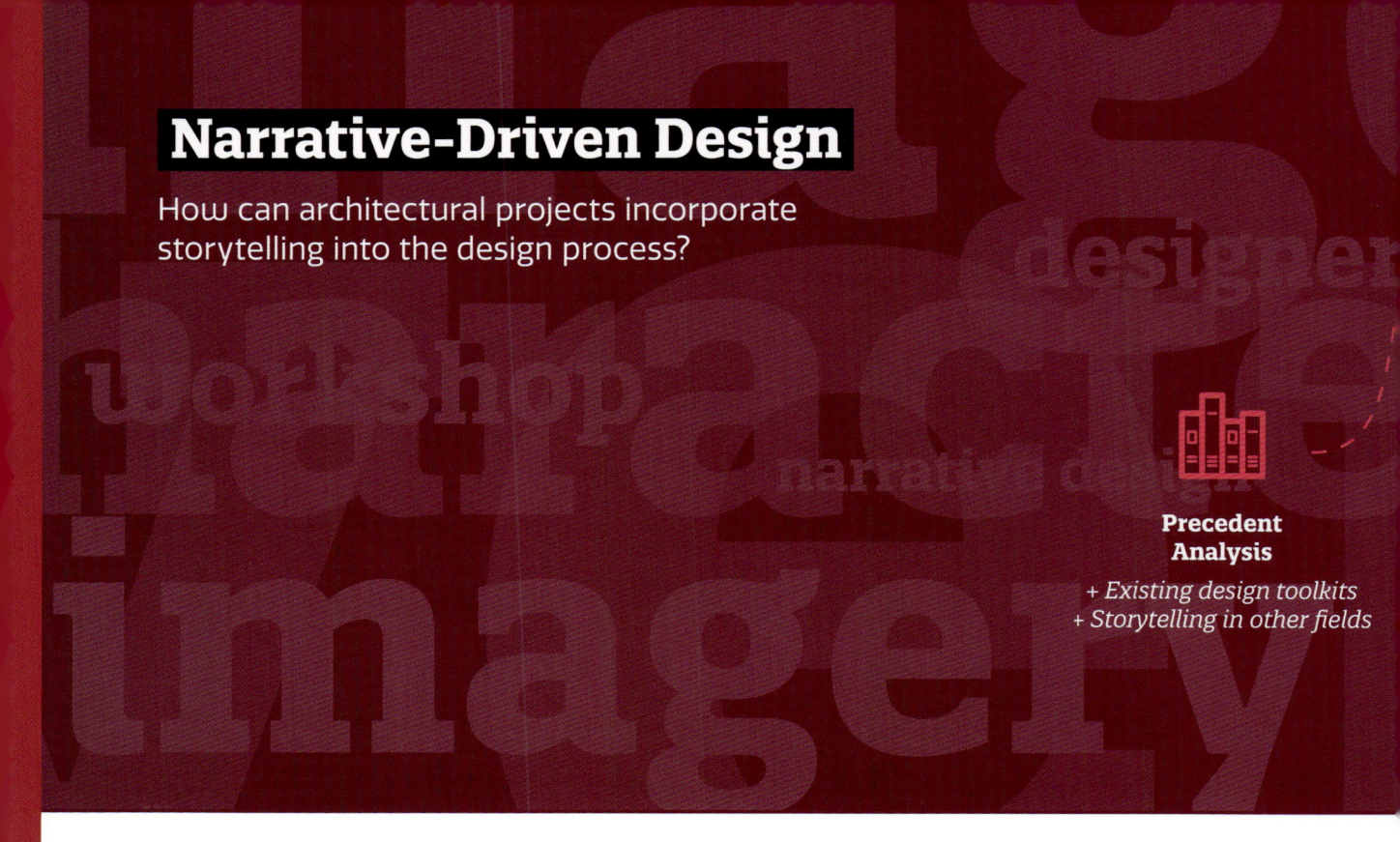

# Narrative-Driven Design

How can architectural projects incorporate storytelling into the design process?

**Precedent Analysis**
+ *Existing design toolkits*
+ *Storytelling in other fields*

**WHAT WE DID**

**We created a narrative design framework to help designers integrate storytelling best practices into their design process.** To accomplish this, we conducted research into the structure and function of a narrative, and examined how storytelling is used in other industries such as branding, advertising, graphic design, entertainment, and service design. We then interviewed several designers with strong narrative-based perspectives to understand their design process. We also studied projects with a strong narrative focus to understand how teams successfully implemented stories in the resulting design solutions. Finally, we held an all-day workshop with a film producer to better understand the elements of a successful narrative.

**THE CONTEXT**

Storytelling is one of the oldest and most essential human activities. Narratives are already being used in the design process, but without a shared or documented approach, leading to mixed results. Too often, project narratives are introduced after a project is complete as a way of documenting what happened or positioning the project after the fact. This misses a key opportunity. Instead, we should leverage the human connection we have to narratives in our work—from a project's inception to its completion.

A narrative approach can help capture **deep-rooted sentiments** about a project, clarify and reinforce the project's goals, and provide an **overall design intent** that guides the entire project team.

**Film Producer Work Session**
+ Learning from a narrative expert

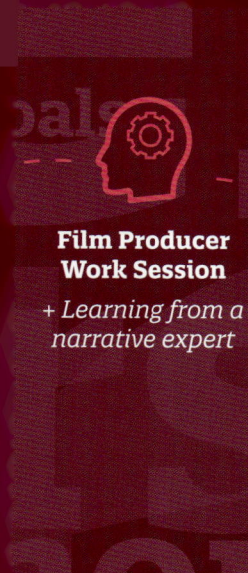

*"Including a story in a building creates a level of meaning and connection to the patron or user that can be engaging and provoking."*

–William A. Browne, Jr., FAIA, LEED AP

**Background Research**
+ What is a narrative?
+ Literature review

**Project Case Studies**
+ Learning from successful projects

**Designer Interviews**
+ Discovering personal process
+ Understanding the need

## THE RESULTS

Four key components of storytelling parallel major parts of the built environment. These components can help a team and/or clients to explore what is important to the narrative of a future place:

**Characters:** the people who will engage with the project, experiencing and reacting to its exterior shape and interior spatial qualities.

**Imagery:** the physical characteristics of a project that will appeal to one's senses, evoke a mood, and elicit an emotional response. Imagery can express an attitude and create iconic, memorable moments.

**Backstory:** the accumulated history of the site that encompasses both the physical context and the human activity that has shaped it.

**Theme:** the underlying message of the project that the architect/designer is conveying with the design; the universal belief that touches on the human experience.

## DESIGN IMPLICATIONS

**Most narrative-based designs incorporate more than one storytelling element.** The case studies we examined indicated that one component usually isn't enough to convey a unified narrative throughout a structure. Designers should consider opportunities to highlight various aspects of the chosen narrative throughout the space.

**A strong, well-defined narrative can serve as a North Star for a project.** A narrative can capture the client's deep-rooted sentiments about the project, reinforce the client's goals, and provide an overall design intent that focuses and directs the entire project team. Additionally, a strong story can make the project memorable and establish a strong vision that helps the project weather inevitable difficulties.

## WHAT'S NEXT

We have developed a prototypical toolkit and narrative guide. The Narrative Design Toolkit can help architects and designers gather meaningful information, find inspiration, and connect with the client's vision. The toolkit will help to introduce clients to the narrative design process. We will test the toolkit and guide on live projects to evaluate the usefulness of the tools.

**Narrative Design Framework**
+ Tying story to the built environment

**+**

**Narrative Design Toolkit**
+ Resources for the design process and client engagement

# Rapid Workplace Redesign

How can we make workplace design more agile in volatile industries?

**WHAT WE DID**

**We developed a framework and accompanying set of mixed-methods research tools to rapidly design and deliver flexible workplace strategies.**

We used energy sector clients as a pilot to develop the model, and began by holding a series of roundtable discussions with energy sector leaders to understand the emerging forces driving the industry, workplace, and workforce. This helped us grasp the ways that the physical environment, technology, and human behavior intersect in energy workspaces. We then completed pilot projects for three local energy industry clients that were seeking a value-driven approach to workspace. Each pilot had a different scope, enabling us to test our tools and methods on projects of various scales.

**THE CONTEXT**

Organizations are increasingly required to navigate volatile and complex business climates. The energy sector is uniquely susceptible to environmental, economic, technology, societal, and geopolitical disruptions, which have both local and global repercussions. Anything from natural disasters, intelligent automation, infectious diseases, and political turmoil can influence the health and profit of the energy market—and its ability to maintain the employment of its workforce.

According to a recent study conducted by University of Houston researchers, the most recent oil bust resulted in more than 215,000 jobs lost. From a survey of affected former employees, the study found that nearly 90% remained unemployed or had left the energy sector entirely.

Workforce reductions tend to leave excess space and furniture in their wake, often making office environments appear oversized and underutilized. Energy sector workplaces need to convey a robust, healthy culture to attract and retain employees, but often do not have the resources for full-scale renovations or design overhauls.

This poses a dual challenge: a growing shortage of skilled workers drives the necessity to recruit and engage new talent as well as maintain industry veterans, while the volatility means energy sector workplaces must be readily adaptable to staff fluctuations.

> New workplace design and management tools can help accelerate innovation and move the workplace from a "survive" to "thrive" mindset.

## Local disruptors for our clients

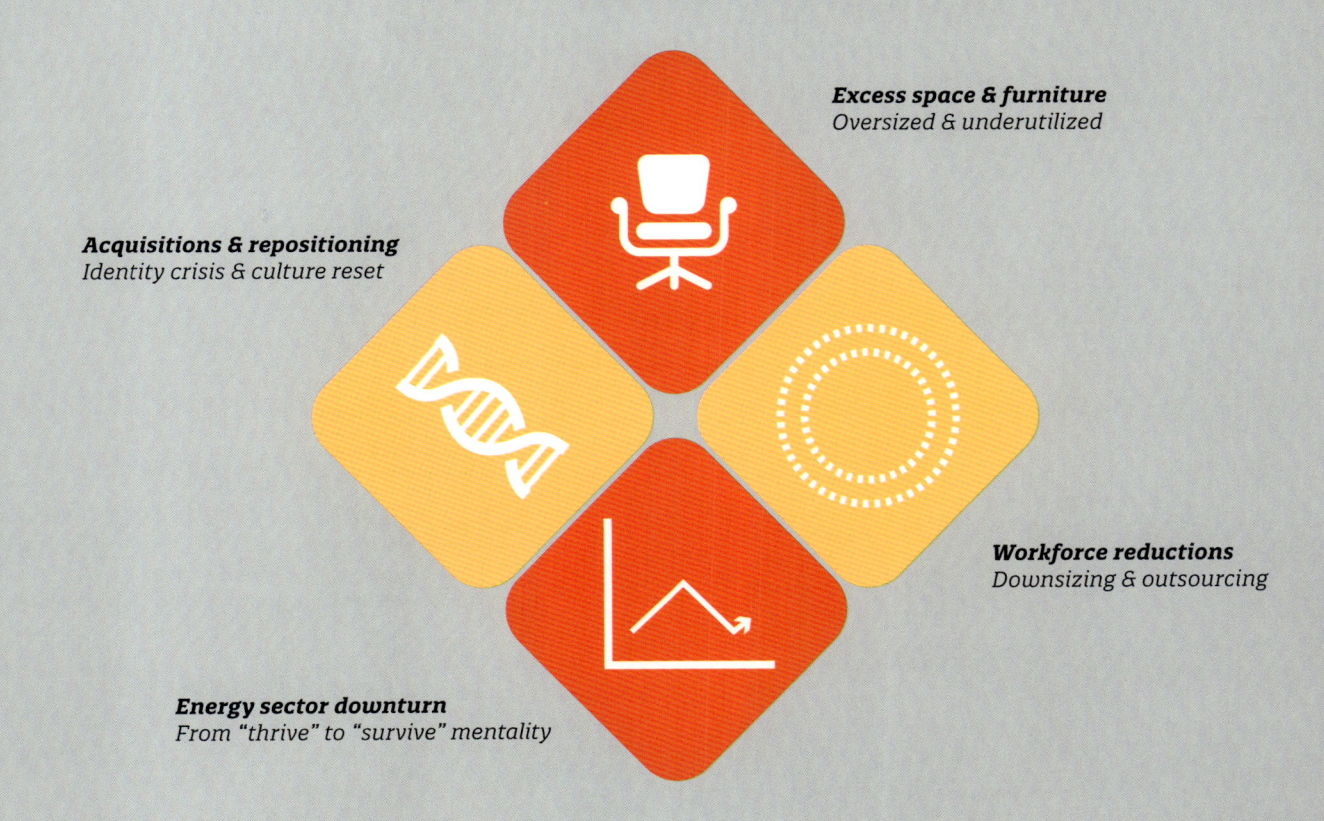

**Excess space & furniture**
Oversized & underutilized

**Acquisitions & repositioning**
Identity crisis & culture reset

**Workforce reductions**
Downsizing & outsourcing

**Energy sector downturn**
From "thrive" to "survive" mentality

### Energy sector disruptors

The energy sector is susceptible to a variety of disruptive events and circumstances.

| | | | |
|---|---|---|---|
| **Environmental disruptors** | Natural disasters | Extreme weather events | Biodiversity loss |
| **Economic disruptors** | Intelligent automation | Digital reality VR/AR/MR | Cyber dependency |
| **Technology disruptors** | Fiscal crisis | Asset bubbles | Unemployment/ underemployment |
| **Societal disruptors** | Unemployment underemployment | Food/water crisis | Immigration/ involuntary migration |
| **Geopolitical disruptors** | Infectious diseases | Social instability | Institutional failure |

**THE RESULTS**

**We envisioned a new process to engage the client and iterate rapidly.** Our goal was to deliver successful pilot projects using existing furniture and resources within organizations. Engaging everyone with an active role from the onset made the design process smoother. This early participation brought diverse and extensive insight, as well as improved buy-in later in the process.

**A mixed-methods toolkit supports rapid iteration, user engagement, and measurable results.** The tools used in our pilot projects included the following:

- Surveys and scorecards that allowed us to gain pre- and post-project perspectives through customized workplace surveys.

- Ethnographic interviews that enabled us to understand individual experience and personal rituals in the workplace.

- Focus groups and workshops to discuss how teams and communities use workspace to collaborate and learn.

- On-site observation to document how specific actions, environments, information, objects, and users create a holistic workplace.

**We organized our discussions around a simple framework: individual, team, and community.** By planning around these zones, the new, flexible environments increased the variety, choice, and capacity of the pilot floors, no matter the scale of the project. One client's total workstations increased from 171 to 233, an increase of 35%. Another client's workstations increased from 40 to 62, an increase of 55%.

**DESIGN IMPLICATIONS**

**Start smart and with a purpose. It all starts with a "why?"** A clear starting point clarifies the vision, strategy, and metrics that will define the parameters of the project. Rapid solutions are achievable if such logistics are worked out in advance—particularly when stakeholders are engaged broadly and early.

**Reimagine, remix, and rethink the way space can be used.** Organize and layer clear zones to address individual, team, and community functions. Build new typologies using components from the existing inventory of furniture. Vary high and low tech to support a variety of collaboration styles.

**Consider user types and profiles, as well as the organization's brand or identity.** Who will make up the departments or teams using the pilot? What are their specific needs and concerns? Are they engaged throughout the design process? Pilots are a change management opportunity. Poor communication about the project's intent can hinder success and even create resistance.

*"You can't say to someone, 'I want you to think differently, build differently, behave differently...now go back to your desk.'"*

—David Kidder, Co-Founder & CEO, Bionic

**RE-IMAGINE THE MODEL**
Organize clear zones to address individual, team, and community functions

| | | |
|---|---|---|
| INDIVIDUAL | Resident neighborhood | Nomadic camp |
| TEAM | Meeting commons | Specialty zones |
| COMMUNITY | Resource center | Socialize hub |

**RE-MIX THE FURNITURE**
Build new typologies using components from the existing inventory of furniture

**RE-THINK THE MEASURES**
Identify metrics to support a business case around choice, productivity, and well-being

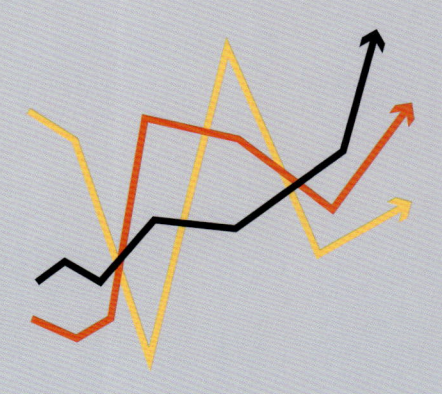

**WHAT'S NEXT**

Staying agile in the face of disruption is a conversation happening in C-suites across the globe. Many clients are rethinking how their space supports their business model, decision-making process, and workforce, especially in the wake of climate change–related weather events. We want to apply our learnings to explore design resilience in the face of major disruptions—both natural and man-made. Additionally, as built prototypes for flexible working, further studies can inform how these environments are envisioned, designed, and delivered.

# Building Repositioning Strategies

How can we codify the range of repositioning strategies employed in today's market?

**WHAT WE DID**

**We conducted an audit of projects involving the repositioning of buildings, from which we generated an exhaustive list of repositioning strategies.** This enabled us to create a list of typologies to inform future work. The subject city of our research, New York, is an epicenter of global real estate, and through using one of the planet's largest real estate markets, our findings are applicable to most markets. In all, we worked with 35 clients and over 50 buildings to shape our ideas into an actionable framework.

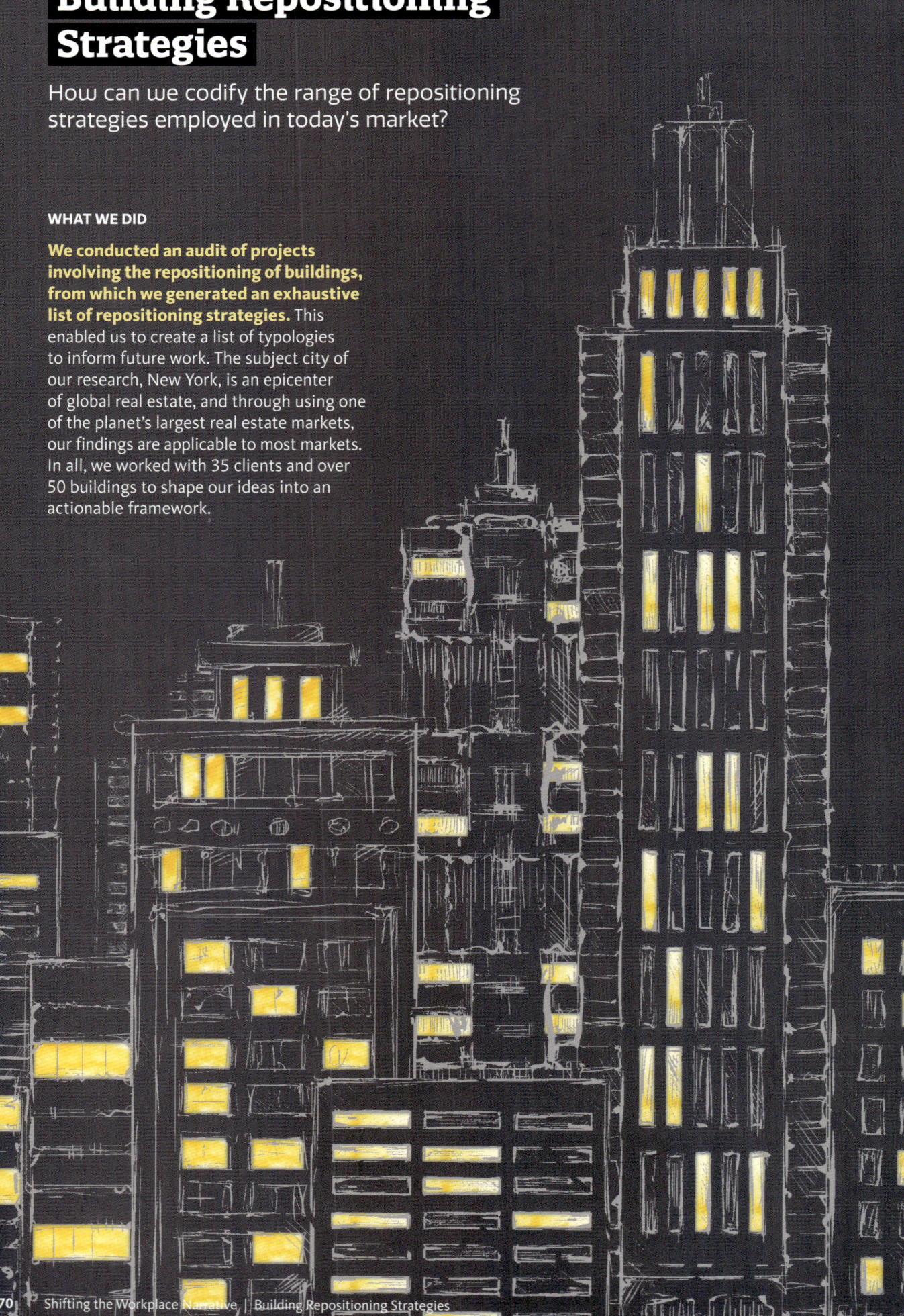

# The right building repositioning strategy needs to align with the values of your tenants.

**THE CONTEXT**

Money is the bottom line of any building reposition; landlords purchase income streams, not buildings. The goal in any repositioning is to deliver the greatest value, but as trends in tenancy shift, the ways of delivering that value become less defined. According to CBRE Fast Forward, 88% of tenants want more from their landlords, or more sophisticated amenities and a greater sense of community. The types of amenities being considered are expanding and in addition to material changes, there is a trend toward interbuilding communities. Networking through serendipitous interactions between people from different companies is an element of workplace happiness—a service that landlords are beginning to deliver.

The shift in repositioning and amenities strategies follows broader trends in work and the workplace. For both how and where we work, the pace of change has evolved. We work faster and we work with immediacy, and talent is moving around more. Since 1955, there has been a 52% increase in Fortune 500 company turnover. This has real implications for real estate decision makers, including a reduced ability to forecast outside the short term: 63% of real estate decision makers plan less than three years out. This is driven by real estate shifts in specific markets. In our subject city, New York City, real estate in Brooklyn has become more expensive than in Manhattan; the downtown area has transitioned from a finance hub to a technology focus; and the Meatpacking District has transitioned from heavy industry to a luxury market.

**THE RESULTS**

Amidst the changing market tides, if we clearly spell out our options for building repositioning, we will be one step ahead of the inevitable and unforeseen change in circumstance. We created a menu of seven key real estate repositioning solutions. Each service is an actionable approach, and choosing an approach will vary according to geography, target clients, and financial position. As we illustrate each strategy under *New Services*, we acknowledge that in many circumstances, more than one strategy will be leveraged.

We are using these typologies to establish metrics of efficacy, or a quantitative understanding of each strategy. For example, our *Neighborhooding* intervention led brokers to market our interventions at a blended rent increase of $30/sf (from $40 to $70/sf). Another owner, after implementing a *Tenancy Products* strategy, sold its property for $516 million, just four years after purchasing it for $160 million. Looking forward, we will continue to categorize and contextualize each case story, mapping out the idiosyncratic context behind how and why a strategy met, or did not meet, our expectations.

| SEVEN KEY REPOSITIONING SOLUTIONS | NEW SERVICES |
|---|---|
| PROPERTY VALUE DIVERSITY → | VALUE ALIGNMENT |
| TENANT SOPHISTICATION → | VOLUMETRIC LEASING |
| AMENITY REQUIREMENTS → | HOSPITALITY MODELING |
| TENANT FLEXIBILITY → | TENANCY PRODUCTS |
| CO-LOCATION EXPECTATIONS → | ECOSYSTEM CURATION |
| PROPERTY VALUE DIVERSITY → | NEIGHBORHOODING |
| URBAN EXPERIENCE → | STREETSCAPE ENGINEERING |

DESIGN IMPLICATIONS

# Value Alignment

A spectrum of values across real estate typologies requires a targeted approach. Landlords that leverage this strategy acknowledge the tipping point where leveraging a new building outfit, or class upgrade, is used to achieve rents that outweigh the initial investment.

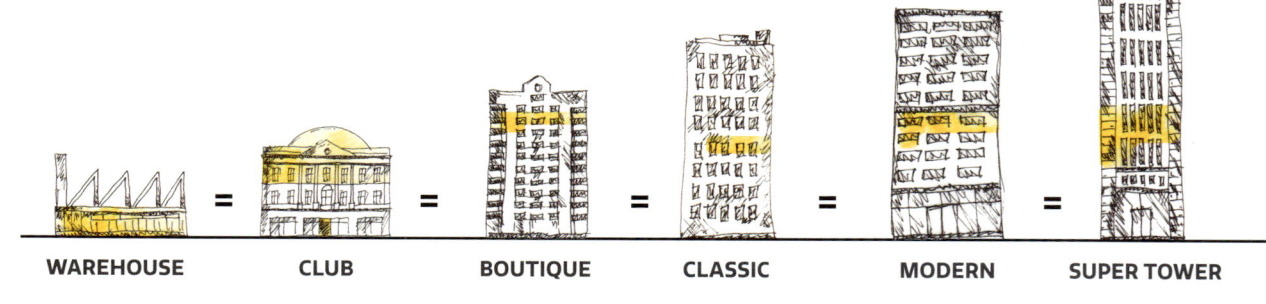

WAREHOUSE = CLUB = BOUTIQUE = CLASSIC = MODERN = SUPER TOWER

# Volumetric Leasing

Changing demands require a new volumetric products-based approach to repositioning. Evolving tenant demands prompt a new volumetric approach to repositioning, or Volumetric Leasing. This approach confects tenancy like a puzzle, understanding that space requirements run the gamut—a scope from single-tenancy to highly segmented micro-office spaces. And most tenant-block solutions will achieve a middle ground.

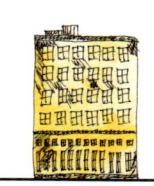

**FLAGSHIP**
Single-Tenant Building

**COWORKING**
Business-Ready Office Suites

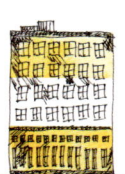

**DUPLEX**
Volumetric Double-Height Spaces

**TOWNHOUSE**
Adjacent Tenants with a Common Core

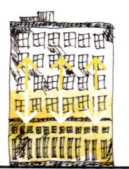

**CO-LOCATION**
Academic and Industry

**ECOSYSTEM**
Single-Floor Environments

# Hospitality Modeling

The millennial generation and technology industry have inspired new employee demands. One differentiation between building classes is amenities. While falling under the same umbrella of capital improvements, an amenity focus acknowledges the services, perks, and notable spaces that distinguish the eminent from the quotidian. Both a growing millennial generation in the workforce and a booming technology industry are forcing landlords and building management to consider more robust amenities.

**17%** of an average tenant's portfolio is amenities
–Gensler

**79%** of millennials would buy an experience over a product
–Eventbrite

# Tenancy Products

Population not capacity defines a successful property. Properties need to have the flexibility to accommodate different client types. These tenancy products may include white box or livable space.

**52%** of real estate decision makers plan less than three years out
–Gensler

**63%** increase in Fortune 500 company turnover since 1955
–Wired

172  Shifting the Workplace Narrative | Building Repositioning Strategies

## Ecosystem Curation

Ecosystem curation brings together education and industry into shared spaces to deliver on community building. This service offering relates to a theme of diversity.

Co-location expectations are putting education and industry together in shared spaces to create a sense of community.

## Neighborhooding

Neighborhooding is remapping cities to create defined, distinct, and valued places. Context is key. Each property operates within a unique environment. Strategies lead to a re-address, re-orient (for example, a different neighborhood, Financial District to Tribeca), or re-brand.

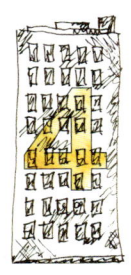

**RE-ADDRESS**
53rd St. to 3rd Ave.

**RE-ORIENT**
Financial District to Tribeca

**RE-BRAND**
17th St. to Union Square North

## Streetscape Engineering

While overhauled amenity options can be costly, a cost-effective solution may include leveraging retail spaces to minimize workplace amenities. This approach is called Streetscape Engineering. While this option does include the capital to render a space for retail use, a paying tenant could potentially offset the initial investment. Design solutions require streetscape engineering, or including frontages, arcades, beacons, pavilions, concourses in design.

**FRONTAGES**
5 Penn Plaza
Storefront

**ARCADES**
101 Franklin
Retail Lobby

**BEACONS**
1 Vanderbilt
Observation Deck

**PAVILIONS**
GM Building
Apple Cube

**CONCOURSES**
601 Lexington
Marketplace

### WHAT'S NEXT

Now that we have a framework of terms and relevant case studies, we can implement our framework across different markets and properties. There is power in categorization: when every group participant speaks the same language, we are empowered with quicker and better decision-making. Further, our framework of repositioning strategies is exhaustive, therefore designers can ensure all strategies are considered before action.

There are many drivers of value, such as the many factors that play into wealth being drawn into a particular market or demographical shifts. As we develop more case studies, our microscope of understanding becomes finer and finer; we will move closer to a whole understanding of the cost of renovations and conversions across time.

# Future-Proofing Design Strategies

How can understanding future scenarios encourage innovative design today?

**Our process helps clients conceptualize relatable futures using narratives built on interrelating trends.**

**WHAT WE DID**

**We developed and piloted a methodology to outline, analyze, and prototype future business scenarios as part of the design and decision-making process.**

It is imperative to ensure the resiliency and performance of our core design strategies over time, particularly in a business climate that is increasingly divergent and fast-paced. By broadening the scope of research beyond real estate and taking on a divergent approach to find disruptive change, we sought to decode the changing needs of human experiences.

Our process helps clients conceptualize relatable futures using narratives built on interrelating trends. Each trend contains spatial, behavioral, and emotional layers that can be workshopped to solicit bold design for future-proof solutions. This process is designed to synthesize trends into workable scenarios, and to workshop solutions for projects across the spectrum of industries, sectors, and design platforms.

In our first beta test, we developed future workplace-focused "worlds" based on the impact of identity, technology, and environment. Each world was designed to help participants imagine and prepare for the workplace of tomorrow. These worlds can serve as an effective design story for teams and clients to use when searching for a future-forward design solution.

**THE CONTEXT**

At the core of this research effort was the idea that while you can't predict the future, you can invent it. Too often, cognitive biases inhibit us from seeing past our immediate environment, relationships, customers, or variables. With the increasing pace of change, even the most experienced design professionals may miss important signals if rigorous processes don't help filter the noise.

Our goal is to help designers and clients create proactive, informed solutions with the future in mind. We believe every business should have a command of disruptive economic, social, and environmental forces, and find a way to build change-resilient design strategies. In other words, *every organization must be in the business of inventing its future.*

# Trend Research

In assessing today's most salient trends, three core themes emerge: identity, technology, and environment. The graphics below illustrate the magnitude of each theme and the networked relationship between trends.

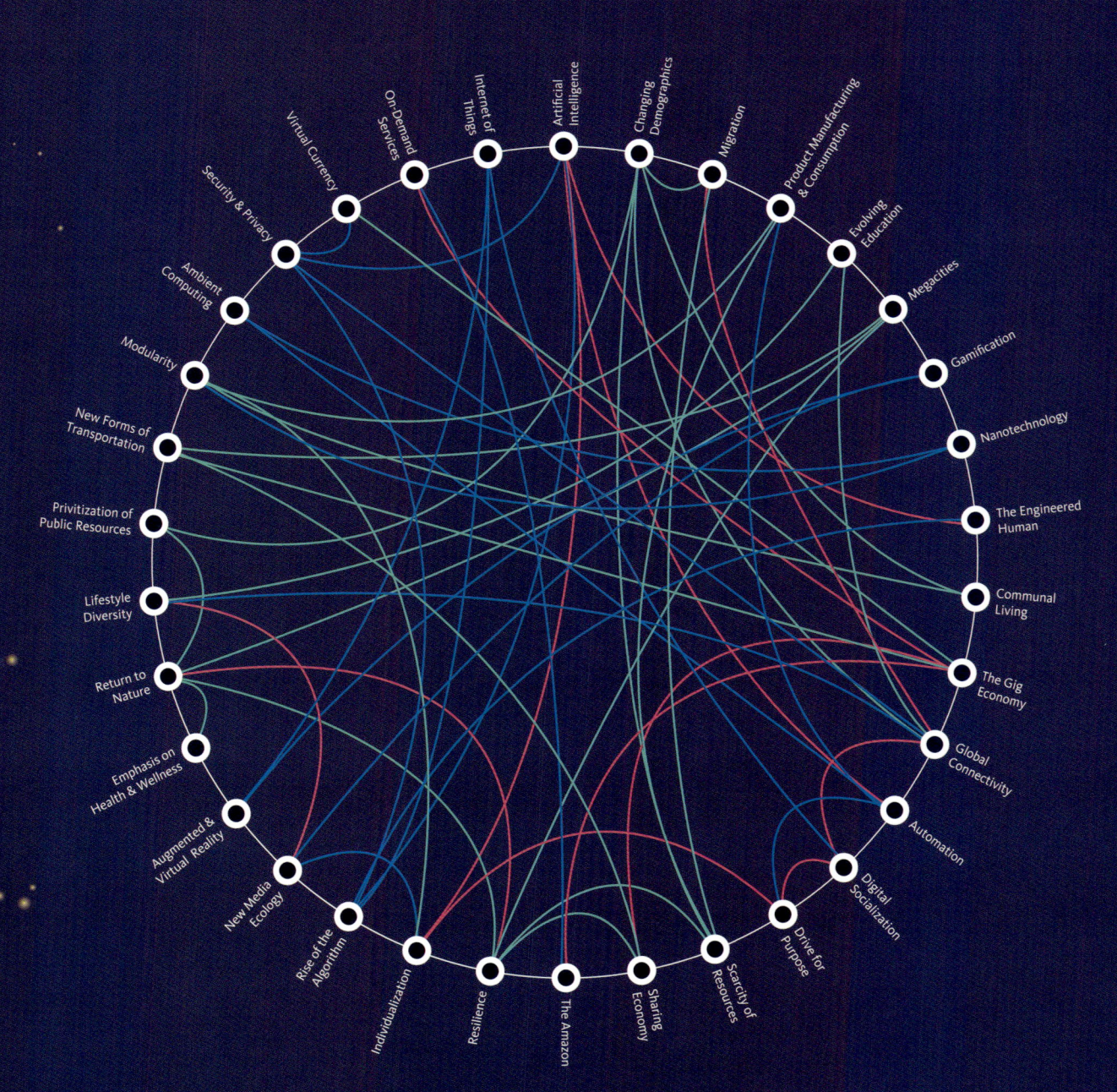

Identity · Environment · Technology

- Artificial Intelligence
- Changing Demographics
- Migration
- Product Manufacturing & Consumption
- Evolving Education
- Megacities
- Gamification
- Nanotechnology
- The Engineered Human
- Communal Living
- The Gig Economy
- Global Connectivity
- Automation
- Digital Socialization
- Drive for Purpose
- Scarcity of Resources
- Sharing Economy
- The Amazon Effect
- Resilience
- Individualization
- Rise of the Algorithm
- New Media Ecology
- Virtual & Augmented Reality
- Health & Wellness
- Return to Nature
- Lifestyle Diversity
- Privatization of Public Resources
- New Forms of Transportation
- Modularity
- Ambient Computing
- Security & Privacy
- Virtual Currency
- On-Demand Services
- Internet of Things

**THE RESULTS**

Our methodology for the creation of disruptive, conceptual future worlds forms the basis for productive, exploratory analysis and ideation around the future. Our three-phase process is structured as an interactive, in-person workshop. The workshop begins with a trend analysis activity, with the goal of dispelling cognitive biases and opening possibilities of the future. Each trend has a thorough historical backdrop and fictional players.

Participants are then led through a process of synergizing this context into an informed narrative of what the future looks like. A "change triggers" exercise explores participants' reactions to world narratives and our potential approaches to design. The beta test of our workshop—run in Gensler's Washington, D.C., office—also provided insight into how to refine our futures-strategy process moving forward.

### Phase 1: Exploration

Armed with a comprehensive understanding of trends, users, and disruptors that extend the boundaries of a given problem's space, we begin to formulate themes that distill order from chaos. Intersecting these themes and layering in a client's business goals provides a springboard for concepting and scenario modeling. Results from Phase 1 should outline a gap analysis of current and future business expectations, a highlight of critical user needs, and a map of signal pressures over a stretch of time.

### Phase 2: Scenario Modeling

Designed as an immersive, co-creative process, Phase 2 involves building highly-practical backdrops for exploring how a business might respond when certain economic certainties, cultural norms, and operating assumptions are turned on their heads. These tangible yet provocative scenarios allow us to envision new directions and spatial models for our clients. Depending on the engagement, this phase could result in a set of future concepts, scripted experiences that illustrate future user needs, or even podcasts that allow users to fantasize about future narratives.

### Phase 3: Implementation

After we've clarified the frontier and concepts from the future, we turn our focus to the tactical moves we can make today. Working with design teams, we create phasing plans, rollout strategies, and design solutions that make our clients more change-resilient and future-ready. This could include spatial recommendations for future-proofing designs, change management required to adjust to futures, or targeted avenues for design exploration.

**DESIGN IMPLICATIONS**

**Futures thinking turns weaknesses into opportunities.** When disruptions can be addressed proactively, design teams can continually set new best practices that speak to each client's unique needs. In this way, the process is a form of innovation, and an opportunity to feed a larger thought-leadership business or create a knowledge IP profit center focused on the future of opportunities in design.

**Trends are only the beginning of the conversation.** Trends are, by definition, near-term documentation of processes already happening. Our process predicates a more sophisticated exploration process, unpacking the difference between flash-in-the-pan headlines, trend signals, and larger mega-trend trajectories.

**We need to envision multiple future worlds.** Our process calls for multiple viewpoints, or different vantage points on what may matter in the future. By understanding that each future can play out on a spectrum from probable to provocative, we can welcome new and diverse voices into our process.

**Our goal is to help our clients invent their own ideal.** Beginning a design project with an exploratory vision of the future can yield more innovative design approaches and solutions. This process can be applied to existing engagements to "futurize" design conversations and inform larger organizational strategies.

**WHAT'S NEXT**

As we continue to hone these methods, our goal is to expand our work with clients whose goal is to change the status quo and proactively confront disruption. As we apply our methodology more, we will continue to build a stronger interface between strategy and built reality, connecting future value to design. Ultimately, we look forward to building a network of future innovative thinking across the firm and proliferating an alternative approach to strategy.

# RBAN EXPERIENCE

gining the spaces that define
ere from stores and hotels
itals—as people's needs and

## TRAVEL AND LEISURE

**Exploring Multigenerational Travel**

**Research Team**

Florent Duperrin
Anna Kirkham
Thue Thuy Tran
Amii Yokouchi

**The Impact of Airbnb on Hospitality**

**Research Team**

Prince Ambooken
Vincenzo Centinaro
Lorraine Francis
Steven Harrell
Todd Heiser
Lisa Hibler
Hilary Ingram
Nathan Klinge

## ENHANCED EDUCATION

202 **A Toolkit for Active Learning Environments**

**Research Team**

Keith Besserud
Allison Bulgart
Ashley Claussen
Pedro Coivo
Sarah Jones
Patricia Nobre
Stephanie Park
Mark Thaler
Meghan Webster

208 **A Comparative Analysis of Enhanced Classrooms**

**Research Team**

Pedro Coivo
Kenneth Fisher
Patricia Nobre

## COMMUNITY INSTITUTIONS

**212 A New Model for the Public Library**

**Research Team**
David Broz
Amber Cao
Mahe Hameed
Anthony Harris
Caroline LeFevre
Allison Marshall
Sara Rothholz Weiner
Bevin Savage-Yamazaki
Meghan Webster

**216 The Future of USPS Real Estate**

**Research Team**
Eric Bieber
Reid Brockmeier
John Cassidy
John Ferns
Ryan MacCrea
Shixa Patel
Brooke Rho

## OPTIMIZING HEALTH CARE

**220 A Model for Integrated Ambulatory Care Clinics**

**Research Team**
Amy Carter
James Crispino
June Deng
Ju Hyun Lee
Kelley Tapia
Richard Tyson
Nicholas Watkins

**224 Enhancing the Waiting Room Experience**

**Research Team**
Lucy Arledge
Kim Brown
Michael Crawford
Tama Duffy Day
Carina Mohammed
Louise Russell
Bonny Slater
Kevin Todd
Nick Watkins

**Research Partners**
Interior Elixir
Unity Health Care

**228 Optimizing Exam Room Design**

**Research Team**
Jin Chung
Tama Duffy Day
Joy DeWitt
Randy Guillot
Jill Mahaney
Linda Mysliwiec
Bonny Slater
Katie Smith
Nicholas Watkins

**Research Partners**
Elizabeth Melas (Rush University Medical Center)

# Retail Experience Index 2018

What can brick-and-mortar stores do to embrace a changing retail landscape?

**49%**
of shoppers are visiting to get a specific task done

**19%**
of shoppers are visiting to discover or learn something new

**10%**
of shoppers are visiting to seek inspiration or personal growth

**7%**
of shoppers are visiting for entertainment or to have fun

**15%**
of shoppers are visiting to socialize or be around people

Creating a Rich Urban Experience | Retail Experience Index 2018

## Five core intentions

Our "experience modes" offer a framework for understanding how users are engaging with stores today. Examples of these core intentions include:

**TASK**
Running an errand

**DISCOVERY**
Browsing to see what's new

**ENTERTAINMENT**
Having fun

**SOCIAL**
Shopping with friends and family

**ASPIRATION**
Seeking personal growth

### WHAT WE DID

**We explored the factors that make a great retail experience.** We measured metrics relating to physical space (functionality, ambience, and amenities), interaction (staff and technology), and expectation (product, brand, and context) to understand what combination of elements formed a great experience. Respondents rated their overall experience, likelihood of referring the store to family and friends, likelihood to return, and product quality. We then benchmarked the quality of a specific experience against average and great experiences across the United States.

### THE CONTEXT

The retail industry remains in an unprecedented state of flux. Store closures and calls for "the death of retail" or "the end of malls" seem to happen every day. At the same time, a new wave of retailers—often with their roots in e-commerce—are investing in physical presence as their businesses expand and evolve. What's becoming clear is that retail is in the midst of a dramatic shift in both the purpose and the form of physical stores.

### THE RESULTS

**The purpose of physical stores has shifted to engagement and connection.** Brick-and-mortar stores offer an opportunity to humanize brands and create community, while also promoting and highlighting product quality and value. In fact, a store's product display, organization, and design have a signficant and quantifiable impact on the quality and value a person will attribute to the products being sold.

**To many customers, online and in-store experiences are just different touchpoints for the same brand.** When set up correctly, a brand's various touchpoints with its customers complement each other, weaving a common thread of experiences across platforms. Creating memorable moments is a key to inspiring repeat business.

**Consumers are armed with more information than ever today, and their expectations have never been higher.** They expect in-store content, products, and technology to be fresh—and their experience suffers if they think it's stale. For optional items like curated content or interactive technology, if stores cannot keep it up to date, it's probably not worth having.

## 2x

People who do more than one activity in a store rate that store as one of their favorite places nearly twice as often.

## 1.6x

Millennials are 1.6 times less likely to be in task mode than baby boomers.

## 2x

Millennials are twice as likely to be in entertainment mode than baby boomers.

**Experience varies by generation.**
Percentage of respondents reporting a great experience by generation.

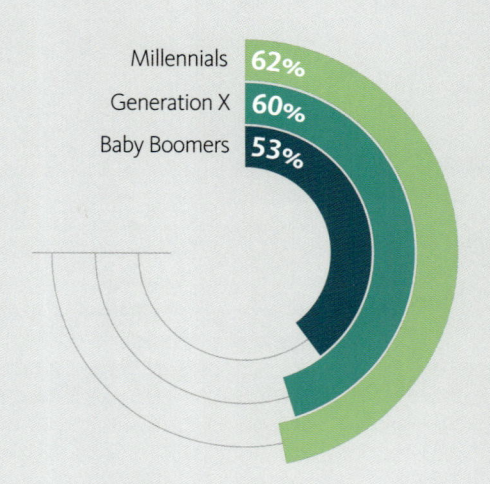

Millennials 62%
Generation X 60%
Baby Boomers 53%

### DESIGN IMPLICATIONS

**Embrace the blur.** Everyone is (and wants to be) doing everything, everywhere. Only half of shoppers today are in task mode. Others are seeking an escape from the everyday, a connection to a larger purpose, or an opportunity to learn something new. With the rise of e-commerce, it's no surprise that people visit stores for reasons other than getting something done. Allowing shoppers to perform a wider range of activities also supports the bottom line: people who do activities beyond task are more likely to have a great experience, recommend the store they visited, and make a repeat visit.

**Break older shoppers out of task-focused mindsets.** The needs, expectations, and behaviors of millennials are a main focus for many retailers for good reason. This generation of influencers and trendsetters represents a massive population with growing buying power. But they're not the only ones shopping, and for older generations, experiences often miss the mark. Experience ratings get progressively lower with age. One reason: shopping for fun is concentrated in younger generations, while boomers and Gen X shoppers are generally in task mode, even when making seemingly aspirational/ luxury-focused purchases.

**Great design expands experience.**

Percentage of respondents who do more than one activity:

- ■ Poorly designed stores
- ■ Well-designed stores

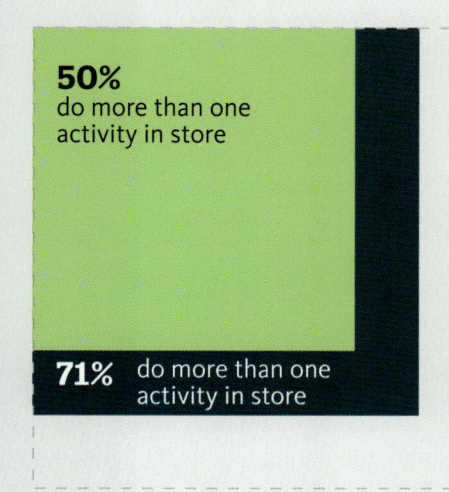

**50%** do more than one activity in store

**71%** do more than one activity in store

**Technology forms a strong impression.**

Percentage of respondents who had a great experience:

- ■ Places without the latest technology
- ■ Places with the latest technology

**39%** had a great experience

**76%** had a great experience

**Make shopping easy. Simplifying tasks creates the necessary foundation of broader emotional engagement.** When customers can easily locate needed items, they'll have more time to browse, engage, and discover new things. As online and offline continue to merge, where customers buy is less important than how they feel. Give them places to have fun, socialize, connect, and get inspired—and their business will come along with it.

**WHAT'S NEXT**

Physical stores are not going away any time soon—they are just changing. Retailers are transitioning to embrace customers who are anything but strict in their purpose for what they want from the retail experience. In an age when brick-and-mortar stores face continuous challenges from new competitors and new technologies, we will continue to investigate the latest trends of the retail experience.

# Museums Experience Index 2019

How can we better understand the interests and expectations of museum visitors?

**33%**
history museum/ historical attraction

**9%**
cultural heritage

**9%**
natural history

**11%**
children's

**25%**
art or design

**13%**
science or technology

### Where People Visited

Research based on 2,000 survey respondents who visited 850+ different museums across the U.S.

**50%**
of respondents go to museums at least twice per year

184    Creating a Rich Urban Experience  |  Museums Experience Index 2019

## What brings people to museums?

Respondents' identified their primary reason for visiting museums by experience mode.

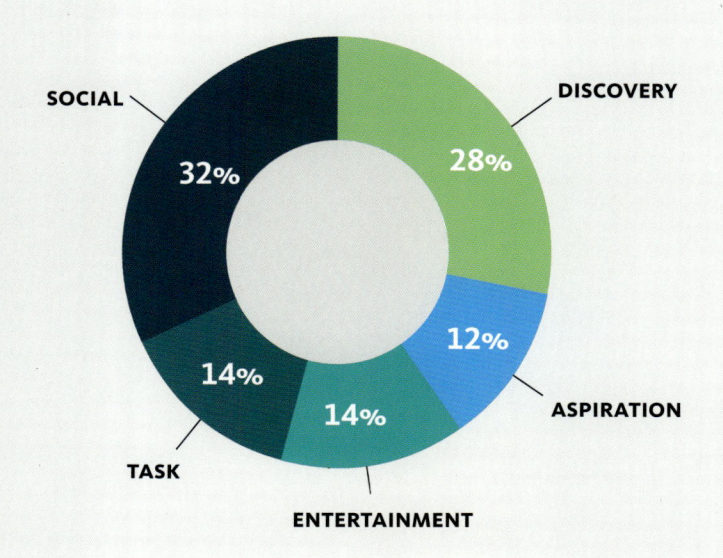

- SOCIAL 32%
- DISCOVERY 28%
- ASPIRATION 12%
- ENTERTAINMENT 14%
- TASK 14%

## 2x

People are twice as likely to visit museums for social reasons than task-oriented ones.

### WHAT WE DID

**We analyzed the museum-going experience—from preparation and planning to post-visit engagement—to understand the importance of museums as social and cultural institutions.** We began our research by conducting a yearlong study of the evolving relationship between museums and their constituencies. We also created a toolkit that could be deployed by one of our team members in any museum to study flow, visitor experience, and design. We then connected with a range of museums interested in better understanding how their audiences experienced their museums. Finally, we analyzed the results of an online, panel-based survey of over 2,000 respondents across the U.S.

### THE CONTEXT

Museums continue to play an integral role in our communities. The National Endowment of the Arts reports that one in five Americans attended at least one art exhibit or gallery over the past 12 months. However, like any other institution, museums must adapt to stay relevant. Shifting demographics, evolving visitor expectations, and technological innovations present unique challenges. Institutions are rethinking and reworking their spaces to craft memorable, engaging experiences. When done right, these changes can boost interactivity and increase revenue stability, ensuring that museums continue to occupy an important place in the public consciousness.

## Museums are places for discovery, inspiration, and growth—but that's not all.

### THE RESULTS

**Visitors expect museums to offer immersive and informative experiences; however, our analysis shows that most users do not visit museums with a specific experience in mind.** Typically, their goals are more abstract. Nearly half of respondents identified having fun, doing something exciting, or being inspired as their primary reason for visiting a museum. Even those who visited with a specific objective rarely confined their experience to a single exhibit. The adventure of the museum experience comes not only from the excitement of the exhibits, but also from not knowing what you'll see next.

## Should museums have technology?

Respondents' answer to whether they prefer a tech-centered experience or not.

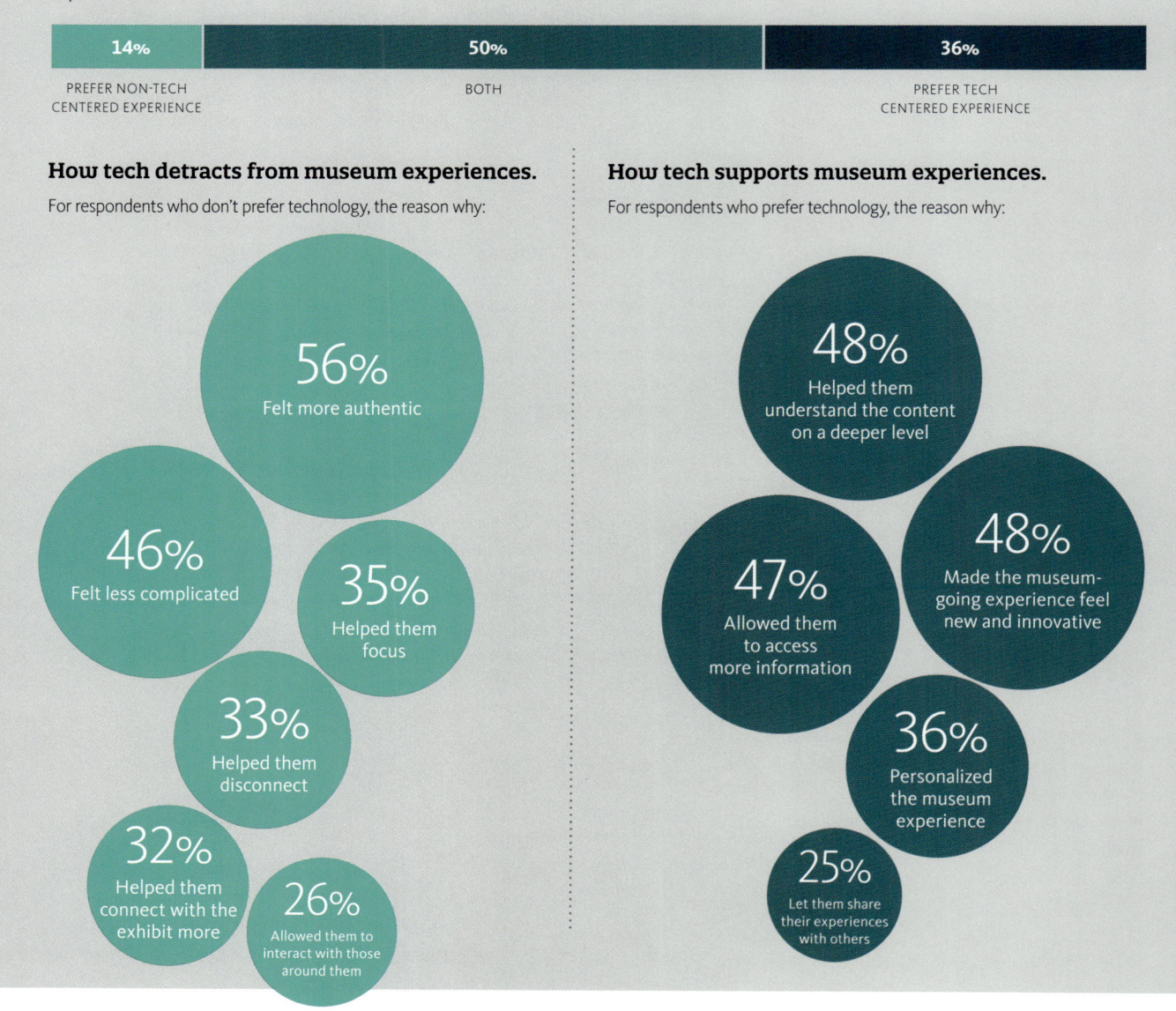

| 14% | 50% | 36% |
|---|---|---|
| PREFER NON-TECH CENTERED EXPERIENCE | BOTH | PREFER TECH CENTERED EXPERIENCE |

### How tech detracts from museum experiences.

For respondents who don't prefer technology, the reason why:

- **56%** Felt more authentic
- **46%** Felt less complicated
- **35%** Helped them focus
- **33%** Helped them disconnect
- **32%** Helped them connect with the exhibit more
- **26%** Allowed them to interact with those around them

### How tech supports museum experiences.

For respondents who prefer technology, the reason why:

- **48%** Helped them understand the content on a deeper level
- **48%** Made the museum-going experience feel new and innovative
- **47%** Allowed them to access more information
- **36%** Personalized the museum experience
- **25%** Let them share their experiences with others

### DESIGN IMPLICATIONS

**Museum visitors bring high expectations but unstructured intentions—they expect to be able to do everything.** Visitors rarely visit a museum with a specific itinerary in mind. Institutions need to create spaces that support a variety of intentions, encourage dialogue, and foster a sense of community. Ideal spaces intersperse places to relax among the exhibits and other engagement activities. This ensures that a visitor can wander through exhibits and seek out unexpected, enjoyable experiences without feeling depleted or suffering from sensory overload.

**Museums face a contradiction of expectations—visitors expect technology integration but also see value in a reflective, off-line experience.** Innovative technologies should be woven into museum exhibits without compromising the authenticity and intimacy of the visitor experience. Our research shows that the optimal balance of technology depends on museum type. Unsurprisingly, visitors to science/technology museums want tech-centered experiences. Visitors to art/design museums prefer experiences that do not integrate technology. Respondents across all six museum types want a balance of tech and non-tech integrated elements.

## How diversity affects the museum experience.

Over 25% of respondents perceived the museum they visited lacked diversity or accessibility; for these respondents, the museum offered a worse experience.

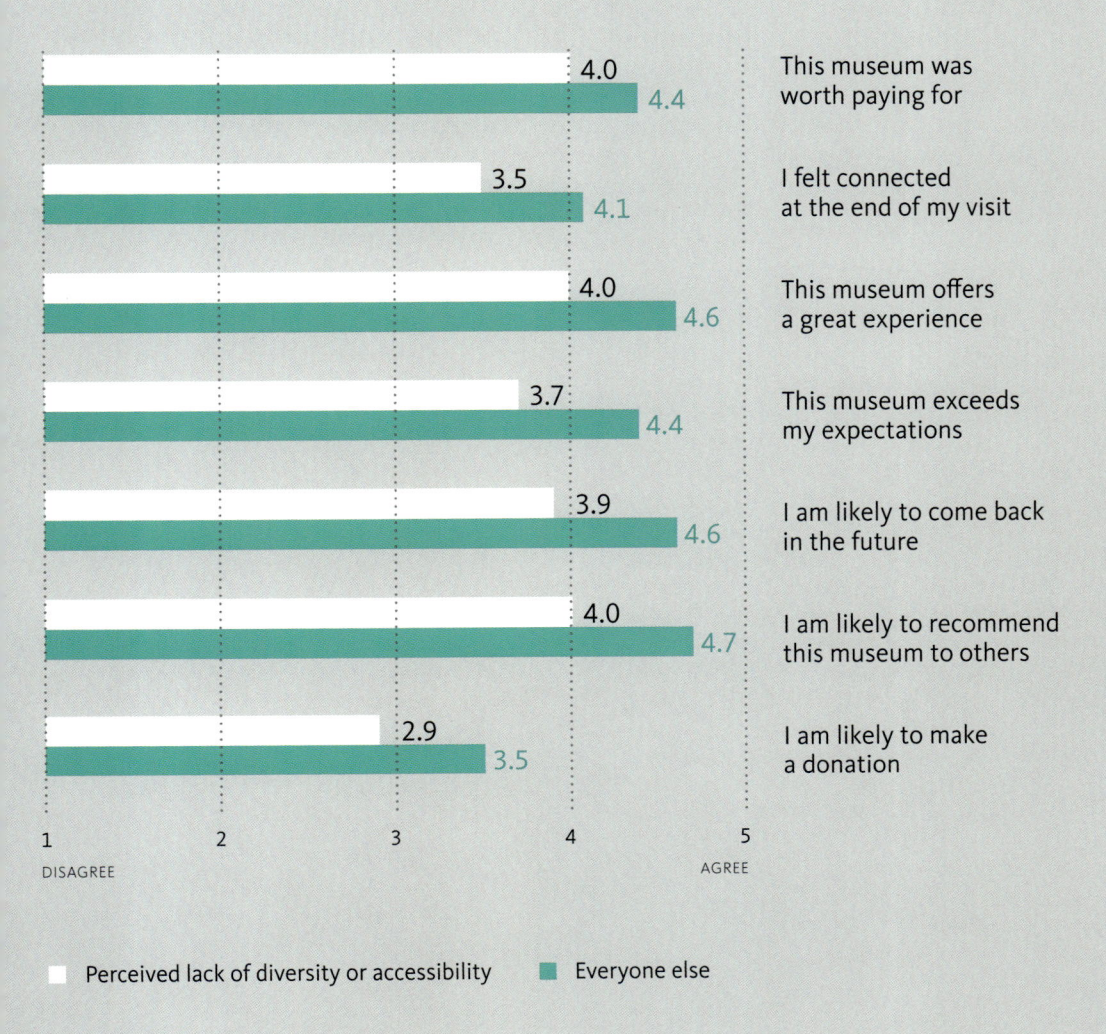

| Statement | Perceived lack of diversity or accessibility | Everyone else |
|---|---|---|
| This museum was worth paying for | 4.0 | 4.4 |
| I felt connected at the end of my visit | 3.5 | 4.1 |
| This museum offers a great experience | 4.0 | 4.6 |
| This museum exceeds my expectations | 3.7 | 4.4 |
| I am likely to come back in the future | 3.9 | 4.6 |
| I am likely to recommend this museum to others | 4.0 | 4.7 |
| I am likely to make a donation | 2.9 | 3.5 |

1 DISAGREE — 5 AGREE

☐ Perceived lack of diversity or accessibility  ■ Everyone else

**Museums must maintain their role as safe places for all—focusing on this responsibility will keep them relevant.** Visitors expect museums to foster an environment of inclusivity and accessibility. Institutions that are inaccessible or don't cater to a diverse audience are consistently ranked lower in key metrics. Gender-inclusive restrooms, railings, clear interpretive labels and navigational signage, and trigger warnings can all boost perceptions of inclusivity. However, the features of inclusive design are ineffective if visitors don't know they exist. For example, only 19% of people we surveyed knew there were gender-inclusive restrooms available in the museums they visited.

**WHAT'S NEXT**

Visitors to museums have high expectations, and we must continue to monitor how museums can offer new ways to experience their spaces. Museums are places for discovery, inspiration, and growth, but we must also focus our attention on how to a) best integrate technology, and b) design museums as safe spaces for all people.

# Hospitality Experience Index 2018

How can hotels exceed expectations for what makes a great experience?

**82%**
of people go to hotels to have fun

**69%**
of business travelers also do leisure-related activities during their stay

**58%**
of Baby Boomers choose hotels based on places they've stayed before

**41%**
of people use hotels as a place to work somewhere quiet

**38%**
of business travelers share their hotel experience on social media

**26%**
of hotels have iPad check-in available

# 1.8x
Millennials are 1.8 times more likely than boomers to use hotels as a place to find inspiration.

# 2.9x
Millennials are 2.9 times more likely than boomers to use hotels as a place to meet clients.

# 2.8x
Millennials are 2.8 times more likely than boomers to use hotels as a quiet place to work.

**WHAT WE DID**

**We examined the myriad factors affecting the guest experience within hotels today to determine which components matter most—from design features to elements of service, technology, and marketing.**
Gensler's Hospitality Experience Index is the culmination of a multiyear, mixed-methods research effort leveraging ethnographic research and a 1,200-person survey to find patterns in how we interact with hotel environments.

**THE CONTEXT**

Today's hotels are the embodiment of our everything/everywhere lifestyles. Whether guests are traveling for business or leisure, hotels are supporting a wide range of activities—from the traditional work trip or vacation to social events and remote work. To be successful in a market permeated by choice, hotels must understand how to support this increasingly wide range of intentions and activities while maintaining individuality and authenticity.

**THE RESULTS**

**We found that a suite of six design variables prove most important when predicting a great hotel experience:**

**Beauty** When executed correctly, beautiful designs positively influence a user's first impression and boost perceptions of the value of the services associated with a space.

**Comfort** Numerous factors—from the comfort of the hotel bed to the overall comfort of a hotel's furnishing and common areas—proved to be drivers of a great experience.

**Authenticity** Hospitality spaces are considered to be authentic when the design reflects a broader brand or mission, takes inspiration from its broader neighborhood and cultural context, and possesses a compelling backstory or history.

**Intimacy** Addressing scale in creative and targeted ways, making spaces feel more welcoming and homelike, and creating experiences that feel individualized are a few ways to foster intimacy in hospitality spaces.

**Inspiration** Spaces that are designed to inspire and spur creative thinking offer some of the best experiences—connecting guests to nature, creating places that support a diverse range of demographics, and providing activities that broaden perspectives are all ways to inspire guests.

**Latest technology** Places that use the latest technology to improve and streamline user visits consistently offer better experiences, and also make spaces appear new and innovative.

**38%**
of business travelers shared their experience on social media during their hotel/resort stay.

**25%**
of leisure travelers shared their experience on social media during their hotel/resort stay.

**69%**
of business travelers also did leisure-related activities during their hotel/resort stay.

**20%**
of leisure travelers also did business-related activities during their hotel/resort stay.

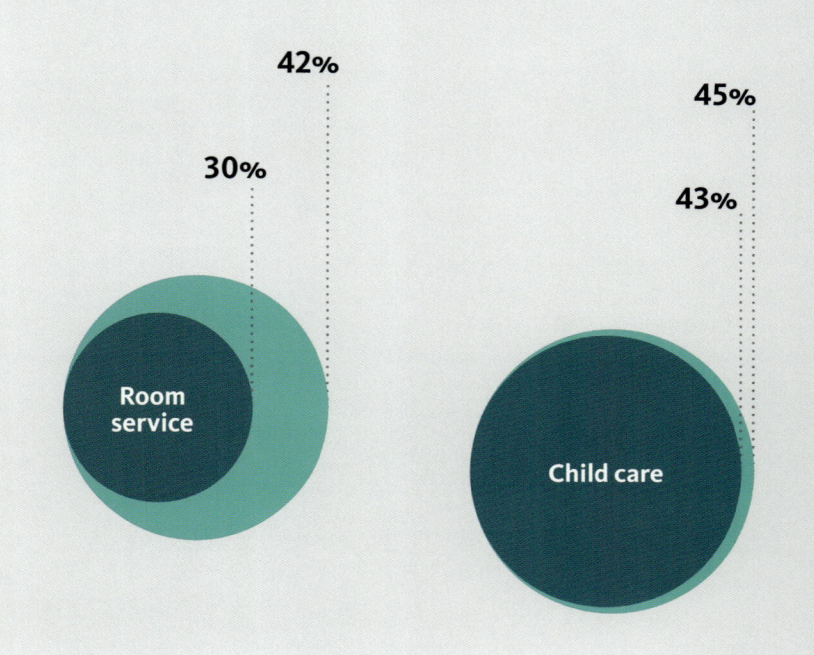

30% / 42% — Room service

43% / 45% — Child care

**DESIGN IMPLICATIONS**

**Solving task mode makes an experience good.** Going beyond that makes an experience great. Hotels that offer a great experience optimize basics like comfort and safety, while integrating technology, luxury amenities, and a beautiful and aspirational aesthetic. Getting the fundamentals right and providing an exceptional task-based experience are paramount concerns for today's hotels—and the foundation on which they build trust with their customers, encouraging them to explore and engage in broader ways.

**The best hotels support business, lesiure, and the growing blur between them.** The differences between business and leisure travel are illuminating. Business and leisure travelers report similar levels of satisfaction with their overall hotel experiences and are similarly likely to have had a great experience during a recent stay. Business travelers are, however, more critical of the overall hotel and are more likely to see their rooms as cluttered. Leisure travelers, by contrast, are more critical of spaciousness, comfort, and the ability of their room to host guests or other activities.

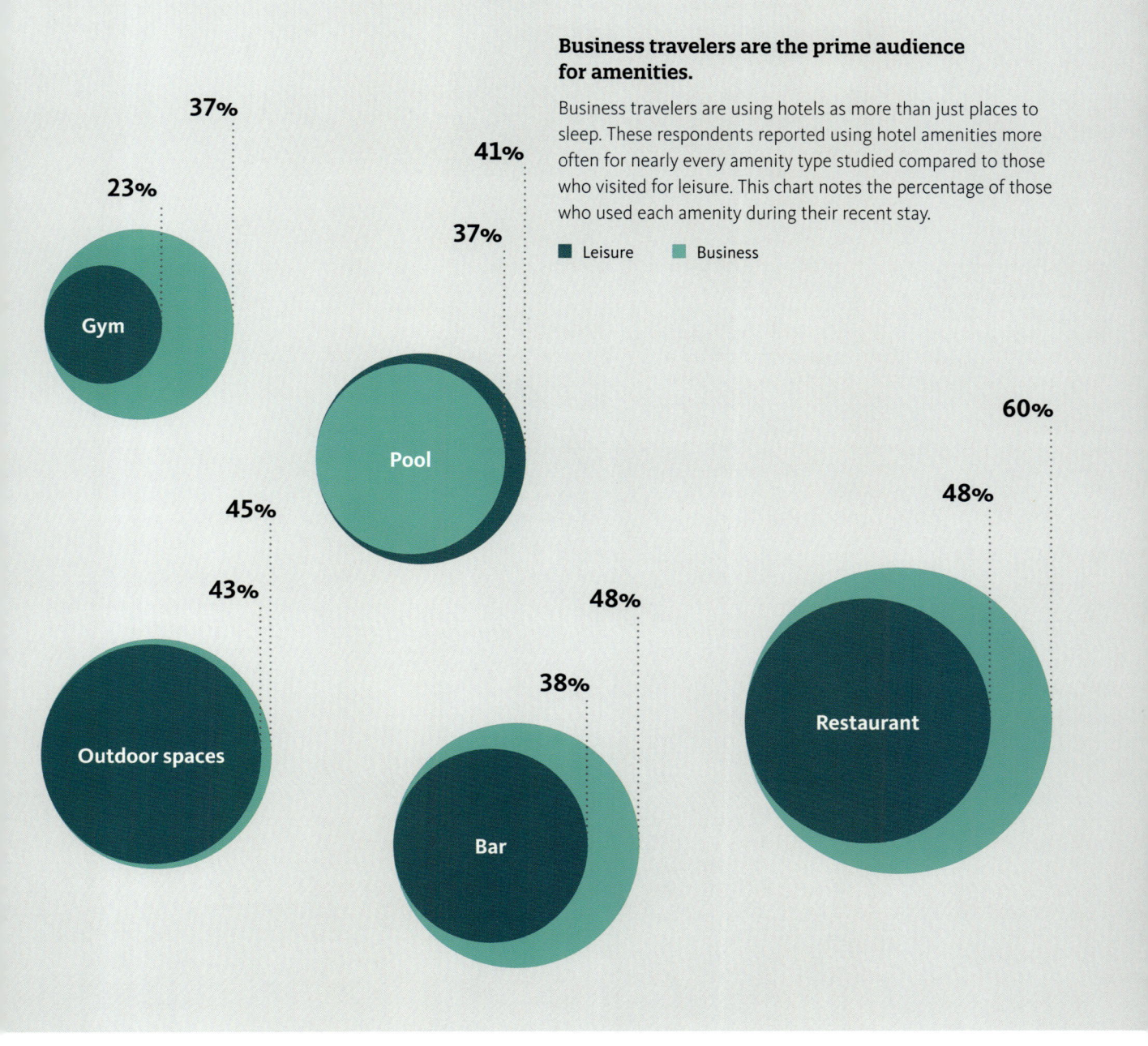

## Business travelers are the prime audience for amenities.

Business travelers are using hotels as more than just places to sleep. These respondents reported using hotel amenities more often for nearly every amenity type studied compared to those who visited for leisure. This chart notes the percentage of those who used each amenity during their recent stay.

■ Leisure   ■ Business

- Gym: 23% / 37%
- Pool: 37% / 41%
- Outdoor spaces: 43% / 45%
- Bar: 38% / 48%
- Restaurant: 48% / 60%

**Expectations have an outsized impact on the overall quality of their experience.** Expectations are set well before guests walk in the door—and make a big difference. The process of choosing where to stay impacts how guests create the first impression to any hotel. Recommendations, online ratings, and routine are key variables that drive hotel choice. Familiarity with the hotel and recommendations are the two top reasons people select their accommodations.

**WHAT'S NEXT**

Hotels are performing well—but that doesn't mean there isn't room for improvement. We articulated clear ways that hotels can offer an even better user experience. The latest trend today is the blending of business and leisure travel. But this dynamic will inevitably change, so we will continue to investigate the evolving balance of what makes a great hotel experience.

Creating a Rich Urban Experience

**Kimpton Aertson Hotel**
Nashville, Tennessee

As the interior designer for the 180-key boutique hotel, Gensler created an atmosphere that spoke to Kimpton's mission to help guests feel as if they were in a comfortable and stylish home, rather than a generic hotel. A focus on a carefully curated mix of textures, materials, and space conveys the rustic and eclectic charm of Nashville. The hotel incorporates a natural palette, and seemingly handmade elements, that offer visitors an authentic experience.

# Exploring Multigenerational Travel

How can travel accommodations support multigenerational travel?

**WHAT WE DID**

**Multigenerational travel, or "3G travel," is on the rise—and most of today's travel accommodation options aren't designed to support it.** To better understand the needs of 3G travel, we investigated its behavioral drivers through a focus on residents of the United Kingdom. We then examined consequential shifts in industry and design.

We launched a 15-minute, online survey focused on people who had taken a recent vacation with members of at least two other generations. Results totaled 300 respondents including employees from our Gensler London office, consultants, clients, suppliers, and London Metropolitan University Interior Design students.

After aggregating our dataset, we categorized travel type by location and accommodation to garner insights into the motivators behind different choices. To add a layer of nuance to this information, we conducted in-depth research into the social and cultural influences behind travel habits of different generations.

**THE CONTEXT**

Multigenerational travel is recognized as a fast-growing trend and an important area of market growth for the hospitality industry. In 2014, more than 12.5 million people in Britain (18%) had been on a 3G holiday, or a trip consisting of at least three generations. And more than a third of the UK (35%) intended to take a 3G holiday over the next 12 months. The 3G travel trend continues to grow: Mark Warner reports a 12% rise in the last five years and Thomson Research shows that 38% of British individuals have traveled with both their parents and kids.

Despite the significance of 3G travel, the UK currently has a timid approach to acknowledging or understanding the phenomenon. Few are able to produce hard data about what factors are driving the growth in 3G travel, and what it means to the market.

Differences in the values and behavior of millennials are often noted as one driver. Millennials value experiential products, like traveling, more than previous generations. As this generation ages and forms families

> 3G travelers reported that before traveling to the airport or their destination, *they are more likely to congregate at home rather than an alternative meeting point.*

of their own, they are maintaining this drive toward experience as they seek multi-generational travel opportunities. For many, this is a missed opportunity—while major hotel brands realize the impact of millennials, 3G travel has not acquired similar attention.

The growing population of boomers also plays a contributing role, particularly since they still control a significant portion of disposable income. Millennials with growing families may be driving the trend, but in many cases it's the parents and grandparents who are footing the bill—a nuanced situation in which the needs of multiple groups must be balanced.

## THE RESULTS

While there have been large nominal increases in the amount of 3G travelers from year to year, the UK hospitality market has yet to catch up. To meet this trend head-on, the hotel industry should merge 3G knowledge into business models. Importantly, 3G travelers still prefer hotels to Airbnb or luxury options. Why? Hotels are flexible enough to promote togetherness as well as independence, and should continue to leverage this capability over competing alternatives.

The most important thing to understand about 3G travel: the desire to spend more time with family is what it's all about. 3G travel is an investment in a shared family experience—understanding and designing under that framework is imperative to delivering on the needs of this travel segment. And with highly variable age ranges, these accommodations will ultimately need to satisfy a diversity of expectations.

When 3G travelers decide on a destination, location is the most crucial factor—all age groups must enjoy the chosen place. When selecting hotel accommodations, hotel location ranks 20 basis points higher (92% choose a hotel because of location) than cost. However, there may be differences in capability and specific interests. So to maintain the willingness of travelers to pay more for hotels vs. other accommodation options, hotels should leverage a location's high-quality services, food quality, and cultural interests alongside a wide range of activities.

**DESIGN IMPLICATIONS**

### Remove impediments to family time.

3G travelers want hotels to provide services that minimize wasted time so they can maximize family time. **Among our survey respondents, 57% believe that a hotel should handle the collection, checking, and transfer of luggage.**

### Use food to your advantage.

Eating—both in and out of the hotel room—is the most important activity that families do together, followed by sightseeing and exercising. Not all meals are sought outside the hotel room: **45% of respondents want a small kitchen included in their hotel room, and 34% want a dining table.**

### Create spaces for togetherness.

Successful 3G design strategies emphasize time spent with the family. Of our respondents, **80% would like a balcony or communal space, and 58% would like a large living space.** Larger rooms and multi-room or family reunion packages are a good starting point.

### Help them be alone and together.

Respondents value both private spaces and spaces that foster collective engagement. Not only do individuals require time to themselves, **63% of respondents bring work even on a vacation, so will need quiet, individual spaces.**

196   Creating a Rich Urban Experience | Exploring Multigenerational Travel

Hotels are flexible enough to promote togetherness as well as independence, and should continue to leverage this capability over competing alternatives.

## WHAT'S NEXT

Rethinking hotel accommodations to meet the needs of 3G travelers is just the beginning. We need to better understand and better accommodate behaviors related to this trend. For example, 3G travelers reported that before travelling to the airport or their destination, they are more likely to congregate at home rather than an alternative meeting point. This trend shows the intersection between multigenerational travel as it relates to ancillary industries like transportation. When it comes down to it, there are many moving parts. Even small behavioral choices can significantly impact how businesses shift to accommodate 3G travelers.

Finally, travel and hotel industries must be cognizant of the profound cultural differences that mediate travel experiences. For example, cultural norms yield various 3G travel group sizes—family makeup and relative dynamics impact travel needs. Research into these variations across cultures, and future trends, is a necessity.

# The Impact of Airbnb on Hospitality

How is the hospitality industry responding to the rise of Airbnb?

**WHAT WE DID**

**Airbnb is a fast-growing phenomenon. To fully appreciate the magnitude of recent industry shifts, we mapped the history of Airbnb, its impact on the hospitality industry, and regulations positioned against the company.**

Our research showcased Airbnb and the hotel industry from both a customer focus and a business perspective. We surveyed Airbnb users on how financial and value-based decisions can lead to choosing Airbnb over alternatives. For congruence with our survey, we launched a questionnaire for leading hotel brands and Gensler's hospitality clients to gauge Airbnb's impact on those hotel brands. Finally, we facilitated conversations with our hospitality clients. We analyzed where the hospitality industry is today, what challenges exist, and what its vision is for the future.

**After denial, there is acceptance:** The hospitality industry has reckoned Airbnb's disruption, embracing new models of immersion, authenticity, and dynamic consumer options.

**THE CONTEXT**

In less than a decade, Airbnb became a ground-shaking market disruption to the hospitality industry. A new paradigm has formed: people, not businesses, are creating their own presence in the hospitality sector.

Although the advent of Airbnb has challenged lasting traditions of the hospitality and travel industries, the company targets different groups than traditional businesses. This means that Airbnb is not solely poaching business from traditional products, but embracing a new target population. For example, of those who use Airbnb, 66% are traveling in groups; 91% want to "live like a local"—an idea that Airbnb has used to position itself above traditional hotel brands; and 74% of Airbnb properties are outside the main hotel districts.

As a sharing platform, Airbnb is meant to catalyze a global, positive paradigm shift. However, the company has faced challenges in many cities, including major cities where finding affordable housing is so difficult—and residents blame Airbnb for driving up prices by removing apartments from the market. But an analysis by FiveThirtyEight demonstrated that there has yet to be a significant impact on apartment rents. Despite the rise of Airbnb, hotel occupancies are up. However, for a firm that began as a travel air mattress company less than a decade ago, many assert that it is only a matter of time before empirical consequences are a reality.

## What makes Airbnb unique?

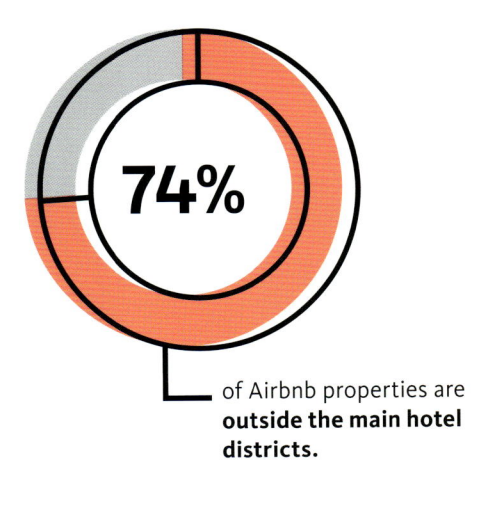

**74%** of Airbnb properties are **outside the main hotel districts.**

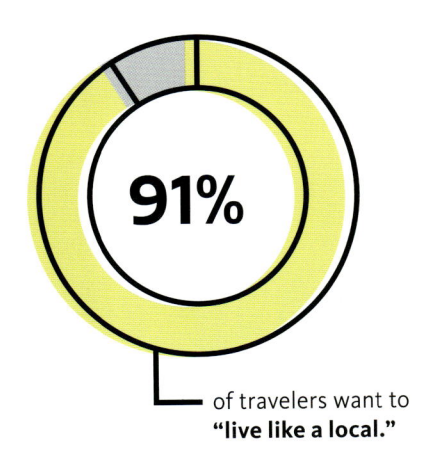

## Airbnb created a new market and demand.

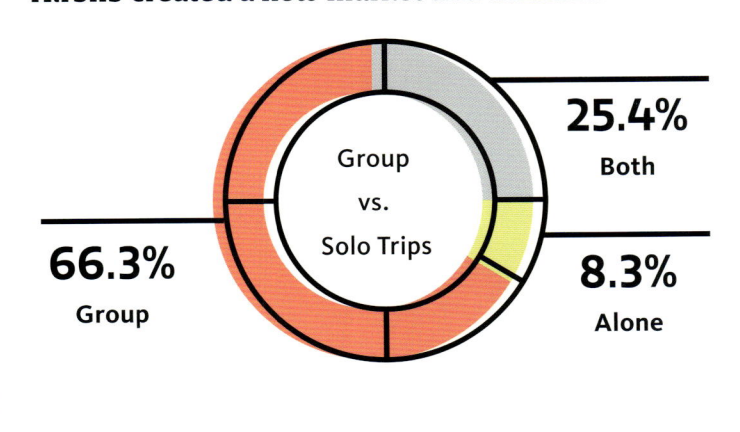

Group vs. Solo Trips

**66.3%** Group
**25.4%** Both
**8.3%** Alone

**91%** of travelers want to **"live like a local."**

**7  Nights**

Seven nights is the average length of stay for the 10% of the business travel market that is switching to Airbnb. Twice as long as stays in traditional hotels.

Save up to **37%**

In some cases, companies can save up to 37% by using Airbnb.

199

## THE RESULTS

Airbnb users make decisions based on financial incentives, and prefer unique experiences that are more prevalent in the Airbnb model. Across the board, consumers asserted that Airbnb is far more cost-effective for groups traveling with friends or family. Both pricing and flexibility are integral selling points. Traditional hotel designs are based on limited accommodation models such as King, Double, or Suite. In contrast, because Airbnb users are staying in the home of a "local," there is the feeling of an authentic or more immersive experience.

Hotels are also trending toward immersive experiences. Brands are integrating guest-only experiences such as intimate concerts, on-site restaurants helmed by celebrity chefs, and personal access to mixologists. Another upcoming change is room design: hotels are transitioning to re-creating a sense of home. The hotel industry plans to bolster amenities and services that Airbnb does not provide. Although Airbnb can offer cheaper prices, hotels provide consistent and predictable comfort and services. While Airbnb is accountable to provide basic needs, there is a shroud of uncertainty around the quality amenities like bedding and security. Hotel brands are targeting millennials through smaller rooms with more affordable prices. The hospitality industry will continue to respond to Airbnb's growing presence.

Most hotel brands reported minimal effect on room rates or the hotel brand. However, Airbnb is still relatively new. In the second half of 2016, Airbnb achieved profitability for the first time. Across the world, there are over 2 million people staying in an Airbnb rental on any given night. A 2018 report by the National Bureau of Economic Research found 1.5% lower hotel revenues in the ten U.S. cities with the largest Airbnb presence.

## The hotel industry and Airbnb are learning from each other and establishing new trends.

### DESIGN IMPLICATIONS

**Consumers buy experiences.**
While hotel room rates and occupancies are strong, change is on the horizon for hotel brands. Hotels report that flexible social hubs, coworking spaces, and coauthored small group spaces are becoming more prevalent. Airbnb is not complacent either. The company is working with community leaders to forge local, symbiotic business relationships.

**There is an arms race to engage consumers through technology.**
Hotels are focusing on becoming more flexible by improving the ease of booking, and are looking to share existing amenities and unreserved rooms online through third-party apps. Hotels have also tapped local artists and journalists to develop apps and content for local hotels like Soho Beach House, Miami. Airbnb has leveraged social media and innovative positioning to double down on the local experience. The company plans to launch new services to help users curate their experiences. Users can book additional services such as personal chefs, chauffeurs, and bike tours.

**Corporate responsibility is a significant trend.** There is a strong focus on community and neighborhood connection through social responsibility programs. Through its Host community program, Airbnb opened a channel for individuals to provide free housing following environmental disasters and terrorist attacks. Omni Hotels' Say Goodnight to Hunger program donates to Feeding America for every guest who books directly through Omni's website. The program reportedly supplied three million meals in the first 60 days.

**Business and luxury travelers are the next battleground.** Another Airbnb target population is business travelers. Companies can save up to 37% by using Airbnb. Airbnb has partnered with corporations such as Hyundai and Domino's to streamline the process for their employees to book through Airbnb. These trends directly compete for a hotel's target audience. While the hotel industry looks to maintain its hold on the luxury market, Airbnb has purchased Luxury Retreats, a full-service villa rental company. In 2019, the firm purchased HotelTonight, its largest acquisition to date.

**Understanding emerging models and future scenarios.**

### 1 Group Travel

Flexible social hubs, coworking spaces, and coauthored small group spaces are becoming more prevalent in traditional hotels.

### 2 Service Oriented

A marketplace of on-demand services allows Airbnb guests to arrange personalization during their stay.

### 3 Design & Experience

Airbnb has leveraged its social media and innovative positioning to expand into creating Airbnb experiences.

### 4 Responsibility Driven

A significant trend across all sectors, corporate responsibility focuses on community and neighborhood connections using social responsibility programs.

**WHAT'S NEXT**

Airbnb is mapping its future, yet across the country, the ball is rolling on legislative measures positioned against key tenets of its business model. Looking forward, everything from the frequency of short-term leases to market share is subject to increased scrutiny. Inevitably, the hospitality industry will shift according to how Airbnb and its users are regulated.

Airbnb plans to strengthen its commitment to community-based generosity. In 2016, Airbnb launched Samara, a Google X–like division, whose mission is to tackle the company's most ambitious projects. For example, the division designed Yoshino Cedar House, a communal housing project in rural Japan, and encourages Airbnb users to host refugees through the firm's Open Homes platform.

# A Toolkit for Active Learning Environments

Can we quantify the impact of active learning environments on student outcomes?

**WHAT WE DID**

**Our mission was to develop a toolkit to test the correlation between space and learning.** Capitol Federal Hall—the new Gensler-designed School of Business building at the University of Kansas—served as a beta-test, leveraging both quantitative and qualitative instruments that spanned observations, surveys, and IT information. Our broad range of measurement tools substantiated both the perceptions and the reality behind learning, space dynamics, and student and faculty behavior.

As we worked with University of Kansas to overhaul their facilities, we measured and grounded enhancements in actual behavioral and perceptual change. Our goal was to establish the degree to which a given space influences learning, by testing subjects before and after the new facility opened.

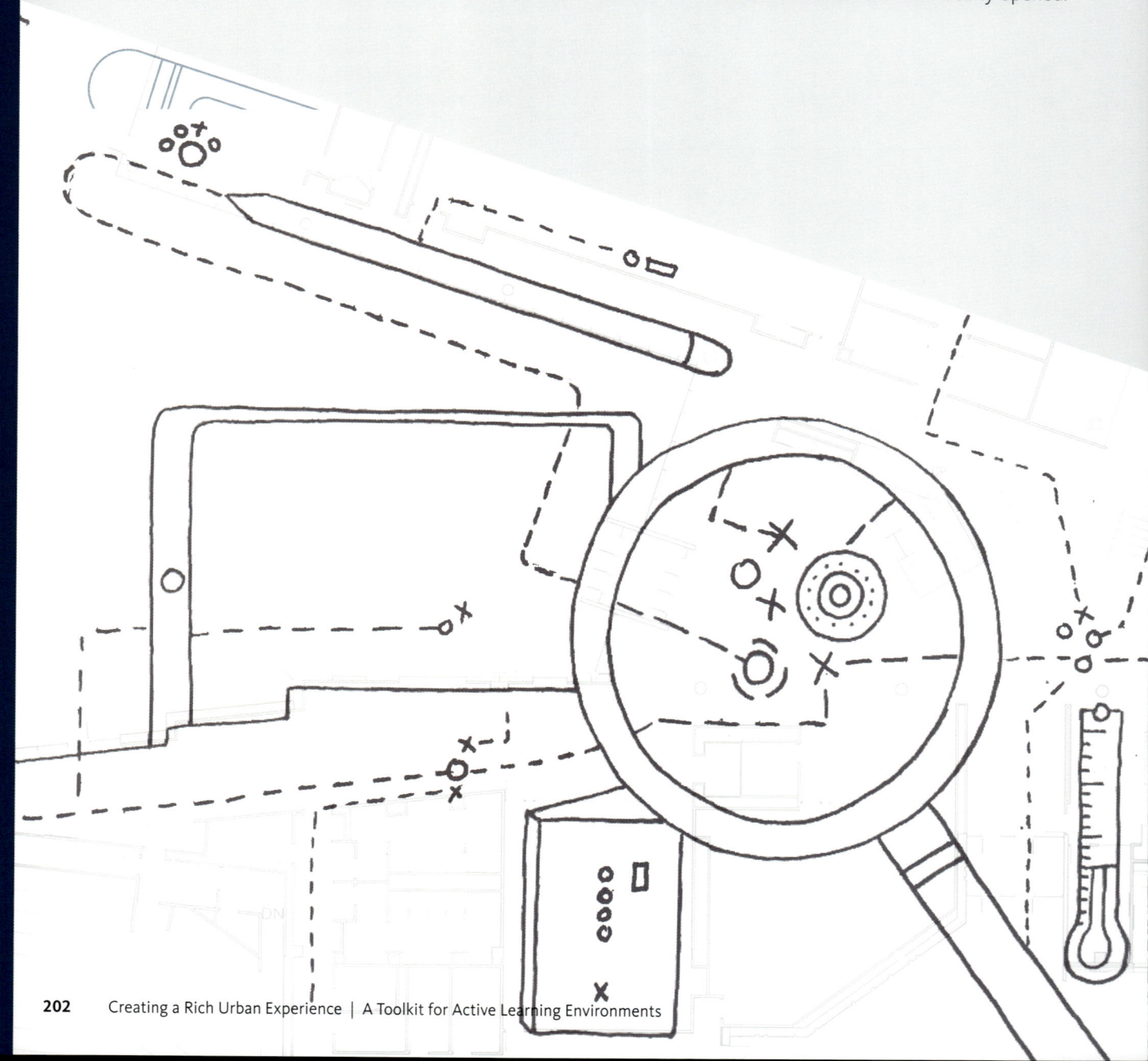

To add another layer of nuance, we surveyed students and faculty members to see what mattered most to them across a wide range of activity-based and space-based indicators, then analyzed the differences between groups. We developed the set of indicators from a composite of primary and secondary research, including Gensler's own history of education research focused on space. Learning indicators include variables such as creativity, self-direction, fundamental literacies, ownership, and choice. Physical indicators include variables such as lighting, acoustics, temperature, and layout.

## To stay competitive, educational institutions need to scrutinize how every aspect of the campus could improve (or hinder) the student experience—and the built environment is a key aspect.

### THE CONTEXT

As educators face increased pressure to improve student performance on shrinking budgets, the ability to pinpoint exactly how and why design solutions enhance learning is paramount. The Great Recession was a major blow to states funding higher education.

Research shows the inextricable link between the environment and learning, with variables ranging from air quality and temperature to furniture layout, lighting, noise, and flexibility. However, most prior studies have targeted K–12 institutions; there is a shortage of research at the higher education level.

On average, states are spending nearly 20% less per student than before the recession.

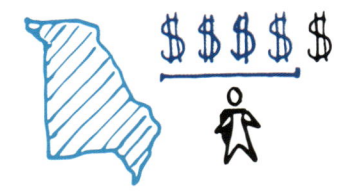

At the same time, institutions are competing for new students at unprecedented levels.

Since 2000, the number of enrollees in American colleges and universities has increased 25%.

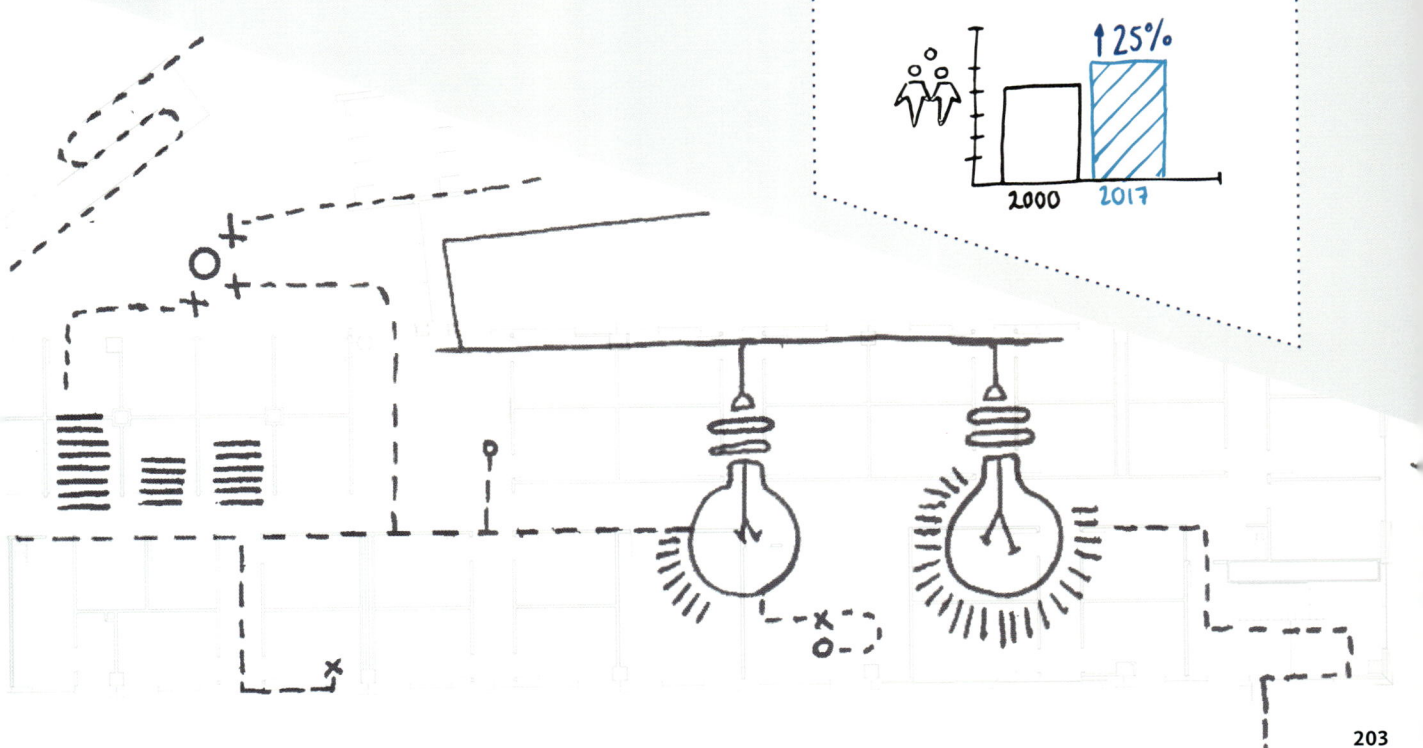

## THE RESULTS

- Feel Connected
- Socialize
- Experience
- Collaborate
- Share/Teach
- Reflect
- Acquire

### Visibility and Engagement

All users reported benefitting from the new space, and felt that visibility and engagement increased. Students also felt their culture changed for the better with an increase in participation and utilization of services since the move to the new facility.

### Teachers' vs. Students' perceptions

Zoning focus work and collaborative activity is critical to success. Both students and faculty felt that focus work could be better supported—and separation of activities may need to be encouraged. Within the classroom, focus work and collaboration often compete in a zero-sum game—a space that favors collaboration can hurt focus. Outside of the classroom, however, enhanced openness and room configurations create interdepartmental, serendipitous interactions. Depending on the area, a priority of either focus or collaboration should be sufficiently supported so that the two aren't at odds with each other.

### Focus work vs. Collaboration

Students adapted quickly to connectivity and collaboration. Some clear perceptual differences emerged between students and faculty, however. Students put a greater value on connectivity and collaboration, while instructors emphasized focus and quiet zones. The faculty who relied most heavily on pedagogical strategies in which quiet and separation are valued saw less impact. They felt the environment supported their focus work, but didn't find the collaboration spaces to be as useful as students did. Broadly, students appeared to adapt more quickly to the new environment—and have welcomed the opportunities for spontaneous interactions and connected learning. However, students noted a need for more quiet study space too.

**DESIGN IMPLICATIONS**

## Balancing focus and collaborative space is critical...as we have seen in the workplace.

In general, students benefited from collaborative, open design while faculty preferred focus time and private space. However, although focus time and private space appeared to be more critical for faculty members, both groups felt focus work could be better supported. This conclusion reflects what we've seen in the workplace, as revealed in Gensler's 2016 Workplace Survey. The key is supporting workflow for both groups while increasing serendipitous student-faculty interaction.

## Choice is important, but limitless choice can actually detract from learning.

For classrooms, students and faculty stated that they want less choice in the future. A side effect of an interconnected layout is a deficit in personalized atmosphere.

## Faculty-student interaction is a strong marker for enhanced learning.

All users reported that the enhanced environment of the building increased connectivity and visibility. This heightened engagement of the School of Business with the rest of the KU campus brought multiple groups and individuals to the building, many of whom are not part of the School of Business. An increased sense of possibility and opportunity coupled with the interdisciplinary convergence of users instills a strong foundation for those learning indicators that form the basis of our research, including creativity, critical thinking, and problem-solving.

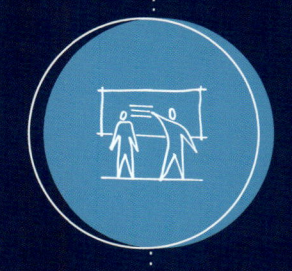

## Change management and user choice are key.

Change management is a key requirement for success in a changed environment. How do we introduce individuals to a built environment that calls for different interactions and behaviors? All users would benefit from a change management process to orient them to the building and the new tools.

**WHAT'S NEXT**

Our next step is to continue to refine our toolkit for the pre- and post-occupancy assessment of education spaces. The ideal toolkit balances data types and is widely applicable. An integral benefit of the toolkit is the interdependence of each tool, and acknowledging the cost of implementation.

**We found that surveys, observations, and ethnography offer the greatest ROI between cost and impact, while the use of data can require greater institution dependent customization.**

We are focused on the evolution of our survey tool and creating a wider diversity of beta-test cases. We also see opportunities to improve and expand our use of focus groups and ethnographic methods to facilitate informal and interactive group discussions around user experience. The regular sessions will be designed to engage the group in understanding how their needs, aspirations, and experiences are developing in the new space. Information technology visualization is an area for improvement, requiring a collaboration with higher education institutions to access information that relates student habits and patterns. This information includes room reservation logs, email and calendar logs, and timecard stamps. Once we aggregate and visualize student habitual information, we will be able to better utilize the spaces we have.

Creating a Rich Urban Experience

**Lynn University**
Boca Raton, Florida

Gensler's master plan for Lynn University reimagines its 115-acre campus by enhancing under-utilized real estate, improving campus walkability, and embracing sustainable initiatives. Upgrades to aging facilities will further enable connectivity and expansion, as Lynn moves toward improving the student experience and creating spaces where students can live and learn together.

# A Comparative Analysis of Enhanced Classrooms

How do enhanced classrooms improve the learning experience?

**WHAT WE DID**

**We partnered with seven universities in Brazil to track 272 students as they transitioned from traditional classrooms to enhanced learning spaces, then we studied the impact the environment had on learning.** We began with a pre-survey to communicate the fundamentals of our research design and to understand the many layers of learning within the program. In a mixed-methods approach, we collected observational data, ran surveys, and conducted focus groups with the learners and educators in the traditional space. We then engaged the same methodology after the students moved to the new environment to measure the impact of the new space.

Traditional classrooms had a rigid structure: a well-defined front of room, furniture not easily moved, and features designed to support a front-of-room, lecture-based learning style. The enhanced space included nontraditional features such as multiple displays; no clear front and back; three-way partitioned, height-adjustable tables that allow for different learning modes; and reconfigurable seating and learning settings.

**THE CONTEXT**

Our research taps an ancient epistemological question: what is the process through which an individual comes to learn new things? Pedagogical approaches have evolved from the Socratic method, to critical pedagogy and the inseparable nature of personal experience, social context, and education. Only recently has psychology included social context under concepts of learning such as social cognitive theory.

Our study builds on existing research that demonstrates the relationship between the built environment and learning. The conditions under which someone receives information can reinforce the information. For instance, the consequences of poor room temperature or inadequate lighting have been correlated with the decreased ability of students to retain information. **On the other hand, a progressive learning environment pushes students to learn information in novel ways—classrooms can facilitate learning through one's peers, the teacher, and technology.**

For our research, we focused on how students acquire, collaborate, focus, and convey. We triangulated individuals' learning processes with the content being taught, the learning tools, and the environment through which the individual learns. In social cognitive theory, this is referred to as a "triadic" approach.

Multiple presenters

Teachers noted that students were "learning for themselves" in the enhanced classroom.

Efficacy across learning modes increased by an average of 30% in the enhanced spaces.

Ergonomic furniture

**THE TRADITIONAL CLASSROOM**

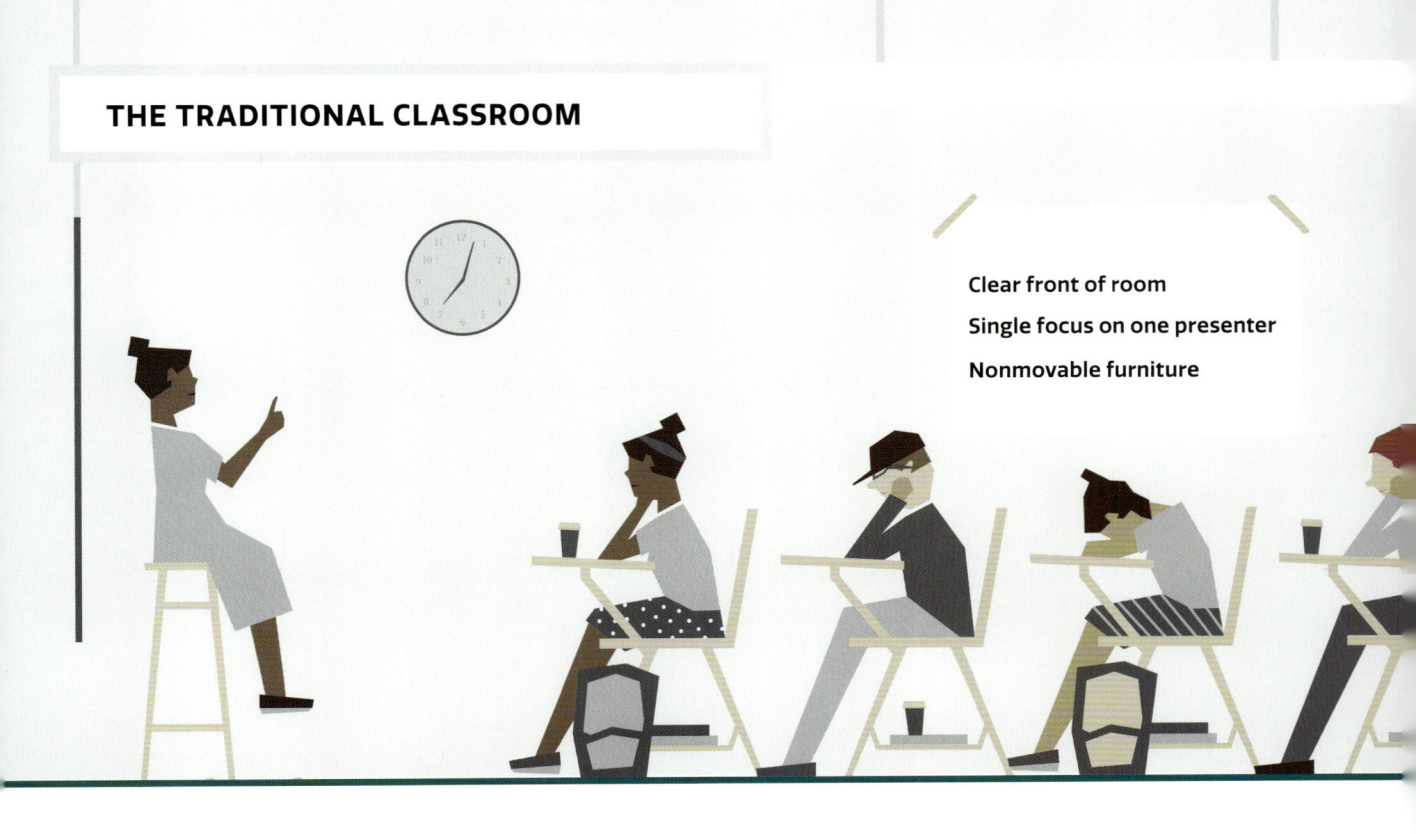

Clear front of room
Single focus on one presenter
Nonmovable furniture

# Increasing choice and flexibility in classroom design can enhance student engagement and promote deeper learning.

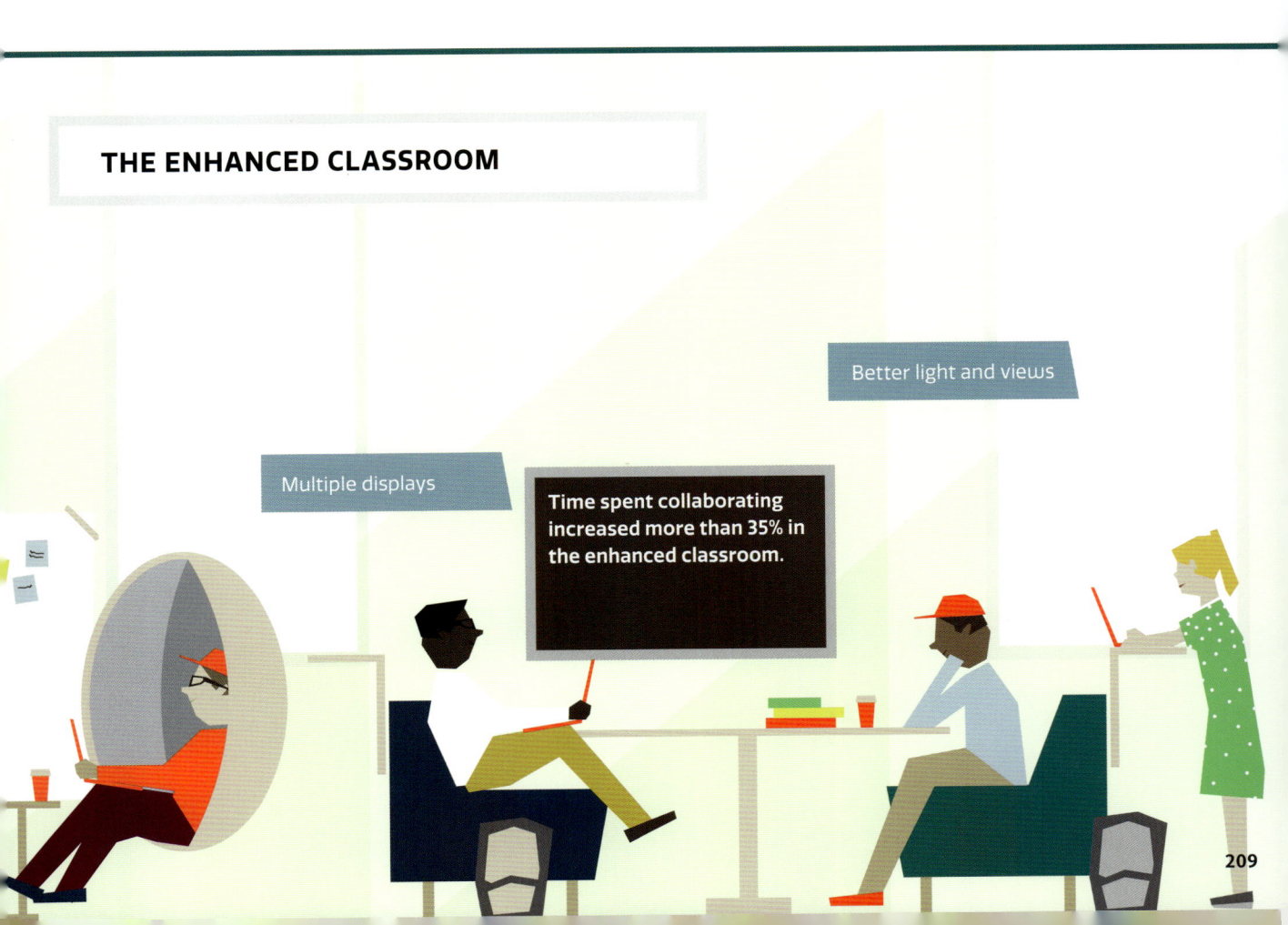

**THE ENHANCED CLASSROOM**

Better light and views

Multiple displays

Time spent collaborating increased more than 35% in the enhanced classroom.

209

**THE RESULTS**

Our primary finding: behaviors changed along with a change in space. We witnessed large increases in collaboration. This led to a pedagogical distinction between traditional and nontraditional workplaces: students in the enhanced space spent less time learning from the teacher and more from one another and by themselves. In essence, the flow of information was coordinated to include both teacher-to-student and student-to-student information flows. The new space created new opportunities for student-to-student learning.

Students reported an increase in the efficacy across all learning modes—that is, an enhancement in their ability to focus, collaborate, acquire, and convey information in the enhanced space.

Students and teachers pointed out how the enhancement of the tools and technology enables nuanced and interactive learning and allows for the role of presenter and learner to seamlessly shift between teacher and student.

Choice is also key. While students and teachers often don't exercise the full range of choices at their disposal, both groups resoundingly wanted the ability to choose. In fact, the mere existence of choice improved satisfaction.

Students and teachers differed in fulcrum point placement for the balance between teamwork and individual work. Students reported teamwork as key to engaged learning, while teachers ranked "focus" most highly, demonstrating a balance any successful environment would have to accommodate.

**DESIGN IMPLICATIONS**

**Students and teachers thrive in environments that facilitate open-ended learning.** Both recognize the need for new ways of learning that go beyond a one-way transmission from teacher to student. While the objective of grasping knowledge will not change, we need multiple pathways to get there—and the flexibility and open nature of space can be a key component in the transition to personalized learning.

**Enhanced environments create a sense of ownership.** Students in our enhanced classroom formats reported higher productivity and were more engaged. Technology further blurs the boundary between teachers and students, giving them a platform to consolidate learnings from teachers, on their own, and from each other.

**Connectedness enhances engagement.** Our research showed a significant increase in the ability to learn from other students in the enhanced environments. Though students felt supported in learning and working by themselves, the expanded options to work collaboratively heightened their feeling of connectedness to other students and to their own education.

Creating a Rich Urban Experience | A Comparative Analysis of Enhanced Classrooms

**Time Distribution
Among Learning Modes**
*Derived from observational analysis, average of all schools*

■ traditional classroom
■ enhanced learning space

**Efficacy of Space
for Each Learning Mode**
*As reported by students*

■ traditional classroom
■ enhanced learning space

| mode | traditional classroom | enhanced learning space |
|---|---|---|
| focus | 51% | 85% |
| collab | 50% | 88% |
| acquire | 63% | 88% |
| convey | 55% | 93% |

**WHAT'S NEXT**

Students crave the freedom to define their own learning trajectory. The environments in which they learn should support that objective. A self-regulated learning style that acknowledges students' proactive nature sets a guiding framework.

It is hard to quantify the effect a positive attitude can have on learning. We found that creating choice through classroom design increased learning indicators such as creativity, inclusivity, and agency—factors that are also associated with overall happiness. Further exploration can help us better understand the interplay between positive thinking and positive learning behaviors.

Our research demonstrated a clear preference for enhanced environments, but we also want to identify which environmental features are most salient. We should conduct more research to discern the building features most important in enhancing the learning experience.

> *"Creativity flourishes best in a unique kind of social environment: one that is stable enough to allow continuity of effort, yet diverse and broad-minded enough to nourish creativity in all its subversive forms."*
>
> —Gerard Fischer, University of Colorado

# A New Model for the Public Library

How must libraries adapt their services, programming, and partnerships to serve their communities?

**394** Survey Responses

**4** Panel discussions in cities across the country

**34** One-on-one interviews at the 2018 American Library Association annual conference

Panel event in Minneapolis shown

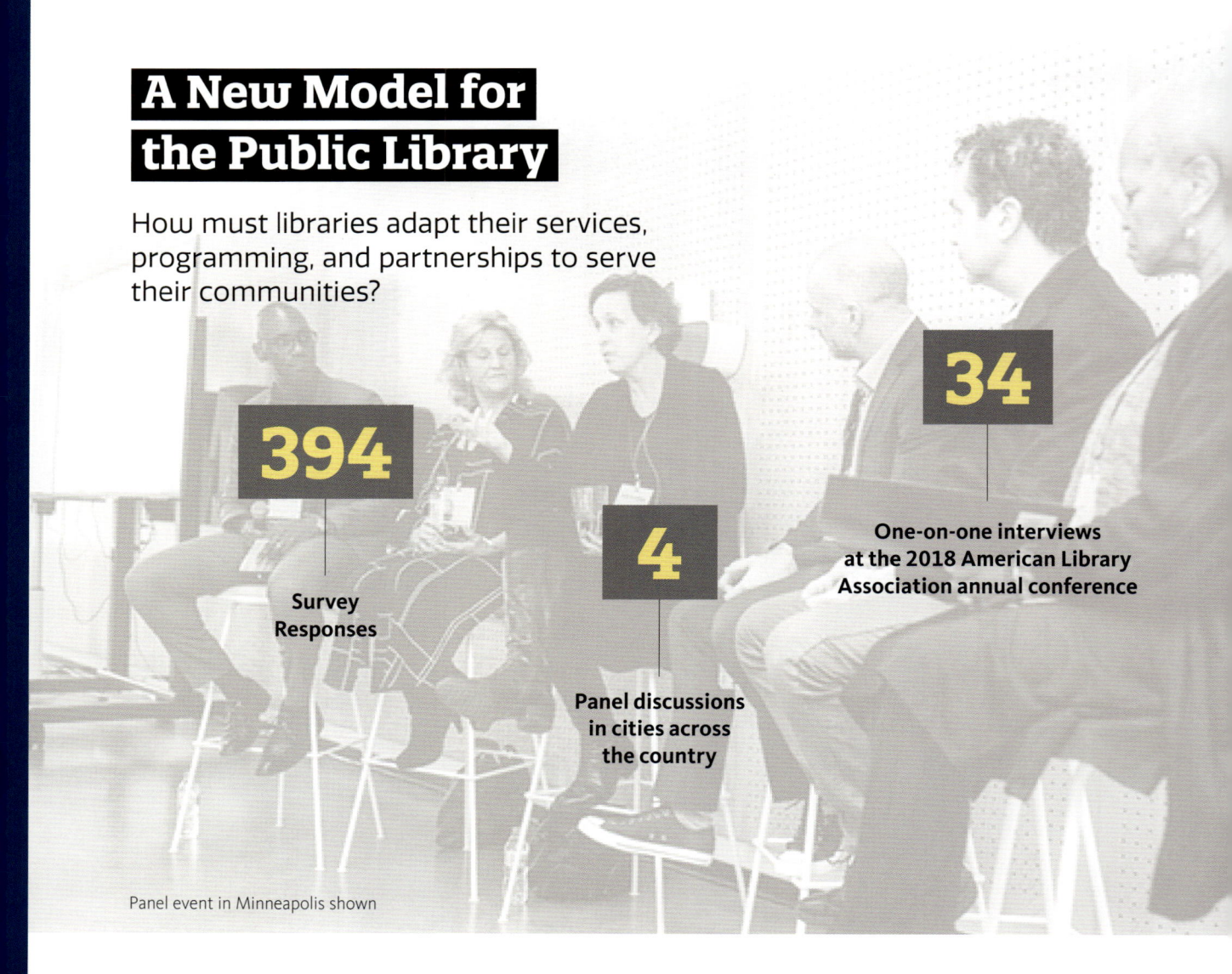

### WHAT WE DID

**We explored the macro- and micro-level trends impacting public libraries and developed a set of design strategies to support the institution's evolving role in communities.** To achieve this, we developed a trend report, hosted a series of panel discussions across the country, and evaluated the results of a web-based survey.

We created the trend report by analyzing current surveys, reports, and studies that examine the future of economies, cultures, and society. We also considered perspectives on community engagement, media technology, civic action, and forecast scenarios for the future of libraries. This research enabled us to identify a range of themes that guided our design strategies and recommendations.

Panel events in New York, Houston, Minneapolis, and Washington, D.C., were attended by library thought leaders, administrators, and academics. We also distributed a web-based survey to library professionals. These endeavors helped us gain an understanding of the salient issues, priorities, and challenges confronting libraries.

## Library programs and services should focus on equity, social connection, and community resilience.

**THE CONTEXT**

Since its inception, the public library's most basic mission has been to make resources and information universally accessible to all. Data shows that these institutions continue to serve as important pillars of communities. According to a recent survey conducted by the Pew Research Center, millennials are visiting libraries more than any other generation, and two-thirds (65%) of respondents 16 and older said that closing their local public library would have a significant impact on their local community. However, the institution is currently in a period of evolution, driven by a reordering of social infrastructure and disruptions in the media landscape. These shifts are triggering fundamental changes in the nature of librarianship, program operations, and the design of library spaces.

Community needs are changing. The disruption of the social compact has catalyzed the growing focus on equity and a need for social cohesion. Digitized and social media have transformed the way we produce and consume content, and have also redefined what constitutes both public and social space. Automation and globalization have greatly impacted the workforce, prompting pressing needs for skills development, educational advancement, and bridging institutional gaps for nontraditional learners. Additionally, the increased mobility of workers and the growth of the freelance economy have redefined notions of the workplace. To ensure that they continue to play an important role in the cultural life of our cities and communities, library systems will need to leverage and reposition their existing facilities to respond to these emerging changes.

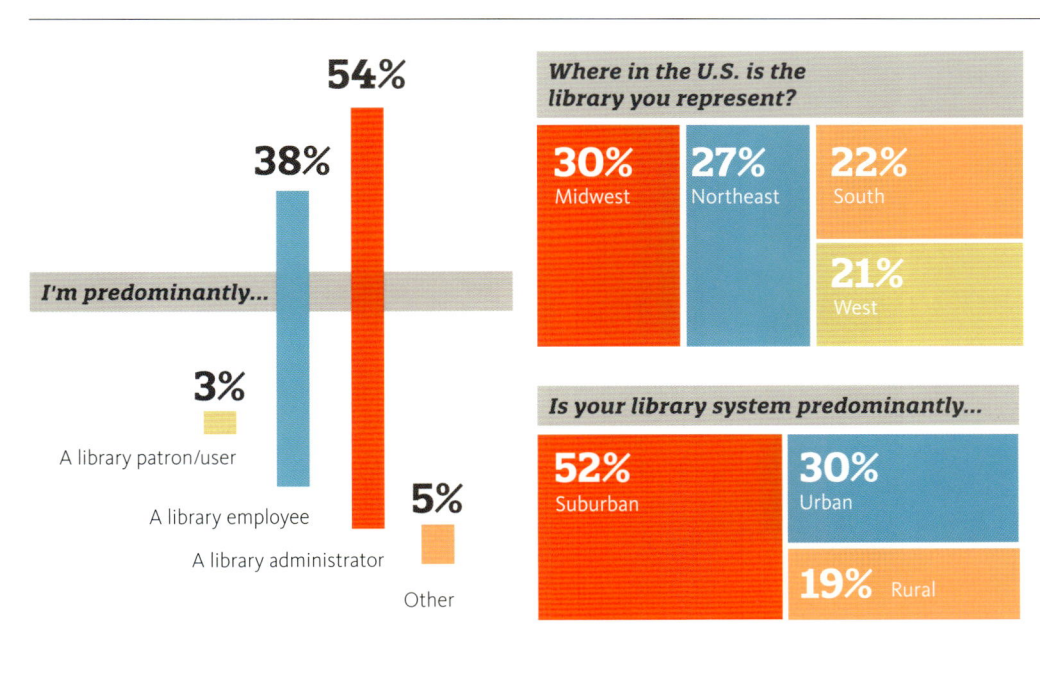

*I'm predominantly...*
- A library patron/user: 38%
- A library employee: 54%
- A library administrator: 3%
- Other: 5%

*Where in the U.S. is the library you represent?*
- Midwest: 30%
- Northeast: 27%
- South: 22%
- West: 21%

Our survey generated responses from library professionals and patrons across the country.

*Is your library system predominantly...*
- Suburban: 52%
- Urban: 30%
- Rural: 19%

*As you plan your capital budget, what are the top-three priorities?*
- Staffing and workplace: 48.5%
- Physical infrastructure maintenance: 46.2%
- Enhancing technology: 45.8%
- Remodeling existing facilities: 40.5%
- Reconsidering use of existing facilities: 38.5%
- Rethinking/enhancing collections: 28.2%
- Sustainability: 26.6%
- Accessibility: 23.3%

Enhancing technology was identified as a top priority in budget planning by survey respondents, exceeded only by staffing and workplace concerns, and physical infrastructure.

**THE RESULTS**

**The nature of librarianship must continue to evolve to serve the needs of diverse populations.** Libraries are central to communities' network of social environments and public spaces. Larger concentrations of people are settling in cities, attracted by greater employment opportunities and more attractive lifestyles. As cities become more densely populated, libraries will confront issues resulting from social dislocation, homelessness, chronic unemployment, and substance abuse. Library staff will need to include a greater share of social workers, health care advisors, therapists, and community organizers.

**Libraries are people-centered, not collections-centered.** Public libraries' service offerings need to address diversifying populations and different learning styles. Both the aging cohort of baby boomers and the rise of millennials present generational challenges that institutions need to address. Additionally, increasing levels of migration cause deeper demographic shifts. Libraries will need to devise programming and design interventions that accommodate a broad range of interests and educational/informational needs. While collections are still important, the needs of library users should be the first consideration when deciding how to allocate space. Patrons need areas to create, collaborate, socialize, and learn.

**Libraries should be viewed as part of a broader system of allied institutions.** Libraries will increasingly partner with private companies, philanthropic organizations, and government agencies to coordinate the delivery of goods and services. They should also consider exploring partnerships with public schools, community colleges, and vocational schools to accommodate the growing demand for a more robust continuing education and skills-based learning infrastructure. Furthermore, developing pop-ups, temporary outposts, and creative placemaking programs will also extend the presence of libraries throughout communities.

---

Of our survey participants, 95% felt there was a role for social and community-based services at the library.

**Is there a role for access to social and community-based services at the library?**

95% Yes

---

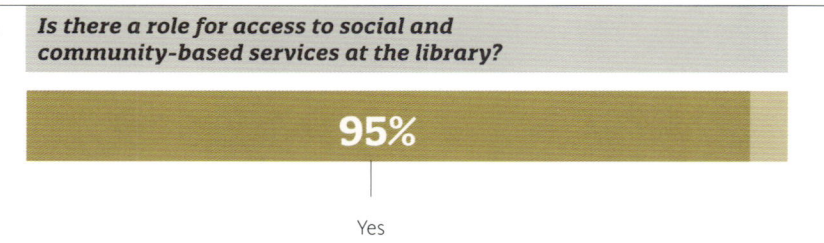

Access to resources, community services, and education disparities were identified as the top-three community issues to address.

**What are your top-three community issues to address?**

- 77% — Access to resources
- 40% — Community services
- 40% — Education disparities
- 40% — Recreational activities
- 31% — Immigrant and multilingual services
- 24% — Homelessness
- 22% — Mental health
- 11% — Language support
- 10% — Food disparities
- 2% — First-responder community aid site

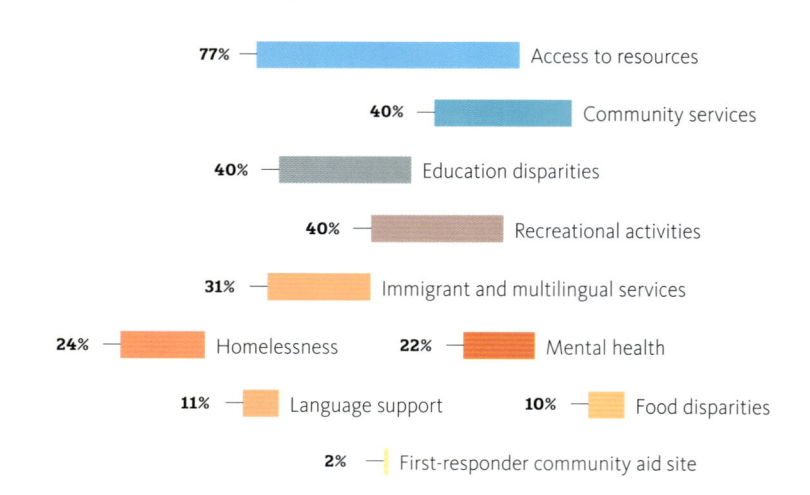

**DESIGN IMPLICATIONS**

### The design of public libraries should promote a sense of ownership, belonging, and safety.

The ideal library design creates a hub for community resilience and growth. When developing strategies to leverage existing library space, designers should look for opportunities to embrace the outside world and encourage patrons to share their ideas. Celebrating community achievements and promoting social equity are key. As the public becomes more conditioned to high levels of personalization in their cultural, civic, and work environments, it is critical that library designs support spatial and cultural diversity.

### Libraries will need to integrate physical and virtual environments.

In the coming decades, digital media will complement books as the predominant format for most library collections. Additionally, as virtual and augmented reality experiences come to serve as reliable media for conveying information, libraries will need to leverage those tools to take advantage of new models of education and pedagogy.

### Library design must be adaptable and flexible.

Libraries will occupy a myriad of roles in the coming decades. These institutions will need to function as offices, classrooms, laboratories, and social/recreational centers. As library programming diversifies to accommodate generational and demographic shifts, designers should create rooms that flex and grow depending on activity. Library design needs to enable areas of individual focus within active, public settings. Additionally, as libraries are key centers of thought and information-sharing, collaboration zones are critical.

### Library spaces need to accommodate a broader range of production modes alongside 3D printers, CNC routers, and laser cutters both analog and digital.

As libraries play a larger role in supporting content creation with the proliferation of makerspaces and incubators, they continue to provide access to robust digital platforms for sharing these goods and connecting communities of makers and sharers. This ensures that libraries occupy a prominent place in the ecology of media production and maker culture.

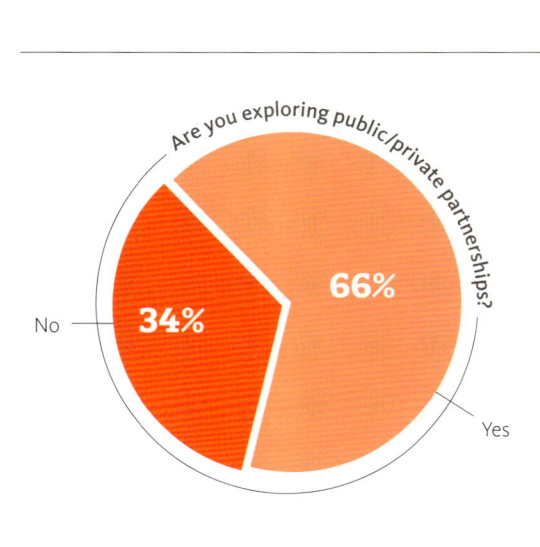

**Are you exploring public/private partnerships?**
- No: 34%
- Yes: 66%

**Are these partnerships revenue-producing?**
- Yes: 25%
- No: 75%

Two-thirds of library professionals say they are exploring private/public partnerships. Of these partnerships, 75% are non-revenue-producing.

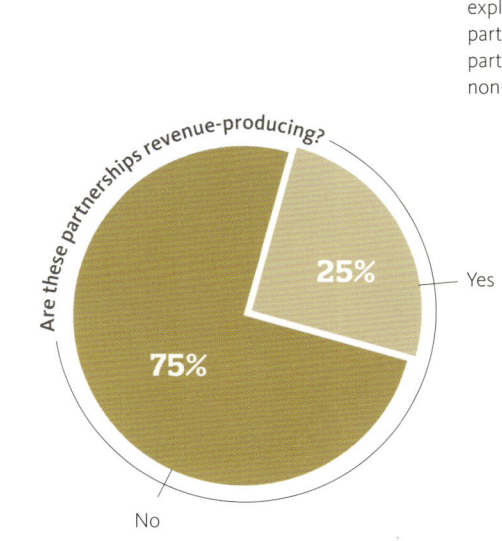

**WHAT'S NEXT**

We will develop an engagement framework and a set of concrete design strategies that address different learning styles and methodologies—as well as the needs of vulnerable individuals who are drawn to the library as a respite. We will also look for opportunities to engage directly with local populations to ensure that investments are in line with community needs.

# The Future of USPS Real Estate

How can we reimagine USPS's mission of connecting people to evolve with an aging real estate paradigm?

**WHAT WE DID**

**We evaluated shifting value propositions for physical post offices in the U.S., and what that means for our communities as well as for the real estate portfolio of the U.S. Postal Service (USPS).**

We connected with external experts to advise our research process, and conducted primary and secondary research into the history and current state of the post office. We documented how the post office has historically served as a catalyst for enterprise, industry, and communication. We analyzed how the post office has created or amplified a sense of identity and place in America—and for the communities it represents.

Ultimately, we understood USPS as a series of systems and assets; we used this understanding to establish a framework for community and site selection parameters. Now, as the USPS considers how best to use its existing real estate, it can ensure that its future real estate strategy keeps with the USPS mission of bringing communities together.

**THE CONTEXT**

The USPS, and its physical post office locations, is an American institution. By the numbers, it covers 100% of American addresses, accounting for 2.7 billion annual visits. The Postal Service has 35,000 facilities across the country, occupying 200 million square feet of real estate. However, pension payouts and federal money issues have driven USPS into the red for the past 12 years. Over that period, the rise of e-commerce has precipitated the transition of USPS from a mail-dominated to a package- and parcel-dominated business. Although this has increased gross revenues, because of the outsize cost of package and parcel shipping and handling, it has decreased overall profits.

Pressure to change comes from all angles. Amazon and FedEx have dampened revenue streams by using similar, if not the same, logistical networks as USPS to carry out consumer deliveries. These major competitors are testing autonomous deliveries and other means of streamlining logistical patterns. Additionally, technology has replaced traditional mail with emails and text messages. These shifting communication patterns have forced the USPS to restructure its logistical network—commissioning new delivery modes to reach 100% of all U.S. addresses.

USPS has adjusted to this new paradigm by reducing the number of total offices and routes as well as investing in its fleet—greatly expanding the number of vehicles and delivery points. As a backdrop to USPS's shifting business model, the institution has often been politicized in national conversations as a social symbol or a symptom of financial irresponsibility. Currently, a federally appointed task force is looking at ways to privatize, sell assets, and sell facilities.

The value of post offices derives from their unique position in the community ecosystem.

The U.S. Postal Service covers **100%** of American addresses, and accounts for **2.7 billion** annual visits.

USPS has **35,000** facilities across the country, occupying **200 million** square feet of real estate.

Technology has replaced traditional mail with emails and text messages.

## RESULTS

To design the future of the post office, we must address the supply chain, the community, and the physical post office in tandem. We broke these issues down into nine key factors that define the postal ecosystem. The community and the post office interact through the supply chain of shipping and receiving. Three main factors influencing the supply chain are communication, transportation, and consumer trends. The main factors influencing the community are development trends, legislation, and demographics. And customer interface, context, and operations are three main factors of influence for the post office.

We then developed a Power BI tool to help visualize site parameters such as vacancy, renter-occupied housing, and average rent, helping us identify existing opportunities for implementation. Using U.S. Census data, we defined parameters for site selection by reimagining and supplementing the USPS mission of communication, diversity, logistics, and delivery. Traditional postal services are needed less each year, but myriad community issues remain that could instead be prioritized. Our tool also includes other socioeconomic variables such as unemployment, poverty, and food deserts to repurpose USPS facilities to better serve and align with community needs.

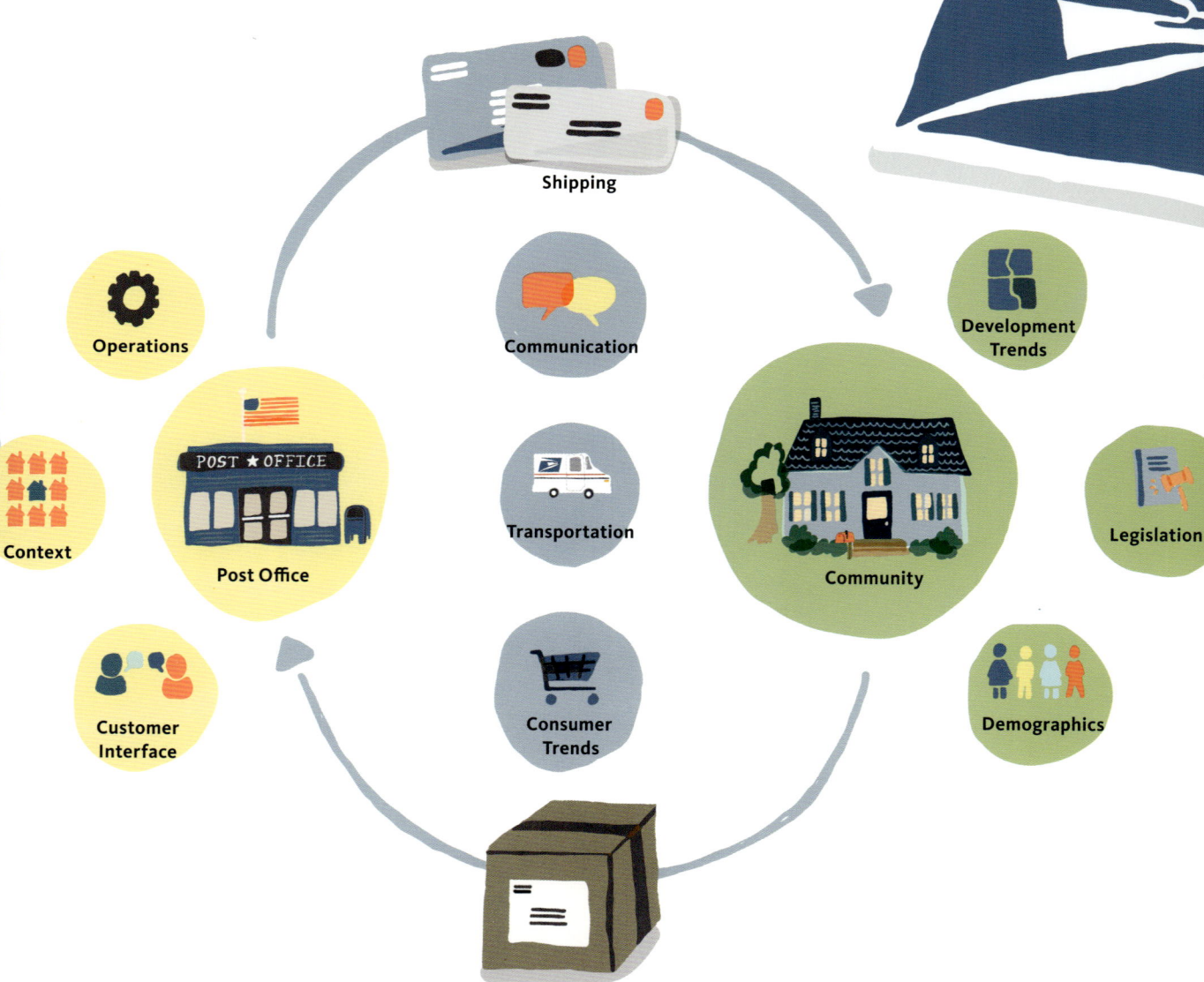

Creating a Rich Urban Experience | The Future of USPS Real Estate

*USPS is not falling out in popularity:*
**20% of millennials report that they visit a post office at least once per week.**

**DESIGN IMPLICATIONS**

**We believe the USPS can evolve to once again be a focal point for American communities by adapting its mission to its contemporary context.** Once a gathering point for locals, post offices have fallen out of being an exchange point for serendipitous interactions. In a future where liquidating real estate is likely, we know that we must work to preserve USPS architecture, because of its community value and placemaking identity. Even though the connection between the post office and the community has atrophied, USPS has a foothold in every community in the country. We should ensure that properties don't become fully privatized, so they remain or can be repurposed to play a role in civic life.

**The current shift from single-use to multi-use spaces has created opportunities to reuse and adapt the post office per community needs.** Post offices are strategically located on main streets and near train stations, originally planned around geography and distribution efficiencies. Once identified as a central point around which a community was built, today's postal service is now broken into several underutilized branches of service. Federal zoning has restricted redevelopment of these civic facilities, many of which are historic properties. Designed around associated program and area requirements, these facilities were strategically planned based on parameters such as volume of mail to daily services like retail, workrooms, offices, and loading docks—many of which are now outdated.

**The future of the post office should be built directly around community needs.** Throughout its history, the USPS has routinely analyzed its consumers to realign its business model. USPS can recalibrate this entrepreneurialism to optimize existing facilities according to the communities its consumers represent. As it conducts this analysis, prioritizing investment in at-risk communities should be paramount, as this is where the greatest opportunity—and need—exists.

**WHAT'S NEXT**

USPS is not falling out in popularity: 20% of millennials report that they visit a post office at least once per week. That means we have to fast-track our implementation process, finding new case studies that cover various scenarios given different scales of adaptive reuse interventions. Our next step is to codify use of our Power-Bi Tool to select USPS sites located in at-risk communities—to propose and visualize the most community-responsive design solutions.

# A Model for Integrated Ambulatory Care Clinics

How can we engage health care consumers to reshape care and communities?

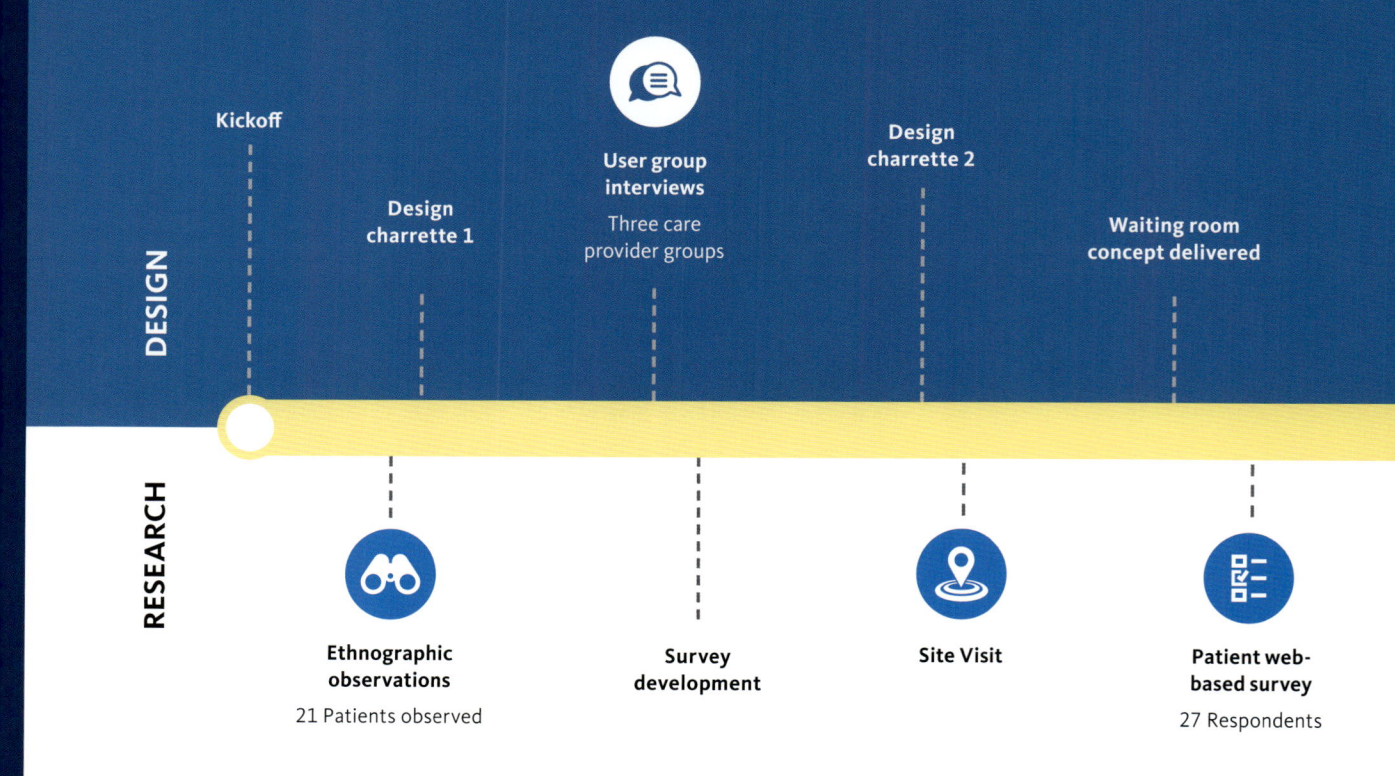

**DESIGN**
- Kickoff
- Design charrette 1
- User group interviews — Three care provider groups
- Design charrette 2
- Waiting room concept delivered

**RESEARCH**
- Ethnographic observations — 21 Patients observed
- Survey development
- Site Visit
- Patient web-based survey — 27 Respondents

### WHAT WE DID

**We partnered with Mount Sinai's PeakHealth practice to reimagine the workflow, experience journey, and design of an intensive ambulatory care clinic.** We employed a mixed-methods research strategy including user group interviews from three care provider groups, behavioral mapping, and structured interviews with healthcare consumers of the practice. We researched the digital technology utilization, exam room, waiting area layout and features, patient experience, engagement, emergency department utilization—identifying what worked and where opportunities were missed, to engage health care consumers in their care. Our findings informed a mock-up of a future examination room within the framework of the health care consumer's journey over time and into the community.

### THE CONTEXT

Mount Sinai is a global, integrated health care system. PeakHealth has served medically vulnerable and underserved patients of the local community for three years. Prior to PeakHealth, health care consumers independently navigated health insurance, multiple chronic conditions, and complex psycho-social effects. At PeakHealth, health care consumers are supported by a network of care providers who administer a complex care package. It is this contingent of consumers—those who make up only 20% of overall patients but constitute 80% of health care costs—whom Mount Sinai targets with PeakHealth's personalized model of care.

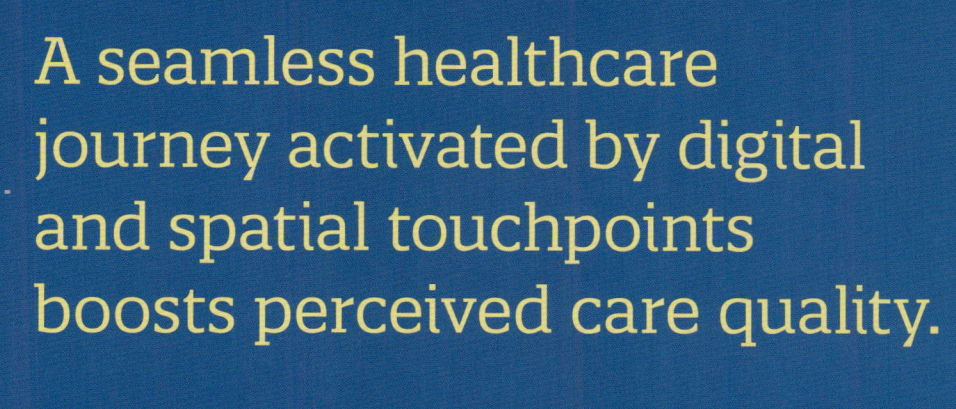

# A seamless healthcare journey activated by digital and spatial touchpoints boosts perceived care quality.

**Exam room construction**

**AV camera installation completion**

**PeakHealth moves into new exam room**

**Next-gen exam room design**

**Update on research**

**Research peer review**

**Exam room ethnography**

**Ethnography review and analysis**

**Final report**

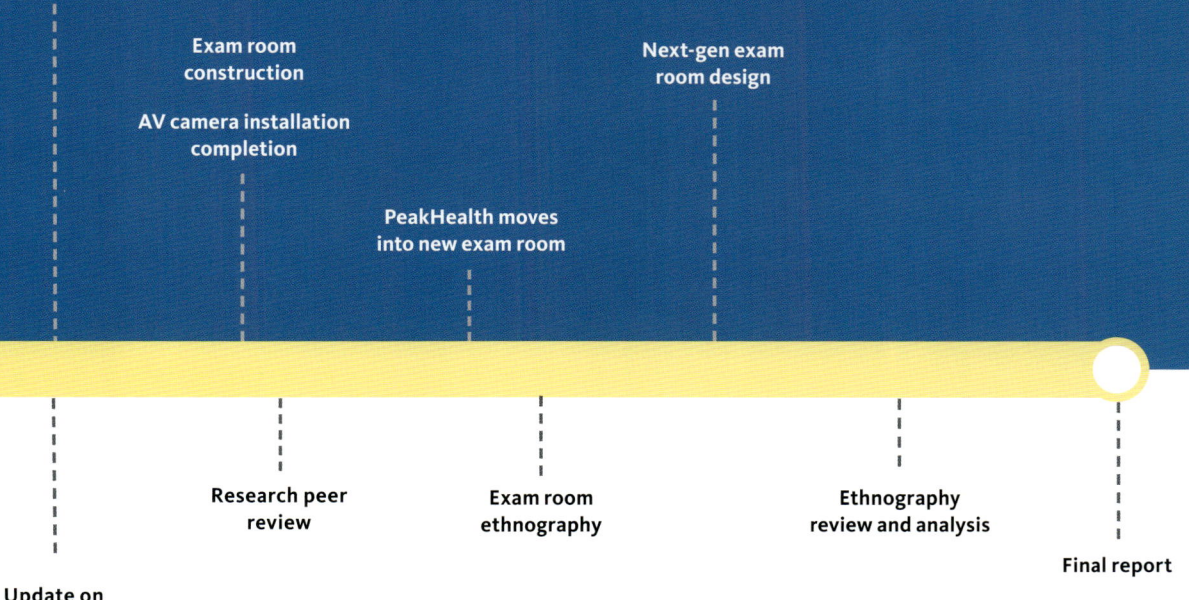

## THE RESULTS

When talking about patient experiences, wait times and the patient-doctor relationship often take center stage. However, their overemphasis prohibits a more holistic understanding of the health care consumer's navigation within the care system, including first encounter, education, collaboration, digital tools, social networks, and ultimately care maintenance and prevention. Interaction points—primarily between care providers and health care consumers—are integral to the quality of care yet isolated from the continuum of a health care consumer's experience. Once outside a clinic, the health care consumer is typically on their own to remain informed and motivated to follow through.

We envision a seamless health care experience of meaningful touchpoints, activated by digital and spatial engagements. Both spatial and digital design build trust and community from the waiting area and exam room through to digital interfaces within the patient's community. Design interventions that target a sense of control, a sense of welcoming and teamwork, and particularly, tools for communication, have substantial impacts on perceived care quality and patient-provider interactions.

Performance and outcomes also hinge on perceptions of an exam room's design, equipment, and furnishings, with statistics indicating opportunities to limit unnecessary ER visits and missed appointments. Specifically, the patient's ability to see the exam room computer screen—which is a facilitator for the patient-care provider engagement—is linked to less missed appointments. Of our participating health care consumers, 37% reported they did not see the computer screen.

**66%**
*of patients have missed or skipped an appointment*

DESIGN IMPLICATIONS

**Tools for communication,** whether digital or analog, are lacking in the clinical space. The existing computer screen is not conducive to patient-provider engagements.

**37%**
of patients did not see the computer screen

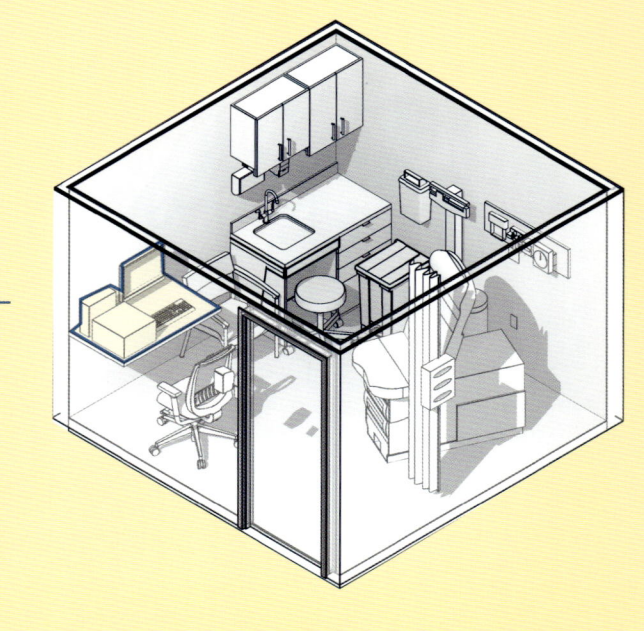

The **patient's first impression** of the space and perception of control over the exam room experience impacts his or her perception of care quality.

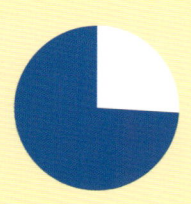

**26%**
of patients used a cane, walker, or wheelchair

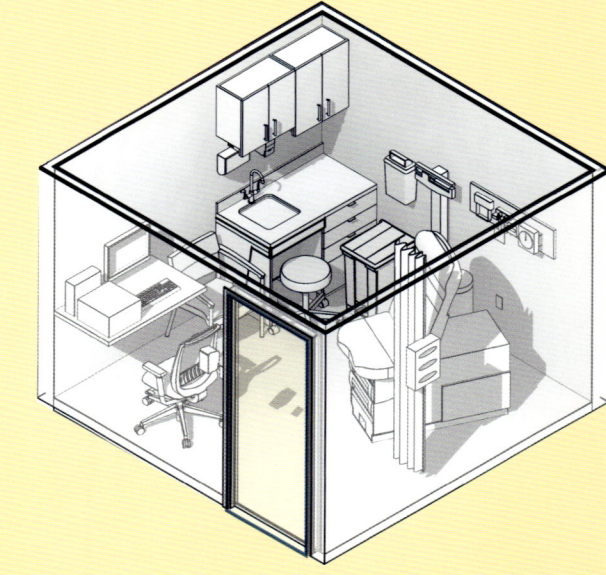

The **size and layout** of the exam room can impact how the patient feels during their visit. Lack of space for guests and assist devices can be frustrating for the patient.

**33%**
of patients have an accompanying guest or caretaker

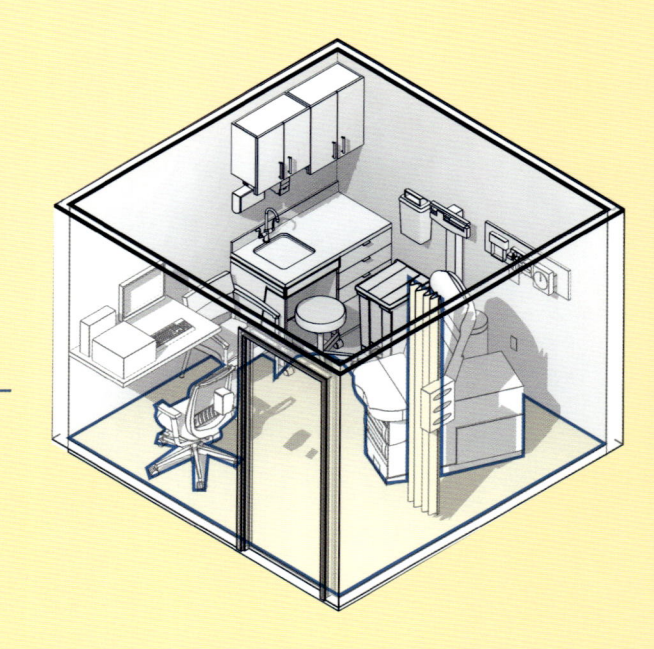

Creating a Rich Urban Experience | A Model for Integrated Ambulatory Care Clinics

### Our approach to design must be more than a redesigned health care clinic layout.

Digital assistant services that capture biometrics and body stats from vitals to nutrition are integral to a holistic care plan. Outside the clinic, care continues with prescribed activity, notifications, and additional interactions with the care team. These steps help health care consumers become more proactive in their own well-being.

### Social opportunities should be embedded in physical space, encouraging engagement and support among health care consumers and care providers.

Design areas for education, training, and support groups with reconfigurable layouts. Position digital screens in accessible locations to share educational material and provide a personalized welcome in the exam room. Finally, separate spaces with sliding glass partitions for privacy when necessary and arrange seating to encourage conversations and interactions.

### In the exam room, the feeling of spaciousness impacts the patient visit.

A lack of space for guests and assist devices can be frustrating for the health care consumer. Most patients bring belongings with them, and many require walkers or wheelchairs for mobility. Crowdedness can make the healthcare consumer feel uncomfortable, and therefore, less likely to fully engage in the patient-care interactions. Health care consumers may even opt for the emergency department if the design and layout do not appear to be conducive to their patient-care experience.

### The average visit lasts just over one hour—over 70% of which is spent in the waiting room.

Space planning and physical attractiveness can reduce patient anxiety, noise, and facilitate positive interactions between guests and staff while fostering workflow efficiencies through self-registration and other techniques. Activities are typical—sitting, talking, or using electronics—however, people cluster around outlets instead of spreading proportionately. Moreover, assist devices take up space and block usage of the entire waiting area. A welcoming and personable experience is design-influenced. Attention to lighting, casework, monitors, and furniture can impact privacy, storage, visibility, and conversations.

**WHAT'S NEXT**

We must contextualize our findings with the greater community services such as housing, workplace, wellness centers, pharmacies, and relevant space types. Mount Sinai PeakHealth's concierge model of care profoundly moves the needle toward livable cities. The ongoing research and design project's findings have universal application across consumer types and places with design and digital design technologies at the heart of consumers' communities. Here they can be accessed at the right time and right place.

# Enhancing the Waiting Room Experience

How can community feedback inform and improve waiting room configurations?

**WHAT WE DID**

**We leveraged a waiting room redesign opportunity for Washington, D.C.'s Unity Health Care to test the impact that different furniture and design configurations can have on patient, visitor, and employee satisfaction.** By reviewing academic literature on everything from technology and evidence-based design to community health and well-being, we found several standard waiting room features that had not yet been substantially investigated. These features became our areas of focus: seating arrangement, seating choice, artwork, amenities, cultural relevancy, visibility, line of sight, and wayfinding.

Our research included three main phases: pre-occupancy assessment, design interventions, and post-occupancy evaluation. In pre-occupancy stages, we used both self-reported information and objective measurement tools in formulating what our design should achieve. We issued a staff survey to gauge baseline feelings toward the waiting room with a Likert scale, which asked level of agreement on statements such as "the waiting room feels warm and inviting." The customer base of Unity's Brentwood Health Center was included in interactive exercises to help us understand their aesthetic preferences and interlinkages with the Brentwood community through art. We used behavioral mapping to determine communication patterns and seating preferences. Sunbrella, a textile manufacturer, partnered with Gensler to finance the redesign and assist with the waiting room research.

As a tool for evaluating how best to redesign the waiting room, we established hypotheses that predicted how each feature could enhance communication, comfortable waiting, staff happiness, and design.

## HYPOTHESES

- An improved furniture arrangement encourages increased communication among patients.
- Art inspired by the community can calm the clinical feel of the waiting experience.
- Diversity in furniture styles and more comfortable seating choices for patients improves experience.
- Artwork representative of the community increase staff happiness.
- Community engagement in the design process can bring creative new solutions.
- An enhanced waiting room reduces perceived wait time.

## DATA COLLECTION METHODS

**SURVEY**
(QUANTITATIVE)
Staff and Patient Evaluations

**OBSERVATION**
(QUALITATIVE / QUANTITATIVE)
Behavioral Mapping

**INTERVIEWS**
(QUALITATIVE)
Community Engagement
Staff Engagement

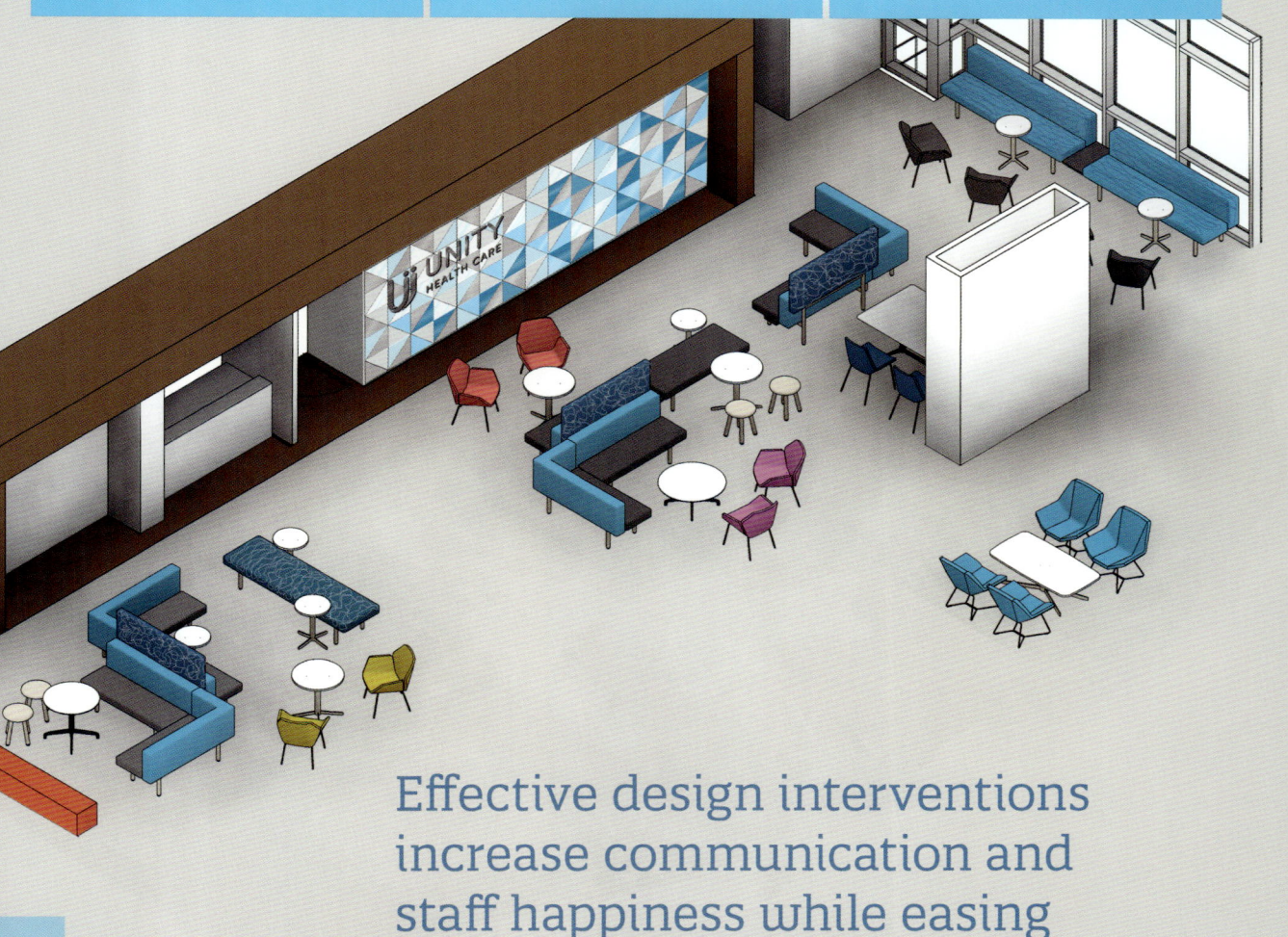

Effective design interventions increase communication and staff happiness while easing perceived wait times.

### THE CONTEXT

Unity Health Care is Washington, D.C.'s largest nonprofit health and social services organization, serving each of the District's eight wards. This facility includes medical, behavioral, and oral care; a teen clinic; and innovative programs such as Produce Prescription and Park Rx programs.

The facility serves more than 10,000 patients annually, many of whom constitute D.C.'s most vulnerable citizens. Brentwood is a neighborhood where people self-describe as "helpful, friendly, and welcoming." Unity Health Care accommodates the needs of a robust and growing constituency, doing so effectively while reflecting community identity.

## THE RESULTS

Pre-occupancy survey, observation, and behavioral mapping results showed a waiting room in need of change. We created design solutions and a re-orchestrated process from informed hypotheses, and through post-occupancy evaluations, we found substantial shifts in the right direction.

## DESIGN IMPLICATIONS

### A comprehensive discovery process leverages traditional and creative research methods.

Surveys and interviews are necessary, but are not the only means to assess what changes to make. Through thought-provoking exercises, we explored color, pattern, and poetry to understand the nuances of the unique community members. We could then integrate the community's creativity in the furniture, upholstery, macramé art, and quilt wall, incorporating pattern preferences and inspirational words from those exercises.

### Insights from post-occupancy analysis should drive future design iterations.

We found that our design interventions led to greater user satisfaction with the waiting room experience. This finding shows that design interventions can make a large experiential impact and ultimately improve patient satisfaction scores.

### Project goals should marry the operational and the experiential.

We knew that we had to make pragmatic changes to seating arrangements, wayfinding, and other room components that help streamline the user experience. However, the impacts of our design were more than pragmatic—enhancing patient satisfaction and staff happiness.

## DATA ANALYSIS

The new waiting room demonstrated a

# 100%

increase in communication

---

Community input directly impacted decisions on color, pattern, furniture selections, and art.

---

With increased color and waiting room art, staff happiness increased by

# 45%

Patient and staff engagement in the design process provides opportunities for higher patient satisfaction scores.

---

**Complaints about wait time decreased by**

# 25%

despite no change in perceived wait time

---

When diverse seating types were provided, modular sofas were preferred.

**WHAT'S NEXT**

Future research should explore the fluidity of patient experience with a focus on community-driven design and its impact on satisfaction scores. With each iteration of our research methodology, we will expand our ability to hold our interventions to the highest standards.

# Optimizing Exam Room Design

How can you tailor exam room design to the needs of an organization?

**WHAT WE DID**

**As part of the creation of ambulatory design standards for Rush University Medical Center, we conducted a detailed study of optimal exam room design tailored to the needs of their organization.** Before putting pen to paper, our team of leaders from Gensler's Health & Wellness practice area toured three existing Rush facilities and studied post-occupancy evaluations related to them. We reviewed all materials on Rush's current paradigm of facility guidelines.

We modeled floor plans to determine exam room and workstation spaces, and defined each space using an onstage/offstage corridor model. We then developed actual prototypes for testing: four exam rooms and two caregiver work zones for practitioner and patient evaluation. With a space type like exam rooms, there are myriad variables with complex interactions with one another. Even if we are on the beat of the latest literature, only in case-by-case testing can we reach our goal of an ideal patient and practitioner experience.

To optimize patient experience and functionality, we conducted an app-based survey to gather feedback on each prototype. Our survey included a questionnaire and written responses. Respondents included physicians and nurses, facilities managers, environmental service managers, leadership, and certified medical assistants. In total, nearly 200 people provided input over a two-week period. We supplemented our survey with discussions with a steering committee who considered 33 additional variables that ranged from floor materials to sink and cabinet positioning. After our survey and discussion phases, we analyzed respondent answers and ran an analysis of chi-square testing.

Finally, we created a fifth prototype exam room that is a hybrid representation of our research outcomes. Survey results, written responses, and steering committee discussions helped aggregate each configuration and product choice.

## Research Process

**1.** Information Gathering/ Hypothesis Formation

**2.** Design + Build Four Mockups

**3.** Survey + Analysis

**4.** Steering Committee Feedback

**5.** Design + Build Hybrid Mockup

**6.** Create Guidelines

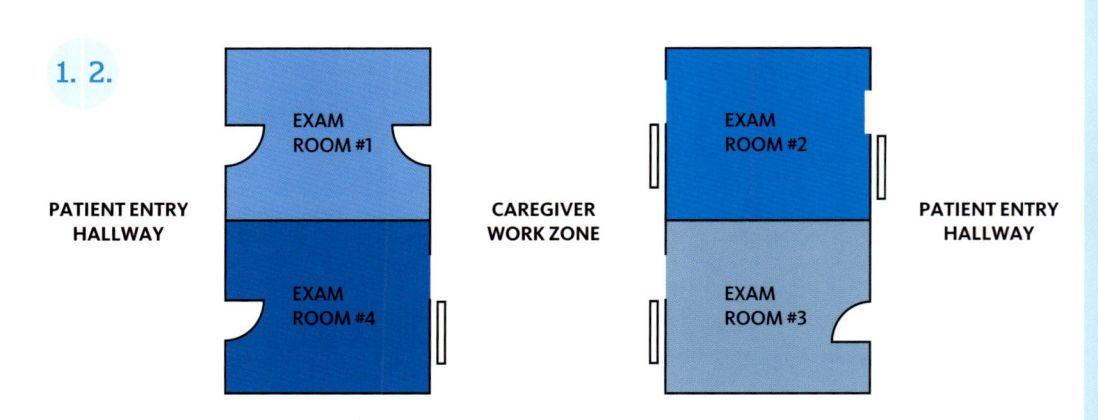

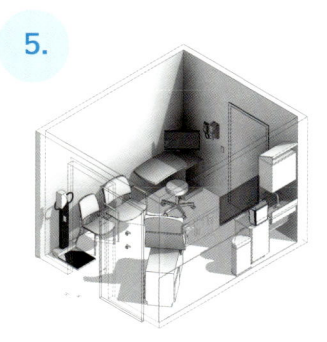

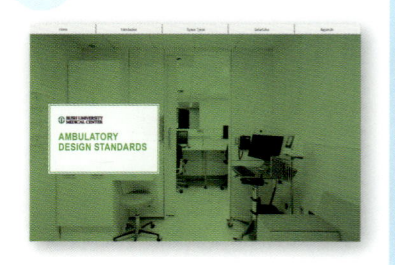

1. 2.
EXAM ROOM #1 | EXAM ROOM #2
PATIENT ENTRY HALLWAY | CAREGIVER WORK ZONE | PATIENT ENTRY HALLWAY
EXAM ROOM #4 | EXAM ROOM #3

3. 4. 5. 6.

# Testing the patient and provider experience improves the performance of our design solutions.

**THE CONTEXT**

Rush University Medical Center standards articulate a flexible, progressive, and patient-centric design. A "high-tech" aesthetic promotes knowledge exchange between patients and providers. Plurality is key: our design solutions acknowledge multiple practice models and future flexibility. Further, in all exam room prototypes, we promote privacy, the patient-provider relationship, and greater productivity.

With a growing shift toward ambulatory care, businesses must raise the bar. The Rush brand assures consistent messaging, signage, interior finishes, as well as standard infrastructure that is easy to navigate and is recognized as a Rush ambulatory practice.

Within the exam room, patients have evolving expectations. In keeping with practicality and economy, the exam room should make patients feel safe and dignified. This means that configurations for display monitors, vital sign equipment, or sinks must create a positive experience for both patients and practitioners.

The dialogue continues on what constitutes the ideal clinic planning module. Our prototype exam rooms are constructed within an onstage/offstage model, a design that leads a patient to their room through onstage hallways. Meanwhile, offstage areas are not included in the patient experience. These spaces are allocated for more private work and collaboration, and provide exclusive and convenient exam room access for providers. An onstage/offstage model necessitates two doors for each exam room, adding some complexity to our design plans. Operationally, however, an onstage/offstage model reduces travel distances for staff, which results in less patient waiting time—a clear improvement to the patient experience.

Evidence-based design, as a pre-occupancy research tool, builds best practices by engaging the people most likely to be affected by our decisions: the end user.

Hybrid Mockup

**42%**
of respondents think a modular casework and storage solution allows the most versatility in work types.

**40%**
of respondents think a powered exam table with arm accessories allows the greatest flexibility.

**THE RESULTS**

We conducted chi-square tests, frequencies, and content analyses to identify which variables were most important, and how those variables interacted with each other. Put simply, we sought an understanding of which rooms were most desirable—and which features made them so. Ranging from 99 to 120 square feet, each room varied by layout, door and wall types, millwork, and equipment. The rooms that ranked highest had a prodigious configuration of devices for workflow, viewing, and documentation needs. Across the board, exam room properties that promote flexibility are desirable.

Our findings helped us create a "hybrid" design room. Our chi-square test demonstrated eight design features correlated with improving the patient-provider relationship. These features include the design of the provider work area, and patient seating in relation to the patient-provider exchange. The lines of sight and visibility between a patient, practitioner, and guests are key elements. We view the significance of these variables as illustrating the importance of patient-provider interactions.

**DESIGN IMPLICATIONS**

### Creating guidelines sets the stage for better experiences.

Only by developing prototypes, gathering feedback, and conducting analysis could we come to actionable findings. Respondents often reinforced what we know from experience and secondary research. For example, our baseline for exam room design should be inclusive to all individuals, and should be flexible enough to accommodate specialty-specific needs. To accommodate the idiosyncrasies of practitioner workstyles and patient experiences, we must include both patients and practitioners in our research methods.

### Testing helps us maximize value in every square inch.

Although we need to provide flexibility for workstyle preferences, even the slightest adjustment of sink and cabinet space can be consequential. Sliding doors are preferred for both functionality and appearance. Evidence-based design has demonstrated that sliding doors also optimize space, so in a design scheme where every inch matters, sliding doors are key. Further, our results show that design impacts patient-provider orientation, a key determinant of a positive experience. Wherever permissible, design solutions should be flexible; for example, monitors that are reported by many as too high can be made more adjustable in future exam room versions.

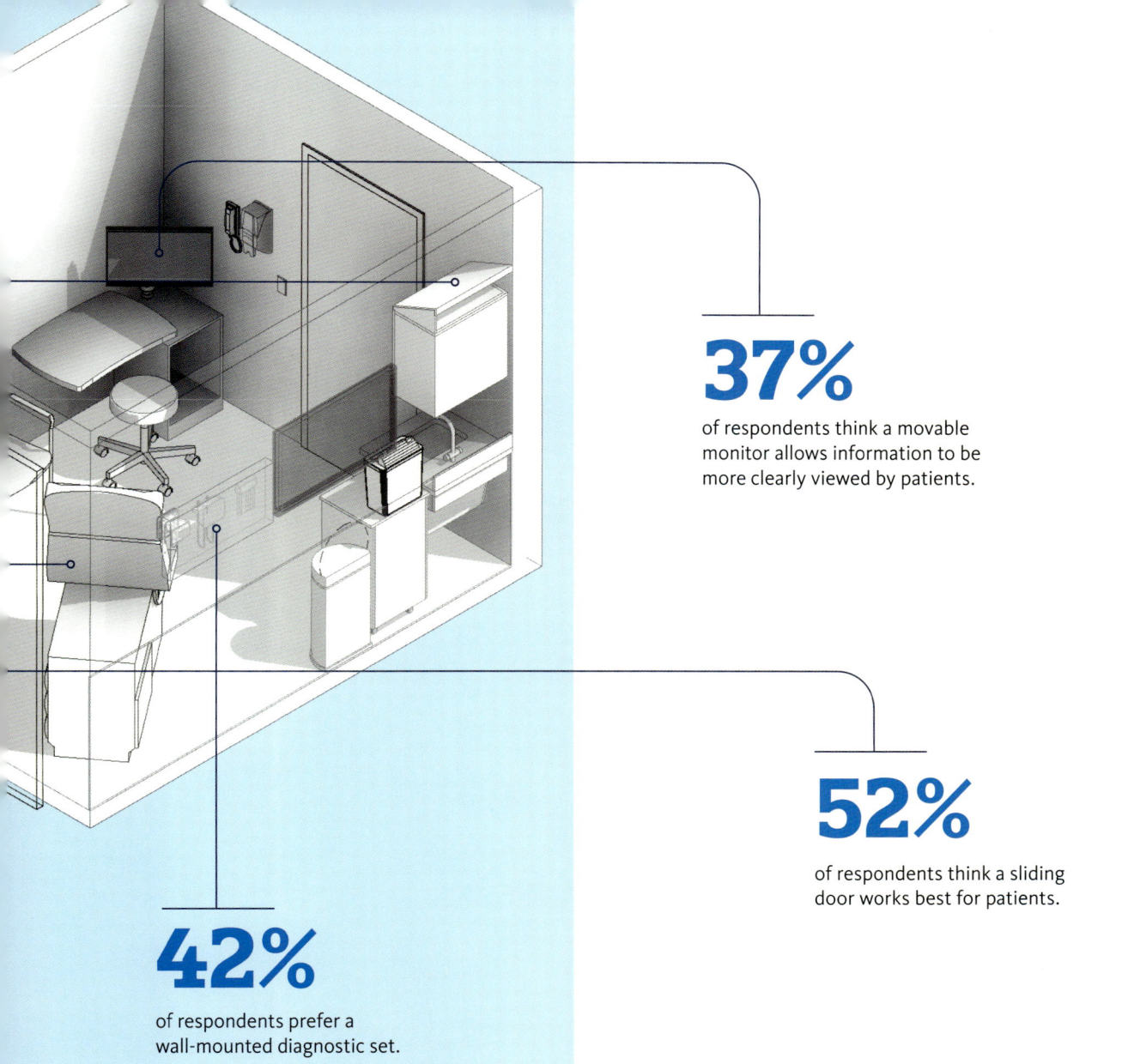

**37%**
of respondents think a movable monitor allows information to be more clearly viewed by patients.

**52%**
of respondents think a sliding door works best for patients.

**42%**
of respondents prefer a wall-mounted diagnostic set.

## Evidence-based design is an iterative process.

There is an ongoing dialogue on best health care design practices, and an expanding body of research that supplements design with backing data. Projects such as ours fill in knowledge gaps or contested best practices, such as the decentralized nurse station, general safety standards, and even the onstage/offstage model that our study operates within. Our research includes a level of analysis that should be applied to similar case studies. Because patient and health care professional expectations are constantly changing, evidence-based design principles will never be set in stone. It is only through rigorous and continuous research that we can create a great patient experience.

### WHAT'S NEXT

The final exam room prototype will be modified according to our research findings. It was only through a multiphased research process that we landed substantiated results. Going forward, our iterative research model that includes patient and provider feedback, analysis, and discussion will allow us to address multiple space types in a similar manner.

Our standards guidelines are not written to be an immovable strategy of caregiving and efficiency. They are a flexible strategy that can be easily modified as new research findings and new conversations on best practices unfold.

## BUILDING INTELLIGENT CITIES

The new technologies being rapidly integrated by our cities are giving us deeper insight into the human experience than ever before.

**SENSED ENVIRONMENTS**

234 **Building Intelligent Retail Places**

**Research Team**
Ryland Auburn
Daniel Bender
Stephanie Benkert
Raymond Bourraine
Islay Burgess
Chang-Yeon Cho
Michelle DeCurtis
Sean Drepaul
Ian Friedman
Rachel Ganin
Johnny He
Kathleen Jordan
Kelley Tapia
Zach Trattner
Richard Tyson
Peter Wang
Nicholas Watkins
Nathan Welch
Inwon Yoon

238 **Spatializing Our Data**

See Intelligent Retail Places Research Team

240 **IoT Technology in the Workplace**

**Research Team**
David Briefel
Islay Burgess
Chang-Yeon Cho
Johnny He
Stephanie Park
Ben Prager

**MACHINE LEARNING**

244 **Machine Learning Design Strategies**

**Research Team**
Nilesh Bansal
Chang-Yeon Cho
Russell Gilchrist
Sean McGuire
Jonathan Sandoval

**CONNECTED REAL ESTATE**

248 **Real Estate and the Intelligence Economy**

**Research Team**
Federica Bertoncini
Steven Folkes
Jessica Garcia
Wes LeBlanc
Duncan Lyons
Jose Luis Sánchez-Concha
Levi Schoenfeld
Gervais Tompkin
Richard Tyson

# Designing Intelligent Retail Places

How can we use spatial data to facilitate better retail experiences?

**WHAT WE DID**

**We applied mixed-methods research at a confidential flagship retail location to correlate customer engagement (behavior, interactions, and sentiment) and spatial characteristics (connectivity, visibility, and activation) with retail outcomes (quality of experience, purchase behavior).** This integrated approach included surveys, field observations, shop-along interviews, and spatial analytics. We leveraged proprietary, mobile surveys validated from prior Experience Index (EXI) research to capture the individual, in-store experience across core metrics. We measured and analyzed spatial dimensions and mapped the customer journey by gathering in-store movement and behaviors, and analyzed patterns using machine learning processes.

**THE CONTEXT**

Retailers are reimagining their brick-and-mortar assets with greater speed and agility as customers expect more from retail experiences. Some brands have responded with increased in-store technology, while others have reduced their physical footprint and investment. Retailers' primary goal should be creating value for customers and meeting their expectations around brand engagement, purchasing, and positive staff interactions.

Integrating sensors and IoT technology into physical spaces clarifies the customer journey. By leveraging these technologies, retailers may elevate their value beyond just products and sales figures—increasing brand loyalty, recognition, and connection. While relevant stakeholders are still researching how best to leverage and analyze that data, using new data to connect engagement, purchasing behavior, and staff-interaction experiences directly to how stores are designed, merchandized, and operated is key to increasing these forms of brand value.

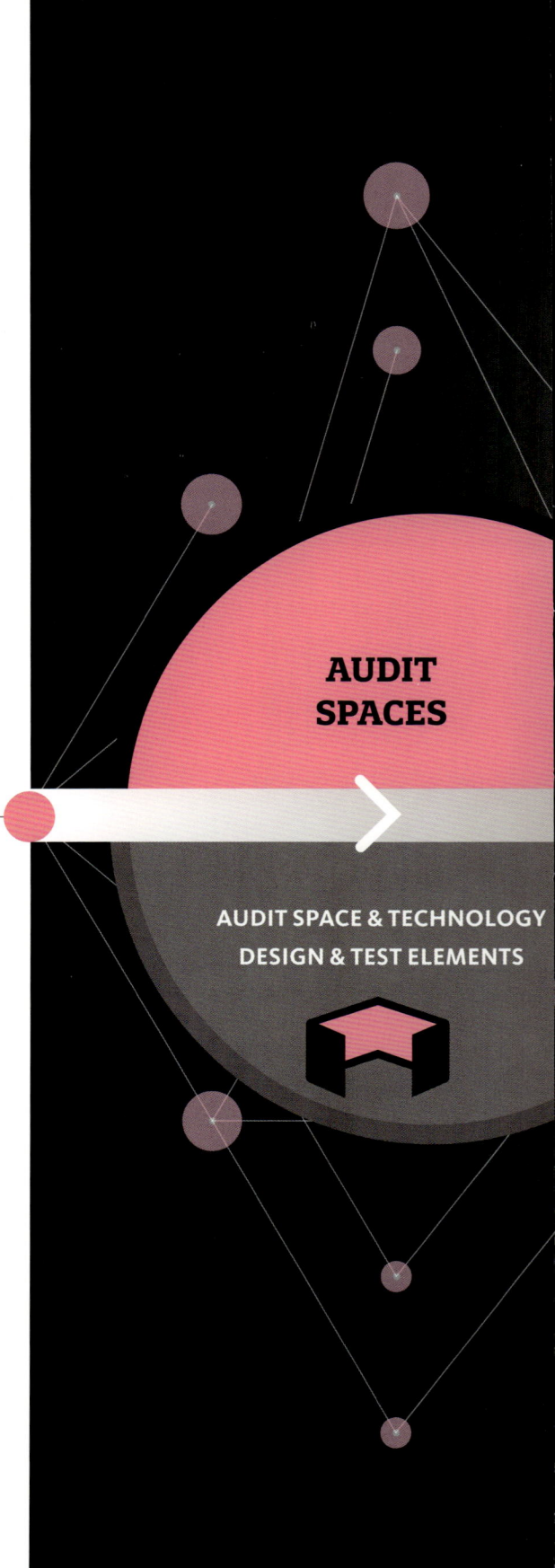

**AUDIT SPACES**

AUDIT SPACE & TECHNOLOGY
DESIGN & TEST ELEMENTS

## OUR PROCESS

We applied mixed methods to correlate shopper perception, shopper flow and behavior, and the contribution of spatial configuration to retail outcomes.

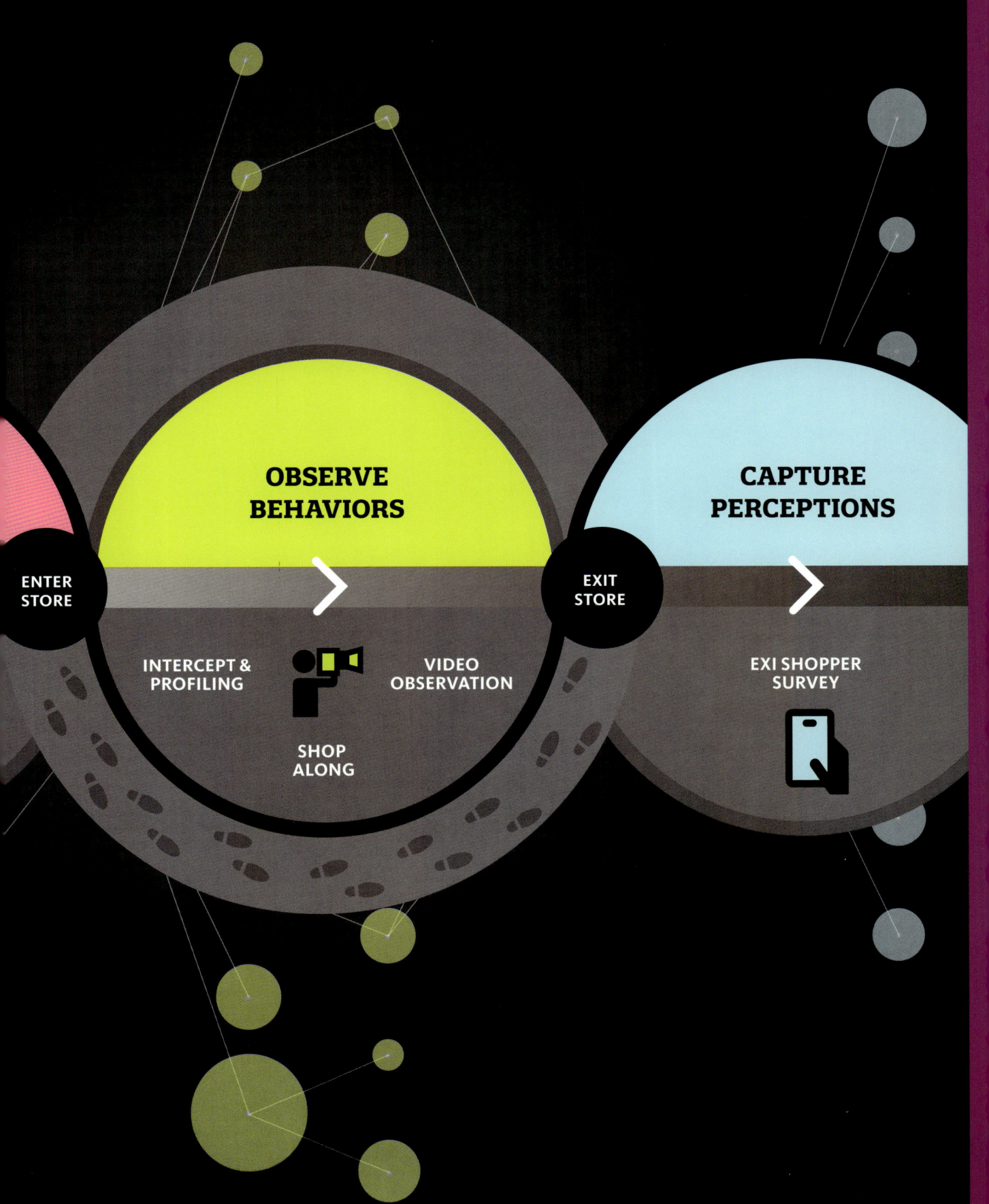

**ENTER STORE**

**OBSERVE BEHAVIORS**
- INTERCEPT & PROFILING
- VIDEO OBSERVATION
- SHOP ALONG

**EXIT STORE**

**CAPTURE PERCEPTIONS**
- EXI SHOPPER SURVEY

**THE RESULTS**

We delivered new insights into the relationships between places, people, and business through a technology-enabled, mixed-methods approach. Combining quantitative, qualitative, and spatial data helps identify correlations between customer engagement and spatial characteristics to reveal unique design opportunities for space, brand, service, merchandising, and operations. Gathering this data in real time helps us consider spaces as "living labs" that leverage in-store experiments to test hypotheses and generate feedback on an ongoing basis. This provides continuous opportunities to test layout, merchandising, and staffing to calibrate the store for fluid customer expectations.

**2x**
Faster in-store customer journey post-occupancy

**3x**
Group shoppers are 3x more likely to purchase

**DATA PREP**
TRANSCRIBE & CLEAN DATA

**ANALYSIS**

**BEHAVIORAL RESEARCH**
Mode switching
Product interation
Dwell time
Wait time
Staff interaction

**PERCEPTION RESEARCH**
Satisfaction
Experience
Recommendation
Contextual inquiry

**SPATIAL RESEARCH**

Visibility
Compactness
Connectivity

> **INSIGHTS**

**6 pts** Higher EXI score with staff interaction

**7.5%** Increase of in-store visibility post-occupancy

**DESIGN IMPLICATIONS**

**Spatializing data helps translate brand and merchandising aspirations into design and operational strategies.** Our integrated, mixed-methods approach creates the ability to understand and manage the customer journey. We can position merchandise, such as anchor products, based on customer intentions with optimized impact. We can study operational efficiencies including the coordinates of staff interactions, staffing protocols, and assurance that staffing plans are staffing plans are aligned with design and layout.

**Connecting data to space provides greater insight into the customer journey, facilitating design decisions that are more evidence-based.** This retail store pilot will become one of a succession of case studies used to benchmark and evaluate cross-retail type performance. Ultimately, we can compare project-specific metrics to those in similar industries or retail contexts.

**WHAT'S NEXT**

Brand identity can have different interpretations in diverse contexts. We are exploring the implications of variations in sentiments and behaviors based on spatial layout, design quality, and merchandising strategy. In doing so, we may identify core customer expectations, or brand "DNA," across multiple locations.

**Spatializing Our Data**  In this confidential retail store, our mixed-methods research included ethnography to map the customer journey through the store—tracking when customers transition through different modes of experience (below), and aggregating customer journeys to develop heat maps that display the frequency of visits to store areas (right).

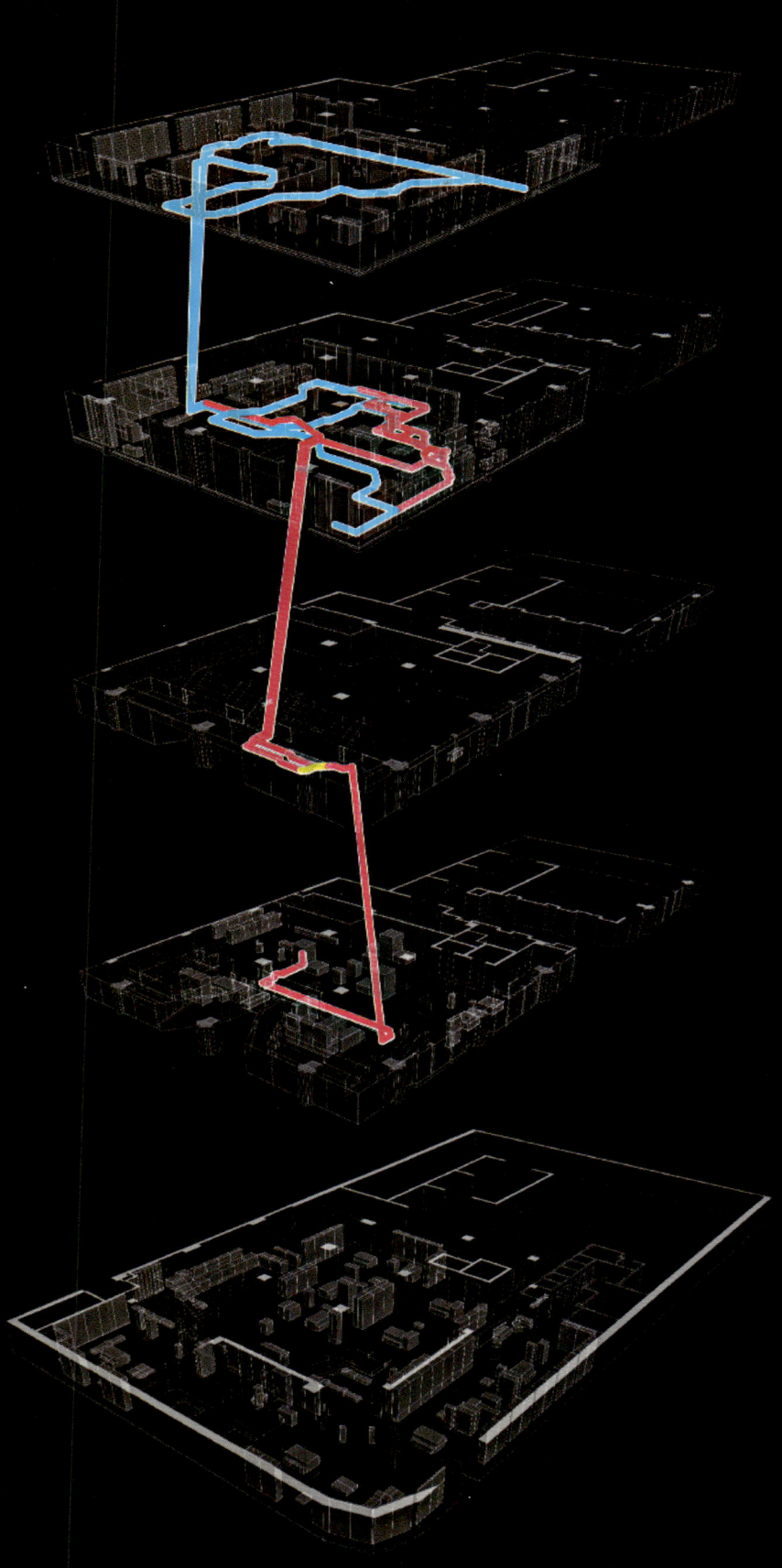

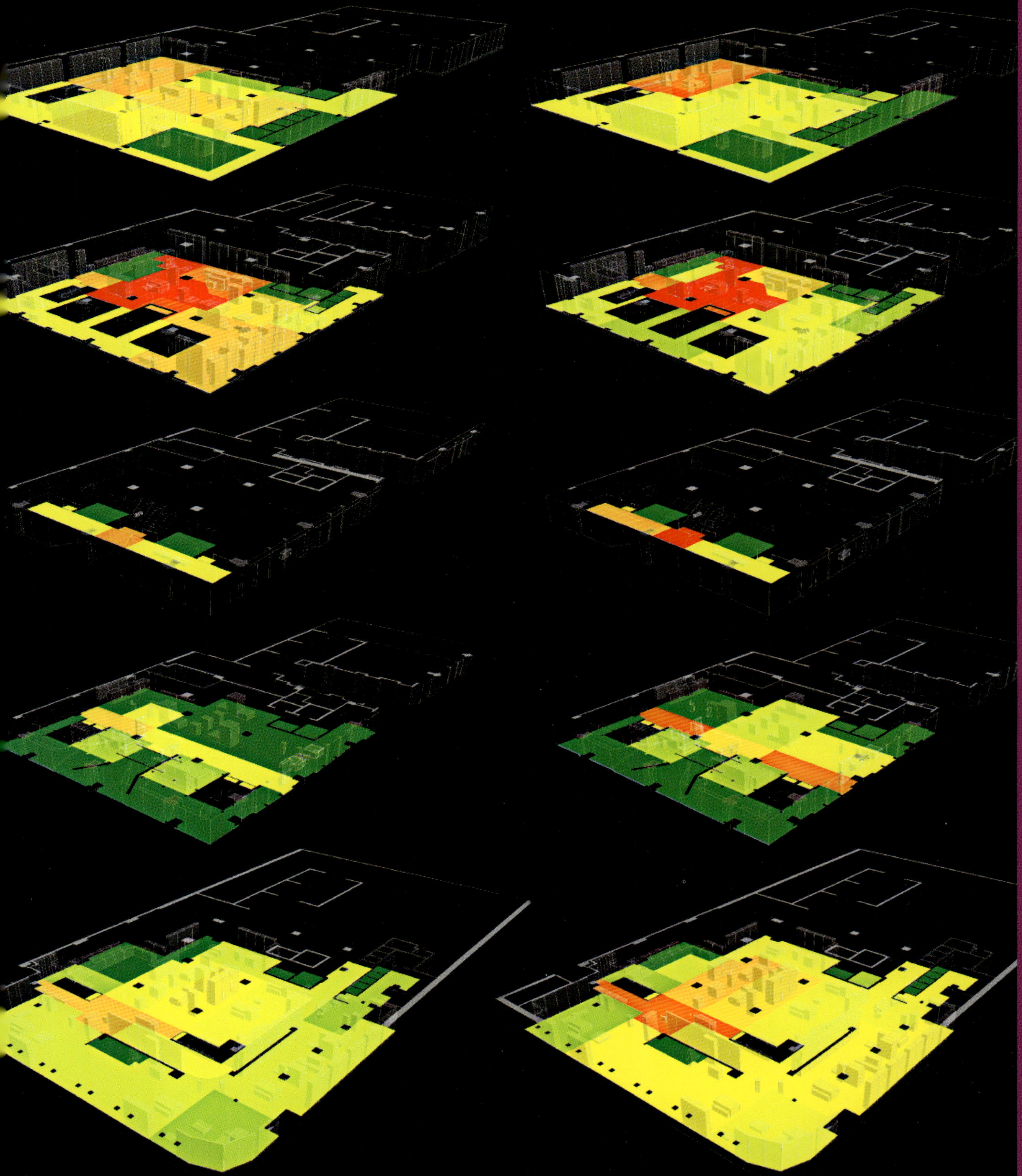

# IoT Technology in the Workplace

How can IoT sensing drive evidence–based design?

**WHAT WE DID**

**We piloted the integration of IoT sensor information into an evidence-based design approach, using Gensler's New York office as a case study.** To do this, we outfitted the office with 1,500 sensors connected to lighting and electrical outlets, creating a network that tracks daylight levels, occupancy, temperature, and energy consumption relative to spatial features. Our pilot analysis focused specifically on lighting and occupancy data, and analysis of that data as part of a mixed-methods approach including survey (WPIx[SM]), observational (Observe[SM]), and room booking data to capture occupancy on one floor of Gensler's New York office. We then outlined next steps for data visualization, a dashboard, and further methodological refinements to make our framework a reality.

**THE CONTEXT**

The impact of IoT is beginning to be felt. Affordable sensors only became available in the past few years, paralleling the growing symbiosis between design, users, and technology.

By 2025, the number of connected devices is expected to triple (75 billion) from today's count (23 billion). IoT technology has been utilized under many different situations: Bill Gates spent $80 million to build a Smart City in an Arizona desert; Samsung is launching a baggage-sensor product to help users track luggage; offices around the world are installing employee tracking devices. The technology offers an ongoing stream of data on space utilization, energy usage, health, and other contingencies that may inform our decision-making. But the technology is relatively new, and documentation of IoT outcomes is scant.

The multitude of use cases mirrors the diverse information types provided by IoT. In the office environment, this can range from individual occupant data to information owned by the landlord or facility management (BMS, temperature, CO2, turnstile and elevator usage, utility, and sensor data). This data becomes more powerful when paired with other data types such as information technology data (card swipes, logins, emails, and meeting rooms) and human resources data (productivity, PTO, demographics, and personnel data).

## The rapid adoption of sensor technologies is transitioning workplaces to "living laboratories."

## WPIx<sup>SM</sup>

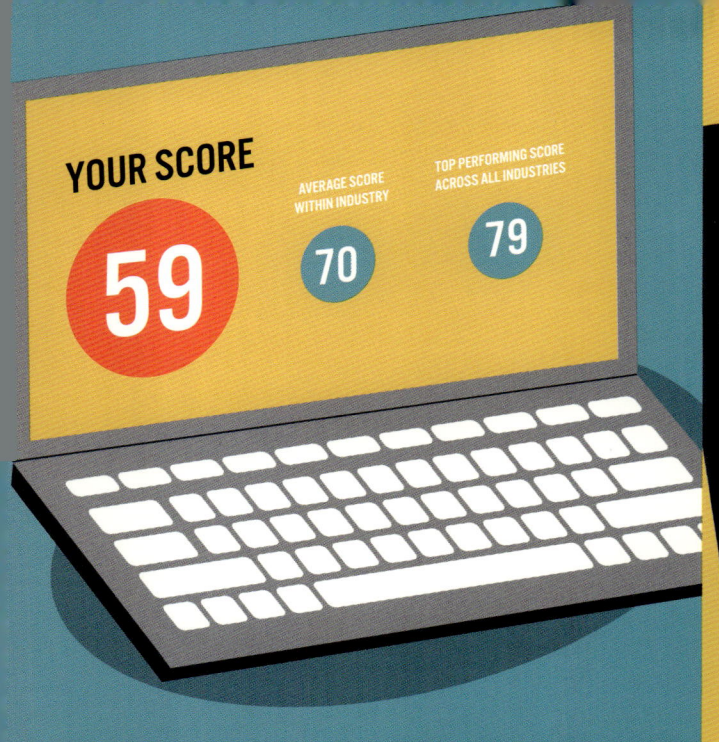

The WPIx is a survey tool that measures people's current work patterns, how they see the effectiveness of physical space and its related characteristics, and the impact of the workplace environment on key business drivers such as employee satisfaction and organizational commitment.

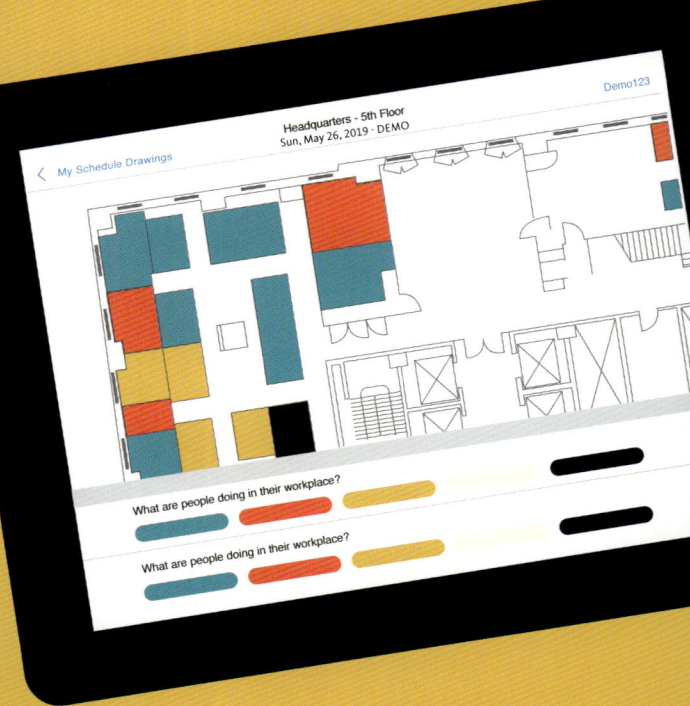

## Observe<sup>SM</sup>

Observe combines floor plans and survey criteria, allowing workplace activity and utilization data to be collected directly onto floor plans.

## IoT Overhead Sensors

Information from overhead sensors is the starting point for activity analysis, capturing real-time movement over the course of the workday.

## Room Booking

Room booking information can be explored to measure room utilization, and over time, utilization patterns can help leverage strategies for space maximization.

**THE RESULTS**

We devised a data structure that aggregates data from multiple sources. Gensler's Observe is an iPad app that combines floor plans and survey criteria into one platform, allowing workplace activity and utilization data to be collected directly onto floor plans. This data integrates with WISP, a SaaS space and occupancy management solution that combines data with interactive floor plans for real-time reporting, and the WPIx, Gensler's pre- and post-occupancy survey tool. In our pilot, we integrated this data with overhead sensor data using Enlighted, an IoT system solutions provider specializing in commercial real estate. We created spatial parameters using building information modeling (BIM) coordinates and connected this information to datasets for analysis.

The datasets we produce help us explore how we work, operate, and adapt to space across time. Our research resulted in a series of recommendations on how to frame "living labs," or organic case studies for future evaluation. Our work is open-ended: we call for an iterative and flexible approach to connect the quantitative findings from each new dataset.

We laid the groundwork for making the workplace tangible. We conceptualized a dashboard, centralizing the capabilities of different methodologies under one user interface. Our interpretation of aggregated data is accomplished through visualization and analysis. By aggregating raw data, we created custom visualizations, or representations of the evolution of space use and data across time. Visualizing data organizes the abstract and fragmented into a sensory experience of what is happening in space.

**DESIGN IMPLICATIONS**

**Before we use IoT, we must know what we want from it.**
We must answer key questions by mapping out the path from questions to solutions. At the end of the visioning process, there is a synthesis of findings that reveal system components answering each of the business needs identified. Designing and employing an IoT system is complex, requiring a scientific process and bridges that link cross-discipline expertise and system components. Successful applications of IoT will synergize experts of spatial and human centered design, integrators of engineering and technology in the built environment, and trusted consulting groups.

**Frame analyses by how we observe variable parameters.**
The nature of our data—time and space—can be infinitely large; therefore, we must restrict our data points for clarity and usefulness. Further, we must merge multiple variables into a singular path, creating a model for information trending. We need to record commissioning settings and calibrate the system accordingly through each iteration. In so doing, we will develop a baseline truth by testing sensors in a control state manually. We can then check coverage—or the radial range that sensors cover—and track the timing of intervals for data capture and coordination.

**Applied IoT creates a more granular vision of space.**
IoT can be leveraged to continuously monitor occupancy and utilization—the basis for future decision-making. We can develop a volume of raw data that can be analyzed for actionable variables such as desired occupancy rates. And paired with pre- and post-occupancy data, we can gather information on how to make a better user experience. Ultimately, the goal is to sense, analyze, and adjust according to an ongoing, feedback-driven process.

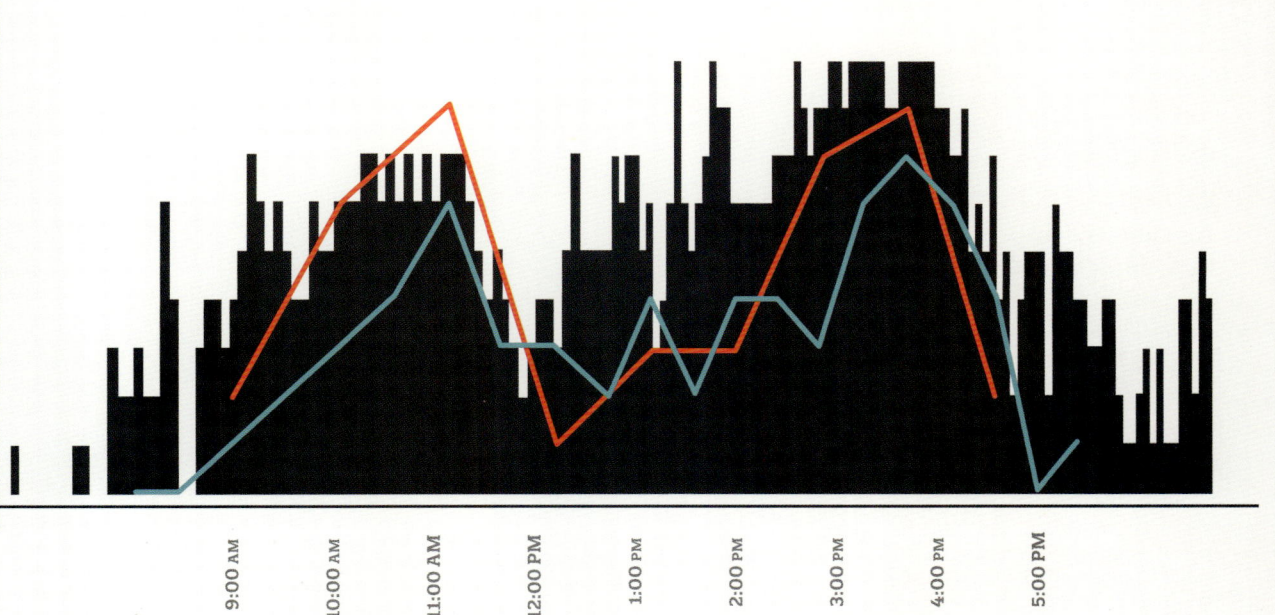

● Room Reservations ● Overhead Sensor ● Activity Analysis

**Number of Meeting Rooms Occupied**

9:00 AM — 10:00 AM — 11:00 AM — 12:00 PM — 1:00 PM — 2:00 PM — 3:00 PM — 4:00 PM — 5:00 PM

**Time of Day**

**WHAT'S NEXT**

Even though data is produced from the organization whose spaces and people are mapped, data ownership issues remain. Data belongs to different groups and is kept under careful lock and key. It's important to have buy-in across the organization in order to have access to the potentially sensitive data being tracked, and the metrics they are supposed to stand against. To create an effective interface, we need access to raw data points, not processed or digested information. Data access must be pre-negotiated with third parties, in line with analytical goals.

Once we have access to IoT technology, there is a critical sequence of validation at each stage of data collection, storage, and analysis—correction protocols for any information error or misrepresentation. Assuming that technology is reporting data correctly without affirmation can introduce bias. Our research addressed this concern by manual data collection of the same information as the sensors. Teams should include a diverse set of participants to ensure cross-disciplinary perspectives from architectural design, BIM, data and information technology, operations, HR, engineering and construction, and resilience and sustainability.

# The Value Opportunities of Machine Learning Design Strategies

How can machine learning enhance the process of architectural design?

**WHAT WE DID**

**We explored the nature of machine learning and its potential applications to architectural design.** Our exploration included identifying potential entry points for the applications and identifying design tasks that could most benefit from machine learning technology. We then developed two pilots that apply machine learning methods as a tool to improve the decision-making process: one focused on architectural visualization and the other on survey comments analysis.

Based on these pilots, we focused our efforts on the survey comments analysis because it proved to have the highest probability for design application. We utilized machine learning to create topic models that analyzed and graphically clustered comments from Gensler Workplace Performance Index surveys into defined themes, visually clustering the results around commonalities such as natural light and noise. We evaluated over 234,000 comments in a matter of seconds. We also explored opportunities to create targeted topic models and analyses by industries for more granular insights.

**THE CONTEXT**

Machine learning programs learn from experience according to a task and a performance measure—they require repeatable tasks, clear outcomes, and large amounts of data to be successful. In design, the application of machine learning is mostly focused on task automation, and is only beginning to find links with the creative process. By applying machine learning analyses to behavioral and perceptual data, as well as to data focused on the connection between people and space, we hope to identify design elements that might get overlooked in traditional design processes—thereby establishing new areas of value.

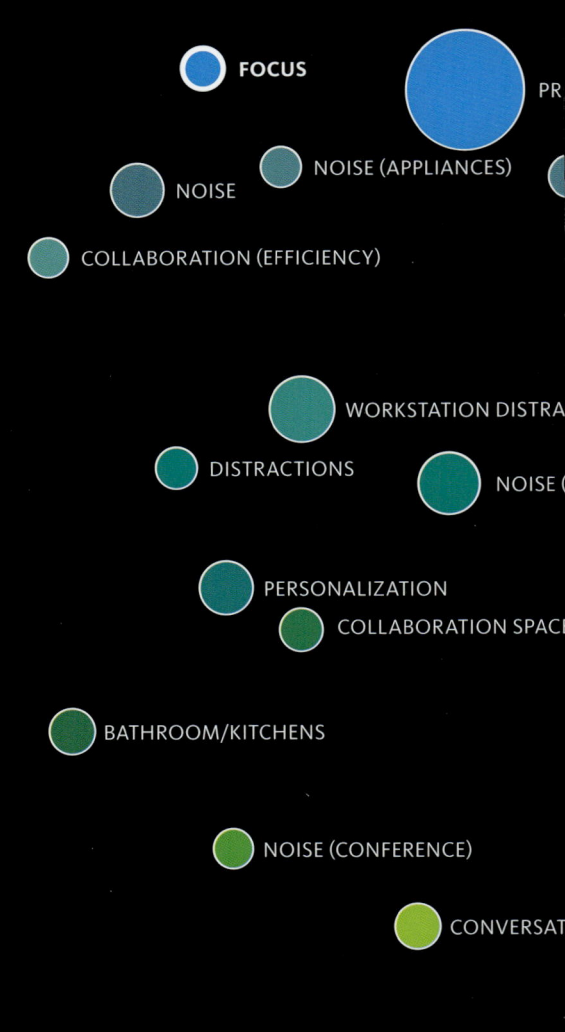

**THE RESULTS**

The biggest opportunities are those focused on learning about human experience in space. In our workplace data, we found multiple comment clusters around furniture-, fixture-, and equipment-focused variables (FF&E), as well as larger, singular clusters around overall spatial qualities such as workstations and amenities. The multiple, distinct FF&E topics proved to be both nuanced and potentially valuable in making design decisions, providing new insight into the best balance between the quality of space and cost of finishes from the perspective of users.

In these analyses, we analyzed overall term frequencies paired with the estimated term frequency within a selected topic. Our analysis differentiated words into clusters, or unique topics. We then created a platform utilizing natural language processing (NLP) libraries to reanalyze survey comments with greater specificity. We found space-related insights through analyzing both industry-wide and company-specific preferences. Through this study, the use of natural language processing enabled our team to understand user preferences and identify key design trends, shaping the spaces we design.

## SURVEY COMMENTS CLUSTER ANALYSIS

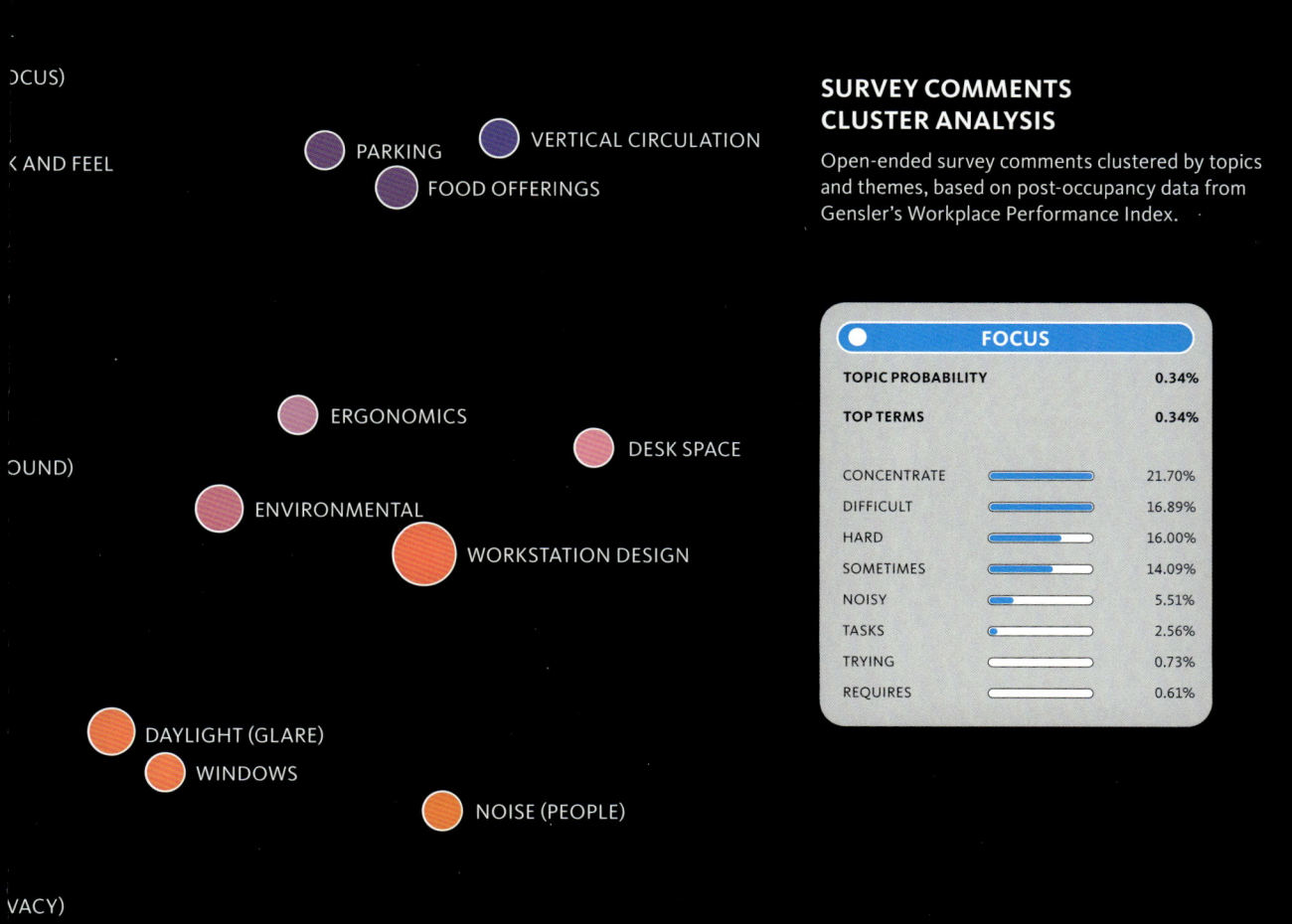

Open-ended survey comments clustered by topics and themes, based on post-occupancy data from Gensler's Workplace Performance Index.

- PARKING
- VERTICAL CIRCULATION
- FOOD OFFERINGS
- ERGONOMICS
- DESK SPACE
- ENVIRONMENTAL
- WORKSTATION DESIGN
- DAYLIGHT (GLARE)
- WINDOWS
- NOISE (PEOPLE)

**FOCUS**

| | |
|---|---|
| TOPIC PROBABILITY | 0.34% |
| TOP TERMS | 0.34% |
| CONCENTRATE | 21.70% |
| DIFFICULT | 16.89% |
| HARD | 16.00% |
| SOMETIMES | 14.09% |
| NOISY | 5.51% |
| TASKS | 2.56% |
| TRYING | 0.73% |
| REQUIRES | 0.61% |

## Natural language processing captures user feedback rapidly and in realtime.

### DESIGN IMPLICATIONS

**We are on a path toward a more empathetic design process.** Pre-occupancy topic modeling can pinpoint existing workplace concerns by analyzing nuances of how we work. This method empowers us with a deep understanding of how users interact with the built environment. Post-occupancy modeling serves to benchmark and preemptively address possible concerns.

**Machine learning is a broad and complex field, with numerous opportunities for implementation.** Natural language processing is an apt starting point—an area that will capture open-end feedback in a rapid, real-time basis. By finding variation across industries, we will achieve benchmarks against which individual companies can initiate predictive analyses.

**Machine learning provides a clear, holistic, and quantifiable articulation of why a floor plan may work.** We want to definitively—and with granularity—describe how specific design elements impact experience. By doing so, we create a unique value proposition for each design element, a value proposition that changes in real time according to both space and people.

### WHAT'S NEXT

The largest dataset and the best-suited algorithms are competitive advantages. These sorts of analysis have laid the foundation for predictive analytical methods that have the potential to become the centerpiece for how we think about design and experience.

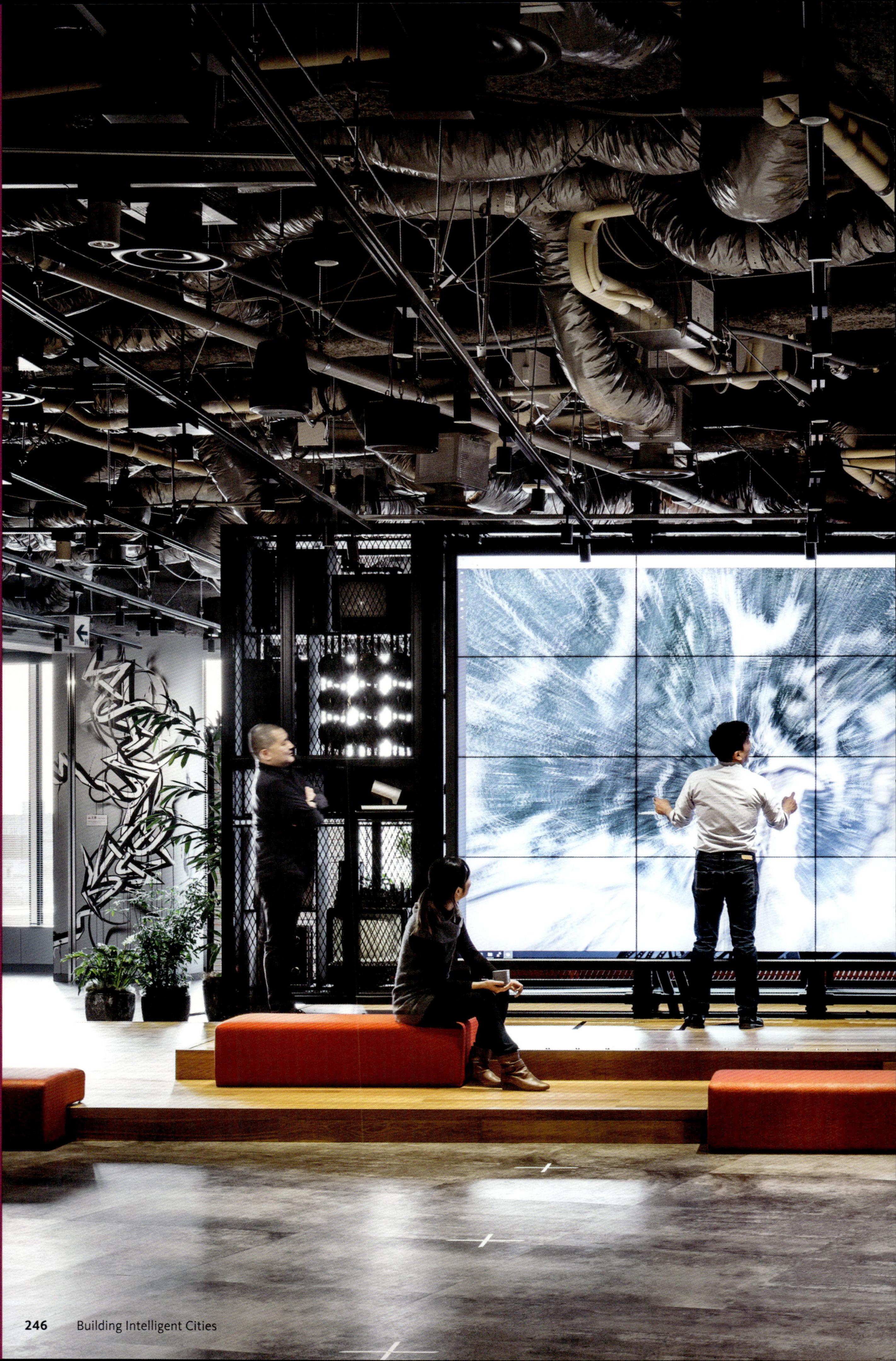

**Accenture Innovation Hub**
Tokyo, Japan

Accenture opened its Tokyo Innovation Hub as an experience-driven, state-of-the-art facility where employees collaborate with clients to turn new ideas into reality. The lower-level "neighborhood" is a space for clients, researchers, and entrepreneurs to collaborate and create. The design of the upper level is based on a traditional Japanese merchant house and provides a relaxing home atmosphere with a detached space for extended collaborative work sessions.

247

# Real Estate and the Intelligence Economy

Is the real estate industry smart enough for the intelligence economy?

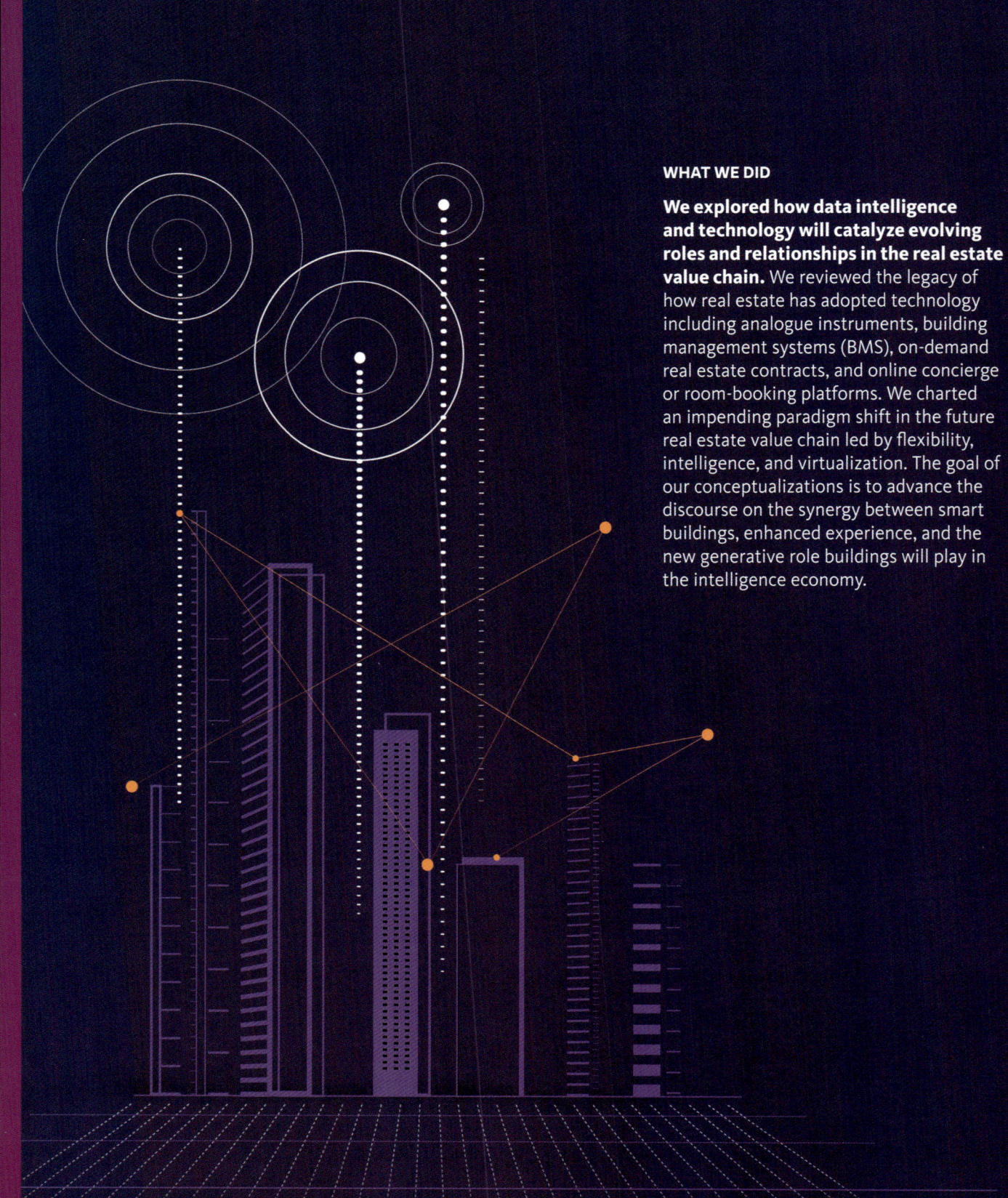

**WHAT WE DID**

**We explored how data intelligence and technology will catalyze evolving roles and relationships in the real estate value chain.** We reviewed the legacy of how real estate has adopted technology including analogue instruments, building management systems (BMS), on-demand real estate contracts, and online concierge or room-booking platforms. We charted an impending paradigm shift in the future real estate value chain led by flexibility, intelligence, and virtualization. The goal of our conceptualizations is to advance the discourse on the synergy between smart buildings, enhanced experience, and the new generative role buildings will play in the intelligence economy.

# The proliferation of building data and the emphasis on experience is poised to disrupt the traditional real estate value chain.

**THE CONTEXT**

The same digital transformation and on-demand service disruption that has restructured other industries is now poised to transform real estate by changing the roles and relationships of stakeholders in relation to one another, and ultimately the structure of the real estate value chain. We see the proliferation of building data and the evolving interest in experience intersecting in new ways that not only could revolutionize the way we design and live, but could transform the traditional real estate value chain into a responsive network of nonlinear value creation.

## The promise of "smart" or "intelligent" buildings is at the crux of this new value chain.

But smart buildings are still nascent; a well-packaged app bundle does not yet exist to harvest user data. And this new "intelligence," while enhancing convenience and accessibility, has yet to fundamentally shift personalization, flexibility, or our ability to design and anticipate user behavior proactively and adaptively.

**THE RESULTS**

# In this convergent future, all stakeholders—tenants, financers, developers, designers, and operators—will have a more direct, data-driven role to play in a real estate ecosystem as new value is placed on building data and its use.

The increasing granularity of our data and insights about people, behavior, and economics will be brought about by an emergent, sensor-rich environment that will deliver deeper, richer, and real-time understandings of end users.

Success in this convergent future will require the ability to anticipate future needs, use data to differentiate experiential value, facilitate richer interpersonal interactions, and democratize participation and ownership. Many signals already exist today: coworking and flexible contracts are already impacting leasing and ownership structures. Virtual and collective entities are being tasked with creating, aggregating, and analyzing assets and intelligence, disrupting traditional waterfall ownership models.

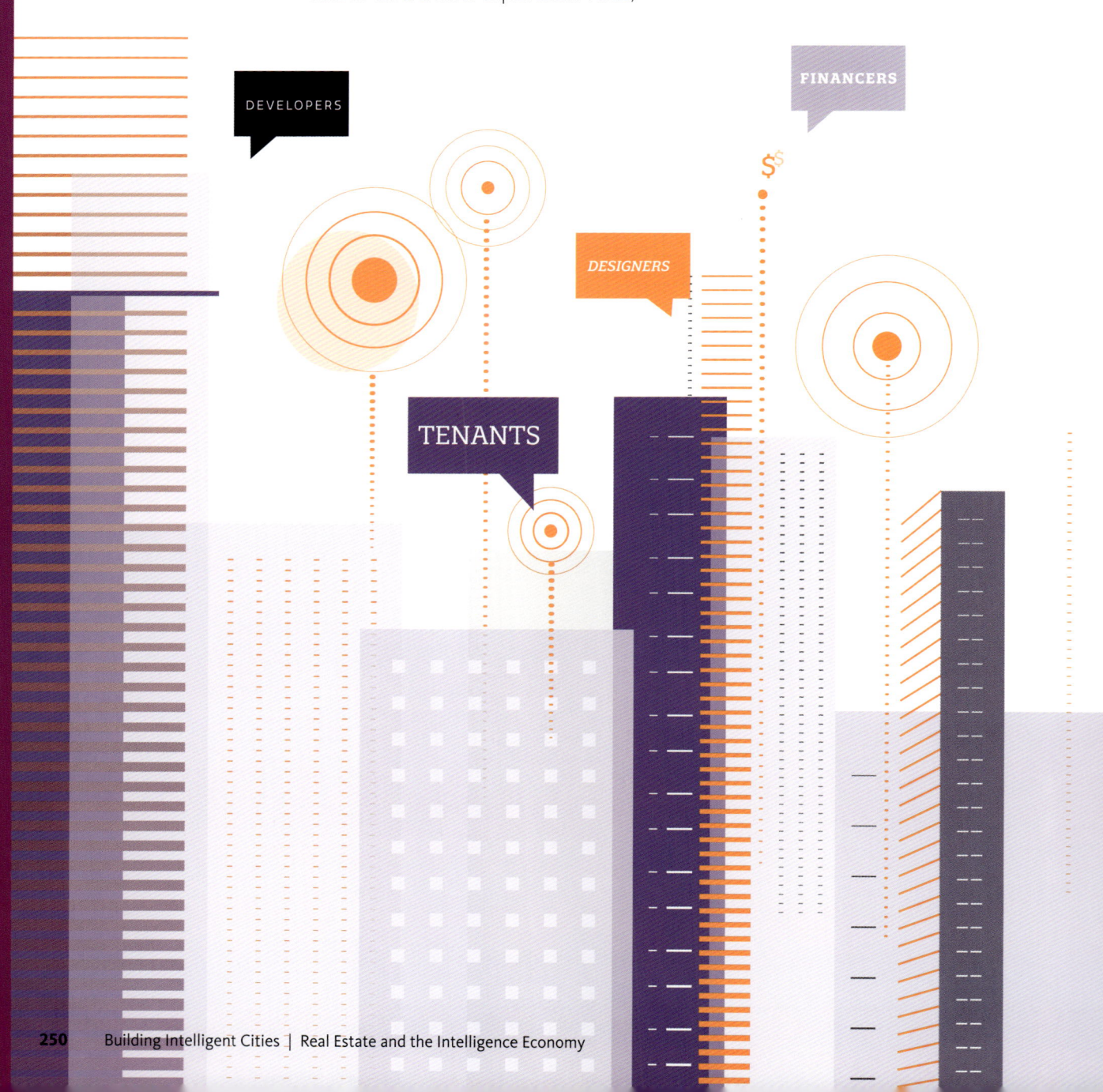

**DESIGN IMPLICATIONS**

**We must design for the convergence of physical and virtual realities.**

In the future, the most integral design consideration will be how to manage the physical and virtual realities into an interface of built and digital platforms. This new frontier will require that we consider spaces, services, and interactions in tandem—and leverage data and intelligence to explore their interconnections.

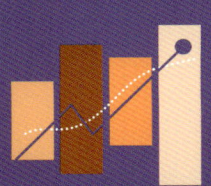

**The dynamics of operational expenditures are changing.**

New differentiation opportunities will be achieved by crafting a strategy to integrate digital assets, provide data services, and host platforms that provide intelligence to users and companies. This represents a blurring of the traditional lines between operational and capital expense spending, which are often siloed today.

**Those who intelligently manage their assets will facilitate better experiences.**

Future prestige may be staked upon the robust virtual network of relationships between tenants, owners, managers, and the community.

**The intelligent, on-demand future will require more adaptable environments.**

The full-scale virtualization of real estate assets, or the creation of "digital twins," will support business models that adapt to rapidly shifting needs.

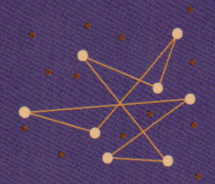

**Players in the real estate value chain will need to plan for handling data ownership and data management.**

In a near future world of on-demand building services and experiences, building data may become more valuable than the buildings themselves.

**WHAT'S NEXT**

IoT, machine learning, AI, and flexible on-demand services are just beginning to restructure the value chain and stakeholder relationships in the real estate industry. We need deeper user-centric investigations into how digital participation transforms value.

In particular, when design and experience shift from being periodic to continuous activities, designers will need to assume new roles and build great digital relationships with place and the social networks that define a place.

# APPENDIX

# RESEARCH TRENDS

Research proposal topics vary over time, as this visualization of our submissions topics from 2013–2019 shows. In 2019 alone, the Institute received over 175 research grant proposals.

| 2013 | 2014 | 2015 | 2016 | 2017 | 2018 | 2019 |

- URBAN STRATEGIES AND DESIGN
- TRANSPORTATION
- RESILIENCE/SUSTAINABILITY
- EDUCATION, CIVICS, AND CULTURE
- CRITICAL FACILITIES
- HEALTH AND WELLNESS
- HOSPITALITY
- SPORTS AND CONVENTION CENTERS
- RETAIL
- BRAND DESIGN
- CONSULTING AND REAL ESTATE SERVICES
- MIXED USE
- OFFICE BUILDINGS
- WORKPLACE
- PRODUCT DEVELOPMENT
- CLIENT RELATIONSHIPS
- DESIGN PROCESS

254  Appendix

# HISTORY OF THE
# GENSLER RESEARCH INSTITUTE

The Gensler Research Institute supports a diverse range of practitioner-led global research projects focused on enhancing the human experience and shaping the future of cities. In 2019 alone, we funded 34 research grants, including industry-leading research efforts such as the ongoing Workplace Surveys and Experience Index research, and the upcoming City Design Index.

We published our first research report, the UK Workplace Survey, in 2005, which revealed the connection between workplace design and employee productivity. Those insights underscored the importance of pursing research investigations outside of day-to-day project work, in turn leading to the launch of the first U.S. Workplace Survey in 2006. Gensler formally established our research program in 2007, and in 2008 launched our first request for proposals (RFP) targeted to practice area leaders around the firm.

In 2011, we transformed the RFP process by opening it up to all Gensler people, which dramatically expanded project diversity. This also helped us expand our global footprint; in 2013, we funded our first projects in China, India, and Latin America. Many of our teams also began partnering with academic institutions, clients, industry peers, or not-for-profit organizations, multiplying the impact of our data and insights. This breadth of work was documented in our first Research Catalogue, published in 2014, with a second volume published two years later.

The significant growth and influence of our program in recent years prompted a renaming to the Gensler Research Institute in 2018. Our establishment as an institute and publication of this third volume of the catalogue mark a new era—one that extends beyond inquiry to application through advanced data analytics and data spatialization that will inform the next generation of urban design and planning. Our continued goal is to envision and empower the future by generating new insights to fuel, inform, and inspire innovative design solutions that make the world better and more resilient for everyone.

Christine Barber
Director, Gensler Research Institute

## ABOUT GENSLER

Gensler is widely considered the world's leading design firm—our breadth of expertise, global scale, and unwavering focus on the human experience are what make us different. We impact millions of people's lives every year by designing the spaces in which they live, work, and play. We're also taking on the toughest challenges facing cities, including climate change, mobility, smart city technology, and issues of housing and homelessness.

**1965** — San Francisco · Houston · Denver · **1975** · Los Angeles · New York · Washington, DC · Newport Beach · **1985** · London · Boston · Atlanta · Detroit · Morristown · Tokyo · **1995** · Chicago · La Crosse · Baltimore · Dallas · **2000** · Charlotte · San Jose · Seattle · Phoenix · Shanghai · Las Vegas · San Diego · **2005** · Costa Rica · Tampa · Austin

*In 1954, Buckminster Fuller—the mind behind the iconic Geodesic Dome—revealed the "Fuller Projection Map," also known as the "Dymaxion Map," which shows the entire planet as an island in one ocean, splits no continents, and more accurately presents the shapes and sizes of land areas.*

# BIBLIOGRAPHY

### Design Solutions for Homelessness

Marcellino, E. (2019). "LA County Approves $460 Million in Homeless Initiatives." NBC Los Angeles. Retrieved from https://www.nbclosangeles.com/news/local/LA-County-Set-to-Approve-460-Million-in-Homeless-Initiatives-509914871.html

Smith, D. (2016). "Proposition HHH would raise funds to build homeless housing in L.A." Los Angeles Times. Retrieved from https://www.latimes.com/local/california/la-me-ln-prop-hhh-qa-20161017-snap-story.html

Smith, D. (2019). "How close is L.A. to building 10,000 houses for homeless people?" Los Angeles Times. Retrieved from https://www.latimes.com/local/lanow/la-me-ln-hhh-spending-commitments-20190421-story.html

### A New Model for Intergenerational Living

AARP (Producer). (2017). AARP Network of Age-Friendly Communities Program Cycle.

Burbank, J., & Keely, L. (2014). "Baby Boomers and Their Homes: On Their Own Terms." Retrieved from http://demandinstitute.org/baby-boomers-and-their-homes/

Coughlin, J. (2015). Mapping the Community of the Future. Point of View.

Generations United. (2007). "The Benefits of Intergenerational Programs: Fact Sheet."

Harrell, R., Lynott, J., Guzman, S., & Lampkin, C. (2014). "What is Livable? Community Preferences of Older Adults." Retrieved from https://www.aarp.org/ppi/issues/livable-communities/info-2015/what-is-livable-AARP-ppi-liv-com.html

Harvard.edu. "Housing America's Older Adults: Meeting the Needs of an Aging Population." (2014). Retrieved from https://www.jchs.harvard.edu/housing-americas-older-adults-2018

Henkin, N. Z., Patterson, T., Stone, R., & Butts, D. (2017). "Intergenerational Programming in Senior Housing: From Promise to Practice." Retrieved from https://www.gu.org/resources/intergenerational-programming-in-senior-housing-from-promise-to-practice/

Institute for the Future. (2007). "Boomers: The Next 20 Years." Retrieved from http://www.iftf.org/our-work/health-self/aging/boomers-the-next-20-years/

Irving, P. (2016). "Millennials Shape the Future of Aging." Retrieved from https://encore.org/blogs/paul-irving/

Irving, P. (2018). "Silver to Gold: The Business of Aging." Retrieved from http://milkeninstitute.org/reports/silver-gold-business-aging

Lampkin, C. (2012). "2011 Boomer Housing Survey." Retrieved from https://www.aarp.org/home-family/livable-communities/info-10-2012/boomers-housing-livable-communities.html

Leinberger, C. B., & Rodriguez, M. (2016). "Foot Traffic Ahead: Ranking Walkable Urbanism in America's Largest Metros." Smart Growth America.

Milken Institute. (2016). "The Future of Aging: Realizing the Potential for Longevity." Retrieved from https://www.giaging.org/documents/Milken_Future_of_Aging_report_May_2016.pdf

Milken Institute. (2016). "The Power of Purposeful Aging: Culture Change and the New Demography."

Saiz, A., & Salazar, A. (2017). "Real Trends: The Future of Real Estate in the United States."

Senior Housing News. (2017). "The Urban Opportunity: Senior Living Development and Design in the City."

Stambolian, J., Blanchard, J., Thomas, W. H., Hively, J., & Stambolian, B. (2018). "Aging in Community: A New Perspective."

World Health Organization. (2007). "Checklist of Essential Features of Age-friendly Cities." Retrieved from https://www.who.int/ageing/publications/Age_friendly_cities_checklist.pdf

### Hong Kong's Next Generation of Senior Living

Hong Kong Housing Society. "Ageing-in-Place Scheme." (2019). Retrieved from https://www.hkhs.com/en/our-business/elderly-housing/ageing-in-place

Mok, J. (2018). "Hong Kong faces challenge in how to manage its ageing population." South China Morning Post. Retrieved from https://www.scmp.com/news/hong-kong/education/article/2146677/hong-kong-faces-challenge-how-manage-its-ageing-population

Senthilingam, M. (2018). "This urban population is leading the world in life expectancy." CNN. Retrieved from https://www.cnn.com/2018/03/02/health/hong-kong-world-longest-life-expectancy-longevity-intl/index.html

### Converting Office Buildings for Residential Use

Banister, J. (2017). "U.S. Office Vacancy Rose in Q1 For The First Time in Seven Years." BisNow. Retrieved from https://www.bisnow.com/national/news/office/national-office-vacancy-rose-for-the-first-time-since-2010-in-q1-75194

Department of Small and Local Business Development. (2019). "Business Improvement Districts." Retrieved from https://dslbd.dc.gov/service/business-improvement-districts-bids

Cushman & Wakefield. (2018). "Office Q3 2018." MarketBeat: Washington, D.C.

Zamorano, L., & Kulpa, E. (2014). "People-oriented cities: Mixed-Use Development Creates Social and Economic Benefits." World Resources Institute. Retrieved from https://www.wri.org/blog/2014/07/people-oriented-cities-mixed-use-development-creates-social-and-economic-benefits

### Achieving Inclusivity in the Design Process

Goren, W.D. "Understanding the Americans with Disabilities Act, Fourth Edition." October 2013. ABA Book Publishing.

Martin, H. "Lawsuits targeting business websites over ADA violations are on the rise." Los Angeles Times. 2018. Retrieved from: https://www.latimes.com/business/la-fi-hotels-ada-compliance-20181111-story.html

ADA National Network. "ADA Checklist for Existing Facilities." 2016. Retrieved from: https://www.adachecklist.org/doc/fullchecklist/ada-checklist.pdf

### Designing Gender Inclusive Restrooms

Anthony, K. H., & Dufresne, M. (2007). "Potty Parity in Perspective: Gender and Family Issues in Planning and Designing Public Restrooms." Journal of Planning Literature, 21(3), 267.

Human Rights Campaign. (2017). "Restroom Access for Transgender Employees. Workplace." Retrieved from https://www.hrc.org/resources/restroom-access-for-transgender-employees

Molotch, H., and Noren, L. (2010). Toilet: Public Restrooms and the Politics of Sharing: NYU Press.

Neu, R., & Keane, M. "Building a Better Bathroom." Strategies for Success, 2.

Schuster, M. A., Reisner, S. L., & Onorato, S. E. (2016). "Beyond Bathrooms—Meeting the Health Needs of Transgender People." The New England Journal of Medicine, 2016 (375), 3.

Tobia, J. (2017). "Why All Bathrooms Should Be Gender-Neutral." Time, 1, 1.

World Health Organization (2017). "Sanitation." Media Centre. Retrieved from http://www.who.int/mediacentre/factsheets/fs392/en/

### Local Development in Sub-Saharan Africa

Ibrahim Index of African Governance. (2019). Retrieved from http://mo.ibrahim.foundation/iiag/

Kirk, A. (2016). "What Africa will look like in 100 years." The Telegraph. Retrieved from https://s.telegraph.co.uk/graphics/projects/Africa-in-100-years/

Metcalfe, J. (2016). "Looking Down at Nairobi's Explosive Growth." CityLab. Retrieved from https://www.citylab.com/life/2016/09/nairobi-kenya-population-growth-urbanization/502361/

Nairobi City Water and Sewerage Company. (2019). Retrieved from https://www.nairobiwater.co.ke/index.php/en/

S&P. (2018). S&P Global Ratings.

The Architectural Association of Kenya. (2019). Retrieved from https://aak.or.ke/

The World Bank. (2019). "Ease of Doing Business in Nigeria." Retrieved from http://www.doingbusiness.org/en/data/exploreeconomies/nigeria#

United Nations Development Programme. (2018). "Global Human Development Indicators." Retrieved from http://hdr.undp.org/en/content/human-development-index-hdi

United Nations Development Programme. (2019). "About Kenya." Retrieved from http://www.ke.undp.org/content/kenya/en/home/countryinfo.html

UNEP. (2018). "Nairobi and its Environment." Retrieved from https://na.unep.net/atlas/kenya/downloads/chapters/Kenya_Screen_Chapter5-End.pdf

World Council on City Data. (2019). Retrieved from https://www.dataforcities.org/

### Investigating Downtown Neighborhood Resurgence

CoStar Market Analytics. (2019). Retrieved from: https://www.costar.com/products/costar-market-analytics

Esri. (2019). "Tapestry Segmentation." Retrieved from: https://www.esri.com/en-us/arcgis/products/tapestry-segmentation/overview

JLL. Cities Research Center. (2019). Retrieved from: http://cities-research.jll.com/cities-research

### A Framework for Holistic Urban Planning

International Organization for Migration. (2018). "World Migration Report 2018." Retrieved from https://www.iom.int/wmr/world-migration-report-2018

United Nations. (2019). "Sustainable Development Goals." Retrieved from https://www.un.org/sustainabledevelopment/sustainable-development-goals/

### Impact by Design

ACEEE (2015). "Energy Efficiency in the United States: 35 Years and Counting." Retrieved from https://aceee.org/research-report/e1502

Amann, J. T. (2017). "Unlocking Ultra-Low Energy Performance in Existing Buildings." ACEEE.

Architecture2030 (2017). "Architecture2030." Retrieved from http://architecture2030.org/about/

Berwyn, B. (2016). "Germany Reasserts Climate Leadership, Outlines Path to Carbon-Neutral Economy by 2050." InsideClimate News. Retrieved from https://insideclimatenews.org/news/17112016/germany-climate-change-carbon-neutral-economy-cop22-paris-agreement

BREEAM (2018). "Refurbishment and Fit-Out: Homes and Commercial Buildings." Retrieved from https://www.breeam.com/discover/technical-standards/refurbishment-and-fit-out/

City of Cambridge. (2018). "The Path to Net Zero Cambridge." Retrieved from http://www.cambridgema.gov/~/media/Images/CDD/Climate/NetZero/netzero_20150408_infographic.jpg

City of Vancouver. (2018). "Greenest City Action Plan." Retrieved from https://vancouver.ca/green-vancouver/greenest-city-action-plan.aspx

City of Vancouver. (2018). "Targets and actions." Retrieved from https://vancouver.ca/green-vancouver/goals-and-target.aspx

Climate Change Adaptation. (2018). "Climate change impact on buildings and constructions." Retrieved from http://en.klimatilpasning.dk/sectors/buildings/climate-change-impact-on-buildings.aspx

Climate Solutions. (2017). "New Coalition Formed to Advance Zero Energy Buildings in Oregon." Retrieved from www.climatesolutions.org

D'Agostino, D., et al. (2017). "Towards Nearly Zero Energy Buildings in Europe: A Focus on Retrofit in Non-Residential Buildings." Energies 10(1):1.

Directorate-General for Internal Policies, European Parliament. (2018). "Boosting Building Renovation: What Potential and Value for Europe?" European Parliament.

Domonoske, C. (2018). "California Sets Goal of 100 Percent Clean Electric Power By 2045." Energy. Retrieved from https://www.npr.org/2018/09/10/646373423/california-sets-goal-of-100-percent-renewable-electric-power-by-2045

Energiesprong. (2018). "What is Net Zero Energy?" Retrieved from http://energiesprong.eu/net-zero-energy-home-makeovers/

# BIBLIOGRAPHY

EPA (2015). "Executive Order 13693, Planning for Federal Sustainability in the Next Decade." Retrieved from https://www.epa.gov/greeningepa/executive-order-13693-planning-federal-sustainability-next-decade

EPA (2018). "The Inside Story: A Guide to Indoor Air Quality." Retrieved from https://www.epa.gov/indoor-air-quality-iaq/inside-story-guide-indoor-air-quality

European Commission. (2018). "Energy Renovation: The Trump Card for the New Start for Europe." Retrieved from https://ec.europa.eu/jrc/en/publication/eur-scientific-and-technical-research-reports/energy-renovation-trump-card-new-start-europe

European Commission. (2018). "Towards nearly zero energy buildings in Europe: a focus on retrofit in non-residential buildings." EU Science Hub. Retrieved from https://ec.europa.eu/jrc/en/publication/towards-nearly-zero-energy-buildings-europe-focus-retrofit-non-residential-buildings

Government of Sweden. (2018). "The climate policy framework." Retrieved from https://www.government.se/articles/2017/06/the-climate-policy-framework/

Gov.uk (2013). "Energy saving measures boost house prices." Retrieved from https://www.gov.uk/government/news/energy-saving-measures-boost-house-prices

International Energy Agency. (2018). "Buildings." Retrieved from https://www.iea.org/buildings/

Hallegatte, S., et al. (2013). "Future Flood Losses in Major Coastal Cities." Nature Climate Change 3(9): 5.

McKinsey & Company. (2011). "Urban world: Mapping the economic power of cities." Retrieved from www.mckinsey.com

New York City Council. (2018). "A Local Law to amend the administrative code of the city of New York, in relation to requiring that all city-owned buildings be powered by green energy sources by 2050 Int 0598-2018." Retrieved from www.legistar.council.nyc.gov. No. 598

Office of Governor Edmund G. Brown, Jr. (2012). "Executive Order B-18-12. Executive Order B-18-12." Retrieved from https://www.gov.ca.gov/2012/04/25/news17508/

Passipedia (2018). "EnerPHit – the Passive House Certificate for retrofits." Retrieved from https://passipedia.org/certification/enerphit

Reuters (2017). "Inner-city living makes for healthier, happier people, study finds." The Guardian. Retrieved from https://www.theguardian.com/society/2017/oct/06/inner-city-living-makes-for-healthier-happier-peoplestudy-finds

Ross, K. (2017). "Costa Rica Sets Carbon Neutral Goal." Renewable Energy World. Retrieved from https://www.renewableenergyworld.com/articles/2017/01/costa-rica-sets-carbon-neutral-goal.html

Roys, M., et al. (2016). The full cost of poor housing: IHS BRE Press.

UNHCR (2018). Global Report 2017: UNHCR.

United Nations. (2018). 2018 Revision of World Urbanization Prospects: United Nations.

U.S. Department of Energy (2015). "A Common Definition for Zero Energy Buildings. Energy Efficiency & Renewable Energy." Retrieved from www.energy.gov

U.S. Green Buildings Council. (2018). "LEED is green building." U.S. Green Building Council. Retrieved from https://new.usgbc.org/leed

Wong, S. (2017). "Sweden commits to becoming carbon neutral by 2045 with new law." New Scientist. Retrieved from https://www.newscientist.com/article/2138008-sweden-commits-to-becoming-carbon-neutralby-2045-with-new-law/

Zhang, X. and F. Wang (2017). "Analysis of embodied carbon in the building life cycle considering the temporal perspectives of emissions: A case study in China." Energy and Buildings 155: 9.

**Gensler's Path to Net Zero**

Architecture 2030. (2019). Retrieved from https://architecture2030.org/

Paris Pledge for Action. (2019). Retrieved from http://www.parispledgeforaction.org/

The American Institute of Architects. (2019). "The 2030 Commitment: Are you up for the challenge?" Retrieved from https://www.aia.org/resources/202041-the-2030-commitment

United Nations Global Compact. (2019). Retrieved from https://www.unglobalcompact.org/

World Green Building Council. (2019). "The Net Zero Carbon Buildings Commitment." Retrieved from https://www.worldgbc.org/thecommitment

**Designing Dynamic Facades to Conserve Energy**

U.S. Energy Information Administration. (2019). "How much energy is consumed in U.S. residential and commercial buildings?" Retrieved from https://www.eia.gov/tools/faqs/faq.php?id=86&t=1

**Urban Strategies for Coastal Resilience**

Agency for Toxic Substance and Disease Registry. (2018). "CDC's Social Vulnerability Index (SVI)." Retrieved from https://svi.cdc.gov/

ArcGIS Online. (2019). Retrieved from https://www.arcgis.com/index.html

Cadmapper. (2019). Retrieved from https://cadmapper.com

City-Data. (2019). "Miami, Florida (FL) income map, earnings map, and wages data." Retrieved from http://www.city-data.com/income/income-Miami-Florida.html

Environmental Protection Agency. (2018). "Smart Growth and Preservation of Existing and Historic Buildings." Retrieved from https://www.epa.gov/smartgrowth/smart-growth-and-preservation-existing-and-historic-buildings

Holtz, D., Markham, A., Cell, K., and Ekwurzel, B. (2014). "Historic Sites at Risk." Union of Concerned Scientists. Retrieved from https://www.ucsusa.org/sites/default/files/legacy/assets/documents/global_warming/National-Landmarks-at-Risk-Full-Report.pdf

Horowitz, A. (2013). "The Effects of Sea Level Rise on Historic Districts and the Need for Adaptation."

Goucher College. Retrieved from https://mdsoar.org/handle/11603/2629

Miami21. (2019). Retrieved from http://www.miami21.org/

National Low Income Housing Coalition. (2019). Retrieved from https://nlihc.org

National Oceanic and Atmospheric Administration. (2019). Retrieved from https://www.noaa.gov/

Renken, R.A., et al. (2005). "Impact of Anthropogenic Development on Coastal Ground-Water Hydrology in Southeastern Florida, 1900-2000. Geological Survey Circular 1275." Retrieved from https://archive.usgs.gov/archive/sites/sofia.usgs.gov/publications/circular/1275/cir1275_renken.pdf

**Preserving Urban Ecosystems**

American Forests. (2000). "Urban Ecosystem Analysis For the Houston Gulf Coast Region: Calculating the Value of Nature." American Forests, December 2000, 12.

Elmqvist, T. et al. (2013). Urbanization, Biodiversity and Ecosystem Services: Challenges and Opportunities: Springer.

Rosenzweig, C. et al. (2009). "Mitigating New York City 's Heat Island: Integrating Stakeholder Perspectives and Scientific Evaluation." American Meteorological Society, September 2009, 16.

**Underground Retail and Rooftop Farming**

Arup. (2014). "Cities Alive: Rethinking green infrastructure." Retrieved from https://www.arup.com/perspectives/cities-alive-rethinking-green-infrastructure

Department of Health. (2007). "Guidelines for Implementing a Healthy Cities Project in Hong Kong." Retrieved from Department of Health.

Environmental Impact Assessment and Thermal Performances of Modern Earth Sheltered Houses. Environmental Engineering and Management Journal, 13(10), 8.

Goetz, S., & Rupasingha, A. (2006). "Wal-Mart and Social Capital." American Journal of Agricultural Economics, 88(5), 6.

Jarosz, L. (2008). "The city in the country: Growing alternative food networks in Metropolitan areas." Journal of Rural Studies, 2008(24), 14.

Labs, K. (1976). "The Architectural Underground." Underground Space, 1, 22.

McCormick, M. (2014). "The Ironic Loss of the Postmodern BEST Store Facades." Retrieved from https://www.failedarchitecture.com/the-ironic-loss-of-the-postmodern-best-store-facades/

Mohan, G. (2017). "As California's labor shortage grows, farmers race to replace workers with robots." Los Angeles Times. Retrieved from http://www.latimes.com/projects/la-fi-farm-mechanization/

Rupasingha, A., Goetz, S. J., & Freshwater, D. (2006). "The production of social capital in US counties." The Journal of Socio-Economics, 35(2006), 19.

Surls, R., & Gerber, J. (2016). From Cows to Concrete: The Rise and Fall of Farming in Los Angeles: Angel City Press.

Tantardini, M., Guo, H., & Ganapati, N. (2017). "Social Capital and Public Financial Performance: Lessons from Florida." Public Performance & Managment Review, 40(3), 24.

Tundrea, H., Maxineasa, S. G., Taranu, N., Budescu, M., B., Gavrilescu, M., & Simion, I. M. (2014).

Wines, J. (2016). "The Point is to Attack Architecture." In V. Belogolovsky (Ed.), City of Ideas. Arch Daily.

**The Effects of Living Walls**

AMA (2017). "Steps Forward: Optimizing Space in Medical Practices: Design For Meaningful and Efficient Patient Visits". Retrieved from https://www.stepsforward.org/modules/space-design

ASHRAE. "Chapter 11 Air Contaminants." 2013 ASHRAE Handbook--Fundamentals. Retrieved from https://www.ashrae.org/technical-resources/ashrae-handbook.

Cormier, S. A., S. Omnicki, W. Backes, and B. Dellinger. "Origin and Health Impacts of Emissions of Toxic Byproducts and Fine Particles from Combustion and Thermal Treatment of Hazardous Wastes and Materials." (2016). Environmental Health Perspectives, 810(7), 206.

Erdmann, C. A., K. C. Steiner, and M. G. Apte. (2002). "Indoor Carbon Dioxide Concentrations and Sick Building

Syndrome Symptoms in the BASE study revisited: Analyses of the 100 building dataset." US Environmental Protection Agency, Aug. 2014. Web. 26 July 2016.

"Frequent Questions." Fine Particle (PM2.5) Designations. Retrieved from https://www.epa.gov/sites/production/files/2014-08/documents/base_3c2o2.pdf

"Health Effects of Particulate Matter." World Health Organization, 2013. Web. 26 July 2016.

Joshi, Sumedha M. "The Sick Building Syndrome." Indian Journal of Occupational and Environmental Medicine. Medknow Publications, 12 Aug. 2008. Web. 26 July 2016.

Kobayashi, Kent D., Andrew J. Kaufman, John Griffis, and James McConnell. "Using Houseplants To Clean Indoor Air." College of Tropical Agriculture and Human Resources (CTAHR). College of Tropical Agriculture and Human Resources (CTAHR), Dec. 2007. Web. 26 July 2016.

Mo, Li. "Assessing the Capacity of Plant Species to Accumulate Particulate Matter in Beijing, China." Assessing the Capacity of Plant Species to Accumulate Particulate Matter in Beijing, China E0140664 10.10 (2015): n. pag. PLoS. Web. 11 Aug. 2016.

"Shanghai Air Quality Survey." Survey. Gensler Shanghai. 1 April 2015.

"UCSB Science Line." UCSB Science Line. The Regents of the University of California, n.d. Web. 08 Aug. 2016.

"Volatile Organic Compounds' Impact on Indoor Air Quality." Volatile Organic Compounds' Impact on Indoor Air Quality. US Environmental Protection Agency, n.d. Web. 26 July 2016.

**Implementing the Circular Economy**

Accenture. (2014). "Circular Advantage: Innovative Business Models and Technologies to Create Value in a World without Limits to Growth." Retrieved from https://www.accenture.com/t20150523T053139__w__/us-

# BIBLIOGRAPHY

en/_acnmedia/Accenture/Conversion-Assets/DotCom/Documents/Global/PDF/Strategy_6/Accenture-Circular-Advantage-Innovative Business-Models-Technologies-Value-Growth.pdf

Berry, M.A., and Rondinelli, D.A. (2017). Proactive Corporate Environmental Management: A New Industrial Revolution. Academy of Management. Retrieved from https://journals.aom.org/doi/pdf/10.5465/ame.1998.650515

Bruvoll, A. (1998). "Taxing virgin materials: An approach to waste problems." Resources, Conservation and Recycling, 22 (1-2), 15-29. Retrieved from https://www.sciencedirect.com/science/article/pii/S0921344997000402

Dietz, B.A. (2005). "Life cycle assessment of office furniture products." Retrieved from http://css.umich.edu/sites/default/files/css_doc/CSS05-08.pdf

Mithun Architects+Designers+Planners and Lady Bird Johnson Wildflower Center at the University of Texas at Austin. (2007). Construction Carbon Calculator. Retrieved from http://buildcarbonneutral.org/

### Forecasting Design Shifts Under Future Vehicle Technologies

Deloitte. (2018). "Gearing for change: Preparing for transformation in the automotive ecosystem." Future of Mobility. Retrieved from https://www2.deloitte.com/content/dam/insights/us/articles/3474_Future-of-mobility-gearing-for-change/DUP_Future-of-mobility-gearing-for-change.pdf

Morgan Stanley. (2019). "The EDGE: Autonomous Vehicles." Retrieved from https://www.morganstanley.com/im/en-us/financial-advisor/insights/investment-insights/the-edge-autonomous-vehicles.html

Morris, C. (2019). "Gloal Electric Vehicles Sales Are Rising Exponentially." InsideEVs. Retrieved from https://insideevs.com/news/343633/global-electric-vehicles-sales-are-rising-exponentially/

### Projecting Future Parking Demands of Autonomous Vehicles

Acitelli, T. (2017). "Boston developments without parking: It's a trend!" Curbed. Retrieved from https://boston.curbed.com/2017/6/19/15820274/boston-development-without-parking

Baumgardner, K. (2018). "Beyond Google's Cute Car." The Future Now.

Deloitte. (2018). "Gearing for change: Preparing for transformation in the automotive ecosystem." Future of Mobility. Retrieved from https://www2.deloitte.com/content/dam/insights/us/articles/3474_Future-of-mobility-gearing-for-change/DUP_Future-of-mobilitygearing-for-change.pdf

Walker, A. (2017). "Self-driving cars may need rental car companies to go mainstream." Curbed. Retrieved from https://www.curbed.com/2017/6/28/15877298/avis-waymo-self-driving-cars-driverless-rentalImage

### Investigating Parking in the Age of Automation

Chuang, T. (2016). "ParkiFi mashes IoT and data analytics to offer better sense of where to park downtown." The Denver Post. Retrieved from http://www.denverpost.com/2016/11/09/parkifi-where-to-find-parking-spotsdowntown-denver/

Citron, R. (2017). "The Future Of Smart Parking Is Integration With Automated Technology." Forbes. Retrieved from https://www.forbes.com/sites/pikeresearch/2017/01/26/smart-parking/#526ff3462f62

Deng, D., et al. (2015). "A Cloud-Based Smart-Parking System Based on Internet-of-Things Technologies." Digital Object Identifier, 10, 11.

Shoup, D. (2011). "Free Parking or Free Markets." Access Magazine, Spring 2011.

### Understanding Airports through Social Data

Leasca, S. (2017). "Airlines Will Make $82 Billion Off Those Extra Fees You Paid in 2017." Travel and Leisure. Retrieved from https://www.travelandleisure.com/airlines-airports/airlines-profit-from-extra-fees

### Japan's Railway Retail Hubs

East Japan Railway Company. (2017). "Annual Report 2017." Retrieved from https://www.jreast.co.jp/e/investor/ar/2017/pdf/ar_2017-all.pdf

East Japan Railway Company. (2015). "Basic Summary of Town Development of the Shinagawa Development Project." Retrieved from https://www.jreast.co.jp/e/press/2015/pdf/20150801.pdf

Tokyo Metropolitan Government. (2018). "New Tokyo. New Tomorrow. The Action Plan for 2020." Retrieved from http://www.metro.tokyo.jp/english/about/plan/index.html

Urban Planning Section Minato City. (2015). "Minato City Community Development Master Plan." City Development Support Department. Retrieved from https://www.city.minato.tokyo.jp/sougoukeikaku/kankyo-machi/toshikekaku/kekaku/documents/summary06en.pdf

Yamamoto, N. et al. (2016). "Tokyo's Third Places : Exploring ways to improve work/life balance for Tokyo's busy workforce." Gensler Research Institute. Retrieved from https://www.gensler.com/uploads/document/499/file/GenslerResearch_WorkLivePlayInTokyo_lores_2016.pdf

### U.S. Workplace Survey 2019

Advanced Workplace Associates. (2018)."Advancing the Debate on Open Plan Offices." Retrieved from https://www.advancedworkplace.com/advancing-debate-on-theopen-plan-office/

Bernstein, E. S., & Turban, S. (2018). "The impact of the 'open' workspace on human collaboration." Philosophical Transactions of the Royal Society B., May(2018), 8.

Bureau of Labor Statistics. (2017). "Women in the labor force: a databook. United States Department of Labor." Department of Labor. Retrieved from https://www.bls.gov/opub/reports/womens-databook/2016/home.htm

Bureau of Labor Statistics. (2019). "Current Population Survey." Department of Labor. Retrieved from https://www.bls.gov/cps/

Dunn, A. L. (2018). "An architect's defense of open plan offices." Fast Company. Retrieved from https://www.fastcompany.com/90218754/in-defense-of-open-offices

Fry, R. (2018). "Millennials are the largest generation in the U.S. labor force." Pew Research Center. Retrieved from http://www.pewresearch.org/fact-tank/2018/04/11/millennials-largest-generation-us-labor-force/

Harter, J. K., Schmidt, F. L., Agrawal, S., Plowman, S. K., & Blue, A. (2016). "The Relationship Between Engagement at Work and Organizational Outcomes. 2016 Q12Meta-Analysis: Ninth Edition." Gallup.

Lindberg, C. M., Srinivasan, K., Gilligan, B., Razjouyan, J., Lee, H., Najafi, B., . . . Sternberg, E. M. (2018). "Effects of office workstation type on physical activity and stress." Occupational & Environmental Medicine, 2018(75), 7.

McLaurin, J. P. (2018). "The Open Office Isn't Dead." Gensler. Retrieved from http://www.gensleron.com/work/2018/7/26/the-openoffice-isnt-dead.html

Semuels, A. (2017). "Poor Girls Are Leaving Their Brothers Behind." The Atlantic. Retrieved from https://www.theatlantic.com/business/archive/2017/11/gender-education-gap/546677/

### Germany Workplace Survey 2019

Addison, J. T., Bryson, A., Teixeira, P., Pahnke, A., & Bellmann, L. (2013). "The Extent of Collective Bargaining and Workplace Representation: Transitions Between States and Their Determinants. A Comparative Analysis of Germany and Great Britain." Scottish Journal of Political Economy, 60(2), 29.

Aridogan, S. (2018). "Why German companies fail at digital innovation." Retrieved from https://global.handelsblatt.com/opinion/why-germancompanies-fail-in-digital-innovation-901367

Buehler, R., Jungjohann, A., Keeley, M., & Mehling, M. (2011). "How Germany Became Europe's Green Leader: A Look at Four Decades of Sustainable Policymaking." Retrieved from https://www.thesolutionsjournal.com/article/how-germany-became-europes-greenleader-a-look-at-four-decades-of-sustainable-policymaking/

Dakers, M. (2017). "Secrets of growth: the power of Germany's Mittelstand." The Telegraph. Retrieved from https://www.telegraph.co.uk/connect/small-business/driving-growth/secrets-growth-power-ofgermany-mittelstand/

Eurostat. (2016). "Share of Member States in EU GDP." Retrieved from https://ec.europa.eu/eurostat/web/products-eurostat-news/-/DDN-20170410-1

The Federal Government. (2017). "Germany's National Sustainable Development Strategy." Retrieved from https://www.bundesregierung.de/breg-en/issues/sustainability/germany-s-national-sustainabledevelopment-strategy-354566

GTAI. (2018). "Economic Overview Germany: Market, Productivity, Innovation."

Hoyler, M., Freytag, T., & Mager, C. "Advantageous fragmentation? Reimagining metropolitan governance and spatial planning in Rhine-Main." Built Environment, 32(2), 12.

Luthi, S., Thierstein, A., & Bentlage, M. (2013). "The Relational Geography of the Knowledge Economy in Germany: On Functional Urban Hierarchies and Localised Value Chain Systems." Urban Studies, 50(2).

Musser, G. (2009). "The Origin of Cubicles and the Open-Plan Office." Retrieved from https://www.scientificamerican.com/article/the-origin-of-cubicles-an/

Nink, M., & Schumann, F. (2018). "German Workers: Satisfied, but Not Engaged." Retrieved from https://www.gallup.com/workplace/236165/german-workers-satisfied-not-engaged.aspx

Wever, K. S., & Allen, C. S. (1992). "Is Germany a Model for Managers." Harvard Business Review.

World Economic Forum. (2017). "Germany recycles more than any other country." Retrieved from https://www.weforum.org/agenda/2017/12/germany-recycles-more-than-any-other-country/

### Latin America Workplace Survey 2017

Chamorro-Premuzic, Tomas, and Michael Sanger. "What Leadership Looks Like in Different Cultures," Harvard Business Review. Retrieved from https://hbr.org/2016/05/what-leadership-looks-like-in-different-cultures, May 06, 2016.

Kington, Ani. "Proxemics and Communication Styles." Retrieved from https://www.interexchange.org/articles/career-training-usa/2013/05/06/ proxemics-and-communication-styles/

Steelcase. "Engagement and the Global Workplace: Key findings to amplify the performance of people, teams and organizations." Steelcase Global Report, 2016.

Mackenzie, M.L. 2010. "Manager communication and workplace trust: Understanding manager and employee perceptions in the e-world." International Journal of Information Management, Vol. 30.

Brew, Frances P. and David R. Cairns. 2004. "Do culture or situational constraints determine choice of direct or indirect styles in intercultural workplace conflicts?" International Journal of Intercultural Relations, Vol. 28:331-352; 2004.

### Emotional Security in the Workplace

Block, P. (2018). Community: The Structure of Belonging. Berrett-Koehler Publishers.

Damasio, A. (2018). The Strange Order of Things: Life, Feeling, and the Making of Cultures: Vintage.

Greer, L. (2018). Personal interview.

Isaacson, K. (2018). Personal interview.

Little, W. (2018). Personal interview.

### Prioritizing Psychological Well-Being

Asay, G.R.B., Roy, K., Lang, J.E., Payne, R.L., Howard, D.H. (2016). "Absenteeism and Employer Costs Associated With Chronic Diseases and Health Risk Factors in the US Workforce." Preventing Chronic Disease, 13.

Centre for Mental Health. (2019). "Mental health problems at work cost UK economy £34.9bn last year, says Centre for Mental Health." Retrieved from https://www.centreformentalhealth.org.uk/news/mental-health-problems-workcost-uk-economyps349bn-last-year-says-centre-mental-health

Gallup. (2013). "State of the American Workplace: Employee Engagement Insights for US Business Leaders." Retrieved from https://www.google.com/url?sa=t&rct=j&q=&esrc=s&source=web&cd=1&ved=2ahUKEwjBsdD2vZv

# BIBLIOGRAPHY

iAhUZd8KHW85C7MQFjAAegQIARAC&url=http%3A%2F%2Fwww.gallup.com%2Ffile%2Fservices%2F176708%2FState_of_the_American_Workplace_&usg=AOvVaw3lKtf7vLkShE2xAJzlKwC

Global Organization for Stress. (2019). "Stress Facts: Stress Related Facts and Statistics." Retrieved from http://www.gostress.com/stress-facts/

Health and Safety Executive. (2019). "Working Days Lost in Great Britain." Retrieved from http://www.hse.gov.uk/statistics/dayslost.htm

National Alliance on Mental Illness of Massachusetts. (2015). "Bad for Business: The Business Case for Overcoming Mental Illness Stigma in the Workplace." Retrieved from http://ceos.namimass.org/wp-content/uploads/2015/03/BAD-FOR-BUSINESS.pdf

### Balancing Density and Employee Engagement

Gallup. (2012). "Q12 Meta-Analysis." Retrieved from: https://www.gallup.com/workplace/229424/employee-engagement.aspx?g_source=link_wwwv9&g_campaign=item_236927&g_medium=copy

### Work Styles and Spatial Preference

Gardner, H. (1993). Frames of Mind: The Theory of Multiple Intelligences (Twentieth-Anniversary ed.): Basic Books.

### Designing Effective Research Buildings

Gertner, J. (2013). The Idea Factory: Bell Labs and the Great Age of American Innovation: Penguin Books.

Lee, K., Brownstein, J.S., Mills, R.G., and Kohane, I. S. (2010). "Does Collocation Inform the Impact of Collaboration?" PLOS ONE. Retrieved from https://doi.org/10.1371/journal.pone.0014279.

Lehrer, J. (2012). "Groupthink: The Brainstorming Myth." The New Yorker.

Leslie, Stuart W. (2010). "Laboratory architecture: Building for an uncertain future." Physcis Today, 63(4), 40-45. Retrieved from https://physicstoday.scitation.org/doi/10.1063/1.3397042.

### Adaptive Life Science Lab Design

Blanchard, R. (2015). "The Core of Flexibility." Laboratory Design Magazine.

Brase, W. C. (2012). "Smart Laboratories Cut Energy Consumption by Half." Retrieved from UCI Environmental Health and Safety website: https://www.ehs.uci.edu/programs/energy/SmartLabsCutEnergyConsumptionbyhalf.pdf

Campesi, J. G. a. C. (2013). "Lab Construction Outlook: Costs Stable and Trending Upward." Laboratory Design Magazine.

Kray, R. (2015, 2/20/2015). "New Methods for Optimizing Flexibility in Research Environments." Laboratory Design Magazine.

MIT Institute Archives & Special Collections. (1998, March 2, 1998). "Celebrating the History of Building 20." Retrieved from https://libraries.mit.edu/archives/mithistory/building20/

Mollo-Christensen, E. (2016, July, 2016). "Strategic Flexibility for Lab Tenants." Laboratory Design Magazine.

Shah, K. (2015). "Value of Incorporating Flexibility in Lab Buildings: A Real Options Approach." Massachusetts Institute of Technology, Retrieved from https://mitcre.mit.edu/theses-abstracts-2015/value-of-incorporatingflexibility-in-lab-buildings-a-real-options-approach

Unlisted. (2014). "How to Estimate the Cost of a Laboratory Renovation." Retrieved from https://www.aspenational.org/resource/resmgr/Techical_Papers/2015_June_TP.pdf

### Narrative-Driven Design

Ampatzidou, C., & Molenda, A. (2014). "Building Stories: The Architectural Design Process as Narrative." Paper presented at the International Digital Storytelling Conference. http://www.cristina-ampatzidou.com/building-stories-the-architectural-design-process-as-narrative-conference-paper/

Browne, W. (2010). "Storytelling in Architecture." Planetizen.

San Francisco International Airport. (2013). "The Principles of R.E.A.C.H.: Revenue Enhancement and Customer Hospitality." Retrieved from http://media.flysfo.com.s3.amazonaws.com/pdf/about/b2b/SFO-principles-of-REACH.pdf

Sisson, P. (2017). "Architecture's Increasing Role in Branding and Advertising." Curbed.

Suri, C. (2017). "Inside the Rise of Emotional Design." Architectural Digest.

van Meel, J., & Thomassen, M. (2013). "How to Write A Compelling Design Brief Using Narrative." Metropolis.

### Rapid Workplace Redesign

World Economic Forum. (2018). "The Global Risks Report 2018, 13th Edition." Retrieved from http://www3.weforum.org/docs/WEF_GRR18_Report.pdf

### Building Repositioning Strategies

CBRE. (2019). "Fast Forward 2030." Retrieved from https://www.cbre.com/research-and-reports/future-of-work

Perry, M. J. (2019). "Only 53 US companies have been on the Fortune 500 since 1955, thanks to the creative destruction that fuels economic prosperity." American Enterprise Institute. Retrieved from http://www.aei.org/publication/only-53-us-companies-have-been-on-the-fortune-500-since-1955-thanks-to-the-creative-destruction-that-fuels-economic-prosperity/

### Future-Proofing Design Strategies

Chambers, J. C., Mullick, S. K., & Smith, D. D. (1971). "How to Choose the Right Forecasting Technique." Harvard Business Review, July 1971.

Future, I. f. t. (2016). TYF2016: "The Future is a Rite of Passage." Retrieved from http://www.iftf.org/our-work/global-landscape/ten-year-forecast/2016-ten-year-forecast/

Kleining, G., & Witt, H. (2000). "The Qualitative Heuristic Approach: A Methodology for Discovery in Psychology and the Social Sciences." Rediscovering the Method of Introspection as an Example. Forum: Qualitative Social Research, 1(1).

Malhotra, S., Das, L. K., & Chariar, V. M. (2014). "Design Research Methods for Future Mapping." International Conferences on Educational Technologies, 2014(1), 10.

Trend Watching. "5 Trends for 2019." Retrieved from https://trendwatching.com/quarterly/2018-11/5-trends-2019/

Trend Watching. "Your Big Idea." Retrieved from https://trendwatching.com/quarterly/applying-trends/consumer-trend-canvas/

### Museums Experience Index 2019

Ariely, D., & Norton, M. I. (2009). Conceptual Consumption.

Annual Review of Psychology, 60, 28.

Baumeister, R. F., & Newman, L. S. (1994). "How Stories Make Sense of Personal Experiences: Motives That Shape Autobiographical Narratives." PSPB, 20(6), 676.

Diener, E. (2000). "Subjective Well-Being: The Science of Happiness and a Proposal for a National Index." American Psychologist, January 2000.

Hassenzahl, M. (2008). "User Experience (UX): Towards an experiential product quality." Paper presented at the IHM 2008, Metz, France.

Hassenzahl, M., Eckoldt, K., Diefenbach, S., Laschke, M., Lenz, E., & Kim, J. (2013). "Designing Moments of Meaning and Pleasure: Experience Design and Happiness." International Journal of Design, 7(3), 10.

Kahneman, D. (2000). "Objective Happiness." Well Being, 23.

Partala, T., & Kallinen, A. (2012). "Understanding the most satisfying and unsatisfying user experiences: Emotions, psychological needs, and context." Interacting with Computers, 24, 9.

Sheldon, K. M., Elliot, A. J., & Kim, Y. (2001). "What is Satisfying About Satisfying Events? Testing 10 Candidate Psychological Needs." Journal of Personality and Social Psychology, 80(2), 15.

### Retail Experience index 2018

Ariely, D., & Norton, M. I. (2009). "Conceptual Consumption." Annual Review of Psychology, 60, 28.

Baumeister, R. F., & Newman, L. S. (1994). "How Stories Make Sense of Personal Experiences: Motives That Shape Autobiographical Narratives." PSPB, 20(6), 676.

Chang, C.-T. (2015). "Tugging on Heartstrings: Shopping Orientation, Mindset, and Consumer Responses to Cause-Related Marketing." Journal of Business Ethics, 127(2015), 15.

Desmet, P., & Hekkert, P. (2007). "Framework of Product Experience." International Journal of Design, 1(1), 9.

Diener, E. (2000). "Subjective Well-Being: The Science of Happiness and a Proposal for a National Index." American Psychologist, January 2000.

Edmans, A. (2016). "28 Years of Stock Market Data Shows a Link Between Employee Satisfaction and Long-Term Value. Organizational Culture." Retrieved from https://hbr.org/2016/03/28-years-of-stock-market-datashows-a-link-between-employee-satisfaction-and-long-term-value

Hassenzahl, M. (2008). "User Experience (UX): Towards an experiential perspective on product quality." Paper presented at the IHM 2008, Metz, France.

Hassenzahl, M., Eckoldt, K., Diefenbach, S., Laschke, M., Lenz, E., & Kim, J. (2013). "Designing Moments of Meaning and Pleasure: Experience Design and Happiness." International Journal of Design, 7(3), 10.

Kahneman, D. (2000). "Objective Happiness." Well Being, 23.

Partala, T., & Kallinen, A. (2012). "Understanding the most satisfying and unsatisfying user experiences: Emotions, psychological needs, and context." Interacting with Computers, 24, 9.

Sheldon, K. M., Elliot, A. J., & Kim, Y. (2001). "What is Satisfying About Satisfying Events? Testing 10 Candidate Psychological Needs." Journal of Personality and Social Psychology, 80(2), 15.

Watermark Consulting. (2015). "The 2015 Customer Experience ROI Study: Demonstrating the business value of a great customerexperience." Retrieved from https://www.watermarkconsult.net/docs/Watermark-Customer-Experience-ROI-Study.pdf

Wieczner, J. (2017). "How Buying Stock in the Best Companies to Work for Helped This Investor Crush the Market. Finance." Retrieved from http://fortune.com/2017/03/09/best-companies-to-work-for-stocksinvest-esg-parnassus/

### Hospitality Experience index 2018

Ariely, D., & Norton, M. I. (2009). "Conceptual Consumption." Annual Review of Psychology, 60, 28.

Baumeister, R. F., & Newman, L. S. (1994). "How Stories Make Sense of Personal Experiences: Motives That Shape Autobiographical Narratives." PSPB, 20(6), 676.

Chang, C.-T. (2015). "Tugging on Heartstrings: Shopping Orientation, Mindset, and Consumer Responses to Cause-Related Marketing." Journal of Business Ethics, 127(2015), 15.

Desmet, P., & Hekkert, P. (2007). "Framework of Product Experience." International Journal of Design, 1(1), 9.

Diener, E. (2000). "Subjective Well-Being: The Science of Happiness and a Proposal for a National Index." American Psychologist, January 2000.

Edmans, A. (2016). "28 Years of Stock Market Data Shows a Link Between Employee Satisfaction and Long-Term Value." Organizational Culture. Retrieved from https://hbr.org/2016/03/28-years-of-stock-market-datashows-a-link-between-employee-satisfaction-and-long-term-value

Hassenzahl, M. (2008). "User Experience (UX): Towards an experiential perspective on product quality." Paper presented at the IHM 2008, Metz, France.

Hassenzahl, M., Eckoldt, K., Diefenbach, S., Laschke, M., Lenz, E., & Kim, J. (2013). "Designing Moments of Meaning and Pleasure: Experience Design and Happiness." International Journal of Design, 7(3), 10.

Kahneman, D. (2000). "Objective Happiness." Well Being, 23.

Partala, T., & Kallinen, A. (2012). "Understanding the most satisfying and unsatisfying user experiences:

# BIBLIOGRAPHY

Emotions, psychological needs, and context." Interacting with Computers, 24, 9.

Sheldon, K. M., Elliot, A. J., & Kim, Y. (2001). "What is Satisfying About Satisfying Events? Testing 10 Candidate Psychological Needs." Journal of Personality and Social Psychology, 80(2), 15.

Watermark Consulting. (2015). "The 2015 Customer Experience ROI Study: Demonstrating the business value of a great customer experience." Retrieved from https://www.watermarkconsult.net/docs/Watermark-Customer-Experience-ROI-Study.pdf

Wieczner, J. (2017). "How Buying Stock in the Best Companies to Work for Helped This Investor Crush the Market." Finance. Retrieved from http://fortune.com/2017/03/09/best-companies-to-work-for-stocksinvest-esg-parnassus/

**Exploring Multigenerational Travel**

AAA. (2014). "Multi-generational vacations on the Rise, AAA says." Newsroom. Retrieved from http://newsroom.aaa.com/2014/06/multi-generational-vacations-rise-aaa-says/

Chipkin, H. (2016). "Millenials leading multigenerational travel." Operations. Retrieved from http://www.hotelnewsnow.com/Articles/25735/Millennials-leading-multigenerational-travel

Lee, Y.J. & Gretzel, U. (2014). "Cross-Cultural Differences in Social Identity Formation through Travel Blogging." Journal of Travel and Tourism Marketing, 31, 18.

Hawthorne, F. (2016). "3-Generation Family Trips Gain New Appeal but Can Bare Old Tensions." New York Times. Retrieved from https://www.nytimes.com/2016/03/06/business/retirementspecial/3-generation-family-trips-gainnew-appeal-but-can-bare-old-tensions.html

Ottsen, C.L. & Berntsen, D. (2015). "Prescribed journeys through life: Cultural differences in mental time travel between Middle Easterners and Scandinavians." Consciousness and Cognition, 37, 14.

Weidenfeld, A., & Ron, A. (2008). "Religious Needs in the Travel Industry." University of Exeter, 5.

Wong, J. et al. (2014). "Effects of power and individual-level cultural orientation on preferences for volunteer tourism." Tourism Management, 42, 9.

**The Impact of Airbnb on Hospitality**

Benner, K. (2016). "Airbnb Ends Fight With New York City Over Fines". New York Times. Retrieved from https://www.nytimes.com/2016/12/03/technology/airbnb-ends-fight-with-new-york-city-over-fines.html

Chandler, A. (2016). "Reality is Messier Than Uber and Airbnb Want It to Be". The Atlantic.

Gallagher, L. (2017). "Airbnb Unveils a Platform for Housing Refugees. Fortune Magazine". Retrieved from http://fortune.com/2017/06/07/airbnb-refugees-housing/

Lin, H.-Y., Wang, M.-H., & Wu, M.-J. (2017). "A Study of Airbnb Use Behavior In The Sharing Economy. International Journal of Organizational Innovation", 10(1), 11.

Staff. (2017). "Among private tech firms, Airbnb has pursued a distinct strategy." The Economist. Retrieved from https://www.economist.com/news/business/21722653-its-culture-cohesive-and-its-finances-disciplined-amongprivate-tech-firms-airbnb-has

Farronato, C. and A. Fradkin (2018). "The Welfare Effects of Peer Entry in the Accommodation Market: The Case of Airbnb." The National Bureau of Economic Research March 2018(1): 69.

Gerdeman, D. (2018). "The Airbnb Effect: Cheaper Rooms For Travelers, Less Revenue For Hotels." Forbes. Retrieved from https://www.forbes.com/sites/hbsworkingknowledge/2018/02/27/the-airbnb-effect-cheaper-rooms-for-travelersless-revenue-for-hotels/#35b990f0d672

**A Toolkit for Active Learning Environments**

Hayashi, A., & Tobin, J. (2011). "The Japanese Preschool's Pedagogy of Peripheral Participation." Journal of the Society for Psychological Anthropology, 39, 26.

Hudson, J. (2017). "A Primary-School Classroom for a New Public-School Majority". Retrieved from http://www.theatlantic.com/sponsored/allstate-2017/a-primary-school-classroom-for-a-new-public-schoolmajority/1190/?utm_source=TL

Murray, L., McCallum, C., & Petrosino, C. (2014). "Flipping the Classroom Experience: A Comparison of Online Learning to Traditional Lecture". Journal of Physical Therapy Education, 28, 8.

Oreopoulos, P. (2017). "Behavioral Barriers to Education." NBER Report, 1, 5.

**A Comparative Analysis of Enhanced Classrooms**

Hayashi, A., & Tobin, J. (2011). "The Japanese Preschool's Pedagogy of Peripheral Participation." Journal of the Society for Psychological Anthropology, 39, 26.

Hudson, J. (2017). "A Primary-School Classroom for a New Public-School Majority." Retrieved from http://www.theatlantic.com/sponsored/allstate-2017/a-primary-school-classroom-for-a-new-public-schoolmajority/1190/?utm_source=TL

Murray, L., McCallum, C., & Petrosino, C. (2014). "Flipping the Classroom Experience: A Comparison of Online Learning to Traditional Lecture." Journal of Physical Therapy Education, 28, 8.

Oreopoulos, P. (2017). "Behavioral Barriers to Education." NBER Report, 1, 5.

**A New Model for the Public Library**

Greenspan, E., et al. (2018). "Civic Infrastructure: Sustaining and Sharing the Value of Parks, Libraries, and Other Public Assets." PennPraxis. Retrieved from https://www.design.upenn.edu/sites/default/files/uploads/PennPraxis_CivicInfrastructure_Vol2.pdf

Horrigan, J. (2016.) "Libraries 2016." Pew Research Center. Retrieved from https://www.pewinternet.org/2016/09/09/libraries-2016/

Institute of Museum and Library Services. (2018). "Public Libraries in the United States: Fiscal Year 2015." Retrieved from https://www.imls.gov/sites/default/files/publications/documents/plsfy2015.pdf

International Federation of Library Associations. (2016). "IFLA Trend Report 2016 Update." Retrieved from https://trends.ifla.org/files/trends/assets/trend-report-2016-update.pdf

Klinenberg, E. (2018). Palaces for the People: How Social Infrastructure Can Help Fight Inequality, Polarization, and the Decline of Civic Life: Crown.

Mattern, S. (2014). "Library as Infrastructure." Places Journal.

Rosa, K. (2018). "The State of America's Libraries 2018: A Report from the American Library Association." Retrieved from http://digital.americanlibrariesmagazine.org/html5/reader/production/default.aspx?pubname=&edid=7cdd130c-a197-42b4-8842-3e2feb88ccf7

Taylor, P., et al. (2016.) The Next America: Boomers, Millennials, and the Looming Generational Showdown: PublicAffairs.

### The Future of USPS Real Estate

United States Postal Service. (2019). "FY2018 Annual Report to Congress." Retrieved from: https://about.usps.com/who-we-are/financials/annual-reports/fy2018.pdf

### A Model for Integrated Ambulatory Care Clinics

Mount Sinai. "Addressing the Incidence of Multiple Chronic Conditions." (2018) Retrieved from: https://inside.mountsinai.org/blog/addressing-the-incidence-of-multiple-chronic-conditions/

### Enhancing the Waiting Room Experience

Cusack, P., Lankston, L., & Isles, C. (2010). "Impact of visual art in patient waiting rooms: survey of patients attending a transplant clinic in Dumfries." Journal of the Royal Society of Medicine, 1(6), 1.

Fried, D. (2014). "Lessons from Waiting Rooms. Software Advice." Retrieved from https://www.softwareadvice.com/resources/reducing-patient-wait-times/

Jowsey, T., Yen, L., Ward, N., McNab, J., Aspin, C., & Usherwood, T. (2012). "It hinges on the door: Time, spaces, and identity in Australian Aboriginal Health services." Health Sociology Review, 21(2), 10.

Karnik, M., Printz, B., & Finkel, J. (2014). "A Hospital's Contemporary Art Collection: Effects on Patient Mood, Stress, Comfort, and Expectations." Health Environments Research and Design Journal, 2014(3), 60.

Morgan, J. (2015). "Waiting rooms may be a missed opportunity in facility design." Health Facilities Management. Retrieved from https://www.hfmmagazine.com/articles/2032-waiting-rooms-may-be-a-missed-opportunity-infacility-design

Nemschoff. (2014). "Winning Strategies for Waiting Rooms." Retrieved from: https://www.nemschoff.com/uploads/case-study-files/Nemschoff_Insight_2014_11_12.pdf

Sherwin, H. N., McKeown, M., Evans, M. F., & Bhattacharyya, O. K. (2013). "The waiting room wait: from annoyance to opportunity." Canadian Family Physician, 59(5), 3.

### Optimizing Exam Room Design

AMA (2017). "Steps Forward: Optimizing Space in Medical Practices: Design For Meaningful and Efficient Patient Visits". Retrieved from https://www.stepsforward.org/modules/space-design

Burcher, P. (2015). "The Patient-Doctor Relationship: Where Are We Now?" University of Toledo Law Review, 46(Spring 2015), 7.

Clark, T., Edwards, B., & Stang, L. (2017). "Body of Evidence for Research-based Solutions." Retrieved from https:// www.healthcaredesignmagazine.com/trends/perspectives/body-evidence-research-based-solutions/

Freihoefer, K., Nyberg, G., & Vickery, C. (2013). "Clinic Exam Room Design: Present and Future." Herd Journal, 6, 20.

Pedersen, D. M. (1997). "Psychological Functions of Privacy." Journal of Environmental Psychology, 17, 10.

Trachtenbarg, D. E., Asche, C., Ramsahai, S., Duling, J., & Ren, J. (2017). "The benefits, risks and costs of privacy: patient preferences and willingness to pay." Current Medical Research and Opinion, 33(5), 8.

### Intelligent Retail Places

Baird, N. (2017). "Five Retail IoT Use Cases, When Retailers Finally Get Around to IoT." Forbes. Retrieved from https://www.forbes.com/sites/nikkibaird/2017/04/24/five-retail-iot-use-cases-when-retailers-finally-get-around-to-iot/#323192ff6255

Gilliland, N. (2019). "12 examples of digital technology in retail stores." Econsultancy. Retrieved from https://econsultancy.com/examples-digital-technology-in-retail-stores/

O'Shea, D. (2019). "5 retail technology trends to watch in 2019." Retail Dive. Retrieved from https://www.retaildive.com/news/5-retail-technology-trends-to-watch-in-2019/545662/

### IoT Technology in the Workplace

Garfield, L. (2017). "Bill Gates' investment group spent $80 million to build a 'smart city' in the desert - and urban planners are divded." Business Insider. Retrieved from https://www.businessinsider.com/bill-gates-smart-city-pros-cons-arizona-urban-planners-2017-11

Samsung. (2018). "Track and Locate What Matters Most with SmartThings Tracker." Samsung Newsroom. Retrieved from https://news.samsung.com/us/track-what-matters-most-smartthings-tracker/

Statista. (2016). "Internet of Things (IoT) connected devices installed base worldwide from 2015 to 2025." Consumer Electronics. Retrieved from https://www.statista.com/statistics/471264/iot-number-of-connected-devices-worldwide/

### Machine Learning Design Strategies

Blei, D., Ng, Andrew., & Jordan, M., "Latent Dirichlet Allocation." Journal of Machine Learning Research 3 (2003) 993-1022.

"Project Jupyter." (2019). Retrieved from www.jupyter.org

# INDEX

## A

Accenture Innovation Hub, Tokyo, Japan, 246–247
accessibility, 25, 26, 27, 32–41, 187, 213, 249
   in Canada, 33, 34
adaptability, 21, 108, 156, 158, 160-161, 215, 251
ADA Standards for Accessible Design Checklist, 33
aesthetics
   community, 21
   of disability, 32
   exam room, 229
   façades, 29, 69
   and inclusivity, 35
   laboratory, 154, 160
   and parking, 108
   residential, 29
   and restrooms, 41
   and rooftop farming, 80
   waiting room, 224
Africa, 42–45
aging, 18, 19, 24
Airbnb, 195, 198–199
airports, 110–115
   architecture, 111
   Auckland, New Zealand, 114–115
   baggage, 111
   data, 113
   San Francisco, 113
air quality, 69
   indoor (IAQ), 82–87
Ambrosia project, 14
ambulatory care clinics, 220–223
amenities
   in airports, 115
   bathroom, 40–41
   BoomTown, 23
   and building repositioning, 171, 172, 173
   and business travelers, 191
   city-based, 14, 19
   commercial, 28, 29
   in hotels, 200
   for millennials, 29
   and parking, 96, 100, 104, 108
   and retail, 181
   for seniors, 20
   in waiting rooms, 224
   in the workplace, 123–25, 126–27, 131
Americans with Disabilities Act (ADA), 33
architectural inefficiency, 156
Architecture 2030 Challenge, 59, 61

## B / C

baby boomers, 18–19, 181, 182, 188–89, 195, 214
Barclays Whippany Campus (NJ), 126–27
bathrooms, 38–41
BoomTown Community model, 18–23
Boston (MA), 71, 102, 159
building codes, 34, 38, 39, 58
building materials, 12, 54, 57, 58–59, 78, 80
   recycling and reuse, 53, 58–59, 88–91
building repositioning, 170–73
building skin. See façades
Capitol Federal Hall (Univ. of Kansas), 202
carbon neutral, 57, 60–65, 78, 80
cars. See vehicles
charging stations, 95, 96, 100, 105
Chicago (IL), 46, 48, 64–65, 152
Cincinnati (OH), 46, 48
circular economy, 88–91
City Design Index, 10, 11
classrooms. See learning environments
Cleveland (OH), 46, 48
climate change, 54–90
clinics, 220–23, 229
collaboration zones, 157, 215
community engagement, 80, 119, 220, 221
   and intergenerational living, 18, 25
   with libraries, 212, 213, 214, 215
   with the post office, 218, 219
   with waiting rooms, 224, 225, 226
construction materials. See building materials
consumers, 100, 116, 118, 181, 200, 219
   healthcare, 220–23
consumption patterns, 79
Corktown, Detroit (MI), 46, 49
corporate investment, 49
corporate responsibility, 200, 201
cost savings, 69, 80, 81, 149
Crystal City, Arlington (VA), 50–51
curbside demand, 94
customer experience centers (CECs), 154–55

## D / E

data collection, 225, 240–43, 244, 245, 248–51
daylighting, 66, 78, 240
demographics
   Hong Kong, 26
   U.S., 19, 95, 175, 185, 189, 218, 240
density, 11, 26, 27, 29, 51, 95, 146–51, 156
Designing Common Ground, 32
Detroit (MI), 46, 48, 49
digital experience design, 154
digital participation, 251
disability, 32, 33, 35, 140
diversity, 25, 139, 173, 187, 215, 218
doors, 40, 147, 152, 229, 230
downtowns, 28, 29
   neighborhoods in, 46–51
Dynamo tool, 66, 68

economic development, 31, 42, 43, 44
ecosystem curation, 171, 173
educators, 202–5, 208–11
electric cars. See vehicles
El Pueblo Temporary Homeless Shelter, Los Angeles (CA), 16–17
employee engagement, 122, 146–51, 152
employee productivity. See productivity
employee wellbeing, 140–45
"empty world" concept, 75
energy sector, 166, 167
energy use, 57, 60, 66, 96, 240
   and building façades, 66, 69
energy use intensity (EUI), 58, 60, 61
environmental issues, 43, 70–73, 74–77, 80, 104
examination rooms, 220–23, 228–31
Experience Index, 116, 120, 234

## F / G

façades, 29, 66–69
faculty, 202–5, 208–11
floor plans, 107, 148, 158, 228, 241, 242, 245
floor plates, 29, 31, 108, 146
Florida International University, 70
food, 43, 79–81, 113, 115, 119, 196
Ford Foundation Center for Social Justice, New York (NY), 36–37
furniture
   classroom, 203, 218, 219
   exam room, 230–231
   excess, 166, 167
   and floor plan density, 148
   "hackable," 152
   laboratory, 158, 161
   reuse of, 88–89, 90, 168, 169
   and sustainability, 59
   waiting room, 223, 224, 225, 226
furniture-, fixture-, and equipment-focused variables (FF&E), 90, 91, 245
future of work, 138
future-proofing, 104, 108, 161, 174–177
gender segregation, 38
Gensler Cities Climate Challenge, 59, 60
Gensler Denver, 90
Gensler London, 90
Gensler San Diego, 91
Gensler San Francisco, 91
Gensler Shanghai, 82
Gensler Workplace Surveys, 244
   timeline, 136–37
Gen X, 181, 182
Germany Workplace Survey 2019, 128–31
Glendale (CA), 78
global GDP, 10
Global Workplace Surveys timeline, 136–37
Golden Triangle, Washington, DC, 28, 29, 31
Gotanda Station, Tokyo, Japan, 116–19
greenhouse gas emissions, 28, 56
green rooms, 82–87
green space, 24, 76, 108
Growing Underground, 81

## H / I / J / K

"hacked" buildings, 57
Harbor District, Milwaukee (WI), 49
healthcare, 220–23, 231
heat islands, 75, 76, 104
Helen Hamlyn Centre for Design, 140
holistic approaches, 12, 14, 52–53, 72, 74, 106, 168, 221
homelessness, 10, 12–17, 214
Hong Kong, 26–27
Hong Kong Housing Authority, 27
Hospitality Experience Index 2018, 188–93
hospitality industry, 188–201
hospitality modeling, 171, 172
hotels, 188–93, 198–201
housing, 12–17, 25, 26–27, 28–31, 43, 44, 45
Houston (TX), 70, 71, 75
Human Development Index, 42
inclusivity, 19, 23, 25, 32–41, 230
industrial use, 49
informal spaces, 157
infrastructure, 42–44, 76, 104, 108, 109
intelligent buildings, 249
intelligent spaces, 57, 234–51
interdependency, 75
intergenerational living, 18–25
IoT technology, 234, 240–43
Ivy City, Washington, DC, 22–25
jLabs, Toronto, Canada, 162–63
Kimpton Aertson Hotel, Nashville (TN), 192–93
Kohane, Isaac, 156

## L / M

llaboratory spaces, 156–57, 158–63
   configurations, 161
   cost, 159
   fixed, 159
   flexible, 158
   typologies, 158, 160
Lagos, Nigeria, 42, 44–45
land use, 43, 44, 49, 104
Latin America Workplace Survey 2017, 132–35
learning environments, 202–11
   collaborative, 204, 205, 209, 210
   enhanced, 208–09
   traditional, 208, 209, 210, 211
Lexalytics, 112, 114
libraries, 212–15
lifecycle thinking, 59
lighting power density, 59, 62
living walls, 82–87
London, UK, 70, 81, 88, 90, 140, 142, 194
Los Angeles (CA), 12–17, 22–23, 78, 81
Lynn University, Boca Raton (FL), 206–07
MacArthur Park, Los Angeles (CA), 22–25
machine learning, 234, 244–47, 251
mapping tools, 74, 76
megacities, 52, 175
Mexico City, 28, 132
Miami (FL), 70, 72, 73
Midwest, 46–49
millennials, 20, 29, 172, 181, 182, 189, 194–95, 213, 214, 219
Milwaukee (WI), 46, 48, 49
Minneapolis (MN), 46, 48
MIT Building 16, 156
mobility, 26, 123, 124, 138, 213. See also urban mobility
modular housing, 12–17
multigenerational travel, 194–197
Multiple Intelligences, 152
Mumbai, India, 28
museums, 184–87
Museums Experience Index 2019, 184–87

# INDEX

## N / O

Nairobi, Kenya, 42–43, 45
narrative design, 164–65
National Landing, 95
neighborhooding, 173
neighborhoods, 31, 46–51
net zero, 57, 61–65, 78, 80
Net Zero Building Challenge, 59
New York (NY), 70, 71, 76, 88, 170–74, 240
NYC Infrastructure Plan, 76
occupancy data, 46, 48, 107, 240, 242, 245
office buildings, 95, 96, 105
    conversion of, 28–31
    repositioning, 51
office moves, 89
office space, 28–29, 152, 172. See also workplace
onstage/offstage model, 228, 229

## P / Q

parking, 94, 95, 96–97, 100–09
    and automation, 106–09
    costs, 107
    Future of Parking application, 102–3
    infrastructure, 108
    ParkiFi, 107
    real estate value, 103
    SFPark, 107
    structures, 102, 109
    typologies, 102, 109
patients, 220–31
pattern generation, 66
PeakHealth Practice, 220, 221
pedagogy, 208, 215
pedestrians, 22, 51
People's Energy Welcome Pavilion, Navy Pier, Chicago (IL), 64–65
Permanent Supportive Housing (PSH), 12–15
pick-up/drop-off spaces, 95, 96, 106, 108
pictograms, 40
plants indoors, 82–87
PlaNYC, 76
post-occupancy, 53, 205, 224, 226, 228, 242, 245
post offices, 216–19
pre-fab modular housing, 12–17
pre-occupancy, 53, 205, 224, 230, 242
privacy, 175, 245
    in the classroom, 205
    in clinics, 223
    in exam rooms, 229
    in restrooms, 40, 41
    and travel, 196
    in the workplace, 122, 123, 124, 128, 129, 147, 148, 149, 157
productivity
    in the classroom, 210
    in the laboratory, 159
    in the workplace, 136, 140, 143, 147, 169, 240
project management oversight (PMO), 12, 14, 15
Proposition HHH, 12
public libraries, 212–15
public-private partnerships, 42
public restrooms, 38–41
quiet spaces, 123, 124, 157, 188, 189, 156, 204

## R

real estate, 105, 170–73, 248–51
    USPS, 216–19
    value, 146–51
recycling, 53, 59, 88–91
rents, 29, 31, 46, 49, 172, 199
research buildings, 156–57
resilience, 83, 84, 88, 174
    100 Resilient Cities initiative, 72
    coastal, 70–73
    in design, 56–59, 74
    and the environment, 56–59
    and urban ecology, 74–77
    in the workplace, 139
restrooms, 38–41, 187
retail, 25, 51, 173
    brick-and-mortar stores, 180–83, 234–39
    customer engagement, 234
    economies of scale, 12
    generational differences, 182
    heat maps, 238–39
    Japanese railway station, 116–19
    spatial data, 234–39
    and technology, 234–39
    underground, 78–81
Retail Experience Index 2018, 180–83, 234
reuse, 53, 58, 59, 88–91
ride sharing. See vehicles
rooftop farming, 78–81
rooftop gardens, 24–25
rural restructuring, 80
Rush University Medical Center, 228–31

## S

San Francisco (CA), 71, 88, 94, 107, 142, 159
sanitation, 38, 40, 43, 44, 45
scientific buildings, 156–57
scientific research, 156–57
sea level rise, 70–73
self-driving cars. See vehicles
senior citizens, 18–21, 26–27
sensors, 107, 234–39, 240–43, 250
shading components, 66
shared cars. See vehicles
Shaw Create Centre, Cartersville (GA), 144–45
Shimbashi Station, Tokyo, Japan, 116–19
shopping. See retail
signage, 37, 39, 40, 41, 119, 187, 229
Skid Row Housing Trust, 14, 15
Skyport Mobility Hub, 98–99
social capital, 79, 80
Socio-Economic Ecological Performance Index (SEPI), 52–53
solar analysis, 67
solar insolation, 66, 68
solar panels, 80
South Africa, 42
St. Louis (MO), 46, 48
stores. See retail
storytelling, 164–65
street edges, 51
streetscape engineering, 171, 173
street vending, 25
students, 202–3, 208–4
sub-Saharan Africa, 42–45
Sunbrella, 224
sunshades, 66
Super Panel, 68
sustainability, 23, 45, 52–53, 56, 58, 60–63, 65, 74–81, 83
Sustainable Development Goals (SDGs), 52

## T / U / V

Tampa (FL), 70
teachers, 202–5, 208–11
technology
    in the classroom, 210
    collaborative, 134
    and design strategies, 244–47
    disruptors, 167
    and the future, 175
    in hotels, 189, 200
    IoT, 240–43
    in libraries, 213
    and mapping, 76
    in museums, 186–87
    parking, 102–3, 106–09
    and real estate, 248–51
    in retail, 179, 229–34
    in the workplace, 130–31, 134, 170, 236–39
tenants, 167, 168
thermal comfort, 78, 80, 81
Title VII, 35
toilets, 34–37, 183
Tokyo, Japan, 112–15
traffic congestion, 103
train stations, 112–15
transgender rights, 34, 35
transportation as a service (TaaS), 96
travel, 186–87, 190–197
trend research, 171, 173
underground structures, 78–81
UN Global Compact, 59
United Technologies Digital Accelerator, 86–87
Unity Health Care, Washington, DC, 224–27
Up Top Acres, 81
urban agriculture, 78–81
Urban Agriculture Incentive Zones Act, 81
urban ecosystems, 74–77
urban farming, 78–81
urbanization, 56, 79, 80
urban mobility, 94–119
urban planning, 52–53
urban sprawl, 78–79
urban vitality, 28–29
U.S. Workplace Survey 2019, 122–25
vacancy rates, 29, 46, 49, 159
value alignment, 171, 172–73
vehicles
    autonomous (AV), 94–109
    charging stations for, 95, 96, 100, 105
    electric (EV), 94, 95, 96, 97, 100
    shared, 94, 96, 100, 101, 105
ventilation, 40, 66, 69, 83
volumetric leasing, 171, 172

## W / X / Y / Z

waiting rooms, 223, 224–27
Walker's Point, Milwaukee (WI), 46, 49
Washington, DC, 22–25, 28–31, 70, 81, 95, 224, 225
waste streams, 88–90
wayfinding, 113, 115, 116, 119, 224, 226
windows, 29, 31, 66, 245
worker productivity. See productivity
worker wellbeing, 140–45
workforce reductions, 166, 167
workplace, 122–74
    amenities, 123–25, 126–27, 131
    balanced, 122, 128, 129, 130, 131, 137
    collaborative technology, 134
    collaborative work, 129, 147, 152, 156–57, 161, 168, 247
    configurations, 146–47
    costs, 148–51
    coworking, 123–25
    data collection, 240–43, 244
    density, 146–51
    depression in, 140
    emotional security in, 138–39
    and employee engagement, 122, 146–51, 152
    flexible, 146, 148, 166, 169
    German, 128–31
    global companies, 134, 135
    hybrid settings, 124
    IoT technology in, 240–43
    Latin American, 132–35
    occupancy data, 240, 242
    open plan, 123, 129, 146, 147, 149
    personalization, 152, 245
    preferences, 152, 153
    privacy, 123–24, 128, 129, 147, 148, 149, 152
    psychological wellbeing, 140–45
    redesign, 166–69
    relational homeostatis, 138
    resilience, 139, 169, 174, 175
    and technology, 134–35, 138, 155, 160, 166, 167, 174
Workplace Performance Index (WPI), 122, 124, 132, 136, 152, 240–42, 245
Workplace Surveys timeline, 136–37
work styles, 152, 153
zero net energy, 57, 60–65, 78, 80
zoning, 11, 73, 219

# ACKNOWLEDGMENTS

**EDITORIAL**

**Editor**
Christine Barber

**Managing Editor**
Tim Pittman

**Creative Director**
Laura Latham

**Lead Writers**
Stella Donovan
Kyle Sellers

**Lead Designers**
Minjung Lee
Georgia Wilson

**Design Team**
Do Young Ahn
Federico Alonso
Corina Benatuil
Brooks Cole
Saybel Guzman
Shirley Lei
Vania Lin
Sabrina Mason
Joe Morgan
Megan Murdock
Joseph Navarro
Laia Pose Gratacos
Lauren Ransom
Esteban Rojas
Kevin Steele
Jack Trotman
Adira Weixlmann
Sisi Zhu

**Editorial Board**
Sabrina Blowers
Maddy Burke-Vigeland
Dian Duvall
Jordan Goldstein
Lance Hosey
Diane Hoskins
Sam Martin
Janet Pogue McLaurin
Joan Price
Ray Shick
Thomas Stat
Duncan Swinhoe
Leslie Taylor
Rives Taylor
William Taylor
Gervais Tompkin
Li Wen

**Additional Contributors**
Stephanie Benkert
Justin Chase
Denise Griffiths

**RESEARCHERS**

Lauren Adams
Daichi Amano
Prince Ambooken
Sara Anderson
Hisayuki Araki
Lucy Arledge
Sumita Arora
Russell Baker
Nilesh Bansal
Jeff Barber
Izabella Barlog
Mark Bassett
Kloey Battista
Meaghan Beaver
Ana Benatuil
Corina Benatuil
Daniel Bender
Federica Bertoncini
Keith Besserud
Eric Bieber
Aaron Birney
Mitchell Bobman
David Briefel
Reid Brockmeier
Anthony Brower
Kim Brown
David Broz
Andre Brumfield
Nick Bryan
Allison Bulgart
Islay Burgess
Leonora Bustamante
Alfred Byun
Amber Cao
Laura Carey
Amy Carter
John Cassidy
Vincenzo Centinaro
Justin Chase
Zhifei Cheng
Jane Christen
Jin Chung
Ashley Claussen
Andy Cohen
Robert Cohen
Pedro Coivo

Cindy Coleman
Laura Coyne
Kevin Craft
David Crabtree
Michael Crawford
James Crispino
Carlos Cubillos
Alice Davis
Leeann De Barros
Anna Demuth
June Deng
Joy DeWitt
Ned Dodington
Sean Drepaul
Tama Duffy Day
Florent Duperrin
Paula Eleazar
Mark Erdly
Joel Fariss
John Ferns
Chad Finken
JF Finn III
Kenneth Fisher
Steven Folkes
Nancy Foster
Jackson Fox
Lorraine Francis
David Frank
James Frankis
Jessica Galeazzi
Rachel Ganin
Jessica Garcia
Aaron Gensler
Beth Gibb
Russell Gilchrist
Derek Gilley
David Glover
Sven Govaars
Christopher Gray
Jane Greenthal
Randy Guillot
Kelly Guo
Garima Gupta
John Haba
Shamus Halkowich

Mahe Hameed
Scott Hampton
Audrey Handelman
Adam Harper
Steven Harrell
Anthony Harris
Johnny He
Todd Heiser
Brandon Hendricks
Wesley Hiatt
Lisa Hibler
Marcus Hopper
Lance Hosey
Diane Hoskins
Andy Huang
Robert Hughes
Ju Hyun Lee
Hilary Ingram
Aina Ito
Tom Ito
Brenden Jackson
Maja Jasniewicz
Chris Jerde
Rob Jernigan
Lin Jia
David Johnson
Sarah Jones
Kathleen Jordan
Claire Kang
Ian Kim
Anna Kirkham
Nathan Klinge
Namrata Krishna
Kevin Kusina
Brandon Larcom
Laura Latham
Wes LeBlanc
Brian Ledder
Caroline LeFevre
Thabo Lenneiye
Lawrence Ler
Sharon Lessard
Lee Lindahl
Tom Lindblom
Zheyu Liu

Erik Lucken
Erik Lustgarten
Emer Lynam
Duncan Lyons
Callum MacBean
Ryan MacCrea
Scott Magnuson
Jill Mahaney
Cerise Marcela
Simi Marinho
Lara Marrero
Allison Marshall
Michael Martin
Cheryl Martirez
Melissa McCarriagher
Chesley McCarty
Gail McCleese
Allison McElroy
Sean McGuire
Janet Pogue McLaurin
Melissa Mizell
Carina Mohammed
Carolina Montilla
Kathryn Moore
Ian Mulcahey
Tom Mulhern
Linda Mysliwiec
Zsuzsi Nagy
Gail Napell
Chandkiran Nath
Patricia Nobre
Mina Noorbakhsh
David O'Brien
Kate O'Connor
Katy O'Neill
Corina Ocanto
Tatsuya Oi
Daisuke Okazaki
Erica Oppenheimer
Allison Palmadesso
Sarah Palmer
Stephanie Park
Shixa Patel
Karen Pedrazzi
Pixy Peng

Andrea Peterson
Adriana Phillips
Tim Pittman
Gregory Plavcan
Francesca Poma-Murialdo
Amy Pothier
Ben Prager
Nic Pryor
Emmanuel Ramirez Muro
Daniel Ranostaj
Haley Reddick
Adham Refaat
Brooke Rho
Brett Riegler
Yana Ronin
Sara Rothholz Weiner
Louise Russell
Mara Russo
Pia Sachleben
Naomi Sakamoto
Jose Luis Sanchez-Concha
Ken Sanders
Jonathan Sandoval
Michael Saunders
Bevin Savage-Yamazaki
Erin Saven
Peter Schaefer
Oliver Schaper
Vivian Schapsis
Michael Schneider
Levi Schoenfeld
Leonard Sciarra
Deborah Shepley
Roger Sherman
Karina Silvester
Adam Simmons
Jacob Simons
Bonny Slater
Katie Smith
Olivier Sommerhalder
Julia Spackman
Carolyn Sponza

Andrew Starr
Dean Strombom
Eric Stult
Stephen Swicegood
Sarah Szekeresh
Bill Talley
Kelley Tapia
Mallory Taub
Rives Taylor
Jennifer Thornton
Khue Thuy Tran
Philip Tidd
Kevin Todd
Gervais Tompkin
Allie Trachsel
Zach Trattner
Marco Troncarelli
Richard Tyson
Taro Uchiyama
Nagato Uematsu
Steven Upchurch
Carlos Valera
Kelly Van Oteghem
Diana Vasquez
Thomas Vecchione
Peter Wang
Meghan Webster
Amy Weinstein
Nathan Welch
Scott Wilson
Steve Wilson
Ira Winder
Allison Wong
Christy Wong
Justin Wortman
Jeannie Wu
Nachiko Yamamoto
Andrew Yang
Chang-Yeon Cho
Amii Yokouchi
Inwon Yoon
Summer Yu
Richard Zapata
Daquan Zhou
Greg Zielinski

**IMAGE CREDITS**

All images credited to Gensler unless otherwise noted.

Ai Qing, 180 (bottom)
Andrew Bordwin, 192-193
Blackstation, 56-57
Calzada Visualization, 79, 80
Colleen Tunnicliff, 114-115
Connie Zhou, 122, 144-145, 206-207
Eric Laignel, 184
Gareth Gardner, 128 (left)
Garrett Rowland, 36-37, 86-87, 89
Gensler/Robert Deitcher, 126-127
Gensler/Ryan Gobuty, 91 (top), 180 (top)
Google, 22, 28
Ira Winder, 100-105
JR EAST Railway Lines Network, 117
Nacasa & Partners, 180 (bottom right)
Nick Merrick, 90 (bottom left), 188
OJB Landscape Architecture, 81
Rafael Gamo, 91 (bottom)
Scott Frances, 180 (left)
Shimahara Illustration, 16-17
Tom Arban, 162-163
Tom Harris, 54-65
Tomooki Kengaku, 246-247
Wray Ward/Sunbrella, 226-227